HARD RAINS

CONFLICT AND CONSCIENCE IN AMERICA

Edited by

ROBERT DISCH
BARRY N. SCHWARTZ

PRENTICE-HALL, INC.
Englewood Cliffs, N. J.

13-383901-X

Library of Congress Catalog Card No.: 79-110087

Current printing *(last number):*
10 9 8 7 6 5 4 3 2 1

Printed in the United States of America

PRENTICE-HALL INTERNATIONAL, INC., *London*
PRENTICE-HALL OF AUSTRALIA, PTY. LTD., *Sydney*
PRENTICE-HALL OF CANADA, LTD., *Toronto*
PRENTICE-HALL OF INDIA PRIVATE LIMITED, *New Delhi*
PRENTICE-HALL OF JAPAN, INC., *Tokyo*

PREFACE

In recent years campus disturbances have forced teacher and administrators to reconsider how the university is to fulfill its goal of instructing young minds within a society torn by conflict. For their part, the students debate endlessly how to move the educational institutions to confront and respond to the societal problems they believe are the most important. Ironically, the universities, where the exchange of ideas is held to be of primary value, exhibit a breakdown of communication between these groups.

Any understanding of campus upheaval must take into account the fact that the university is afflicted by the same problems—racism, militarism, generational conflict, violence—that have brought the society to the brink of crisis. Again, ironically, while the university derives its unique role from the ideal that the search for the answers to a better society must be initiated in its classrooms, it has long struggled to remain aloof from the implications of social change. Its faculties generally believe that "solutions" can only be derived from an intimate knowledge of human history and through methods of rational discourse and objective inquiry. The students believe that there must be a vital relationship between the content of their courses and the actions necessary to remedy the dilemmas plaguing our society. We believe both approaches are indispensable to justify the continued existence of the university. The teachers argue for an environment which, at least in theory, makes it possible for men and women to examine ideas without hysteria and with some degree of emotional detachment, while the students want to study those problems which threaten our existence as free and fully functioning human beings. This book tries to accommodate both points of view.

Hard Rains is an intellectually rigorous text which probes deeply into many of the problems that ravage America. It demands careful examination, an open mind, and imaginative applications of thought. It brings to the classroom commentaries on subjects which occupy much student attention but which are excluded, the students claim, from most of the organized study in the college curriculum.

But why in freshman English? Why not in sociology? Or economics? Or political science? Or in technical courses? In the opinion of the editors, the purpose of freshman English—to create better writing—is best achieved when the students care about the material they are asked to engage. Since *Hard Rains* brings the issues discussed in the cafeteria, the dormitory room, and the protest march into the classroom, the editors feel that the students will be sincerely involved and that better writing will be the end result.

The authors chosen for inclusion in *Hard Rains* exemplify the merits of this approach. The literary quality of most of these essays is extremely high, not as a result of the authors' preoccupation with formal rhetoric, but because of the commitment they bring to the investigation of their subjects. The contributors are not necessarily "literary stylists"; the expository composition is superior because they are responsible and dedicated communicators.

As with all complex problems, and those presented here are among the most complex, the student will need to pay attention to subtleties and make the imaginative connections which separate trivial paraphrasing from insightful comprehension of interrelationships. Some of the material in this book is tough; its readers must strive to be tougher still.

Hard Rains is not a "controversy" reader, for it does not sacrifice integrity to the abused notion of "fairness" or "two sides to every question." It attempts to take the student to the point where information requires interpretation, which is the beginning of creative thought. We do not, for example, include a racist to counter arguments critical of racism, or an apologist for pollution to "balance" essays decrying the assault on the physical environment. We have not presented debates on the severity of contemporary problems; but, by assuming their existence, we have begun to examine approaches to their solution. Since *Hard Rains* is not an "either/or" book, when the students have finished reading these essays they will have yet to develop their own critiques and formulate their individual points of view.

Considering the most troubling of problems is not the easiest way to pass a semester. To bring the material of *Hard Rains* into the classrooms is to accept the challenge of discussing the issues which, if unresolved, will destroy American society. We believe that the university must join with its students in the consideration of these problems.

R.D./B.N.S.

CONTENTS

CHAPTER ONE
THE SENSE OF DISRELATIONSHIP

Introduction *1*

The New Hero *3*
Louis W. Cartwright

America the Unimagining *17*
Benjamin De Mott

The Forgotten American *27*
Peter Schrag

The Gangster as Tragic Hero *41*
Robert Warshow

War Stories *46*
Murray Polner

Not Gone But Frozen *62*
Howard Junker

The Cold Society *65*
Nat Hentoff

CHAPTER TWO
EDUCATION AND ITS DISCONTENTS

Introduction *85*

Why the Generation Gap? *89*
Harrison Brown

Is the University to Blame? *95*
Henry Steele Commager

ix

Rebellion as Education   *101*
Kingsley Widmer

The New Reformation   *110*
Paul Goodman

The Humanities and Inhumanities   *121*
Louis Kampf

Letter from a Far Frat   *131*
Herbert Gold

Comes the Cultural Revolution   *136*
James Hitchcock

CHAPTER THREE
THE POLITICS OF MILITARISM

Introduction   *147*

The New Forms of Control   *151*
Herbert Marcuse

The New American Militarism   *164*
General David M. Shoup

Why We Are in Vietnam   *175*
Norman Mailer

The Circle of Deception   *183*
Robert Jay Lifton

Toward an Affirmative Morality   *200*
John F. Wharton

Human Nature and International Relations   *206*
J. William Fulbright

The Battle of the Ants   *213*
Henry David Thoreau

CHAPTER FOUR
RACISM: AFFLICTION AND ORDEAL

Introduction   *217*

Racism and the White Backlash   *221*
Martin Luther King, Jr.

The Ethics of Living Jim Crow   *233*
Richard Wright

Esau and Jacob   *237*
Robert Coles

The White Race and Its Heroes   *243*
Eldridge Cleaver

Old Con, Black Panther, Brilliant Writer
and Quintessential American   *255*
Harvey Swados

Motown Justice   *268*
Edgar Z. Friedenberg

Racism:
The Cancer that is Destroying America   *278*
Malcolm X

CHAPTER FIVE
THE ECOLOGICAL DISASTER

Introduction   *283*

A Fable for Tomorrow   *287*
Rachel Carson

Can the World Be Saved?   *289*
La Mont C. Cole

Polluting the Environment   *295*
Lord Ritchie-Calder

The National Pollution Scandal   *304*
Gaylord Nelson

Eco-Catastrophe!   *314*
Dr. Paul Ehrlich

Death in Our Air   *326*
Ben H. Bagdikian

Oil in the Velvet Playground   *334*
Harvey Molotch

Wasteland   *350*
Marya Mannes

CHAPTER SIX
VALUES AND THE PERSONAL CHOICE

Introduction   *353*

The Decline of Religion   *357*
William Barrett

The Revolt of the Diminished Man   *362*
Archibald MacLeish

Freedom and Responsibility   *371*
Jean-Paul Sartre

Crap Detecting   *374*
Neil Postman and Charles Weingartner

Them and Us: Are Peace Protests Self-Therapy?   *386*
Nat Hentoff

Why Women's Liberation?   *393*
Marlene Dixon

An Interview with Abbie Hoffman and Jerry Rubin   *407*
with Paul Kurtz

The Hero Today   *424*
Joseph Campbell

Post-Trip   *428*
Burton H. Wolfe

EPILOGUE

Of the World in 1984   *439*
Richard E. Farson

Science, Sex and Tomorrow's Morality   *447*
Albert Rosenfeld

Day Million   *459*
Frederick Pohl

HARD RAINS

THE SENSE OF DISRELATIONSHIP

INTRODUCTION

The atmosphere within which our society conducts its daily business, a composite of fear, tension, loneliness, social fragmentation, and futility, diminishes the quality of American life. When alone, we are vaguely aware that many of the activities and affirmations supposedly decisive to our happiness are, in reality, only meaningless gestures.

Thoreau's observation that "Men lead lives of quiet desperation" is confirmed by contemporary existence. R. D. Laing has portrayed modern man in these terms: "The individual in the ordinary circumstances of living may feel more unreal than real; in a literal sense, more dead than alive; precariously differentiated from the rest of the world, so that his identity and autonomy are always in question. He may not possess an overriding sense of personal consistency or cohesiveness. He may feel more insubstantial than substantial, and unable to assume that the stuff he is made of is genuine, good, valuable." If this somewhat pessimistic view of our personal emotions seems exaggerated, it has yet to be explained why, as a society, we have turned to analysts, tranquilizers, pills, alcohol, and narcotics, not to mention the more available anesthesia of television, in order to escape from the tensions of everyday life.

Each day people pass one another feeling "more insubstantial than substantial," feeling no call, indeed no necessity, to act in another's behalf. Avoiding trouble, we habitually compromise our principles for immediate profit. The obsession with overt physical

1

violence, so characteristic of our society, the vanishing qualities of honesty and trust, the absence of communal celebration, create anxieties which lie beyond our understanding. In the face of our own personal confusions we are apt to feel the need for an imposed external order. Numerous theories have been offered to explain the pervasive sense of disrelationship. Some argue that the loss of identity described by Laing is incurred as individuals are assimilated into large corporate structures. Others account for the loss as a result of the particularized work functions that have replaced what Paul Goodman has called "man's work." Still others—Erich Fromm, for example—discuss the authoritarian ethic demanded of us by an increasingly regimented society. Critics of the social system dissect the many ways people are manipulated, while psychologists inform us that to some degree we are disturbed by this manipulation.

The problems discussed in other chapters of this book relate to the dehumanization of contemporary man. The generation gap, which has always existed, is unique to our time in the extent to which the largest younger generation ever rejects the older generation's values. Noise, pollution, and the congestion of our environment have further demoralized us. Racial tension pervades our society and seems to give license to the worst in men. The acceptance of violence and the loss of traditional values both seem to propel us further into an undignified, perhaps less than human existence.

The sense of disrelationship felt by so many citizens and described from various perspectives by some of our best writers and scholars is an intangible problem and differs from the other problems considered in *Hard Rains* because one cannot speak of a "solution." Healing the spirit is not a matter of increased federal assistance. One can only hope that if society begins to deal effectively with the problems that are rooted in the social, economic, and political realities of American life, there will emerge among the people a new sense of purpose, a new attitude toward human relationships, and a new sense of community.

THE NEW HERO

Louis W. Cartwright

How do I feel about America, her education systems, her institutions, her people, her land, her me? What question could be more important for each of us to answer! Yet how can one sufficiently untangle oneself from the living and struggling of this vast human drama in order to answer it?

It is impossible for me to respond to a subject so consuming and elusive in the stride of a professional. I can't focus on one or two aspects, for I haven't yet become an expert in any one field. Nor, as I see it now, will I in the future specialize in order to be able to say that I know a few things. So, I begin this collection of feelings about America by saying that I don't know anything for sure. I don't think I have ever known anything for sure long enough to remember it. America is that way to me: every now and then I see her for an instant to be a certain country, definable and pin-pointable; but before I get my pen raised to plunge, she disappears in a cloud-twist of change.

Since there is no other proof of one's feelings than living according to them, I'd say mine are healthy. I've lived a quarter of a century and thus far haven't been put away. My wife doesn't run back to Mother and I'm finally through trying to get my father to tell me how to live. I'm punctual and pay my debts, and there is a good chance I'll instantly like anyone who is and does the same. I'd say I'm doing pretty

Louis W. Cartwright, "The New Hero" in *To Make a Difference*, edited by Otto Butz. Copyright © by Otto Butz. Reprinted by permission of Harper & Row, Publishers.

well. If nothing accidental occurs I might even reach manhood and find out for myself what it's about—providing I can endure the pace I've set for myself, blaming no one else for anything and not seeking salvation tomorrow but always today, now. All this without TV is fairly difficult, but I have faith.

The bomb frightened the daylight out of my life. For two years I didn't make one decision, one plan that bound more than two days together. I continued doing what I had been doing like a castrated bull pacing indifferently among the cows. How many nightmares did I die in? How many mornings did the sun crash into my bed like a surprise party! Finally, out of a desperation to live, I decided that the bomb didn't matter, that if it came today we wouldn't have to face dying the day after. I might as well make big plans, seeing as how nothing had changed. So I made big plans and still make them. But like hell it hasn't changed! I'm probably more religious now than the most devout Jehovah's Witness, but I have no one to pray to. I am devoted to life, health and future, to preserve these in the nowness of every thought, wish and dream. The only one left to believe in is Man, so I figure we've got to prepare him for the responsibilities of being God. And we've got to start with ourselves. Which means we have to start all over again, look at it all as if we had just arrived like children walking to school for the first time. To these ends, then, my life is a first attempt and my feelings are my only guide.

I trust myself at the intuitive level. Propaganda may be pulling me here and there, and it may not be; I don't know. I don't deal decisions out to distant realities like Vietnam. All I know is I don't have any reasons to kill anyone, and I'm the one who has to have them in order to do it. I can't be pushed or bullied into a war I don't understand. That goes for all things of that nature. The term civil rights means nothing to me, but a person getting unfairly shafted means everything. I'll just have to say I don't have time for sit-ins and marches; I'm too busy learning how to live. Besides, most sit-ins and marches are too popular to be effective; in a sense they've been wasted on too many little points. However, they might be the only method of resistance against the State for those of us who can't afford a lobby. I might be wrong not to march or sit, but I just haven't felt it yet. I might be committing huge mistakes that in two years will rise up and hurl a shadow over my life, force me into that corner from which the only escape is to the analyst or Mr. Tambourine Man. There are so many might-be's in my style of life, too many to waste my time in elaborate and absolute preparation. So I keep open to the front and worry only about my back.

I am not contemporary, popular, in the "new look" of the "Pepsi Generation," and I'm not frightened. This party has been going on so long now, that I think if someone announced that it was over nobody would leave. They'd have no place to go. I get the same feeling when I pass a bar at two o'clock and listen to the homeless begging not to be thrown out. If television were suddenly canceled what would people do? All that free time? Occasionally I feel trapped by the outstanding accomplishments of the Beatles, the overnight success of skateboards and hula hoops . . . I find myself trying to come up with a gimmick to make a million. Then I wake up and grab myself by the collar: What? You want to create another ride for them to spend their time on? Then I begin to blame these heroes who throw the people a bone for their money and model nothing but materialism to our children. But, hell, it isn't them. It's the potential in the situation that pays their type, and the situation has never been anything but a blueprint unraveling; it's we who create the morality from it; by morality I mean the way to be, and the way to be is to choose your hero and dress him in money, and it is still of the people. I guess I'm just lonely believing I got my morality from the Earth: the animal in me and at large is in stride with a higher truth than my intellect can handle. Morality is the intellect's attempt to protect itself against the animal, but it is only an aftereffect of life and the animal knows this. We Americans have always fought the animal by ignoring it. Our morality has been a blindfold to wear in the daytime and a sleeping pill to take at night. I've experimented at living without masks and pills and, no kidding, it's all right. We're pretty damn fine animals when we loosen up the cinch and remove the bit.

·   ·   ·

America has seldom been more than a list of many moving spirits clashing, joining, splitting, some small and violent, others huge and bullying, but it has never been describable in terms of one spirit. (Although the Beatles might take some issue.) Today I see a spirit moving in America almost as widespread as the heavy silence following Kennedy's assassination; this is the spirit of uniformity. It seems to bulldoze everything unique and human down until the ground is flat enough for one hundred square miles of identical houses. And I don't have to wait for history to come along with its approval or condemnation of my opinion; I am the pen-point of history writing, my life is its ink. I am defining myself en route, knowing that before the ink is dry what I've written is already inaccurate, for I am a process of becoming different. And this gives me hope.

I am a rear-engine sports car, a Lotus or a Porsche pushing myself into the future of blind curves and diminishing left-handers. I am prepared for the unexpected, I lunge toward it with hunger, even though I've seen so much I seldom encounter a surprise; however, I am most near death when I begin believing I've seen it all. So I continuously doubt the future. My faith is behind me, not out in front: I am not drawn ahead by the apron strings of Heaven; I am pushing at crashing speeds into the unknowns, whether or not I interrupt any heavens. I've made no contract with God; his promises and threats do not interest or frighten me. A life after death is not separated by dying: I die into dream each night and am sifted or jolted back into life each morning. My power is in me, in all of us. Life is this power.

Self-reliance or -directedness is the first inevitable step out of alienation and solitude, and since solitude is such a shocking realization it leaves a scar or flaw in our subsequent adjustment to life. I call this scar a sense of privacy. You might look on it as a void in one's personality which he fills with his very own ideas of the universe; in here he writes philosophy for himself and his dependents. Here, then, is the factory of self-reliance. Others might look upon this void or room as a guest cottage for God, a place we go to pray, an island of insanity. Indirectly self-reliance is manufactured there no matter what you call it.

The obvious counterpart or concomitant of being self-directed is that I profoundly resent anyone interfering by ordering me to do something or go somewhere. Once my father directed my life; when I left home I took over; on occasion he will ask me to do something for him, but it is no longer an order and he has heard my refusal. The police and the selective service don't respect me and my sense of privacy. This is a real fact, and I know it, so it is again up to me to stay out of their way if I want to remain in charge of my doings. Needless to say, I have been negligent and have put myself in positions where they pushed me. You see, I keep forgetting that they no longer keep the peace; they enforce law and so disturb peace. I forget that they do not deal with humans as being human; they deal with humans as being lawbreakers. I forget that one cannot be innocent or ignorant or have lapses into innocence because those states of being are illegal. I guess I forget because I want to. I don't want to recall that I grew up in a town where I was ordered to show a policeman my identification card three or four times a week. There's no excuse for me forgetting that! I should not take walks at night; I know better.

Also, I loathe the notion America is promoting that one has to go to college in order to "make it." How about those who don't want to? Those who have a couple of dreams of their own that they'd like to try out? When a notion like that becomes almost an unwritten law, a matter of course, then we defeat ourselves: we end up forcing pure character and imagination, our only chance for health and future, into systems of education that return to us a beast who is intelligent only because he has finally been trained to answer with the acceptable notions of our time. Once so potentially brilliant and eager to learn about life, they return to us predictably dull and bored under the oppressive weight of collections of information. We frustrate the creative mind into a desperate submission whereupon it closes up like a clam on the ocean floor and never feels good or free about life again. Some of our young blood isn't meant for college even though it can pass the entrance exams, but where else are they encouraged to go? Into the Army? The parent offers to send him to, and support him through, college only if he goes directly after high school and stays with it for a continuous four years (or is it six, now?). So they go, are never late, are never passionate, sit in classrooms, while the life they felt to be good quietly dies.

I first enrolled in college because I wanted to. This was two years after high school, after I had hitchhiked around America, after having cycled a year in Europe, and worked in a missile factory—after, I'd like to say, I felt that I had earned the readiness for learning. I wanted to learn all about the Greeks, especially Odysseus, for he, like me, had traveled. But I wasn't allowed to take Greek mythology or study the Greek language; I had to take certain *preliminary* courses. I did manage to lie my way into a philosophy class. At the end of that year I felt that I had had enough; I knew that I could learn without having an examination date placed before me for discipline. I still liked learning. So I quit and returned to Europe. My father was astounded and hurt at my courteous refusal of the security of a college degree; he made me feel like I was cheating. But he wished me good luck and a quick return.

My first trip to Europe had been a magic carpet tour; I had enough money, and though I cycled I didn't need to work my way, didn't need to stay any place longer than it pleased me. The second trip was the yes-trip: it was yes to everything, and I was broke. I took jobs doing anything, lived anywhere, ate anything, and learned a great deal about freedom. For instance, I learned that you can cycle all day in the rain and not catch cold if you work hard (and if your clothes get washed). I didn't belong in school, anyone could see that. I needed to try myself in life, see if I could learn how to be. From where I was in the south of France, American middle-class security looked like a sickness, one that most never got over. When I returned home, in spite of the particular mood I was in or my reason for returning, I was full of life and lean as a coyote. I wanted to sleep, then eat, then think.

"But he's got to finish college," I heard my father saying to my mother behind their door that night.

"Let him rest awhile," said mother.

"Hell, rest, he's twenty-one. When I was his age I was supporting my parents."

"We don't need support."

"I don't want his support, I want him to get to work. It's not healthy to sit and do nothing."

I listened to them. My father was right. So was I. He wouldn't give in and neither would I. The last favor I wanted of my parents was time, time to decide what I wanted to try next. Three months later I introduced him to my fiancée, and within a month, married, I left that time and place of my childhood forever.

A year later I wanted to return to school to pursue a new interest, and within a week I hated college. It was stuffy, crowded, tightly scheduled, fast, an authority center where questions were slaughtered quickly and efficiently with brilliant little answers. I had to put away my interests and get in line with the others. It wasn't learning; it was read, memorize and answer, and there wasn't any time for exceptions to the beautiful rules. It was terrible, but I had unwittingly promised myself that I would stick it out. I'd convinced myself that like climbing a long, steep grade, there is a personal benefit gained in reaching the top. So here fulfilling my promise was my only reason for remaining. Endurance.

My reason for enduring became a chant I whisper to myself when it gets worse than bad: you can make it, you made it over the Alps, you can do anything. Don't I have other reasons? Would I come to watch people? I'd rather stand on Market Street. Would I come to learn from teachers? We all know how unnecessary and redundant many professors are, how they never quite come alive before their classes, as if the administration were controlling their oxygen supply. Most classrooms are holding a recital of the text you read last night. But every now and then, one man sneaks through and holds a class on his own that balances off the entire history of inadequate professors. Yes, for that chance (as long as it doesn't get any slimmer) I'd sign up for a full load and attend. But isn't it so very unfortunate that the clothesline of education droops so low between the occasional giants? To this point I append the twin to the statement that all of us shouldn't go to college: all of those who are teaching shouldn't be. Perhaps half of all who populate a campus should be in a trade school or on a ranch. I feel we have sacrificed learning for education, that, as with missiles, we are competing with Russia to graduate people, hit or miss. No! No no no no. We fail beneath the statistical affidavits of our success: there it is in black and white, but there it ain't in the people.

.   .   .

College should be a free place with huge doors that swing open to whomever feels curious about what goes on inside. It shouldn't be a prerequisite to life; it is an aftereffect. I've learned and have been inspired more by my time spent in coffee bars and cafeterias with others than in the hours I've sat in classrooms. But I get no credit for that time. So maybe classes should be held in the college cafeteria. I want it to be that free and slow. The way I describe how a college should be, it becomes obvious that we have very few colleges in America. We have trade schools where one learns how to do psychology and engineering and creative writing, and where curiosity is called game playing and inefficient. After all, if you keep asking those questions, you'll never get out by June!

.   .   .

Some afternoons a few of us would gather for coffee in the cafeteria and discuss our private lives and their progress toward freedom. One would describe his latest LSD trip, another would remind us that marijuana is still a good ride, and someone from another state would say, "Yeah, those are good but haven't you tried mushrooms or cactus?" On and on it would go. I was always the one who after a few rounds began to tell about my latest fishing or hunting trip. I would try to describe it vividly so as to remind them that life is still a pretty good trip. I would "trip out" discussing my trip (they called it "zooming," which means getting carried away). They often wondered what I was taking. After my story I tried to convince them that they didn't need pills to be free, that LSD is most often a pause, time out from facing reality as it will be when they return. However, there were always more of them than of me, so I would lose, so to speak, to someone else's LSD vacation story. Oo! The colors! On those days I left school feeling so very lonely I didn't see why or how I could return.

If you take the pill, then chemically you are *forced* to look *freely* at yourself. It is as if we no longer have it within ourselves to reach out and touch the terrible truths, as if we haven't the faith and guts to get us there on our own. Where is America's confidence? The confidence that doesn't depend on pills and degrees and sunglasses, on the new look and the club card, and approval of the authority. Have our governments and schools done so much for us that we have completely forgotten that we can do some things on our own? Why do the majority of professors have to write out a lecture to read to their class? What happened to "off-the-cuff"?

Maybe it is my fault for not being able to see that we have reached a new level of life where only institutions can handle humanity and where the individual is the element of error that must be canceled out. If that is it then I don't want it. Progress can carry America wherever she wants to go, but I'm glad my feet are on the earth and I enjoy walking.

Whose America *is* this? I no longer feel a part of her. I am a stranger in her schools and indifferent to, or against, her goals (or the possible lack thereof). I've pulled my car off the circuit, quit the race to nowhere; now I drive where I want to, and it is up to me to keep out of her way if I want to keep free. (Isn't that ironic? I have to fight America for my freedom!)

My America is me alive and living, wading upstream, crashing through brush, chasing grunion, watching salmon leap, screeching my brakes on the freeway to watch a flight of Canadian geese, picking up a hitchhiker and asking him where he's going, having coffee with a trucker, finding an arrowhead, and being attacked by a blackbird because I passed too near her nest. America is me getting up tired and driving thirty miles to meet someone on time, or hiking up mountains just to do it. It's the whole country when you look around from a mountain fourteen thousand feet tall. It's feeling as if fences are merely spider webs that cling to your pants legs when you go roaming. It isn't a job at ten thousand a year, a club to drink in, a fast red car, and a pasteboard house; and it isn't going to be that ulcer at forty, either. Sometimes I think *I'm* America.

America: a big place, fragmented by rules into smaller places, further broken up by borders into smaller places, and finally, unfindable on a country map, my town, a peephole through which I interact with and spy on the world—if and when I choose to. If I choose not to, they will try to force me to, and though it would take sixty days for Washington's red paper snake to strike me into her army, I'd rather make them use it than submit like a good son. I'm no son of Washington. Yep! America's a big place, but it barely has room for me. I live on its borders, up against its cultural limits at all times. The cost of living on the border is high: you've got to be wealthy, and wealth here is measured in terms of how little you need to live. How few possessions. I need so little I have to make up reasons for not retiring tomorrow. I'm lean. I'm a tramp playing dress-up. My possessions are souvenirs, they are not necessaries. I do not need the luxuries this country uses to bait its people toward progress. I've learned to despise that word.

For whenever we look about to see what it was we were working for, what do we see: a house that wasn't built well enough to raise our children, broken appliances in the garage, two cars falling apart while only one or two years old, furniture that was once so pretty you felt you had to cover it with plastic, an electric kitchen with a trash box full of TV dinner tins. Is this the only other way to avoid another crash: to build stuff so cheaply it will break down and have to be bought again and again? The other way to keep this economy going is to keep a war going. Is this all to build a home for the brave to preserve freedom? No, I'm afraid no one will buy that one any more. We all know that we don't know why we're doing all the things we do, that we don't like what we do, but we don't know what to do about it. Okay, it is easy to say what is happening, and it is easy to list a few reasons why. But what to do about it? What do we do?

It would be pointless to list ways we could alter this situation unless I thought we would do it, and that is the sorrow that weighs me down: I don't think most Americans want to change; they have faith in these systems. Oh, they might argue this in the bar after work with their friends when it doesn't count, but be sure that the next morning they'll be back at the bench performing some push-button task that in some way supports the sicknesses of our time. Whether it's throwing together pasteboard houses, squeezing food into heat-and-serve tins, printing stories they know are just half-true, creating advertising to further confuse and take advantage of others like themselves who no longer know better. Each one plays a small enough role so he doesn't feel accountable. It's *they* who are doing it, the owners, the board, the office. "Don't look at me, buddy, I just work here."

The other night my wife and I went to a drive-in movie. At the intermission I went to get her an ice water and a coffee. I poured myself the coffee and asked the girl to please fix me an ice water. She turned to the boy cashier: "How much do we have to charge for the large cup?"

He didn't turn his head: "Twenty-five cents," he answered.

I couldn't believe I heard him right. "No," I said, "it's just a cup of ice water."

He turned smilingly: "I know, but it doesn't matter. The cups are on inventory. Every one that goes out of here I have to get twenty-five cents for."

"Look," I said, "the cup probably cost three cents at best. How can you charge a quarter for it? I don't care about inventory."

"But the office made the inventory. It's a rule."

"Well, break the damn rule! It's ridiculous."

"How do I explain it to them? There's supposed to be a quarter for each cup."

"Tell them you stepped on one."

"Nah, I couldn't do that."

"Aren't you part of them?" I asked.

"No, I just work here."

"Oh, you're their slave, then?"

"What do you mean?" he asked.

"You are part of this company. All you'd have to do is leave a note for the inventory saying you sold one cup for a nickel."

"I can't do it, I'm sorry."

"Because of them?"

"Yes."

"You know, friend, you're dead. I don't know why anyone would ever want to talk to you. I couldn't stand behind a counter if I had to point blame to my "they" every time something different came up. Don't you realize that every time you shirk and shrug off responsibility you make yourself smaller? You've already shrunk to a pipsqueak."

He just smiled at me like a baby who thinks it's funny to see anger. So did all the people crowding around, but no one said anything or got too close. They wouldn't have done anything to stop me from killing the dead-boy.

"Look," I said with great tolerance, "I'll give you one more chance. You sell me the cup for twenty-five cents. I'll bring it back, wash it, and you give twenty cents return on it, okay?"

"I can't do it. How would I explain the five cents extra in the drawer?"

"PUT IT IN YOUR POCKET!"

The speechless dead-boy stood expressionless, like he didn't under-

stand a word I had said. I held his eyes sternly as I strode out of the
refreshment room. No one said a word. They didn't even call me a nut
behind my back. On the way back to the car I counted four empty cups
blowing around in the wind.

I know that these kinds of Americans, the ones you'll never hear
about unless they get killed in a spectacular accident, are not strong
enough to begin a battle back to reality, to that state of knowing you
are alone and that each person has his own idea of himself and you,
and that beyond this we know nothing for sure. It is a state of dignity
and responsibility to eternity which includes this moment. Some try
to return to this state of awareness; they sink in despair at the odds
with which they're faced. Others don't try; they sink silently into
systems they don't understand. A few make it. They are put into
institutions for safekeeping. But the dead-boy behind the counter sits
safely inside a stockade made up of fears he doesn't look at. If he
steps out in any direction he's afraid he'll be attacked. He's a nobody
and an anybody. So what'll happen to him? Who'll help him? No
one. So stay there and blame them, blame the boss who isn't here
right now. So, each of us lives on that pinhead surrounded by others
like ourselves who will point at us if we move. That doesn't stop
some from moving but it stops most.

Therefore we needn't be surprised when we read that a woman
was raped in a New York building in front of many witnesses, or that
a man was killed in front of the same. It's the law that you are not
supposed to interfere with the scene of an accident. So better drive
by and be glad it wasn't you who careened off that embankment and
are now crying in pain wishing some fragmented person like yourself
would break the law and stop to help you. When the people of a
country won't or can't help one another then it is no longer a country.

We won't help one another but we are herded off in battalions to
help Vietnam! America, the big meat producer, has something wrong
with her and she blames others for the whyness of the war that she
needs to fight in order to keep her sick economy flowing. Why are
the best of our youths devising huge gambles in order not to be
drafted? Faking homosexuality, psychoses, and nervous breakdowns,
or flatly refusing to go and thereby putting themselves in jail. They
are doing this because they believe there is no longer any cause great
enough to kill others for. They have become responsible to humanity,
for all wars now have a red line, a point beyond which we cannot go
and survive. In this respect the bomb is a blessing, for it gives us an

unarguable reason not to try to prove our points in other countries, spilling blood of people who never heard of America.

When I think of war, of bombs startling children and splashing horror on faces of screaming mothers I nearly go mad with anger! While I'm sitting in the cafeteria having coffee or on a stream at dawn feeling very happy, all of a sudden the image of war goose-steps into my mind and I scream: Why? What for? Who for? A million pettinesses crawl quickly like ants to answer those questions. I know it isn't just America, that there have to be at least two to have a war, that the innocent always get it, and that others make money on it, and that others die in it, and that some don't care a damn about it. Okay, this is reality and I know it, but I'm not relieved of anger. I want of fight something, whatever it is, that creates war. But when I try to express my feelings someone nails me down to the hard facts of life as if these facts were the sacred Part Two of the Ten Commandments. I want to fight these facts.

When I fight I am like all neurotics who have waged a war alone. I have no one to compare myself to, no one out there to keep me honest, no one to tell me to go home when my opposition has disappeared. Often I feel like the kid who gets mad when a bunch of his friends playfully pile on top of him. The madness builds up as their laughter loudens, until it cannot be contained, and the boy explodes with unconquerable strength; he breaks loose and swings. He slugs everyone standing around. And he can't stop himself. America sometimes feels like a hundred bags labeled friendship being piled on top of me; I tear loose and rip them all open just to see them pour out. Of course I don't trust everyone. I trust about ten people, and I trust them to be just who they are, not me. But I don't trust America. It thinks friendship can be won during a party, or at least let's all forget about it and have a good time together. Well, that's it, I can't forget. I can't forget that America doesn't want to mean what it says, that it isn't fighting for freedom, that we are not the great home of the brave. And I can't forget that it is my fault, for the others do not care. I miss the America I dreamt about.

.   .   .

I guess having been banged around by those bags of false friendship has made me sound pretty strong and angry. I even surprised myself. I said that I blame myself for everything and turned right around and began blaming others for not remembering, not having the strength to keep reality in focus long enough to become reacquainted with it. I must now state that I haven't written one sentence against America that was not first composed in self-disgust. At one time or another I, too, forgot about everything painful or challenging. I, too, used the word love as only a technique for snowing a girl into bed. I, too, passed the blame to the *They* of America. I didn't know any better. Oh, I felt different, but feelings aren't necessarily expedient. "You can't get anywhere being honest, Mac." The worst most unhealthy person I see today I wouldn't be able to understand unless I had at one time stood in his shoes. I recognize those shoes. I used to be very sick, and that was when I was considered by my elders to be most healthy. Now I am well and clean, and they consider me to be sick. There is not merely a matter of opinion, either.

Every time I kept quiet, put off something I felt for fear of endangering my standing in a group, I began to hate myself. This hate would build up, collect in some recess of my personality, until I was so divided against myself I would have to break open. If I was right I had to argue and fight. If I was wrong and knew it, I had to break down my old feelings and sweat it out forming new ones that were still strange to me. After about fifteen years of this I have finally learned not to keep quiet, not to postpone, not to let someone else do it for fear of getting myself involved too deeply. I don't want to keep quiet any more, and I won't forget anything to make being noisy easier.

Let me backtrack a moment to pick up the points I've tried to make. First, I don't feel a part of America any more: I don't believe in her reasons; I don't learn from her schools; and her systems and laws have just about controlled the human element out of the experiment. Second, I can't forget the fullness of the world in order to make my life easier. Third, I have promised myself not to keep quiet any longer, for I feel to blame for everything, which makes me responsible. And fourth, I can't be pushed into a war or way of life I don't feel to be true. Death would be sweeter than a deadly lifetime, and I feel that is the goal of American progress, which leaves me out.

Why do I feel to blame?

It is simple: I am not part of the system, and the system's hopes, ends and means, but I am part of the people. I am responsible to them and the land. I am responsible to that part in each that each has forgotten, the dark side of their personalities' moon, their subconscious, their back-forgotten. I get along best with those of us we've locked up because we think we can't get along with them. The ones who can't hide any more because they have no place left to run to, the juvenile delinquents, the drunks, neurotics still at large, and other yet unclassified people who are trying to do what they want to do without causing too much of a disturbance. When I say "the people" I refer to those who still try to enrich their lives by seeking out reality, not evading it. The others who coast along from ride to ride with a pocketful of free passes are the dead weight who have to be awakened to the fact that they are being carried.

. . .

But we still have a chance; all our seeds aren't bad. The few old hero-types who are left will be coming out more and more; they always do when things get bad. As a band of animals drives off the one of them that is sick, so these Americans will drive sick America out of business. They will beg for responsible positions and then gamble them against the truth and health of every little incident with which they have to deal. Professors who refuse to be bullied by administrators, personnel managers who refuse to be blinded by the degree, men who still search for personal character and strength—anyplace you find a person living by principles that grow in scope as he learns you find what I call an American. And yes, he looks primitive and ridiculous standing out there all alone. He is an old hero. And he will die nobly. But the others, the faceless gray murmur in every crowd, will need an expensive funeral, for contrast, so that their mourners will think that they had lived.

. . .

When I ask, Who is the new hero? I'm not looking for a name, a celebrity, any one person. I'm looking for the image we have of our own best self. The new hero is one who is following after this image, but, unlike the donkey that follows after the farmer's carrot, he holds his own carrot out in front, and this keeps him honest. I'm not going to say that Zorba is the hero, or that Bobby Dylan is the hero; but I would say that they and others have by example added to the portrait of a potential hero. You could say that potential is the hero, potential wherever it is found and expressed.

. . .

You see, it all comes back to what is possible for us to do in life, to accomplish, to create, to enjoy. When we systematize life we are saying that any other way outside of the system is impossible, for this and this and this will happen to you. We defend our systems by a stockade of consequences. And then somehow we forget that we created both the system and the consequences; we begin to believe the system is unchangeable, is absolute, is god. In any case, life becomes increasingly impossible outside of certain definitions, and increasingly miserable inside them. How about the exceptions, the human exceptions to the rules? For example, and this is not an extreme example even though it shocks some of us: a father wakes up in the night, his daughter is crying, he finds her suffering from some sickness, so he rushes her to the nearest, not the cheapest, hospital. At the desk they inquire: "Do you have insurance? Do you have any money? Well, I'm terribly sorry but you'll have to see our social welfare personnel and they won't be in until tomorrow morning. There's nothing I can do," she says. The twenty-five-cent paper cup. What would you do in his shoes? Or should I ask, what have you done, for I imagine all of us have run into these counter people. But most of us comply even though some rough beast is raging beneath our breath to break desks, rules and systems and more or less kidnap the help we need. But we comply, we wait for people to do it the system's way, and the clock ticks and we wait and the little girl dies in the man's arms.

And it happens all over on all levels from the grossest to the pettiest —exceptions to the rules are forced to comply. Now I put it to you, *what human being is not an exception to the rule?*

No system should ever become so rigid as to not be able to handle with ease the unexpected. Which is just another way of saying no system should not be able to handle life.

In conclusion, the new hero is out to prove to himself and others that there are ways to live where no *They* is ever blamed, where no rule is ever made that can't be unmade or changed, and where the exceptions make up the reality and beauty of being human.

AMERICA THE UNIMAGINING

Benjamin De Mott

A man in his early fifties, vigorous, strong-faced, well liked in his town; family man, business success (small-city merchandising operation). No reader but a great keeper-up—business papers, hard news, world events, facts that matter. Pleasures? He "gets a kick out of" gadgets and machines—wild stereo layout in the cathedral living

Benjamin De Mott, "America the Unimagining." From the book *Supergrow: Essays And Reports On Imagination In America* by Benjamin De Mott. Copyright ©, 1969, 1968 by the author. This essay first appeared in somewhat different form in *The American Scholar* and is here reprinted by permission of E. P. Dutton & Co., Inc. and the author.

room, complicated ship-to-shore gear on his boat, a genuine systems approach for stock control in the stores. Further pleasures: he's outdoorsy, handy at home, a Dartmouth man, skier, active in business and community clubs, nonchurchgoer, nonpolitical argufier. . . .

At parties he doesn't talk much to women. Also, he stands back a little from his kids. Pleasant-tentative with his bright daughter, straight-arrowish "Dad" with his teen-aged boys. Stands back, too, from the "creative" phases of the business—buying, advertising, display, and so on—leaving this to a younger brother. (Let something "real sticky" turn up anywhere, though, and nobody but himself can cope. Who else, for instance, would be up to a face-off with the old family friend, one of his store managers, when the detective service reports the man is robbing them blind?) As for a personality profile:

"I am more interested in a man's behavior than in his inner life." Check. "In shaping character, externals are more important than inner tendencies." Check. "I sometimes have trouble figuring out the behavior of people who are emotionally unstable." Check. "Math is one of my best subjects." Check. "I think I'm practical and efficient when there's something that has to be done." Check. "I don't have the temperament for the 'romantic' point of view." Check. "I have few emotional problems." Check. "A first principle with me is that it's a man's duty to adjust himself to his environment." Check. "I am a fairly conventional person." Check. "My relations with other people are usually uncomplicated." Check. "My ideas are more often sound and sensible than unusual or imaginative." Check. "I say what I have to say in a few simple words so that I'm easily understood." Check. "There's a lot in the economic interpretation of history." Check. "I find it easier to deal with concrete facts in one special field than with general ideas about man or nature." Check. "I think science offers as good a guide as any to the future." Check. "When I'm working out a problem I try to stick as close as possible to the facts." Check. "I enjoy an intimate conversation with one person more than general conversation with several." No. "When I hear a person talk, I think more about his personality than I do about what he's saying." No. "I think I have a good understanding of women." No. "I love to talk about my innermost feelings to a sympathetic friend." Nah. "I often think I can feel my way into the innermost being of another person." No. "It takes a good deal to make me angry." Check. "Unselfishness and sympathy are more desirable than high ideals and ambitions." False. "I'm apt to make up stories by myself about the private thoughts and experiences of the people I meet." No. "I believe the world may be well lost for love." No. "I live in my imagination as much as I do in the external world." No. "I dislike everything that has to do with money—buying, selling, bargaining." Oh sure. "I like being in the thick of the action." Yes, emphatically. "I like to have people about me most of the time." Yes, emphatically. . . .

Other items (not on the Harvard clinic test) worth noting about this man? One: Inclined to treat characters as functions, he regularly "explains" people by telling you what they do (a parenthetical phrase— Harry's a doctor, Hank's a cop, Lucille's had a pair of twins). Another point: The fellow is good to tie up by on a sloppy night at Southwest Harbor, and makes, in general, a fine summer neighbor—fun outings to the island, family picnics, softball on the sand, sun's over the yardarm, and so on. Further point: When you step away from him, sit in judgment, dwell on his limits, you feel like a heel. You discover again that one of the several reasons for not judging is that the minute it's done, the judge is judged, stands fully visible in his own fatuity and self-congratulation, beyond sympathy, ripe for sentence himself. Yet another item: The man "beheld" is representative. Tens of millions are excluded from his place, just at this moment; going up from the middle in society is where you're likely to find him, not from the middle down. But the excluded millions can't forever escape; even now they are being graded "up" on his curve. Every year the movement of economic life shoots tens of thousands toward him—into his set of mind, his style, his inward truth. He is no "middle-class stereotype," in short: he is an American destination or finish line, the possible end of the race.

Finally, last point about the man: He is in trouble. There's a withering in him, a metaphorical arm gone, some limb, some key part missing, something stunted or ungrown. The present judge speaks quickly, on the run, hoping to hide himself from the next judge: The man just described is, in one flat word, *unfulfilled*.

To say as much is, by instant extension, to discount the seriousness of the famous American commitment to the ideal of individual self-fulfillment. And while such discounting is standard practice among the knowing, it isn't at first glance easy to defend. Granted, the language in which national commitments and values are usually spelled out— the language of civics classes and Scouting Award nights—does beg to be mocked. "The social organization of America is compatible with its free political institutions. . . . America is a society in which equality of opportunity is supported by specific social mechanisms, including classlessness, a wide spectrum of inviolable and equal individual rights guaranteed to all individuals, guarantees of minimum welfare for all and special assistance to any that are at unusual economic disadvantage. . . . Enhancing the dignity of the individual citizen, developing his capabilities for self-fulfillment, is a prime concern of the American government. . . . The environments which help to shape the character of the individual—his home life, education, religious training, occupation, etc.—are in varying degrees matters of public concern. The object of this concern is to develop typical traits of character—independence of spirit, respect for the rights of others, cooperativeness, sense of civic responsibility—and others which will make the individual a better, more constructive citizen." Formulations like these cry out for qualification, amendment, hints of stylish self-restraint. Some humility, please.

But the cry for humility can itself become cant. Spells of living abroad in middle-class communities—leafy Edgbaston in England, say, or a Costa village in Portugal—offer only ambiguous testimony on the matter of the American versus European sense of civic responsibility. But in the area of attitudes and policies concerning education, those ambiguities disappear. The cause of "trained excellence" is Everyman's cause in America; my right to as much education as I can bear goes relatively unchallenged. No events, no crisis, seemingly, can interrupt the national dream of self-realization through mental strife. And no taxpayer protest ever badly smutches this piety. Two years ago, after the peace demonstration at the Pentagon, President Johnson, meeting with a group of teachers at the White House, turned eloquent—some might have said moving—on the subject of self-realization and the school. Appointments this morning, he explained, with the National Security Council and with the President of Mexico—but you, you teachers, you're more important. Whatever else they said about him, the President went on, they would have to say that because of programs he instituted, a million people were in college this year who would not otherwise have had a chance to go. And how much more remained to be done! Four men out of ten on earth could not read or write! He himself was returning to teaching when his political career was over.

The books on the Cabinet Room shelf suggested an absence of a passion for the higher literary culture—O. Henry, a high school physics text, a high school chemistry text, and the like. (There has been no report that President Nixon has replaced them.) The few educational institutions in the country where the idea of standards is well rooted are meritocratic in assumption—which means not only antiaristocratic but antidemocratic as well. By far the larger part of the huge federal expenditures in the field of education supports phases of the defense program. And, more important than any of this, profound inequities still exist in the American system of public education. But from none of this does it follow that the cause or dream in question was a sham. The old programs and the new—Head Start, the regional educational laboratories, the tuition loan bank—have flaws, cannot meet every need. But the motive behind them is, in essence, no more suspect than the motive behind the foundation of the first free public education system on earth. That motive is the nurture of a citizen useful to the community at large but also decently developed for himself—gifts realized, mind awake, wholeness intact. An unmockable aim, in sum: dignity for man.

And yet, and yet: the Product of It All looks out from the mirror and reveals himself to be—stunted. Somewhere—not simply in the stereotype of himself but in his actuality—he is locked in himself; somewhere he is fixed in an inhuman rigidity; somewhere there is a "malfunction." How to account for this? Has the nation from the start been the captive of theories about the formation and nurture of individual selfhood that are wrong-headed—theories that are obstacles in themselves to self-realization? Is there a uniquely American muddle about fulfillment? If so, what is its nature? How is it to be solved?

Stupidity alone answers confidently—but several relevant observations come to mind. Chief among them is that, for complex social, historical, and cultural reasons, the nature of human growth—in particular, the central role of the imagination in determining its rate and quality—has not often been placed clearly before the national view.

Commentators by the hundreds score the country off for garishness, gross materialism, unspirituality; few focus on the poverty of its conception of personal growth. Yet that is the fairer target. The nation prates of self-realization, and rests in near obliviousness that my humanness depends upon my capacity and my desire to make real to myself the inward life, the subjective reality, of the lives that are lived beyond me. The nation feeds itself on rhetoric about "individual rates of progress"—and yet possesses little knowledge, if any, of the steps by which the human being becomes itself, the separate, private acts of the imagination on which the achievement of personhood depends.

And, to repeat, this ignorance or obliviousness is no mystery. Human growth stems from the exercise of our power to grasp another being's difference from within. How can that truism maintain itself among a people convinced of the fundamental sameness of men? As Tocqueville long ago pointed out, the myth of sameness is a keystone in the deep structure of American belief. (Tocqueville's specific point was that the American protest on behalf of "the individual" was rooted in the assumption that all individuals, once free "to be themselves," would desire the same things and feel in the same ways.) And it is a fact that the moral imperative of the imaginative act is rarely proclaimed in American public or cultural life. A Negro singer invited to a White House conference bursts out in condemnation of the guests for the unreality of their proposals, their abstractness when seen in the light of her experience. The First Lady's eyes moisten. Shaken but proud she responds that she "cannot understand" the outburst; she has not had the same experience. And in the morning the country's best newspaper, *The New York Times,* editorially salutes the First Lady for her "candor," agrees that the feelings and sense of life of the black community are beyond our imagining, and consigns all whites to blank, useless, uncomprehending pity.

And the story is not different on the contemporary intellectual scene. It is a French voice—Jean-Paul Sarte's—not an American voice, that is heard urging men to more intelligent conceptions of human growth, demanding that they break free of the notion that others have no life except that which they exhibit when serving as the material out of which we fashion our experience. (". . . there are men who die without—save for brief and terrifying flashes of illumination —ever having suspected what the *Other* is. The horizons of my life are infinitely shrunk.") And among recent philosophers it is a German voice—Max Scheler's—not that of an American, which dares to formulate an equation setting out relations of identity between individual growth, the perfection of love, and a grasp of the full distinctness and separateness of another human being. ("Love calls explicitly for an understanding entry into the individuality of *another* person *distinct in character* from the entering self . . . a warm and wholehearted endorsement of 'his' reality as an individual, and 'his' being what he is . . . In love . . . there is built up, within the phenomenon itself, a clear-cut consciousness of two *distinct* persons. This consciousness is not merely a starting point; it reaches full maturity only as love pursues its course.")

What is more, a backward glance at the American cultural heritage confirms that the most powerful voices of American literary culture have been precisely those which, in one manner or another, have been most committedly hostile to the enterprise of attentive imaginative concentration on the fathoming of individual differences. D. H. Lawrence, in his *Studies,* broods hard on the stunted quality of the selves created in the writing of Poe and Whitman, and attributes it in the end to their incapacity to imagine and value a *separate* otherness. Love was a theme for both, but for neither was it a possibility; each man was drawn by fantasies of merging, total engrossment, loss of awareness of the other as separate—fantasies that teased him into confusing "understanding" with the act of sinking one's soul in another.[1] And wherever the engrosser or merger disappears from American letters, an even more frightening figure—the self-bound man (Captain Ahab is the Prince)—stands forth in his place. In Emerson, for example, self-fulfillment appears to require an absolute denial of others, a massive, unrelenting independence, a readiness for isolation. Responding to a culture of conformity, this sage declared that a man bent on realizing himself must learn to carry himself in separation from otherness—"as if everything were titular and ephemeral but he." Widen the gulf, Emerson cries:

> We must go alone. I like the silent church before the service begins, better than any preaching. How far off, how cool, how chaste the persons look, begirt each with a precinct or sanctuary! So let us always sit.

Or again:

> At times the whole world seems to be in conspiracy to importune you with emphatic trifles. Friend, client, child, sickness, fear, want, charity, all knock at once at thy closet door, and say, "Come out unto us." But keep thy state; come not unto their confusion.

Or yet again:

> Live no longer to the expectation of these deceived and deceiving people with whom we converse. Say to them, O father, O mother, O wife, O brother, O friend, I have lived with you after appearances hitherto. Henceforward I am the truth's. . . . If you are noble, I will love you; if you are not, I will not hurt you and myself by hypocritical attention.

Emerson does allow that he could love another, if the person were noble; and every Emersonian knows how risky it is to fix the man in a single attitude. But separateness, far more often than involvement, is the theme that rouses him to lyricism; the poetry in him inclines

---

[1] A version of this now turns up in Love Generation mystic-union gabble (You-am-I and I-am-you, etc.).

strongly to the view, saying it once more, that becoming a fulfilled man means drawing oneself more tightly, consciously, firmly back within the limits of the primal existent self.

And that view or stance turns up repeatedly in American literature, in popular culture (the art Western), everywhere in American society. (It may even whisper to us in the writings of David Riesman and Nathan Glazer; the utopian archetype of self-realized man described by them as "autonomous" has a definite taste for Emersonian gestures against otherness.) Over and over we are enjoined to find "our own thing," "our own bag," in the hippie phrase. And again and again the success of our search is presumed to depend upon our power to cut ourselves off, to harden the wall around us, not only to march to the beat of our own drum, but seemingly to hear no other sound.

There are, of course, countervoices here and there. Though his message did not cut through, smothered in clichés of life adjustment, John Dewey frequently dwelt on connections between human growth and sound education of the imagination—that instrument by which people gain in "flexibility, in scope, and in sympathy, till the life which the individual lives is informed with the life of nature and society." More than one American research psychologist has convinced himself of the centrality of imagination in the course of human development, and has attempted inquiries into the nurture of the imaginative man —witness the labors of Henry Murray and his associates at Harvard in the late 1930's. "Self-Other" theories of growth, which stress self-dramatization and imaginative role-playing, have a place in the history of American philosophy, owing chiefly to the writings of George Herbert Mead. ("The self by its reflexive form announces itself as a conscious organism which is what it is only so far as it can pass from its own system into those of others, and can thus, in passing, occupy both its own system and that into which it is passing. . . . Shut up within his own world . . . he would have no entrance into possibilities other than those which his own organized act involved. . . . It is here that mental life arises.")

And there is one great, seldom-studied American who put the case for fulfillment as dependent upon imaginative growth in utterly unambiguous terms—I speak of Charles Horton Cooley, a founder of American sociology. In *Human Nature and the Social Order* (1929), Cooley laid it down that:

> . . . the imaginations which people have of one another are the *solid facts* of society. . . . I do not mean merely that society must be studied *by* the imagination—that is true of all investigations in their higher

reaches—but that the *object* of study is primarily an imaginative idea or group of ideas in the mind, that we have to imagine imaginations. The intimate grasp of any social fact will be found to require that we divine what men think of one another. Charity, for instance, is not understood without imagining what ideas the giver and recipient have of each other; to grasp homicide we must, for one thing, conceive how the offender thinks of his victim and of the administrators of the law; the relation between the employing and hand-laboring classes is first of all a matter of personal attitude which we must apprehend by sympathy with both, and so on. . . .

Nor did Cooley stop here—with a mere definition of an appropriate area of inquiry for his field. He went on to assert that the quality of imaginative sympathies is the surest measure of the degree of human growth and fulfillment:

> One's range of sympathy is a measure of his personality, indicating how much or how little of a man he is.

And he was certain beyond doubt that those who deprecated this sympathy, shrugged it off with prattle about *sensitivity,* missed its richly complicated nature and meaning:

> [Sympathy] is in no way a special faculty but a function of the whole mind to which every special faculty contributes, so that what a person is and what he can understand or enter into through the life of others are very much the same thing. We often hear people described as sympathetic who have little mental power, but are of a sensitive, impressionable, quickly responsive type of mind. The sympathy of such a mind always has some defect corresponding to its lack of character and of constructive force. A strong, deep understanding of other people implies mental energy and stability; it is a work of persistent, cumulative imagination. . . .

But if there is a native tradition which understands the nurture of the imagination to be a key to general human growth, it is, by all odds, a minority tradition, far away from the center of popular belief. The weight of the general culture presses continually toward feats of objectification—objectification of labor (the assembly line, time study), of love (sex research), of desire (image-making, consumer research). At the center stands the conviction that fulfillment is deliverance into a function—a job, a title, a carpet, an income, a pool, somebody else's respect. I, the free American, am free to "find my own place," my "social niche," my "professional slot." I go forth from myself, I *go places,* ranch house to White House, dropout to Ph.D., twelve dollars weekly to a hundred dollars a day. And up the line, where I have it made: I "am more interested in a man's behavior than in his inner life"; I believe man's first duty is to "adjust himself to his environment"; I doubt that anyone can "feel his way into the innermost being of another person"; I don't seek inward truths. . . .

Is mockery in order? The objectifying American culture can be damned for having only once in its history concerned itself intensely with the matter of precisely what this or that individual man felt in this or that instant of time (the occasion was the period of witch trials in the seventeenth century, where it was found useful to know the inward workings of the devil). It can be damned as well for having consistently refused to introduce into its elementary educational system those "studies"—improvisation, mime, dance, dramatics—that elsewhere in the West are accepted as the basic human efforts at developing an imagination of otherness. It can be damned, more fiercely, for its incalculable failures of imagination—for example, its incapacity to make real to itself the inward life, man by man, woman by woman, child by child, of its black people.

But there are, here as always in life, qualifications to be entered: If there is no imagination of deprivation among us, there is at least guilt at good fortune, and this has sufficed to rebuild a world or feed a dozen famines. And in any event, it is not seemly for a professing humanist to lay down accusations here, for the American humanist—the teacher and scholar whose texts and knowledge should have been the greatest resources of those in pursuit of the truth of "the other subject" —has himself been a cop-out, an objectifier, a character madly eager to turn art itself into a "body of objective knowledge" to be "mastered" for "career examinations."

The point of substance, in fine, lies beyond accusations or "cultural critiques." It is a matter simply of a general, culture-wide dimming of the lights of inward life, a matter of failed encounters, missed meetings, hands that do not reach out, minds that hear the lock turn in their prison doors.

It is nighttime, the Maine harbor again. A lantern in the rain, motion of shore waters, a welcome, a beginning . . . But we don't go on, neither he nor she nor I. "My ideas are more often sound and sensible. . . . " "I say what I have to say in a few simple words. . . . " No hardrock, an occasional pot putterer, we would nevertheless prefer that people "not get ideas about us." And as for the famous still sad music of humanity, "we" don't hear it much. We don't flow; we hold on tight inside; we do the generous thing over and over, and invariably do it ungenerously; we see and feel and imagine ourselves to be highly responsible, competent, the solid people of the earth, the independents, the resilients, the unwhiners.

And for that idea or vision of self, some among us pay a lot—gouge out their innerness—become less than men.

THE FORGOTTEN AMERICAN

Peter Schrag

There is hardly a language to describe him, or even a set of social statistics. Just names: racist-bigot-redneck-ethnic-Irish-Italian-Pole-Hunkie-Yahoo. The lower middle class. A blank. The man under whose hat lies the great American desert. Who watches the tube, plays the horses, and keeps the niggers out of his union and his neighborhood. Who might vote for Wallace (but didn't). Who cheers when the cops beat up on demonstrators. Who is free, white, and twenty-one, has a job, a home, a family, and is up to his eyeballs in credit. In the guise of the working class—or the American yeoman or John Smith —he was once the hero of the civics book, the man that Andrew Jackson called "the bone and sinew of the country." Now he is "the forgotten man," perhaps the most alienated person in America.

Nothing quite fits, except perhaps omission and semi-invisibility. America is supposed to be divided between affluence and poverty, between slums and suburbs. John Kenneth Galbraith begins the foreword to *The Affluent Society* with the phrase, "Since I sailed for Switzerland in the early summer of 1955 to begin work on this book . . . " But *between* slums and suburbs, between Scarsdale and Harlem, between Wellesley and Roxbury, between Shaker Heights and Hough, there are some eighty million people (depending on how you count them) who didn't sail for Switzerland in the summer of 1955, or at any other time, and who never expect to. Between slums and suburbs: South Boston and South San Francisco, Bell and Parma, Astoria and Bay Ridge, Newark, Cicero, Downey, Daly City, Charlestown, Flatbush. Union halls, American Legion posts, neighborhood bars and bowling leagues, the Ukrainian Club and the Holy Name. Main Street. To try to describe all this is like trying to describe America itself. If you look for it, you find it everywhere: the rows of frame houses overlooking the belching steel mills in Bethlehem, Pennsylvania, two-family brick houses in Canarsie (where the most common slogan, even in the middle of a political campaign, is "curb your dog"); the Fords and Chevies with a decal American flag on the rear window (usually a cut-out from the *Reader's Digest,* and displayed in counter-protest against peaceniks and "those bastards who carry Vietcong flags in demonstrations"); the bunting on the porch rail with the inscription, "Welcome Home, Pete." The gold star in the window.

When he was Under Secretary of Housing and Urban Development, Robert C. Wood tried a definition. It is not good, but it's the best we have:

He is a white employed male . . . earning between $5,000 and $10,000. He works regularly, steadily, dependably, wearing a blue collar or white collar. Yet the frontiers of his career expectations have been fixed since he reached the age of thirty-five, when he found that he had too many obligations, too much family, and too few skills to match opportunities with aspirations.

This definition of the "working American" involves almost 23-million American families.

The working American lives in the gray area fringes of a central city or in a close-in or very far-out cheaper suburban subdivision of a large metropolitan area. He is likely to own a home and a car, especially as his income begins to rise. Of those earning between $6,000 and $7,500, 70 per cent own their own homes and 94 per cent drive their own cars.

94 per cent have no education beyond high school and 43 per cent have only completed the eighth grade.

He does all the right things, obeys the law, goes to church and insists —usually—that his kids get a better education than he had. But the right things don't seem to be paying off. While he is making more than he ever made—perhaps more than he'd ever dreamed—he's still struggling while a lot of others—"them" (on welfare, in demonstrations, in the ghettos) are getting most of the attention. "I'm working my ass off," a guy tells you on a stoop in South Boston. "My kids don't have a place to swim, my parks are full of glass, and I'm supposed to bleed for a bunch of people on relief." In New York a man who drives a Post Office trailer truck at night (4:00 P.M. to midnight) and a cab during the day (7:00 A.M. to 2:00 P.M.), and who hustles radios for his Post Office buddies on the side, is ready, as he says, to "knock somebody's ass." "The colored guys work when they feel like it. Sometimes they show up and sometimes they don't. One guy tore up all the time cards. I'd like to see a white guy do that and get away with it."

What counts

Nobody knows how many people in America moonlight (half of the eighteen million families in the $5,000 to $10,000 bracket have two or more wage earners) or how many have to hustle on the side. "I don't think anybody has a single job anymore," said Nicholas Kisburg, the research director for a Teamsters Union Council in New York. "All the cops are moonlighting, and the teachers; and there's a million guys who are hustling, guys with phony social-security numbers who are hiding part of what they make so they don't get kicked out of a housing project, or guys who work as guards at sports events and get free meals that they don't want to pay taxes on. Every one of them is cheating. They are underground people—*Untermenschen*. . . . We really have no systematic data on any of this. We have no ideas of the attitudes of the white worker. (We've been too busy studying the black worker.) And yet he's the source of most of the reaction in this country."

The reaction is directed at almost every visible target: at integration and welfare, taxes and sex education, at the rich and the poor, the foundations and students, at the "smart people in the suburbs." In New York State the legislature cuts the welfare budget; in Los Angeles, the voters reelect Yorty after a whispered racial campaign against the Negro favorite. In Minneapolis a police detective named Charles Stenvig, promising "to take the handcuffs off the police," wins by a margin stunning even to his supporters: in Massachusetts the voters mail tea bags to their representatives in protest against new taxes, and in state after state legislatures are passing bills to punish student demonstrators. ("We keep talking about permissiveness in training kids," said a Los Angeles labor official, "but we forget that these are our kids.")

And yet all these things are side manifestations of a malaise that lacks a language. Whatever law and order means, for example, to a man who feels his wife is unsafe on the street after dark or in the park at any time, or whose kids get shaken down in the school yard, it also means something like normality—the demand that everybody play it by the book, that cultural and social standards be somehow restored to their civics-book simplicity, that things shouldn't be as they are but as they were supposed to be. If there is a revolution in this country —a revolt in manners, standards of dress and obscenity, and, more importantly, in our official sense of what America is—there is also a counter-revolt. Sometimes it is inarticulate, and sometimes (perhaps most of the time) people are either too confused or apathetic—or simply too polite and too decent—to declare themselves. In Astoria, Queens, a white working-class district of New York, people who make $7,000 or $8,000 a year (sometimes in two jobs) call themselves affluent, even though the Bureau of Labor Statistics regards an income of less than $9,500 in New York inadequate to a moderate standard of living. And in a similar neighborhood in Brooklyn a truck driver who earns $151 a week tells you he's doing well, living in a two-story frame house separated by a narrow driveway from similar houses, thousands of them in block after block. This year, for the first time, he will go on a cruise—he and his wife and two other couples—two weeks in the Caribbean. He went to work after World War II ($57 a week) and he has lived in the same house for twenty years, accumulating two television sets, wall-to-wall carpeting in a small living room, and a basement that he recently remodeled into a recreation room with the help of two moonlighting firemen. "We get fairly good salaries, and this is a good neighborhood, one of the few good ones left. We have no smoked Irishmen around."

Stability is what counts, stability in job and home and neighborhood, stability in the church and in friends. At night you watch television and sometimes on a weekend you go to a nice place—maybe a downtown hotel—for dinner with another couple. (Or maybe your sister, or maybe bowling, or maybe, if you're defeated, a night at the track.) The wife has the necessary appliances, often still being paid off, and the money you save goes for your daughter's orthodontist, and later for her wedding. The smoked Irishmen—the colored (no one says black; few even say Negro)—represent change and instability, kids who cause trouble in school, who get treatment that your kids never got, that you never got. ("Those fucking kids," they tell you in South Boston, "raising hell, and not one of 'em paying his own way. Their fucking mothers are all on welfare.") The black kids mean a change in the rules, a double standard in grades and discipline, and—vaguely —a challenge to all you believed right. Law and order is the stability and predictability of established ways. Law and order is equal treatment—in school, in jobs, in the courts—even if you're cheating a little yourself. The Forgotten Man is Jackson's man. He is the vestigial American democrat of 1840: "They all know that their success depends upon their own industry and economy and that they must not expect to become suddenly rich by the fruits of their toil." He is also Franklin Roosevelt's man—the man whose vote (or whose father's vote) sustained the New Deal.

There are other considerations, other styles, other problems. A

postman in a Charlestown (Boston) housing project: eight children
and a ninth on the way. Last year, by working overtime, his income
went over $7,000. This year, because he reported it, the Housing
Authority is raising his rent from $78 to $106 a month, a catastrophe
for a family that pays $2.20 a day for milk, has never had a vacation,
and for which an excursion is "going out for ice cream." "You try and
save for something better; we hope to get out of here to someplace
where the kids can play, where there's no broken glass, and then
something always comes along that knocks you right back. It's like
being at the bottom of the well waiting for a guy to throw you a rope."
The description becomes almost Chaplinesque. Life is humble but not
simple; the terrors of insolent bureaucracies and contemptuous officials produce a demonology that loses little of its horror for being
partly misunderstood. You want to get a sink fixed but don't want to
offend the manager; want to get an eye operation that may (or may
not) have been necessitated by a military injury five years earlier, "but
the Veterans Administration says I signed away my benefits"; want to
complain to someone about the teen-agers who run around breaking
windows and harassing women but get no response either from the
management or the police. "You're afraid to complain because if they
don't get you during the day they'll get you at night." Automobiles,
windows, children, all become hostages to the vague terrors of everyday life; everything is vulnerable. Liabilities that began long ago cannot possibly be liquidated: "I never learned anything in that school
except how to fight. I got tired of being caned by the teachers so at
sixteen I quit and joined the Marines. I still don't know anything."

At the bottom of the well

American culture? Wealth is visible, and so, now, is poverty. Both
have become intimidating clichés. But the rest? A vast, complex, and
disregarded world that was once—in belief, and in fact—the American
middle: Greyhound and Trailways bus terminals in little cities of
midnight, each of them with its neon lights and its cardboard ham-
burgers; acres of tar-paper beach bungalows in places like Revere and
Rockaway; the hair curlers in the supermarket on Saturday, and the
little girls in communion dresses the next morning; pinball machines
and the *Daily News*, the *Reader's Digest* and Ed Sullivan; houses with
tiny front lawns (or even large ones) adorned with statues of the Virgin
or of Sambo welcomin' de folks home; Clint Eastwood or Julie An-
drews at the Palace; the trotting tracks and the dog tracks—Aurora
Downs, Connaught Park, Roosevelt, Yonkers, Rockingham, and forty

others—where gray men come not for sport and beauty, but to read numbers, to study and dope. (If you win you have figured something, have in a small way controlled your world, have surmounted your impotence. If you lose, bad luck, shit. "I'll break his goddamned head.") Baseball is not the national pastime; racing is. For every man who goes to a major-league baseball game there are four who go to the track and probably four more who go to the candy store or the barbershop to make their bets. (Total track attendance in 1965: 62 million plus another 10 million who went to the dogs.)

There are places, and styles, and attitudes. If there are neighborhoods of aspiration, suburban enclaves for the mobile young executive and the aspiring worker, there are also places of limited expectation and dead-end districts where mobility is finished. But even there you can often find, however vestigial, a sense of place, the roots of old ethnic loyalties, and a passionate, if often futile, battle against intrusion and change. "Everybody around here," you are told, "pays his own way." In this world the problems are not the ABM or air pollution (have they heard of Biafra?) or the international population crisis; the problem is to get your street cleaned, your garbage collected, to get your husband home from Vietnam alive; to negotiate installment payments and to keep the schools orderly. Ask anyone in Scarsdale or Winnetka about the schools and they'll tell you about new programs, or about how many are getting into Harvard, or about the teachers; ask in Oakland or the North Side of Chicago, and they'll tell you that they have (or haven't) had trouble. Somewhere in his gut the man in those communities knows that mobility and choice in this society are limited. He cannot imagine any major change for the better; but he can imagine change for the worse. And yet for a decade he is the one who has been asked to carry the burden of social reform, to integrate his schools and his neighborhood, has been asked by comfortable people to pay the social debts due to the poor and the black. In Boston, in San Francisco, in Chicago (not to mention Newark or Oakland) he has been telling the reformers to go to hell. The Jewish schoolteachers of New York and the Irish parents of Dorchester have asked the same question: "What the hell did Lindsay (or the Beacon Hill Establishment) ever do for us?"

The ambiguities and changes in American life that occupy discussions in university seminars and policy debates in Washington, and that form the backbone of contemporary popular sociology, become increasingly the conditions of trauma and frustration in the middle. Although the New Frontier and Great Society contained some programs for those not already on the rolls of social pathology—federal aid for higher education, for example—the public priorities and the rhetoric contained little. The emphasis, properly, was on the poor, on the inner cities (*e.g.,* Negroes) and the unemployed. But in Chicago a widow with three children who earns $7,000 a year can't get them college loans because she makes too much; the money is reserved for people on relief. New schools are built in the ghetto but not in the white working-class neighborhoods where they are just as dilapidated. In Newark the head of a white vigilante group (now a city councilman) runs, among other things, on a platform opposing pro-Negro discrimination. "When pools are being built in the Central Ward—don't they think white kids have got frustration? The white can't get a job; we have to hire Negroes first." The middle class, said Congressman Roman Pucinski of Illinois, who represents a lot of it, "is in revolt. Everyone has been generous in supporting anti-poverty. Now the middle-class American is disqualified from most of the programs."

"Somebody has to say no . . . "

The frustrated middle. The liberal wisdom about welfare, ghettos, student revolt, and Vietnam has only a marginal place, if any, for the values and life of the working man. It flies in the face of most of what he was taught to cherish and respect: hard work, order, authority, self-reliance. He fought, either alone or through labor organizations, to establish the precincts he now considers his own. Union seniority, the civil-service bureaucracy, and the petty professionalism established by the merit system in the public schools become sinecures of particular ethnic groups or of those who have learned to negotiate and master the system. A man who worked all his life to accumulate the points and grades and paraphernalia to become an assistant school principal (no matter how silly the requirements) is not likely to relinquish his position with equanimity. Nor is a dock worker whose only estate is his longshoreman's card. The job, the points, the credits become property:

> *Some men leave their sons money [wrote a union member to the* New York Times*], some large investments, some business connections, and some a profession. I have only one worthwhile thing to give: my trade. I hope to follow a centuries-old tradition and sponsor my sons for an apprenticeship. For this simple father's wish it is said that I discriminate against Negroes. Don't all of us discriminate? Which of us . . . will not choose a son over all others?*

Suddenly the rules are changing—all the rules. If you protect your job for your own you may be called a bigot. At the same time it's perfectly acceptable to shout black power and to endorse it. What does it take to be a good American? *Give the black man a position because he is black, not because he necessarily works harder or does the job better.* What does it take to be a good American? Dress nicely, hold a job, be clean-cut, don't judge a man by the color of his skin or the country of his origin. What about the demands of Negroes, the long hair of the students, the dirty movies, the people who burn draft cards and American flags? Do you have to go out in the street with picket signs, do you have to burn the place down to get what you want? What does it take to be a good American? *This is a sick society, a racist society, we are fighting an immoral war.* ("I'm against the Vietnam war, too," says the truck driver in Brooklyn. "I see a good kid come home with half an arm and a leg in a brace up to here, and what's it all for? I was glad to see *my kid* flunk the Army physical. Still, somebody has to say no to these demonstrators and enforce the law.") What does it take to be a good American?

The conditions of trauma and frustration in the middle. What does it take to be a good American? Suddenly there are demands for Italian power and Polish power and Ukrainian power. In Cleveland the Poles demand a seat on the school board, and get it, and in Pittsburgh John Pankuch, the seventy-three-year-old president of the National Slovak Society demands "action, plenty of it to make up for lost time." Black power is supposed to be nothing but emulation of the ways in which other ethnic groups made it. But have they made it? In Reardon's Bar on East Eighth Street in South Boston, where the workmen come for their fish-chowder lunch and for their rye and ginger, they still identify themselves as Galway men and Kilkenny men; in the newsstand in Astoria you can buy *Il Progresso, El Tiempo,* the *Staats-Zeitung,* the *Irish World,* plus papers in Greek, Hungarian, and Polish. At the parish of Our Lady of Mount Carmel the priests hear confession in English, Italian, and Spanish and, nearby, the biggest attraction is not the stickball game, but the *bocce* court. Some of the poorest people in America are white, native, and have lived all of their lives in the same place as their fathers and grandfathers. The problems that were presumably solved in some distant past, in that prehistoric era before the textbooks were written—problems of assimilation, of upward mobility —now turn out to be very much unsolved. The melting pot and all: millions made it, millions moved to the affluent suburbs; several million—no one knows how many—did not. The median income in Irish

South Boston is $5,100 a year but the community-action workers have a hard time convincing the local citizens that any white man who is not stupid or irresponsible can be poor. Pride still keeps them from applying for income supplements or Medicaid, but it does not keep them from resenting those who do. In Pittsburgh, where the members of Polish-American organizations earn an estimated $5,000 to $6,000 (and some fall below the poverty line), the Poverty Programs are nonetheless directed primarily to Negroes, and almost everywhere the thing called urban backlash associates itself in some fashion with ethnic groups whose members have themselves only a precarious hold on the security of affluence. Almost everywhere in the old cities, tribal neighborhoods and their styles are under assault by masscult. The Italian grocery gives way to the supermarket, the ma-and-pa store and the walk-up are attacked by urban renewal. And almost everywhere, that assault tends to depersonalize and to alienate. It has always been this way, but with time the brave new world that replaces old patterns becomes increasingly bureaucratized, distant, and hard to control.

Yet beyond the problems of ethnic identity, beyond the problems of Poles and Irishmen left behind, there are others more pervasive and more dangerous. For every Greek or Hungarian there are a dozen American-Americans who are past ethnic consciousness and who are as alienated, as confused, and as angry as the rest. The obvious manifestations are the same everywhere—race, taxes, welfare, students— but the threat seems invariably more cultural and psychological than economic or social. What upset the police at the Chicago convention most was not so much the politics of the demonstrators as their manners and their hair. (The barbershops in their neighborhoods don't advertise Beatle Cuts but the Flat Top and the Chicago Box.) The affront comes from middle-class people—and their children—who had been cast in the role of social examplars (and from those cast as unfortunates worthy of public charity) who offend all the things on which working class identity is built: "hippies [said a California labor official] who challenge the precepts that these people live on." If ethnic groups are beginning to organize to get theirs, so are others: police and firemen ("The cop is the new nigger"); schoolteachers; lower-middle-class housewives fighting sex education and bussing; small property owners who have no ethnic communion but a passionate interest in lower taxes, more policemen, and stiffer penalties for criminals. In San Francisco the Teamsters, who had never been known for such interests before, recently demonstrated in support of the police and law enforcement and, on another occasion, joined a group called Mothers Support Neighborhood Schools at a school-board meeting to oppose—with their presence and later, apparently, with their fists—a proposal to integrate the schools through bussing. ("These people," someone said at the meeting, "do not look like mothers.")

Which is not to say that all is frustration and anger, that anybody is ready "to burn the country down." They are not even ready to elect standard model demagogues. "A lot of labor people who thought of voting for Wallace were ashamed of themselves when they realized what they were about to do," said Morris Iushewitz, an officer of New York's Central Labor Council. Because of a massive last-minute union campaign, and perhaps for other reasons, the blue-collar vote for Wallace fell far below the figures predicted by the early polls last fall. Any number of people, moreover, who are not doing well by any set of official statistics, who are earning well below the national mean ($8,000 a year), or who hold two jobs to stay above it, think of themselves as affluent, and often use that word. It is almost as if not to be affluent is to be un-American. People who can't use the word tend to be angry; people who come too close to those who can't become frightened. The definition of affluence is generally pinned to what comes in, not to the quality of life as it's lived. The $8,000 son of a man who never earned more than $4,500 may, for that reason alone, believe that he's "doing all right." If life is not all right, if he can't get his curbs fixed, or his streets patrolled, if the highways are crowded and the beaches polluted, if the schools are ineffectual he is still able to call himself affluent, feels, perhaps, a social compulsion to do so. His anger, if he is angry, is not that of the wage earner resenting management—and certainly not that of the socialist ideologue asking for redistribution of wealth—but that of the consumer, the taxpayer, and the family man. (Inflation and taxes are wiping out most of the wage gains made in labor contracts signed during the past three years.) Thus he will vote for a Louise Day Hicks in Boston who promises to hold the color line in the schools or for a Charles Stenvig calling for law enforcement in Minneapolis but reject a George Wallace who seems to threaten his pocketbook. The danger is that he will identify with the politics of the Birchers and other middle-class reactionaries (who often pretend to speak for him) even though his income and style of life are far removed from theirs; that taxes, for example, will be identified with welfare rather than war, and that he will blame his limited means on the small slice of the poor rather than the fat slice of the rich.

If you sit and talk to people like Marjorie Lemlow, who heads Mothers Support Neighborhood Schools in San Francisco, or Joe Owens, a house painter who is president of a community-action organization in Boston, you quickly discover that the roots of reaction and the roots of reform are often identical, and that the response to particular situations is more often contingent on the politics of the politicians and leaders who appear to care than on the conditions of life or the ideology of the victims. Mrs. Lemlow wants to return the schools to some virtuous past; she worries about disintegration of the family and she speaks vaguely about something that she can't bring herself to call a conspiracy against Americanism. She has been accused of leading a bunch of Birchers, and she sometimes talks Birch language. But whatever the form, her sense of things comes from a small-town vision of national virtues, and her unhappiness from the assaults of urban sophistication. It just so happens that a lot of reactionaries now sing that tune, and that the liberals are indifferent.

Joe Owens—probably because of his experience as a Head Start parent, and because of his association with an effective community-action program—talks a different language. He knows, somehow, that no simple past can be restored. In his world the villains are not conspirators but bureaucrats and politicians, and he is beginning to discover that in a struggle with officials the black man in the ghetto and the working man (black or white) have the same problems. "Every time you ask for something from the politicians they treat you like a beggar, like you ought to be grateful for what you have. They try to make you feel ashamed."

When hope becomes a threat

The imponderables are youth and tradition and change. The civics book and the institution it celebrates—however passé—still hold the world together. The revolt is in their name, not against them. And there is simple decency, the language and practice of the folksy cliché, the small town, the Boy Scout virtues, the neighborhood charity, the obligation to support the church, the rhetoric of open opportunity: "They can keep Wallace and they can keep Alabama. We didn't fight a dictator for four years so we could elect one over here." What happens when all that becomes Mickey Mouse? Is there an urban ethnic to replace the values of the small town? Is there a coherent public philosophy, a consistent set of beliefs to replace family, home, and hard work? What happens when the hang-ups of upper-middle-class kids are in fashion and those of blue-collar kids are not? What happens when Doing Your Own Thing becomes not the slogan of the solitary deviant but the norm? Is it possible that as the institutions and beliefs of tradition are fashionably denigrated a blue-collar generation gap will open to the Right as well as to the Left? (There is statistical evidence, for example, that Wallace's greatest support within the unions came from people who are between twenty-one and twenty-nine, those, that is, who have the most tenuous association with the liberalism of labor.) Most are politically silent; although SDS has been trying to organize blue-collar high school students, there are no Mario Savios or Mark Rudds—either of the Right or the Left—among them. At the same time the union leaders, some of them old hands from the Thirties, aren't sure that the kids are following them either. Who speaks for the son of the longshoreman or the Detroit auto worker? What happens if he doesn't get to college? What, indeed, happens when he does?

Vaguely but unmistakably the hopes that a youth-worshiping nation historically invested in its young are becoming threats. We have never been unequivocal about the symbolic patricide of Americanization and upward mobility, but if at one time mobility meant rejection of older (or European) styles it was, at least, done in the name of America. Now the labels are blurred and the objectives indistinct. Just at the moment when a tradition-bound Italian father is persuaded that he should send his sons to college—that education is the only future —the college blows up. At the moment when a parsimonious taxpayer begins to shell out for what he considers an extravagant state university system the students go on strike. Marijuana, sexual liberation, dress styles, draft resistance, even the rhetoric of change become monsters and demons in a world that appears to turn old virtues upside down. The paranoia that fastened on Communism twenty years ago (and sometimes still does) is increasingly directed to vague conspiracies undermining the schools, the family, order and discipline. "They're feeding the kids this generation-gap business," says a Chicago housewife who grinds out a campaign against sex education on a duplicating machine in her living room. "The kids are told to make their own decisions. They're all mixed up by situation ethics and open-ended questions. They're alienating children from their own parents." They? The churches, the schools, even the YMCA and the Girl Scouts, are implicated. But a major share of the villainy is now also attributed to "the social science centers," to the apostles of sensitivity training, and to what one California lady, with some embarrassment, called "nude therapy." "People with sane minds are being altered by psychological methods." The current major campaign of the John Birch Society is not directed against Communists in government or the Supreme Court, but against sex education. (There is, of course, also sympathy with the young, especially in poorer areas where kids have no place to play. "Everybody's got to have a hobby," a South Boston adolescent told a youth worker. "Ours is throwing rocks." If people will join reactionary organizations to protect their children, they will also support others: community-action agencies which help kids get jobs; Head Start parent groups, Boys Clubs. "Getting this place cleaned up" sometimes refers to a fear of young hoods; sometimes it points to the day when there is a park or a playground or when the existing park can be used. "I want to see them grow up to have a little fun.")

Can the common man come back?

Beneath it all there is a more fundamental ambivalence, not only about the young, but about institutions—the schools, the churches, the Establishment—and about the future itself. In the major cities of the East (though perhaps not in the West) there is a sense that time is against you, that one is living "in one of the few decent neighborhoods left," that "if I can get $125 a week upstate (or downstate) I'll move." The institutions that were supposed to mediate social change and which, more than ever, are becoming priesthoods of information and conglomerates of social engineers, are increasingly suspect. To attack the Ford Foundation (as Wright Patman has done) is not only to fan the embers of historic populism against concentrations of wealth and power, but also to arouse those who feel that they are trapped by an alliance of upper-class Wasps and lower-class Negroes. If the foundations have done anything for the blue-collar worker he doesn't seem to be aware of it. At the same time the distrust of professional educators that characterizes the black militants is becoming increasingly prevalent among a minority of lower-middle-class whites who are beginning to discover that the schools aren't working for them either. ("Are all those new programs just a cover-up for failure?") And if the Catholic Church is under attack from its liberal members (on birth control, for example) it is also alienating the traditionalists who liked their minor saints (even if they didn't actually exist) and were perfectly content with the Latin Mass. For the alienated Catholic liberal there are other places to go; for the lower-middle-class parishioner in Chicago or Boston there are none.

Perhaps, in some measure, it has always been this way. Perhaps none of this is new. And perhaps it is also true that the American lower middle has never had it so good. And yet surely there is a difference, and that is that the common man has lost his visibility and, somehow, his claim on public attention. There are old liberals and socialists—men like Michael Harrington—who believe that a new alliance can be forged for progressive social action:

> *From Marx to Mills, the Left has regarded the middle class as a stratum of hypocritical, vacillating rear-guarders. There was often sound reason for this contempt. But is it not possible that a new class is coming into being? It is not the old middle class of small property owners and entrepreneurs, nor the new middle class of managers. It is composed of scientists, technicians, teachers, and professionals in the public sector of the society. By education and work experience it is predisposed toward planning. It could be an ally of the poor and the organized workers— or their sophisticated enemy. In other words, an unprecedented social and political variable seems to be taking shape in America.*
>
> *The American worker, even when he waits on a table or holds open a door, is not servile; he does not carry himself like an inferior. The openness, frankness, and democratic manner which Tocqueville described in the last century persists to this very day. They have been a source of rudeness, contemptuous ignorance, violence—and of a creative self-confidence among great masses of people. It was in this latter spirit that the CIO was organized and the black freedom movement marched.*

There are recent indications that the white lower middle class is coming back on the roster of public priorities. Pucinski tells you that liberals in Congress are privately discussing the pressure from the middle class. There are proposals now to increase personal income-tax exemptions from $600 to $1,000 (or $1,200) for each dependent, to protect all Americans with a national insurance system covering catastrophic medical expenses, and to put a floor under all incomes. Yet these things by themselves are insufficient. Nothing is sufficient without a national sense of restoration. What Pucinski means by the middle class has, in some measure, always been represented. A physician earning $75,000 a year is also a working man but he is hardly a victim of the welfare system. Nor, by and large, are the stockholders of the Standard Oil Company or U.S. Steel. The fact that American ideals have often been corrupted in the cause of self-aggrandizement does not make them any less important for the cause of social reform and justice. "As a movement with the conviction that there is more to people than greed and fear," Harrington said, "the Left must . . . also speak in the name of historic idealism of the United States."

The issue, finally, is not *the program* but the vision, the angle of view. A huge constituency may be coming up for grabs, and there is considerable evidence that its political mobility is more sensitive than anyone can imagine, that all the sociological determinants are not as significant as the simple facts of concern and leadership. When Robert Kennedy was killed last year, thousands of working-class people who had expected to vote for him—if not hundreds of thousands—shifted their loyalties to Wallace. A man who can change from a progressive democrat into a bigot overnight deserves attention.

THE GANGSTER AS TRAGIC HERO

Robert Warshow

America, as a social and political organization, is committed to a cheerful view of life. It could not be otherwise. The sense of tragedy is a luxury of aristocratic societies, where the fate of the individual is not conceived of as having a direct and legitimate political importance, being determined by a fixed and supra-political—that is, non-controversial—moral order or fate. Modern equalitarian societies, however, whether democratic or authoritarian in their political forms, always base themselves on the claim that they are making life happier; the avowed function of the modern state, at least in its ultimate terms, is not only to regulate social relations, but also to determine the quality and the possibilities of human life in general. Happiness thus becomes the chief political issue—in a sense, the only political issue —and for that reason it can never be treated as an issue at all. If an American or a Russian is unhappy, it implies a certain reprobation of his society, and therefore, by a logic of which we can all recognize the necessity, it becomes an obligation of citizenship to be cheerful; if the authorities find it necessary, the citizen may even be compelled to make a public display of his cheerfulness on important occasions, just as he may be conscripted into the army in time of war.

Naturally, this civic responsibility rests most strongly upon the

Robert Warshow, "The Gangster as Tragic Hero" from *The Immediate Experience* by Robert Warshow. (Doubleday & Co.) Reprinted by permission of the author.

organs of mass culture. The individual citizen may still be permitted his private unhappiness so long as it does not take on political signifi-cance, the extent of this tolerance being determined by how large an area of private life the society can accommodate. But every produc-tion of mass culture is a public act and must conform with accepted notions of the public good. Nobody seriously questions the principle that it is the function of mass culture to maintain public morale, and certainly nobody in the mass audience objects to having his morale maintained.[1] At a time when the normal condition of the citizen is a state of anxiety, euphoria spreads over our culture like the broad smile of an idiot. In terms of attitudes towards life, there is very little difference between a "happy" movie like *Good News*, which ignores death and suffering, and a "sad" movie like *A Tree Grows in Brooklyn*, which uses death and suffering as incidents in the service of a higher optimism.

But, whatever its effectiveness as a source of consolation and a means of pressure for maintaining "positive" social attitudes, this optimism is fundamentally satisfying to no one, not even to those who would be most disoriented without its support. Even within the area of mass culture, there always exists a current of opposition, seeking to express by whatever means are available to it that sense of despera-tion and inevitable failure which optimism itself helps to create. Most often, this opposition is confined to rudimentary or semi-literate forms: in mob politics and journalism, for example, or in certain kinds of religious enthusiasm. When it does enter the field of art, it is likely to be disguised or attenuated: in an unspecific form of expression like jazz, in the basically harmless nihilism of the Marx Brothers, in the continually reasserted strain of hopelessness that often seems to be the real meaning of the soap opera. The gangster film is remarkable in that it fills the need for disguise (though not sufficiently to avoid arousing uneasiness) without requiring any serious distortion. From its begin-nings, it has been a consistent and astonishingly complete presentation of the modern sense of tragedy.

In its initial character, the gangster film is simply one example of

---

[1] In her testimony before the House Committee on Un-American Activities, Mrs. Leila Rogers said that the movie *None But the Lonely Heart* was un-American because it was gloomy. Like so much else that was said during the unhappy investigation of Hollywood, this statement was at once stupid and illuminating. One knew immediately what Mrs. Rogers was talking about; she had simply been insensitive enough to carry her philistinism to its conclusion.

the movies' constant tendency to create fixed dramatic patterns that can be repeated indefinitely with a reasonable expectation of profit. One gangster film follows another as one musical or one Western follows another. But this rigidity is not necessarily opposed to the requirements of art. There have been very successful types of art in the past which developed such specific and detailed conventions as almost to make individual examples of the type interchangeable. This is true, for example, of Elizabethan revenge tragedy and Restoration comedy.

For such a type to be successful means that its conventions have imposed themselves upon the general consciousness and become the accepted vehicles of a particular set of attitudes and a particular aesthetic effect. One goes to any individual example of the type with very definite expectations, and originality is to be welcomed only in the degree that it intensifies the expected experience without fundamentally altering it. Moreover, the relationship between the conventions which go to make up such a type and the real experience of its audience or the real facts of whatever situation it pretends to describe is of only secondary importance and does not determine its aesthetic force. It is only in an ultimate sense that the type appeals to its audience's experience of reality; much more immediately, it appeals to previous experience of the type itself: it creates its own field of reference.

Thus the importance of the gangster film, and the nature and intensity of its emotional and aesthetic impact, cannot be measured in terms of the place of the gangster himself or the importance of the problem of crime in American life. Those European movie-goers who think there is a gangster on every corner in New York are certainly deceived, but defenders of the "positive" side of American culture are equally deceived if they think it relevant to point out that most Americans have never seen a gangster. What matters is that the experience of the gangster *as an experience of art* is universal to Americans. There is almost nothing we understand better or react to more readily or with quicker intelligence. The Western film, though it seems never to diminish in popularity, is for most of us no more than the folklore of the past, familiar and understandable only because it has been repeated so often. The gangster film comes much closer. In ways that we do not easily or willingly define, the gangster speaks for us, expressing that part of the American psyche which rejects the qualities and the demands of modern life, which rejects "Americanism" itself.

The gangster is the man of the city, with the city's language and knowledge, with its queer and dishonest skills and its terrible daring, carrying his life in his hands like a placard, like a club. For everyone else, there is at least the theoretical possibility of another world—in that happier American culture which the gangster denies, the city does not really exist; it is only a more crowded and more brightly lit country —but for the gangster there is only the city; he must inhabit it in order to personify it: not the real city, but that dangerous and sad city of the imagination which is so much more important, which is the modern world. And the gangster—though there are real gangsters—is also, and primarily, a creature of the imagination. The real city, one might say, produces only criminals; the imaginary city produces the gangster: he is what we want to be and what we are afraid we may become.

Thrown into the crowd without background or advantages, with only those ambiguous skills which the rest of us—the real people of the real city—can only pretend to have, the gangster is required to make his way, to make his life and impose it on others. Usually, when we come upon him, he has already made his choice or the choice has already been made for him, it doesn't matter which: we are not permitted to ask whether at some point he could have chosen to be something else than what he is.

The gangster's activity is actually a form of rational enterprise, involving fairly definite goals and various techniques for achieving them. But this rationality is usually no more than a vague background; we know, perhaps, that the gangster sells liquor or that he operates a numbers racket; often we are not given even that much information. So his activity becomes a kind of pure criminality: he hurts people. Certainly our response to the gangster film is most consistently and most universally a response to sadism; we gain the double satisfaction of participating vicariously in the gangster's sadism and then seeing it turned against the gangster himself.

But on another level the quality of irrational brutality and the quality of rational enterprise become one. Since we do not see the rational and routine aspects of the gangster's behavior, the practice of brutality—the quality of unmixed criminality—becomes the totality of his career. At the same time, we are always conscious that the whole meaning of this career is a drive for success: the typical gangster film presents a steady upward progress followed by a very precipitate fall. Thus brutality itself becomes at once the means to success and the content of success—a success that is defined in its most general terms, not as accomplishment or specific gain, but simply as the unlimited possibility of aggression. (In the same way, film presentations of businessmen tend to make it appear that they achieve their success by talking on the telephone and holding conferences and that success *is* talking on the telephone and holding conferences.)

From this point of view, the initial contact between the film and its audience is an agreed conception of human life: that man is a being with the possibilities of success or failure. This principle, too, belongs to the city; one must emerge from the crowd or else one is nothing. On that basis the necessity of the action is established, and it progresses by inalterable paths to the point where the gangster lies dead and the principle has been modified: there is really only one possibility —failure. The final meaning of the city is anonymity and death.

In the opening scene of *Scarface,* we are shown a successful man; we know he is successful because he has just given a party of opulent proportions and because he is called Big Louie. Through some monstrous lack of caution, he permits himself to be alone for a few moments. We understand from this immediately that he is about to be killed. No convention of the gangster film is more strongly established than this: it is dangerous to be alone. And yet the very conditions of success make it impossible not to be alone, for success is always the establishment of an *individual* pre-eminence that must be imposed on others, in whom it automatically arouses hatred; the successful man is an outlaw. The gangster's whole life is an effort to assert himself as an individual, to draw himself out of the crowd, and he always dies *because* he is an individual; the final bullet thrusts him back, makes him, after all, a failure. "Mother of God," says the dying Little Caesar, "is this the end of Rico?"—speaking of himself thus in the third person because what has been brought low is not the undifferentiated *man,* but the individual with a name, the gangster, the success; even to himself he is a creature of the imagination. (T. S. Eliot has pointed out that a number of Shakespeare's tragic heroes have this trick of looking at themselves dramatically; their true identity, the thing that is destroyed when they die, is something outside themselves—not a man, but a style of life, a kind of meaning.)

At bottom, the gangster is doomed because he is under the obligation to succeed, not because the means he employs are unlawful. In the deeper layers of the modern consciousness, *all* means are unlawful, every attempt to succeed is an act of aggression, leaving one alone and guilty and defenseless among enemies: one is *punished* for success. This is our intolerable dilemma: that failure is a kind of death and success is evil and dangerous, is—ultimately—impossible. The effect of the gangster film is to embody this dilemma in the person of the gangster and resolve it by his death. The dilemma is resolved because it is *his* death, not ours. We are safe; for the moment, we can acquiesce in our failure, we can choose to fail.

WAR STORIES

Murray Polner

—*I think that any other war would have been worth my foot. But not this one.*

—*She was old, like my grandmother maybe. . . . I fired once, twice. She fell dead. You know I killed nine people as an adviser.*

—*It was exciting . . . and it was a man's job—the one job in the world where you're good or you're dead. I was good.*

—*I hope the Vietnamese never forget what we are trying to do for them.*

—*I can't sleep, I'm a murderer.*

GIVE MY REGARDS TO SAIGON

Give my regards to Saigon, remember me to Cholon, too.
Tell all the girls down at the Tu Do Bar that my tour is through.
Tell them that I'm returning, back to the old Z.I.[1]
Give my regards to General Ky and tell him to kiss my ass goodbye.

THIS LAND IS YOUR LAND

This land is your land, but it's not my land.
From the Mekong Delta to the Pleiku Highland.
When we get shot at, the ARVN[2] flee.
This land was meant for the VC!

—*by anonymous G.I.s in Vietnam*

Murray Polner, "War Stories," *TRANS-action Magazine,* Nov. 1969. Copyright © by *TRANS-action Magazine,* New Brunswick, N.J.

[1] Zone of the Interior—i.e., the United States.
[2] The South Vietnamese Army.

Three months after his return to the United States from Vietnam, Stephen Williams went walking in his hometown of Newport, R.I. He was afraid, he now says: out of touch and bewildered. The first thing he noticed was the contrast between his country and town, standing whole and rich, with Vietnam. He wandered aimlessly, past the great mansions, the carpet lawns, the majestic trees, but his mind kept returning to the Vietnamese hovels, to a scene he remembered in which a young woman lay in a grass hammock giving birth, her sense of humor and her humanity still intact. These memories and this town overwhelmed him; he looked back at the mansions and turned away, vomiting.

Williams (the names of veterans have been changed) is a six-foot blond, brown-eyed, open-faced youth who dropped out of his second year of college, enlisted, and later even toyed with the idea of making the army a career. He has come back a different man. "I saw the emptiness in the faces of the Vietnamese people. I saw our own wounded. I saw the refugees. And I came away against the idea of ever using another human being for one's own self-interest."

Stephen Williams is one of the 92 veterans I have recently met and interviewed. Many of these men had enlisted, or been drafted, soon after graduating from high school. Nearly all were white. I had more than one hundred interviews with them, and I discovered that, to a man, their personalities and their outlooks had been profoundly altered by their experiences in Vietnam. In this article I shall present a typology of these men, describe the ways in which they have changed, and then speculate on how they may differ from veterans of previous American wars.

Shortly after I started these conversations, at first in my office and afterwards in the homes of the veterans, I met a field Marine awaiting medical discharge. He had stepped on a land mine near Qui Nhon and had lost his left leg below the ankle. He was only a few months past 19. And he was upset. His mother and his girl friend would not let him talk about the war, and his former parochial school teachers persisted in thinking of him as a war hero.

He had never really equated soldiering with killing. "I joined the Marines because I wanted to go all the way with a fighting unit." But now, back home, he has started to wonder. "I've seen little kids killed. I've seen napalm strikes. You know, it hits the ground, bursts into a fireball, and bounces. Charley was once on a dike wall in a rice paddy. We had been pinned down by small-arms fire for three hours that day and had to call for an air strike. They flew over dropping napalm. It hit mid-way in the rice area but the wind carried it back toward us. Thirteen guys were caught and in an instant they were charcoal."

This young Marine had reached two conclusions. "I think any other war would've been worth my foot. But not this one. One day, someone has got to explain to me why I was there."

When I spoke with him he insisted on anonymity: he was almost out of the Marines, and was afraid of possible reprisals. The last I heard of him, he had apparently settled on a second conclusion, for he was speaking before antiwar rallies and supporting antiwar politicians.

Harold Byrdy, a psychiatrist (his name, and those of the other psychiatrists, are real), was in an excellent position to assess the effects of the war on the fighting man, because from August 1965 to July 1966 he had been attached to the First Cavalry Division in Vietnam. Dr. Byrdy thinks it too much to expect young G.I.s to understand the complexities of international politics while they are in Vietnam. To them, good and evil are represented by the availability of hot showers and cold beer. Combat soldiers are fighting for survival, and if a rare soldier ever thinks or speaks of the political goals of the war, it is generally in terms of conventional anti-Communism. Someone once told me that in his Special Forces team, not one of the 12 men ever spoke of anything but their most immediate concerns, a defensive mechanism possibly, but also a concentration of all their attention on the problem of remaining alive.

Dr. Byrdy had noticed this, too. "Our air strip was built on the site of an old French outpost. The French commandant's manor was still intact. Yet nobody talked about the French legacy, or how it had come to pass that we had become their successors." Only towards the end of their tours, or after they returned home, did many veterans become bitter—those whom Dr. Byrdy calls "the victimized," those who believed they had been misused and lied to. (Special Forces Captain William Chickering, for example, has commented that, at the end of his tour, the wife of a dead soldier wrote and asked him what worthwhile cause her husband had died for. At that point, he finally sensed that something was wrong.)

Another psychiatrist, Arthur Blank, Jr., had served as chief hospital psychiatrist in the 93rd Evacuation Hospital at Bien Hoa, and later in the 3rd Field Hospital near Saigon. He remembered one wounded soldier who was brought in after the Iron Triangle offensive. He had killed about two dozen VC when his best friend alongside was hit badly. Then a grenade landed next to him but didn't go off. He was so paralyzed with fright he couldn't function; the dying buddy reached down and threw it away. The kid as a result became psychotic, evoking a kind of guilt about the event.

After some treatment, the soldier's symptoms vanished and he went back to combat, as happy and aggressive as ever. He had never expressed any political convictions or any doubts about what he was doing. His primary concern was that his platoon buddies think well of him. And this was predictable, Dr. Blank says, for it was asking too much to expect that this boy, weaned on the goodness and the promise of America, believe that his country was engaged in a questionable war in which tens of thousands were being killed needlessly. "If he ever reflects on what he did," Dr. Blank says, "it would only happen after he went home."

Three Kinds of Soldiers

Dr. John Rosenberger never got to Vietnam, but as a psychiatrist at Fort Dix, he spoke with many returnees. His view was that, as in the general population, there were three categories of soldiers. "There are quite a large number of doves, but they offer only tacit and passive opposition—, if that—, while they serve. My own feeling is that they don't seem to carry with them a sense of the tragic. Once they know you're sympathetic, they will chew your ears off about the war. They only want to get out when their time is up."

There were, he thought, just as many hawks at Dix, emotionally anti-Communist and very angry at the doves. He believed that they tended to represent the army's "power élite"—white, Southern, and Protestant—and that they seemed to see things in unambiguous blacks and whites. Cut off from what sociologists call the civilian primary groups, the service hawks had learned to depend upon the military life, often staking their self-respect on its values. It was no accident then that the hawks as soldiers and as veterans bitterly resented anyone who threatened their new loyalties and way of life.

Dr. Rosenberger was most intrigued, however, by the largest bloc of veterans, those he calls "the indifferent," those who are "really hurting in an emotional sense. They're apple-pie Americans, usually bored with politics, patriotic, and waiting out their separations so as to move into the middle-class dream they all share. They perceive this war as especially terrible, but their emotional follow-up is lacking." To Dr. Rosenberger, this is a "crisis of conscience" of which they are unaware. He believes that if these Vietvets were to honestly confront what they experienced, they might conclude that America is committing a ghastly crime in Vietnam.

"Many of the veterans I spoke with," Dr. Rosenberger told me, "thought that something was not quite right about the war. Nobody believed the body counts. Everyone was disgusted with South Vietnamese corruption. A few were even touched by the suffering of the people. And some tried to talk about their feelings, in guarded ways. But what they feared most of all was tarnishing the impeccability of America, which I suppose gave meaning to their sacrifices. And since they cannot bring themselves to do this, they often retreat into indifference—or else try to wipe from their memories what happened. The real tragedy of the war for them, and perhaps for all of us, is that they don't feel the *tragedy* of the war."

One occurrence in particular had upset him. A soldier had murdered a peasant in an especially brutal fashion. After speaking with the soldier, Dr. Rosenberger came away shaken. "The fellow was absolutely untouched by what he had done. He had no emotional reaction. It was this, more than anything else, that finally made me wonder what this war is doing to these men so that they cannot bring themselves to *feel.*"

I met Michael Pearson in a fifth-floor walkup tenement in Manhattan, not far from the United Nations. The halls were noisy with Puerto Rican kids playing. Pearson's apartment was bare except for an overstuffed armchair, a frayed rattan couch with two old, faded blue pillows, and a Dumont 10-inch television set. But Pearson himself was dressed in shirt, tie, and jacket, shaven and well-groomed, and very apologetic about the beer cans and overflowing ashtrays littering the room. "We had a party last night," he explained.

Pearson is 21, intense, almost humorless, and a chain smoker ever since his return home. He is one of six children of an Irish Catholic truck driver, and four years ago, when he decided to quit his Philadelphia high school to join the army, no one at home questioned his decision. Mike's father wished him well, and hoped that when Mike came back he, too, would become a truck driver and join the union. It was a good job, and Mike says that he had every intention of following his father's wishes. But it's out of the question now.

Mike has repeatedly marched with antiwar pickets, fought with cops, and spoken to student groups in this country and Canada. His theme is simple. The South Vietnamese leaders are tyrants, and the United States has emulated many of their most reprehensible tactics.

Although Mike was pleased to discover his ability to speak well in public, he found that his activities did not sit well with his family. His elder brothers had been in the army, as had his father, and at first they considered him a pinko. His father would not speak to him; one brother threatened to beat him up if he showed up in the old neighborhood. Only his mother took his side. She sent him a letter that he still carries in his wallet. "I respect my President," she wrote, "but I love my son, too." Of late, his father and brothers have persuaded themselves that Mike is mentally ill, and they are trying, through his mother, to have him treated by a V.A. psychiatrist.

All this troubles Mike, but he cannot put aside his feelings about Vietnam: "It's only recently that my hands have stopped sweating when I hear a jet." And on the occasions I met with him, he kept protesting how much he wanted to return to Vietnam, but this time as a teacher and healer with a private relief organization. Then, after a lengthy period of talking, he stood up and said: "I can't sleep, I'm a murderer."

He went on: "We were outside Bac Lieu, out on an eight-man patrol along with 15 ARVNs. Our orders were to move ahead and shoot at everything suspicious. My God, how I remember that damned day! It was hot and sticky. The mosquitoes were driving me crazy. And there was this boy, about 8 or 9. He had his hand behind his back, like he was hiding something. 'Grab him,' someone screamed, 'he's got something!' I made a move for him and his hand moved again. 'Shoot!' I fired. Again and again, until my M-2 was empty. When I looked he was there, all over the ground, cut in two with his guts all around. I vomited. I wasn't told, I wasn't trained for that. It was out-and-out murder. When I told that to the base psychiatrist and the Catholic chaplain, they just pooh-poohed it: They said I was only doing my duty. My *duty?* You know, that little boy only had a three-inch penknife, and I had a carbine.

"Another time, in a village, I was serving as an adviser when a woman ran out of her hut with a rifle held high above her head. She wasn't shooting it, only carrying it high, moaning and shrieking and crying, like she was mad. She was old, like my grandmother maybe. Shrieking and crying. One of the ARVNs then began shouting, 'VC! VC!' I fired once, twice. She fell dead. You know, I killed nine people as an adviser. Nine people fighting for their country against us and our stooges. Killing came easy after that."

Death of a Friend

Mike thinks he first began to wonder about why he was in Vietnam when his friend, a Negro, was shot through the temple while on guard duty. "He had tried to start me thinking about the war, but I never wanted to." His last words were to Mike: "My God, why must I die for this?"

After that, Mike says, small things began to bother him. He began seeing connections between apparently unrelated incidents. "Take sadism and killing. I saw the tie-up between the two when I watched the way G.I.s picked on little creatures, like rats and shrews. They set out cages, sometimes as many as 75, and filled them with rodents. Then they'd mock the villagers with simulated Buddhist rituals and pour on gasoline and set the rodents afire. Everyone grinned while the rodents shrieked. For the first time, I saw the connection. It was like a rebirth. When harmless creatures have to be tortured in this way, then it's easy to move over to human beings. And that's exactly what many guys did, cursing and spitting at the Vietnamese kids, beating the men, and using the women."

He reacted so furiously that he was eventually let out of the army with a less than honorable discharge. He's home now, hates home-front defenders of the war, chides career soldiers as parasites 'living off death and killing," and goes on speaking against the war.

Hal Edwards had never really thought about politics. He was married one month before his induction in 1965, and only when he left for Fort Dix did he feel resentment at having been chosen. His father and father-in-law were upset by his dissatisfaction. Both had been in the navy during World War II, and felt that serving was Hal's duty.

"I never talked back to them and neither did my wife," Hal says. "I thought they knew more about those things than I did. But never again!"

At first Hal seems laconic, almost diffident. Yet the more he talks, the more eloquent he becomes. For the first time in his life, he relates, he is reading books—*Catch-22,* Camus, several of Dostoevski's novels, Fanon and the literature of the New Left. And he is now wearing a one-inch lapel button on his field jacket. It reads, "I Support Vietnam Veterans Against the War," and it shows a G.I.'s unstrapped helmet perched upon a rifle embedded in the ground. The button was put out by a group of veterans in Manhattan who, since their return, have spoken and written against the war. Hal has also signed their ads, usually headed "Vietnam Veterans Speak Out," urging negotiations, and claiming that true support for their buddies in Vietnam "demands that they be brought home." Hal has never met any of the thousand or so protesting veterans, but now at least he feels he is not alone. "Before Vietnam (and everything for me is pre-Vietnam), I was in a vacuum, caught up in a machine. Never again. I was wounded twice and saw many of my friends die. I had to ask, finally, 'For what?' "

He was a rifleman, D Company, 3rd battalion, 27th Infantry. "I remember," he says shyly, almost without feeling, "my buddy and I just sitting and talking. He was saying how much he enjoyed life and how much he wanted to go home. He had been a carpenter like his father, and was looking ahead to going into business with him. And then suddenly, like it always seemed to happen in an area supposedly friendly, he was shot. When I looked down at him, his whole throat was ripped out. I think I went into shock." At that moment, he thinks, the meaning of the months of marching, fighting, and just doing nothing suddenly became clear.

"I knew we were killing the country and its people. In any other war, what I have seen might be considered war crimes. The ARVNs were the worst of all. I saw them drown people during interrogation. I saw American troopers go into villages looking for VC and hit the peasants over the head with rifles. I saw the evidence of napalm in our aid stations, where the burned included pregnant women and kids."

One minor incident sticks in his mind. "We were on patrol and someone spotted a farmer and his water buffalo. One guy said they looked suspicious but another said No, he was only a farmer. Well, they argued back and forth for a few moments and then an officer came up. 'They *look* suspicious,' he said. 'Finish them off.' Our tanks opened up and killed them both. Nobody even thought to ask first or ever worry about it later."

When Hal came home he said very little. "I would awaken in the middle of the night and stare out of the window. Several times I dressed and just walked for miles. I felt a tremendous weight on me, something that no one could understand who wasn't there." He told his wife, "I have to go this way." And so, early in 1968, he joined the pickets marching in front of a federal building in Long Island to protest against the war and the draft. He was wearing his faded field jacket, a combat infantryman's badge, his "I Support Vietnam Veterans Against the War" button, and his two Purple Hearts. A cop came up and asked if any of them had ever been in the service. "I said I had and was wounded twice." The cop said, "Too bad you weren't killed."

In *What Price Glory?,* the Maxwell Anderson play about World

War I, Captain Flagg says, "There's something rotten about this profession of arms, some kind of a damned religion connected with it that you can't shake." Bob Darnell apparently shared this feeling. The day after he finished high school he enlisted. And he got a lot of emotional satisfaction, he says, out of the camaraderie and dedication he found among the men of his Marine platoon, and out of combat itself. Bob deeply believes in the cause for which he was sent to fight, and for which he would gladly return if necessary. He is a hawk.

The Hawk's Story

He lives in New Jersey. His father, a World War II veteran, is a fireman; his mother, a British war bride of 1945, is an insurance broker. In high school Bob was a B student but was bored and restless. When he decided to join the Marines, he was overjoyed to receive his parents' approval; they felt it was natural that a young man should serve his nation.

Today Bob speaks proudly of the lessons he has learned from the war: patriotism, independence, and personal responsibility (virtues that he believes were first implanted in him at home). He is also proud of having been in combat.

"I was in Vietnam for ten months and only two were in combat. But if I hadn't fought, I could never again look at myself in the mirror. Luckily, I did get my chance, for this was my war. We had to stop Communism somewhere, to draw a line far from home."

Once in action, he was exhilarated. "I was now doing something for my country. It was exciting. The spirit among the platoon was great and it was a man's job, the one job in the world where you're good or you're dead. I was *good.*"

In his own eyes he has been transformed into an American missionary, the carrier of technological sophistication, as well as political tutelage in the body of a superior and anti-Communist culture. He performed well in a difficult setting and saw scores of atrocities, by VC and ARVN and the North Vietnamese. He says he had also seen Americans torture prisoners, but of that he will never speak publicly or attempt to pass judgment. "I'll always refuse to say anything that can hurt my country."

His warmest memories are of the men he met. He never had any close friends at home, and in the service he was startled at how intimately the men were involved with one another. All of this meant a great deal to Bob, and it helps him talk about the five or so men he killed in battle. "I felt a real joy; in fact, I was up whenever we were shooting, especially when we were winning. The only time I was afraid was when guys around me were getting hit. But as for killing the VC or North Viets, well, it was all so impersonal. Besides, it was what I was trained for. And if you got a kill, it was a platoon status-symbol."

Still, Bob believes that he was basically motivated by a desire to change the lives of the Vietnamese for the better. Indeed, many veterans were heard saying, "I hope the Vietnamese never forget what we are trying to do for them." Don Luce, for many years the head of the International Voluntary Service in Vietnam, said he had heard that line repeatedly; several chaplains have said this was the rationalization they heard most frequently from those G.I.s troubled enough to visit them.

"I'm no killer," Bob would say, "but I do believe that the cause is just." In some instances, he went on, even napalm is necessary: "It's very effective when people are entrenched, seeping down into their caves and suffocating them." More than ever, Bob believes that questions of right and wrong, raised by critics of the war, are irrelevant: "Every time we went to napalm, the ARVN were overjoyed. I know they were. I spoke to them. They said everything would be fine if only the Reds would leave them alone. That's why I can't think of good and evil. We really *helped* those people. In the long run, we gave them something to live for."

George Ryan had enlisted. For him it was almost inevitable: He had long been troubled by a lack of close friends, and by constant anxiety. He was very short—only five feet five. He saw himself as a coward and kept looking for some way to change his life and become a hero. He fought with the 101st Airborne, and came out a sergeant. His superiors thought so highly of him that when his commanding officer was killed, they gave the platoon over to him until a replacement arrived.

George grew up in a family oblivious to his personal problems. During his high-school years in Boston, he found that he couldn't face up to anything demanding: exams, schedules, discipline, and—above all—the physical threats of his peers. He took up smoking "to look tough." (As he spoke of this, he chain-smoked, kept his eyes down, kept calling me "Sir," and clasping and unclasping his hands.) He recalled many occasions when "guys would tear me down and I was afraid to fight back. It was a curse."

So there he was, an undistinguished high-school graduate with no special interests. He ignored his father's pleas that he go to college. Instead he started shopping around for a "real fighting army" and hit upon the Israelis. When they told him that service with them might mean the loss of his American citizenship, he joined the American army—for a three-year hitch. In January, 1964, he reported for basic training.

A series of events changed him forever, he says. (He said he wanted to speak of it, at least once, before time blurred the memory of it forever.) The first two events were comparatively insignificant. In Vietnam he met his cousin, an Air Force mechanic, who was there for a second time. This cousin told him that, after his return home, no one —not even members of his family—made much of his Vietnam days. Later the cousin heard, and was convinced, that antiwar protesters in California were shooting down returning vets as they arrived by plane. Both revelations alarmed George and left him deeply troubled.

Far more important to him, however, was the death of his only close friend, Walter Miller, a machine-gunner from Denver. "Walt was only 18, strong as a bull, and always laughing and happy. But one day, after a bad fight, he just went crazy, stood up, took the machine gun off its tripod, and began firing. A sniper tore off the front of his face and when I looked he was gushing blood and just making sounds. I threw up. Since then I've hated anybody with slant eyes. They killed my best friend."

George kept lighting and relighting cigarettes. Never did our eyes meet.

He had seen the senselessness of brutality, but it was remote, and George did not allow himself to brood about it. An American once kicked a wounded North Viet in the head and penetrated his skull so deeply that his own ankle had been broken. George had watched a Vietnamese suspected of being a VC thrown out of a helicopter. He had heard of the emasculation of a district chief by a VC. Yet the victims remained shadows. Then something different happened to him. He himself became an executioner.

"I was ordered to kill by my sergeant. It was supposed to be good training, but it made me sick at first." His company was near Can Tho, in a small hamlet, and a North Vietnamese had been taken prisoner. George recalls the date—February 6, 1966. "Our platoon had been pinned down for hours but finally the North Viets pulled back, leaving us this wounded guy. He had a very bad wound. Nobody wanted to doctor him or call for a dust-off [evacuation by helicopter], so my platoon sergeant said I should finish him off with my .45. I went up to where he was lying and moaning and waited for 30 minutes, hoping he'd die first. The sergeant then came up and called me chicken, so I fired.

"When I walked back to the other men, they were all proud of me. It was a big thing to kill a North Viet in battle and this, so to speak, was in battle." Does he think of it now? "Now that I mull over it, it's not how many you kill but what your friends think. My buddies said I did a good job and that made me happy. Anyway, if I had refused the order it would have meant being blacklisted. I'd have been called a coward."

George says that he has never questioned what he did, nor would he refuse to do it again if necessary—although he quickly adds, "I wouldn't be happy about it." Why not? He would rather not say, but killing is fine, if you've got a good cause, he tells me. Vietnam was a good cause, and he is glad to have served America. Still, he does admit that *one* incident continues to haunt him.

"It was the fourth or fifth time I had killed. The guy way five feet away when I opened up. I saw the tracers hit, the first into his back and, when he spun around, the rest of the bullets, 19 of them, into his chest." He is disturbed that he fired more than one round, and that "I never felt anything for the guy, not then or now." It worries him. "I tried to feel for him but I can't. He never meant anything to me." He remembers searching the body for papers. "He was an old guy, maybe the same age as my father, about 40."

Fred Schoenwald saw more sustained, intense fighting than any other veteran I interviewed. He was a combat medic in a reconnaissance platoon and had taken part in several of the bigger sweeps: Addleboro, Gadsden, and Junction City I and II. Before entering the army, he had worked with his father and mother in their small delicatessen, and had never given a thought to politics, or even to much outside his small town. In the half-year he has been home from Vietnam he says he never speaks of the war or the army, that "it simply never happened and I never want to hear of it again."

During our several talks he was tense, smoked incessantly, and only with apparent discomfort recalled his 12 months of combat. "I was always afraid. In fact, I can't remember not being afraid. For one thing, a combat medic doesn't know what's happening. Especially at night, everybody screaming or moaning and calling, 'Medic, medic.' I always saw myself dying, my legs blown off, my brains spattered all about, shivering in shock, and talking madly. This is what I *saw* in reality. I used to tell myself anyone wanting to send 18- and 19-year-olds to fight ought to try it on himself or his own sons. But that was crazy talk too, and I soon stopped that." He remembers overhearing a conversation that taught him a lesson. "A guy had been up to Nha-Trang, and in a bar he saw a little sign, 'If you can keep your head while others about you are losing theirs, perhaps you've misjudged the situation.' I interpreted that to mean I should mind my own business." Confronted by what he called a "horror," Fred turned inward, devoting himself to his work. He told himself that with his medical knowledge he was serving his fellow men, American and Vietnamese. Most of all he liked helping the villagers, although the days he spent giving penicillin shots were rare. He once thought it amusing that the only Vietnamese he ever learned were such phrases as "Beat it," "Get out of here," and "Your identification card." It indicated, he says, a contempt for the South Vietnamese, which he is ashamed of now. Once he saw a boy killed in front of his own father, "by mistake." The South Vietnamese were deathly afraid of the Americans, and everywhere he went "I saw hate in their eyes, that we should get out, leave them alone, and not give them trouble anymore."

On the other hand, George Ryan spoke passable Vietnamese, and even served briefly as a company interpreter. At the beginning he liked the people, finding them simple and generous and gentle. But after his friend was killed by the VC, and after several instances of South Vietnamese stealing, he turned bitter. "I began to think of them as gooks. They helped the VC and had no appreciation of what we did for them."

Today both Schoenwald and Ryan feel they have been used, but for different reasons. Ryan has recently started calling his shooting of the wounded prisoner "a sort of atrocity," but won't go further. He still believes California peaceniks gunned down Vietnam veterans, and despises the antiwar critics since "they stole the victory from us." And he goes on proudly wearing his 101st Airborne pin on all his jackets, certain now that he is no longer a coward. He has, however, arrived at a definite aim. "I want to be a peace officer. I'd rather give a guy a break by arresting him than just shooting him. Maybe I've had enough, I don't know. But it was a good cause, and we should have won."

Fred Schoenwald, meanwhile, continues to blot out his experiences. "Deep down I know damn well what happened," he says, "but not *why*. I don't ever want to pursue that 'why.' I don't think I could handle it. My father lived in Germany right through World War II and served in the German army. He has never once talked with me about what he did, and I've never once asked. That's the way it is now. It never happened. It was all a bad dream. I sleep well. I only pray nothing ever happens again to make me lose that sleep. I know I couldn't handle it, not twice in a lifetime."

Many of the men I talked with were easy to classify as doves or hawks, or—like George and Fred—as "the indifferent." But many could not fit into any simple classification. Nick D'Allesandro was one.

Nick had come home from Vietnam deeply shaken. He had always been rough and cruel in his personal relations, and had thought he could "handle anything and be surprised by nothing." He grew up in a Little Italy in Utica, N.Y., where he led a bopping gang. Later he went West and joined a Hell's Angels group near Anaheim, Calif. One day he chainwhipped a truck driver, and a judge gave him a choice: the army or jail.

This young veteran now lives in a West Village tenement with Valerie, a secretary from Ohio. The first thing you see when you enter his place are two large signs. One, on the door facing the hallway, is anti-Johnson, the other, inside, denounces the war. The apartment was in total disorder: no bed, only a mattress, no dishes, only cans and utensils, beer cans and books scattered all about. Nick and Valerie drank beer as we talked. He wore no shirt; she was wearing only a black slip. Many of his sentences were prefaced, army style, with "fuck" and "shit." But despite his obscenities and "cool" vocabulary, he was articulate, and remarkably intelligent. *The Village Voice* was lying on a desk. I mentioned to him that I had written a letter that had been published in that issue. "Shit, we used that for toilet paper." He had read the issue, but this newspaper—like all property and possessions—had lost its meaning. He wanted nothing but Valerie, everything else could go to hell.

He had wound up with two tours as a Green Beret in Vietnam, had fought in Laos and North Vietnam before the Tonkin Gulf incident, had tortured Vietnamese men and women with electric generators applied to their genitals, and yet had emerged from the army opposed to mindless violence. He had refused a third tour and, despite his Bronze Star, almost got thrown out of the Special Forces. He had finally concluded that the war was a disease of the American spirit, and he wanted no more of it.

When he got home, he almost killed a cop who, he says, "tried to kill me first." He received only a suspended sentence because of his war record, but he thinks the cop should have been tried as well. One of his friends says that Nick, like many of the veterans who feel they have been had, is in suspended animation now, caught between his lack of values and his desire for a meaningful approach to life. At one point, Nick said he no longer cared. For the only time Valerie spoke up, "It's a lie. He cares, he really cares. Last night he dreamed he was in a village and the Chinese came down and were about to slaughter them all. He dreams like that all the time." Nick is, one supposes, trying not to forget the war but to transcend it. "People, especially middle-class types, object to my dirty language. But what possible impact can a 'fuck' have on me, a guy who has seen so much in just a few years? Anyone who accepts war and killing for any reason is more obscene than I could ever be."

After Nick was discharged he went to a Midwestern college for a semester and quit; worked six months for a book publisher and quit; and then went to work as a social worker with juvenile gangs, but quit that too—he was so contemptuous of the legality and respectability his supervisors wanted him to preach that instead he started showing the youths how to avoid the draft, and other new ways to break the law.

And so during the day Nick stays inside his tenement apartment, reading, and at night he and Valerie go out and swing. Ambition, accumulation, responsibility have lost whatever little meaning they may have once held for him, and he has become a classical anarchist.

I asked a friend, a professional Air Force pilot with 25 years' service including two tours in Vietnam, what he thought all this meant to himself and to his comrades. Gene Ferguson has three university degrees and studied at the Sorbonne and at Cambridge.

This is a different war, he believes, in that it does not follow the pattern of the past. "When I attended military-college lectures, it was always Holy Writ to stay out of Asia's mud. And we always saw ourselves as saviors or messiahs. And what did we get? Corruption in the ranks that people at home never have faced up to. This is the thing that's really hurting some of my old buddies.

"The war itself is corrupting, and I don't mean this from any esoteric political viewpoint. I mean Air Force guys can make lots of loot, extra Vietnam pay, all untaxed. Flight crews fight each other for Vietnam duty. Guys make one over-flight a month from Laos, Thailand, or a carrier and get extra pay. Loadmasters, absolutely crucial, balk at going to Germany because there's more in it for them in Asia. For those men, the rot has entered their souls.

"For others, this kind of corruption changes them in another way. If a career enlisted man doesn't come back with a commendation medal, or if an officer doesn't get a Bronze Star, then something's wrong with them. They dole it out like candy. Nothing much is required. Commanders report victories because that goes on their

'Officer Effectiveness Reports,' which promotions and appointments are based on.

"Many colonels and majors, for example, would have been kicked out long ago—'involuntarily retired' is the official euphemism—but were kept on because of the war. Promotions? Ordinarily you might wait 8 to 10 years. Now it comes more quickly. So for some it's been a ball.

"For those troubled by the war, who feel bad about the bombing, well, I've seen them try to get close to the people, work in orphanages, dole out food and money, *anything* to compensate. When they get home they don't volunteer for Vietnam any more. They put in instead for R.O.T.C., the Air Training Command, the Air National Guard, Iceland, Alaska, even Thule. At least that protects them for three years. Only the corrupted want to go back. For the medals and the money."

Veterans of the Past

Seventy years ago, in 1898, this country entered a third-rate guerrilla war that lasted almost four years. Some 70,000 American soldiers fought in that war, over 4000 were killed and almost 3000 wounded. Today the Philippine Insurrection is almost entirely forgotten, and those American volunteers who felt impelled to save their "little brown brothers" eventually went home, resumed their lives, and were never heard of again—like all other veterans of all other wars, except, perhaps, Vietnam.

But *will* the same be true of those who fought in Vietnam? Recently, a research psychologist with the Veterans Administration speculated that if history is any guide, this crop will be no different from their fathers and grandfathers. Indeed, Dixon Wecter, a historian, who specialized in the veteran's postwar adjustment, wrote in 1944 that "war colors the main stream of a citizen-soldier's life, but seldom changes its direction."

Vietnam veterans may very well follow the customary pattern, being reabsorbed into American life passively and quietly. But now that I have been talking with a great many of them for quite some time, no longer am I certain that this group will be exactly like all those who went before.

NOT GONE BUT FROZEN

Howard Junker

Ed Hope, 47, is a brusque, stocky Phoenix wig maker who is involved in a finance corporation, a welding shop, and in freezing human bodies after they are "clinically dead." Hope's Cryocare Equipment Corp. has thus far built eight cryocapsules. "Remember," goes an ad in the February *Cryonics Reports,* "if you *do not* make arrangements for *your* cryomic suspension *you* will be buried or cremated when you are dead.") The latest, stainless steel cryocapsules sell for $4,865, with a monthly maintenance charge—for liquid nitrogen and supervision—of $50. At least four bodies have already been frozen, and the prophet of the cryonics movement, Robert C. W. Ettinger, 49, author of *The Prospect of Immortality* and a physics teacher at a Michigan community college, claims to have heard of, but not verified, the freezing of half a dozen more.

James H. Bedford, a 73-year-old retired psychology professor, was the first to be frozen—in Los Angeles, on January 12, 1967. Dr. Bedford died of cancer. He had hoped that one day a cure for his disease would be found and that he could be thawed, cured and thus restored to life. A paperback published this month tells of his freezing (*We Froze the First Man,* by Robert F. Nelson as told to Sandra Stanley). Another body now frozen is that of a 74-year-old Santa Barbara woman, Marie Phelps Sweet, who died of a heart attack last August. Her remains are stored in a Los Angeles mortuary. Dr. Bedford's body is at Cryocare in Phoenix, as are those of a Detroit man frozen some four months ago and a Los Angeles woman frozen at the end of February. Another Los Angeles woman, now dying of lung cancer, has declared her desire to be frozen. The Cryonics Society of California, says Pres. Robert F. Nelson, 31, "is on a twenty-four-hour alert. But she's still holding on." "It's a fact," boasted Ed Hope while attending the First Annual Cryonics Conference held recently at the New York Academy of Sciences, "business is picking up."

It is unlikely that reanimation of an entire body will ever be possible after freezing. Cells, which are mostly water, tend to rupture during the freezing-thawing process. Yet "freeze banks" already store human red blood cells, bone marrow cells, corneas and skin. The storage of

Howard Junker, "Death Cheaters: Not Gone But Frozen," *The Nation,* April 15, 1968. Reprinted by permission of the publisher.

complete organs is still impossible, although researchers have had some success in regaining partial function in cats' brains and various animal kidneys. Death is, by definition, irreversible, but every day the line separating life from death is blurred by the advances of medical science and biological research.

"Traditional interment simply guarantees oblivion," is the way Ettinger puts it. "Freezing at least offers a nonzero possibility of revival." And there are people who do want to take whatever chances there are, now. A Pennsylvania couple has sent Ed Hope tissue samples from their son who drowned last year. The parents anticipate that some day it will be possible to "regenerate" their boy, in much the same way, says Hope, "that a whole carrot can now be grown from a little piece of carrot."

For all its dim future, there is no doubt that freezing provides a more "cosmetic" kind of interment than mere embalmment. Robert Nelson declares that Marie Sweet, frozen last August, "looks absolutely the same now as she did then." Nelson has a weekly opportunity to observe her body because it is not in a cryocapsule. It has been wrapped in cotton, leaving the face exposed, placed in a casket and covered with dry ice. Once a week Nelson must help replenish the supply of dry ice.

Miss Sweet (she was married but retained her maiden name) was a pioneer member of the Life Extension Society, of the Cryonics Society of California and of about forty other messianic organizations, but when she died there was not enough money to buy a cryocapsule. In a 1964 letter to Ettinger she had written: "For the first time in my entire career, I yearn to be wealthy and free to endow an essential work . . . I want to *see it happen*—with all possible speed! Yet here I sit, more or less helpless to speed things up." Early last year she and her husband took out two $25 and one $10 memberships in the California Society, "to help out in attempts to keep the office going." Miss Sweet had also taken out a $3,000 life insurance policy, payable to the Life Extension Society, but the recommended policy to cover freezing and maintenance is $10,000. Ed Hope insists that he cannot afford to offer capsules "as a charity. You've got to keep the whole thing in ratio."

In April of last year, Miss Sweet's husband, Russ Le Croix Van Norden, suffered a heart attack, and preparations for his freezing were made. But after six weeks in the hospital, Van Norden recovered. "I struggled so hard to make sure everything was worked out," he said while sitting in the corridor during the recent New York conference, "that I pulled through." Van Norden, 75, looks like a slim, gentle Konrad Adenauer. A master craftsman, his hands are worn from years of working in wood, silver and wrought iron. His flannel shirt is frayed, his suit is baggy. He refers to his wife as "an arrested entity whom I hope to recover, although I don't know when."

Van Norden bitterly misses his wife and is especially saddened because she died prematurely. "Why did she have to go then?" he asks. "These things aren't ready. They're still so crude." He began to weep in telling of a letter he would have to write, soon, explaining his wife's condition to a young Indian boy whom they had befriended while teaching painting as VISTA volunteers on an Oregon reservation. "When we left," Van Norden recalls, "there were 187 pictures in that school." President Johnson sent a citation, but the Van Nordens were not reimbursed for the $300 they had spent on oils and brushes for the children.

Because the Van Nordens were late in registering for social security —"my wife thought she would never get old"—reduced payments come in now. And Van Norden's small income as a craftsman is hardly enough to support himself, much less pay for his wife's maintenance. Lately, he has been waking up in the mornings with full-scale, dream-like stories in his mind. He speaks them into a tape recorder, and while in New York, for the first time, he unsuccessfully tried to find an agent.

Ettinger appealed for funds for Miss Sweet last year. He admitted that the "circumstances of clinical death were unfavorable," since it had taken three days to make arrangements for the freezing. "In any case," Ettinger continued, "our public image, in my opinion, depends overwhelmingly on one factor only—are we or are we not freezing people? Everything else fades into a vague blur of tiresome argument; in the long run, I am convinced, the only thing that will matter is whether we are acting."

The Cryonics Society of Michigan, of which Ettinger is president, now has a van equipped and ready to go wherever, whenever the "clinical death" of a society member occurs. The New York and California societies hope to have vans by the end of the year. The California society has no telephone listed at present. The New York society is talking about establishing a foundation for cryonic research.

As for Van Norden, at 75 he is ready to be frozen when the time comes. But he would like to persist. He is trying to slow down, to rest his heart. "We have reasons for living into the 21st century," he says. "By then, war would be eliminated. The economy would be adjusted, wealth would be equitably distributed. And the dignity of man would be restored." Then Van Norden pauses, glances at his young listener, for whom the matter is slightly academic. And he says: "I'm still here, but now Marie is frozen."

THE COLD SOCIETY

Nat Hentoff

Four o'clock on a pleasant May afternoon in 1964. Screams freeze a crowded Bronx street. And there she is, in a doorway, naked: a slight young woman trying to fight off a rapist who had begun his assault on the floor above—her eyes blackened, bruises on her neck, blood running from her mouth. Part of the crowd bestirs itself. Some 40 people move closer to the doorway to get a better look. The rapist starts dragging her up the stairs. No one else moves. Until finally two cops appear and race to the rescue. The next day, a businessman on the street, who had watched the event, shrugs when asked why he hadn't intervened. "You look out for yourself today," the citizen says.

Two days later, in Atlantic City, there are screams from two nine-year-old boys, drowning in a bay. Fifty spectators, silent, watch as one man tries to save them. He fails. Why didn't some of the onlookers jump in to help? "Nobody," mutters one of them, "wanted to get involved."

Two months before, Catherine Genovese, returning from work late at night to her home in Kew Gardens, Queens, was attacked and stabbed by a man on a well-lighted street, within a hundred feet of her apartment. Her screams, it was later established, awakened 38 of her neighbors. Twice, as apartment lights went on, the attacker scurried away. Twice he came back, and finally killed her. Not one of the 38 called the police during the 35 minutes between the first attack and the last, although Miss Genovese kept yelling, "Please help me! Please help me!"

The next day, when newsmen asked her neighbors why they had been immobile, a dentist in the building next door to Miss Genovese's was bitter. "You reporters don't care about me," he complained. "Do you realize that my patients, the women, are afraid to come up here

Nat Hentoff, "The Cold Society." Originally appeared in *Playboy Magazine,* Sept. 1966. Copyright © 1966 by HMH Publishing Co. Inc.

now? It's bad for business. And besides, how do know that the girl is not somebody's wife? Everybody looks out for themselves."

Predictably, in an age as scientific and sophisticated as our own, psychiatrists and sociologists participated in a post-mortem examination of the apathy that was an accomplice in the death of Catherine Genovese. Psychiatrist Iago Galdston proclaimed: "I would assign this to the effect of the megalopolis in which we live, which makes closeness very difficult and leads to the alienation of the individual from the group." Dr. Renée Claire Fox, an associate professor of sociology at Barnard College, was more intricate in her diagnosis. The silent 38, she explained, had manifested a "disaster syndrome"— similar to the withdrawal into themselves by victims of such sudden disasters as tornadoes. Hearing a prolonged murder under their windows had destroyed their feeling that the world was "a rational, orderly place, shaking their sense of safety and sureness." Rounding out the board of examiners was a theologian who lived in the neighborhood: "I can't understand it. Maybe the depersonalizing here has gone further than I thought." Having revealed that much of his anxiety, he added hastily, "Don't quote me."

The depersonalizing had indeed gone further than he and most of us had thought. The case of Catherine Genovese is hardly atypical, and despite the feverish soulsearching that followed it, the odds are that residents of her neighborhood would not today react in significantly different fashion to a similar act of violence outside their windows.

The terms—"alienation" and "depersonalization"—used by those trying to understand the death of community that led to the death of Catherine Genovese have become embedded in the common language of our time. Alienation, defined by Eric and Mary Josephson in *Man Alone,* is a "feeling or state of dissociation from self, from others and from the world at large." A man who is alienated, added Dr. Karen Horney, is remote from his own feelings, wishes, beliefs and energies. He has lost the feeling of being an active, determining force in his own life.

Confused about his own identity and his own values, he is also less and less certain that the world is "a rational, orderly place." In *The Uncommitted: Alienated Youth in American Society,* Kenneth Keniston, assistant professor of psychology at Yale Medical School, points out: "There has seldom been so great a confusion about what is valid and good. . . . More and more men and women question what their society offers them and asks in return. . . . The prevailing images of our culture are images of disintegration, decay and despair; our highest art involves the fragmentation and distortion of traditional realities; our best drama depicts suffering, misunderstanding and breakdown; our worthiest novels are narratives of loneliness, searching and unfulfillment; even our best music is, by earlier standards, dissonant, discordant and inhuman."

He continues: "Despite the achievements of many of the traditional aspirations of our society, we commonly feel a vague disappointment that goals that promised so much have somehow meant so little real improvement in the quality of human life. Whatever the gains of our technological age, whatever the decrease in objective suffering and want, whatever the increase in our 'opportunities' and 'freedoms,' many Americans are left with an inarticulate sense of loss, of unrelatedness and lack of connection."

And, as this feeling of a "lack of connection" spreads, there is an increase in another element of alienation—*anomie*. The term, first used by French sociologist Emile Durkheim, means the collapse of rules of conduct, the condition of rootlessness. The result of *anomie* on one level is increased crime, violence, mental illness and sexual deviation.

On another level, *anomie* is represented by the capacity to accept "the unthinkable." As standards of conduct, personal and national, disintegrate, the implications of the H-bomb, for example, become part of the "normal" fabric of society. Already conditioned by the mass genocide committed by the Nazis, not even religious leaders bestirred themselves to concerted opposition when the first atomic bomb was dropped on Hiroshima. And, by now, the very real danger of a nuclear holocaust is accepted as a fact of life. We see and are titillated by *Dr. Strangelove* and *Fail-Safe,* but a residue of cold, resigned fear stays like a lump inside. An "accident" could occur. A confrontation with China could occur.

A psychologist, Dr. Robert Clifton, studied the survivors of the bombing of Hiroshima and found that a "unique" lasting effect of the disaster was "a loss of faith or trust in the structure of existence, and psychologically speaking, no end point, no resolution." Unique to Hiroshima? The loss of trust "in the structure of existence" is hardly limited to the physical survivors of Hiroshima.

Among America's young, for instance, the possibility that the world may quite literally break apart is seen by many of them as a virtual certainty. Chicago broadcaster Studs Terkel tapes a not-untypical conversation with the parents of a nine-year-old girl. "It bothers our daughter," the woman says. "It really does. And to have these remarks come out at home out of a clear blue sky: 'I wish I'd never been born. If the bomb is going to hit, I'm going to enjoy life while I can. I'll do what I please.' Oh, what an answer! And what can you say?"

CBS surveys the nonrebellious 16-year-olds of Webster Groves, a suburb of St. Louis. Seventy-eight percent have bank accounts of their own. Ninety-nine percent know who Dick Van Dyke is, but only 20 percent can identify Ho Chi Minh. And yet more than half of those 688 16-year-olds consider it likely they will live to see a nuclear war.

The signs of alienation, of *anomie* ("I'll do what I please"), are particularly evident among youth. There is increasing withdrawal through the use of drugs. There is the growing number of what novelist–social critic Jeremy Larner calls "the cool ones" who "do not look to the adult world for models. That world is seen as a hostile and artificial place, full of squares who make pointless distinctions of class and race, who work at useless jobs, who give themselves pompous airs, who try to make you as unhappy as they are themselves. . . . It's not hip to take the grown-up world seriously. It's hip to put up with it passively and to use one's own private time in search of experience which will make one inwardly superior. And putting up with it passively is easier with the judicious use of drugs."

When you're high, you're out of reach. "You're in your own world," one Greenwich Village drug taker says in *The Village Voice*. "That out there is life and this over here is me. And there's no connection. Drugs are just another way of alienating yourself. Narrowing yourself, down from the world, from society, from your parents. . . . That alienation could have manifested itself in many ways. I might have become a holdup man instead. Everbody has his own way of dealing with his hang-ups. What about those housewives who take two pills to go to sleep and two more to wake up?"

The New York Times recently reported that teenaged fighting gangs have all but disappeared in the city: according to the *Times,* there hasn't been a rumble in central Harlem or Williamsburg in more than four years. Though the *Times* did not cite cause and effect, it noted that drug taking has increased substantially in these four years, and it reported official disturbance over "the terrible sense of disaffiliation, cynicism and apathy" that now seems to grip ghetto youth.

There are also signs in the music of the young, in the intensifying focus on what Simon and Garfunkel call, in their hit single, *The Sounds of Silence*. This song is about cities where people talk without speaking and hear without listening. Other songs fix a cold eye on the verities and virtues of their parents' world, as in the Animals' *We Gotta Get Out of This Place*—"See my daddy in bed a-dying', see his hair turnin' gray, he's been workin' and slavin' his life away. He's been workin', workin', work, work."

There are signs of alienation and acute restlessness in the changed statistics of suicide among both the young and their elders. We talk comfortably of the allegedly high rates of suicide in the Scandinavian countries, but suicide is now the ninth leading cause of death among men in the United States. Among Americans from 18 to 45, it is the fourth-ranking cause of death. Among teenagers, the suicide rate has risen 50 percent in the past ten years. Child suicides, adds the National Education Association, are increasing at an alarming rate, and now approach two a day.

We read of the activists in the colleges, but there are also the lonely. "You can see their loneliness," says Dr. Rita V. Frankiel, acting director of the Columbia College Counseling Service, "in their lack of personal emotionality, and in the fact that there are so many wearing dark glasses. They feel there is a danger in face-to-face contact and personal involvement. They are the lonely children of lonely parents. Alienated lonely people breed alienated lonely people."

There are signs in the persistent concern of such social critics as Paul Goodman that we are rapidly losing a sense of community, a sense of being an organic part of where we work, where we live, where we try to love. And this sense of community becomes vaguer and vaguer as cities grow bigger and suburbs become more crowded.

The apathy of Catherine Genovese's neighbors was neither singular nor atypical. Nor is it restricted to large American cities. A. M. Rosenthal, former foreign correspondent for *The New York Times* and now its metropolitan editor, emphasizes: "Indifference to one's neighbor and his troubles is a conditioned reflex of life in New York as it is in other big cities. In every major city in which I have lived—in Tokyo and Warsaw, Vienna and Bombay—I have seen over and over again people walk away from accident victims. I have walked away myself."

A district attorney in Queens looks at a reporter questioning him on public apathy and barks, "They talk about an Affluent Society, a Great Society, a Free Society. You know what we really are, chum? We're a Cold Society."

While the sense of community withers, however, so does the sense of personal identity. And the feeling of being an active, determining force in one's own life also diminishes. As Goodman says, people are becoming personnel. In an acceleratingly rationalized, pervasively systematized society, we are numbered—quite literally. Count the numbers through which your existence is proved—by machines. But, at least, we like to believe, there is security in the system itself —the machines *do* work, the systematized cities *do* function, the subways *do* run on time. A central tenet of the new religion of technology is that the system cannot break down. But what if it does? All electricity stopped in New York City for 13 hours in November 1965. People, said the news reports, reacted remarkably well. They were friendlier than usual. They didn't panic. Who says we've lost a sense of community?

Later, however, the reports of social scientists began to appear. Two of them, Arthur and Norma Sue Woodstone, asked in the *Herald Tribune's New York* magazine, "In the Blackout and Transit Strike, How Did New Yorkers REALLY Act?" Quoting from their own and others' studies, they disclosed that "trapped underground, in a black, claustrophobic box in labyrinthian corridors at the height of the city's homeward rush, amid strangers and potential 'ethnic stresses,' the New Yorker barely spoke to his reluctant companion. He often remained seated while ladies stood. If he was standing, he didn't even make himself more comfortable by sitting on the floor or by removing his shoes and wiggling his toes. Instead, he clung to the same strap for hours or with six others struggled for a grip on the pole near the door. . . . The truth is . . . the New Yorkers locked in their streamlined sarcophagi were not calm. They were . . . 'passive.' They were practically catatonic."

Add, then, what will increasingly become a new source of fear, of rootlessness, of insecurity—the Panovsky Law, herewith named after Dr. Wolfgang K. H. Panovsky, director of the Linear Accelerator Center at Stanford. Panovsky warns: "As society becomes more efficient and automated, it inevitably becomes more vulnerable to chaotic disruption."

By the year 2000, predicts scientist and science-fiction writer Isaac Asimov, "People will be living underground in skyscrapers going straight down instead of up. This will totally eliminate the weather problem—but will increase the possibility of great disasters. Can you imagine what would happen if a great public utility—the Con Ed of the year 2000—should have a power failure? Millions of people could die from lack of air."

And even when the system is working, how much place remains for the spontaneity of individuality? When "communicating" with others, we more and more are trying to manipulate each other, and in the process we are often ourselves manipulated in turn. "Fake personalization," observes psychoanalyst Hendrik M. Ruitenbeek, "has replaced real regard for persons."

Alone, in the midst of atomized crowds, we hardly have the space or the chance to even be alone physically. To be private. "Retirement into solitude," adds Ruitenbeek, "has ceased to be an opportunity offered by daily life. Where besides the bathroom can man go to be by himself?"

And, in fact, as population explodes, there is a new term—"mental pollution"—referring to causes of alienation and disintegration, personal and societal. In March 1966, the World Health Organization cited the very noise of cities as a major element in mental pollution: neighbors shouting, television sets playing at full blast and motor traffic, which in itself "so substantially contributes to nervous disease, insomnia, nervous tension, ill temper and accidents."

Beleaguered by noise and crowding, city dwellers, added Dr. Arie Querido, president of the National Federation of Mental Health of the Netherlands, increasingly plunge inward into neuroses, or act out their alienation in cold violence. "Is the city population," he asks, "approaching the state of rats, which, under conditions of experimental crowding, start fighting and devouring each other?"

Further contributing to the alienation and fragmentation of the individual is his sense of being caught up in the swift developments of technology, developments most of us do not understand and could not change if we did. It is not only the bomb that may determine whether we live or die, but also all the other ambivalent "wonders" created by impersonal science. There is every likelihood, for one example, that heredity can now be shaped through control of the genetic code. But who will set the standards? Who will be the breeders? In addition, as science probes more deeply into the brain, more and more forms of behavior are going to be increasingly controllable.

In 1945, J. Bronowski, a scientist, and a team of colleagues examined what was left of Nagasaki and its people after the bomb had been dropped. Bronowski wrote: "Each of us in his own way learned that his imagination had been dwarfed. . . . The power of science for good and evil has troubled other minds than ours. We are not here fumbling with a new dilemma; our subject and our fears are as old as toolmaking civilizations. Nothing happened *except that we changed the scale of our indifference to man.*" (Emphasis added.)

It is that indifference of power to man—the power of the state, the power of economic forces, the power of science—that has been felt with chilling impact in this century. More in this century than in the 19th because the scale of that indifference has indeed changed. And the corollary of that coldness is man's estrangement from himself, and then from his society.

"Things fall apart," William Butler Yeats wrote nearly 50 years ago. "The center cannot hold. Mere anarchy is loosed upon the world."

Not yet "mere anarchy," because, paradoxically, the society is ever more *organized*; but certainly there is growing concern as to how much control the scientists and the technologists themselves have over the power they are multiplying. "During the past two centuries," notes English social scientist Sir Geoffrey Vickers, "men gained knowledge and power" that they used "to make a world increasingly unpredictable and uncontrollable. The rate of change increases at an accelerating speed without a corresponding acceleration in the rate at which further responses can be made; and this brings ever nearer the threshold beyond which control is lost."

Or, put another way, technical knowledge is outrunning social intelligence, and the individual is swept along.

In a rapidly changing, rootless society, frustrations feed on fantasies. One psychiatrist, Dr. Ralph S. Banay, has linked the confusion of fantasy with reality—a confusion heightened by persistent television violence—to the immobility of Catherine Genovese's neighbors on her final night. The murder, he says, gratified the sadistic impulses of the silent witnesses. "They were paralyzed, hypnotized with excitation, fascinated by the drama, by the action, and yet not entirely sure that what was taking place was actually happening."

And *anomie* transcends class divisions. Consider the study of a group of delinquent youngsters, 13 to 17 years old, in Manhasset, Long Island. All come from families with incomes of from $10,000 to $30,000 a year. They represent what the Germans call *Wohlfahrtskriminalitat*—the criminality of prosperity. Their fathers, according to group psychotherapist Norman Epstein, in his report to the American Group Psychotherapy Association, "usually described how they had attempted to impress upon their sons the necessity for diligence, perseverance, social responsibility and respect for the golden rule."

But the boys heard their fathers boast of "shady business conquests, of truancy and sexual prowess in boyhood" and other forms of behavior directly contrary to parental precepts. These middle-class youngsters, finding it difficult to reject the real example given by their fathers, "felt hopeless about becoming a person of worth." Yet they couldn't blame their fathers. "How can you be mad," asked one of the youngsters in the study, "at a man who gives you a car and a TV set, but doesn't give you guidance, decency and honesty?" The middle-class youngster is confronted with parental pressures for conformity while being supplied with permission to chart a course of evasion.

The term "course of evasion" touches only the surface of the void. When one of the fathers bragged at home about his con-quests in the business jungle ("the suckers are so easy to take"), he was the very personification of the chilled rootlessness of many of his contemporaries—and of his children.

Among the young, the result, when not delinquency, when not escape into drugs, is the cool self-interest that characterizes more and more of those who are "making it." Psychoanalyst Robert Coles has worked with the poor, the delinquent and the affluent, specializing in the young. Describing the similarities between law-breaking ghetto youngsters and many middle-class "achievers," Coles says of the latter: "They are interested in their own wel-fare, and relentlessly pursue its achievement. Their actions are not so crude, not illegal, but their self-involvement is no less striking, and their essential disinterest in 'others' . . . no less obvious."

The reasons for the rise of alienation and *anomie*—now seen most clearly in the young—go back to the qualitative changes during the past two centuries in the ways men live and work. Certainly there was insecurity before the Industrial Revolution, but it existed, when it did exist, within a clearly ordered system of values and within a community that was organized on a hu-man scale. Most people grew up within close-knit families that were also strongly interrelated productive units. Furthermore, man was usually involved in the total realization of his work. There was satisfaction in creating entities rather than in being an interchangeable fragment of an assembly line in a huge factory or a huge office.

Everything—production, distribution, even war—was human-size. As for the imponderable questions of the ultimate meaning of life and death, man relied on faith and on God. It was a purposeful universe. Nature was present as part of the total order of existence, and man's contacts with nature were constant and intimate.

Nor was man especially mobile, except in times of war. He

was usually rooted for life to a place, to expanding generations of a family, to a category. But when the feudal system disintegrated and man found himself able to move—socially and geographically —his problems of identity in a rapidly changing world began. By the late 16th and early 17th Centuries, it was possible for more and more men to conceive of themselves as individuals apart from their social categories. For a time, however, the anxieties of individuality were compensated for by the challenge of an open-ended society.

But as the rate of industrialization increased, that feeling of infinite possibility ended for large masses of people. Packed into growing cities, they lost control over the totality of their work and over the pace at which they worked. They became extensions of the machines. As Hannah Arendt puts it, "Unlike the tools of workmanship, which at every given momenɩ in the work process remain the servants of the hand, the machines demand that the laborer serve them, that he adjust the normal rhythms of his body to their mechanical movement." Alienated from his work, he became alienated from other men, because his basic link with them had become the commodities they produced or exchanged.

Even those who didn't become mechanized, who turned into small entrepreneurs or remained craftsmen, were subject to huge, impersonal economic and political forces, forces that could determine whether they survived or failed without reference to the quality of their services or their skills, let alone their needs. If there was an economic order in this new world, it was an order they could neither understand nor control.

At the same time, faith in the ultimate order of the universe and one's place in it also began to crack. The all-encompassing unity of medieval Catholicism was split. Protestantism insisted that man face God alone and for a long time taught that man is inherently evil. Isolated at work, isolated in the city, man was also isolated before God —and unworthy besides. Gradually, as man's identity in the secular world became more and more splintered, he found it harder and harder to find God, because science told him that in time there would be no mysteries. All was secular. All was material. All could be dissected and then controlled.

But in science, too, the center would not hold. In this century there emerged Heisenberg's Principle of Indeterminacy, which showed there are limits to knowing and predicting physical states. And Godel found that every system of mathematics is doomed to incompleteness. And the atom—the ultimate reality we know—has been discovered to be invisible. "The universe," concluded J. B. S. Haldane, one of the most brilliant scientists of the century, "is not only queerer than we imagine—it is queerer than we *can* imagine." Thus no universal laws can be found; only pragmatic formulas for particular questions. Man will never be able to grasp the universe as a whole. Kant was right. There are limits to reason, too. "We have tried to storm heaven," said mathematician Hermann Weyl, "and we have only succeeded in piling up the tower of Babel."

Other gods of this century have failed. Marxism was to provide the means to so analyze and control the secularized society that man eventually—through the class struggle and historical determinism— would achieve the utopia of a classless society. The agent of change would be the revolutionary working class. But in the West, even in the socialist parties of Europe, the working class has become a partner in the mixed economic order, asking for a larger share of the Gross National Product, but basically content with the structure of ownership and production.

The poor remain as possible vindicators of Marx's prophecy, but they are not organized in any meaningful way to force fundamental change, nor is there any historical precedent that they can be. They are not powered by any unifying ideology, certainly not by Marxism. And there is every likelihood that they will in time be absorbed and mollified by the expanding welfare state. In the underdeveloped countries, in China—if there is not world-wide cataclysm—softening materialism will gradually foreclose the last chance for Marx's utopia.

Another bankrupt deity is Freud. Through psychoanalysis, man was to discover more and more of the full range and depth of his being. And by being in contact with his irrationality—that force Marx neglected to recognize—man would be able to control it, sublimating aggression and other potentially destructive drives into constructive pursuits. The flaw is that psychoanalysis often obscured and dampened individuality, rather than liberating the psyche. As Irving Howe describes the usual middle-class analysand, "You go to your analyst to be smoothed down, to be eased off, to be rounded out—not so that you will live up to the image of yourself, which is being frustrated in your social life, but rather so that you will abandon that image of yourself and learn to conform to the images which society imposes upon you."

In a particularly shrewd perception, Michael Wood, an English social scientist, wrote in the periodical *New Society* about the isolating effect of psychoanalysis. In the vocabulary of that wistful science, "one talks about one's insecurity, one's anxieties as if they were alien bodies—the mutinous members of a not very well suited federation." The rhetoric continues that the subconscious, if it is understood, can be a source of liberation. But, Wood adds, this is how psychoanalysis actually works: "The people, the disturbances are always right, and the conscious mind is seen as a kind of fascist guard: the author of an elaborate, lying construct; the enemy of the real self. . . . Morality now is fidelity to the subconscious, to the real, the sincere you. The problem is that you yourself are going to be the last person to know about the real you, because your conscious mind is not on your side. . . . In this shifting, Pirandellian world, neither the self nor the society is a reality, and the inhabitants of this world can only be the most confirmed of relativists."

Split apart by the Age of Industrialization, man was to be put back together again by psychoanalysis. But the gospel of Freud has served for the most part to alienate man even further—from himself and his society. A poignant American phenomenon now is the sizable number of the middle aged returning to an analyst a decade or more after having "finished." The first "treatment" bound up some wounds, but, it became increasingly clear, the patient's identity remained elusive, ghostlike. They return for a last chance at finding the center of themselves, but there is small evidence that the ghost of self will be made flesh.

With no core of certainty in religion, in science, in historical determinism, in psychoanalysis, Western man has also experienced the disintegration of his last fortress—the family. With the coming of industrialization, the family was no longer a coherent economic unit. For the father, the home became separated from the place of work. No longer in control of his work, he was less and less in control of his home. Even in bed.

The rights of women now include female as well as male orgasm; and if the man fails to fulfill that right, his sense of self, already weakened at work, is further assaulted. Kinsey found that some 45 percent of all the married men he interviewed considered themselves inadequate in their sexual performance. And impotence is hardly a rare occurrence in American marriages.

The wife, increasingly well educated, is either imprisoned at home with little chance to fulfill her expectations of herself, or she, too, is out in the world of work, further blurring her children's definition of male and female roles. The sexual identity of "man's work" is itself increasingly blurred. In Western society, Hendrik Ruitenbeek points out, "passivity, compliance and manipulation are traditionally regarded as female characteristics." Now, "with the declining role of direct production and the increasing importance of marketing activities, ability to do, to control things, has become less important as a way of achieving success than ability to manipulate persons."

Emasculated at work, father is also emasculated at home. Consider the television "domestic comedies" of the past decade in the light of Dagwood as seen by Marshall McLuhan in his 1951 book, *The Mechanical Bride:* "Dagwood is a supernumerary tooth with weak hams and a cuckold hairdo. . . . Dagwood is seedy, saggy, bewildered, and weakly dependent. . . . He is an apologetic intruder into a hygienic, and, save for himself, a well-ordered dormitory. His attempts to eke out some sort of existence in the bathroom or on the sofa (face to the wall) are always promptly challenged. He is a joke which his children thoroughly understand."

But they don't understand it thoroughly enough to be sure what *they* are sexually. In dress, it becomes more and more difficult to tell the sexes of the young apart. Writes Jane Tamerin in the *New York Herald Tribune:*

> There was a day when men were men and women all wore dresses,
> But now the girls are wearing pants and the men are bedecked with tresses.
> So, Buddy, tease those curly locks, relax and just enjoy it;
> You'll look pert in your flowered shirt, while your girlfriend tries to boy it.

At a showing of men's sportswear held early this year by the J. M. Fields discount stores, the models were girls. And women, in the past year, have increasingly taken to wearing pants and suits, which more and more men find sexually provocative.

Homosexuality, as can be seen in most large cities, appears to be increasing. In any case, it is certainly more open. And as contrasted with the homosexuals of a decade ago, the majority of today's recruits do not swish and are, in fact, quite difficult to distinguish from their heterosexual contemporaries at work, in the Army or in the colleges.

For those of the young whose sexual proclivities are "normal," there is a marked increase in what one appalled educator calls "genital, not human sex." In an article, "Pop sex," in *The Village Voice,* Marlene Nadle has observed: "In our cool world, feelings have been eliminated by choice and incapacity. Bodies have become things to be cultivated, like the announcer's voice that persuades us we can sell our iridescent fingernails and squeaky-clean hair to the boy next door. And sex has become just a huge, swinging, pop-art image: simplified, often repeated, and isolated from everything else.

"There are perennial understudies," she continues, "playing one-nighters waiting for their chance at love. One girl explained, 'When there is nobody around who matters, sometimes you just have to reach out to somebody. Physical contact is better than no contact at all, although it can make things worse. . . . People have to have sex as a way to approach one another because they don't know how to get through another way.' For the generation after the sexual revolution, casual sex doesn't seem to be much of a question. But it doesn't seem to be much of an answer, either."

Less and less secure about his own identity, even in the act of "love," modern man is unsure—and uncaring—about the identities of others. In his own life, there are more people—contacts, clients, service personnel—but fewer persons. He shuts himself off from the pain of others; and those he does not see, he takes only the most transient notice of. The slums of our cities are as remote and alien to him as the mountains of Tibet. The aged are in separate housing and increasingly in separate cities. Three quarters of the American aged of all colors live in abject poverty, removed from the rest of the "community" as if they were already dead.

It is not that man is inhuman. In his alienation from himself and others, he has become *a*human. The Germans have been accused of criminal passivity while millions were murdered in their concentration camps. But other nations of the world knew what was happening, and only a small number offered asylum while there was still time. In the final desperation of the Jewish revolt in the Warsaw ghetto, not even medical supplies were dropped to the besieged by the Allies. As for the Nazis themselves, the horror of the Eichmann trial was that Eichmann was not a monster, different in kind from the rest of man. "Half a dozen psychiatrists," Hannah Arendt wrote, "had certified him as 'normal.' One found that his whole psychological outlook, his attitude toward his wife and children, mother and father, brother, sisters and friends, was 'not only normal but most desirable'—and finally the minister who had paid regular visits to him in prison . . . reassured everybody by declaring Eichmann to be 'a man with very positive ideas.' "

And what has been learned from the ahuman bestiality of the Nazis? Simone de Beauvoir, speaking of the years of French acts of torture in Algeria, exclaimed: "We have hated the Nazis when they tortured and oppressed us, and we were in the Resistance. We don't understand: the people who have been in the Resistance now do the same thing to the Algerians that the Germans did to us." The Germans had been alienated from themselves and others; now, those who had survived the ruthless *anomie* of the Third Reich were themselves transformers of self-alienation into bestiality. Cold in their violence, they felt no human relationship with their Algerian victims. Torture and death were impersonal.

The depersonalization of victims continues. A Canadian Broadcasting Corporation documentary on the war in Vietnam shows an American pilot caught up in the excitement of doing his job efficiently. His job is dropping napalm bombs. Over the intercom, exulting on his mission's success in driving the enemy into the open, he grins and says, "This is fun."

Warren Rogers, a columnist for the Hearst syndicate, writes from Vietnam: "There is a new breed of Americans that most of us don't know about, and it is time we got used to it. The 18- and 19-year-olds fashionably referred to as high school dropouts have steel in their backbones and maybe too much of what prize fighters call the killer instinct. These kids seem to *enjoy* killing Viet Cong."

What of the future? If the world does not explode, will the society become colder, even more depersonalized? Although arguments continue on the effect of cybernation (computer-directed automation) on job availabilities, there is consensus that the use of the computer will accelerate. And as it does, our present highly organized society will become even more tightly systematized.

Those in power will be those able to speak to the computers, to program them. Meanwhile, computers have started to talk among themselves. There are already self-programing machines that often do more than has been asked of them and are therefore unpredictable. By 1960, the late Norbert Wiener, the MIT professor who invented the word "cybernetics," was able to write about computers that "unquestionably show originality and most definitely escape from the completely effective control of the man who has made them." Computers, moreover, are designing other computers.

Whoever is in control—the technocrats, the machines, or both in an uneasy partnership—can have unprecedented power over the rest of the population. A perilous decline in privacy and in the quality of other civil liberties is all too likely.

Now, as Robert H. Davis, director of the Learning Service at Michigan State University, points out, "Privacy depends as much upon the technical inefficiency of our innumerable information systems as on the concept of the individual's rights. Often we know little about one another, not because the data is unavailable, but because it is so scattered. There are great pressures to centralize and organize the data because it would greatly facilitate the business of the state. Before the invention of the general-purpose computer, the idea of a central electronic dossier on every individual in the country was impracticable. Today, however, it is technically quite feasible."

A mild example of what might very well happen is described in *The World in 1984* by Dr. M. V. Wilkes, Universal Mathematical Laboratory, Cambridge University: "How would you feel if you had exceeded the speed limit on a deserted road in the dead of night, and a few days later received a demand for a fine that had been automatically printed by a computer coupled to a radar system and a vehicle-identification device? It might not be a demand at all, but simply a statement that your bank account had been debited automatically. Many branches of life will lend themselves to continual computer surveillance."

Right now, as John Pemberton, Jr., national executive director of the American Civil Liberties Union, emphasized in *The Playboy Panel: Crisis in Law Enforcement* (March 1966), privacy is being invaded with increasing subtlety. "Our technological revolution is spawning dozens of new eavesdropping devices every year. Sooner or later, inevitably, miniature television transmitters like the ones in *Dick Tracy* will be developed and we will have entered the era of *1984* with Big Brother's eye on us day and night. And don't think certain police officials will hesitate to use it. In California they even bugged a bedroom shared by the speaker of the California Assembly and his wife. Any assumption that wire tapping and eavesdropping has been or will be confined to criminals is naïve."

Nor is only wire tapping on the rise. "Surveillance technology" includes the growingly sophisticated use of personality testing, "truth serums," brain-wave analysis and closed-circuit television.

If, however, new generations are born into a society in which individuality, spontaneity and privacy are increasingly rare, might they not take these cold but firmly directed rules of the game for granted? If there is not a nuclear war, material wants will be filled by the omnipresent welfare state, "It is by no means impossible," Donald Michael projects in *The Next Generation,* "that those growing into and out of [such a society] will be at least as comfortable and content as we are with our world. After all, many people now live indifferently, apathetically . . . with decaying cities, racial inequities, megaton weapons and the population explosion, as members of the bureaucratic rat race, with their private lives on file, and so on through a catalog of society's failures which would have depressed a reader of an earlier day."

It is equally possible that in such a world, anxiety-creating alienation and *anomie* can be done away with. Dr. Glenn T. Seaborg, chairman of the Atomic Energy Commission, foresees within the next 30 years pharmaceuticals able to change and maintain the personality at any desired level. Removed from even the semblance of decision-making concerning their work and the operations of the state, the population at large will be able to go further and further inside themselves, searching after new sensations, including new sexual experiences, through the use of cheap, safe, nonhabit-forming chemicals. The Age of Kicks will have arrived.

But the thrust for individuality, for spontaneity without drugs, for the right and power to make basic decisions about one's own life remains. In East Germany, a young poet, Wolf Biermann, is in trouble with the state because of poems subversive of what the East German press calls "the new age." Poems like:

I don't want to see anyone!
Stop standing there!
Don't stare!
The collective is wrong.
I am the individual.
The collective has isolated itself
From me.

The odds against the Biermanns, East and West, are high and are growing higher. But there is some justification for hope that the man of the future may not be entirely conditioned by the computer-powered state, by his other rationalized institutions or by drugs.

Significantly, today's dissenting young in the West are pressing not only for an end to poverty and war, but just as urgently, for decentralization of decision-making, for radical changes in the nature of education, for new, more humane definitions of work. Unlike their counterparts of the 1930s, they are radically questioning the Welfare State in its present, nascent form, and are working toward ways by which men can live in dignity as well as in economic security. They form "community unions" in the ghettos in which the decision-making is by "participatory democracy." No one stays in a position of leadership permanently. Identities are forged and strengthened through existential, nonmanipulative contacts with others.

Moreover, it is possible, say educational theorists John Holt and Paul Goodman, to so educate generations to come as to reverse the alienating effect of contemporary education. There is a case to be made that despite all the forces contributing to alienation—from the bomb to the dissolving family—the next generations could preserve and expand their individualities if school were not a lock step of accelerating pressures to be "right" and thereby to get into the "right" schools and the "right" jobs.

As of now, John Holt maintains in *How Children Fail,* our schools "fail to develop more than a tiny part of the tremendous capacity for learning, understanding and creating with which children were born and of which they made full use during the first two or three years of their lives." Man is still perfectible.

If, as Marshall McLuhan hopes, the whole educational system can change from instruction to discovery, with the students as researchers, man in the Age of Cybernation may be able to find a center of identity and the beginning of a returned sense of community. Technology can bring unprecedented abundance, but it need not necessarily further atomize man in his materialistic comfort. If technology is democratically controlled and if the abundance it creates is allocated to *human* resources—such as a massive radicalization of the schools—the increased leisure it will bring can be so creative as to be infinitely more fulfilling than most of what has been known as work up to now.

John R. Platt, associate director of the Mental Research Institute at the University of Michigan, sounds the possibility that "continuing education for much of the population may become a lifelong activity. . . . Many adults may fix up a laboratory room in their houses, where they can work every day at some scientific project, some study in crystallization or in embryology . . . that could offer a lifetime of unfolding discovery."

Others would be able to explore the creative arts. And not only on Sunday. Man would again be interconnected with nature, for, says Platt, "nature is infinite to us, for it includes the human brain itself. After all the myriad galaxies of the astronomers are charted as well as we want to chart them, we will still go on studying the multimyriad complexities of the brain that has measured them." Not—if the society is humane and its members organically interrelated—in order to control others, but to learn and fulfill our own capacities.

In satisfying and deepening contact with himself, man would thereby be able to relate to others without withdrawal or fear. He might even know joy again. "One of the hardest things in this century," says actor-writer Eddie Albert, "is to be truly joyful: I don't mean pleasure; I mean joy. To know pure delight. They knock it out of you too soon."

But for technology to be transformed into a humanistic utopia— where the joy of discovery will have full play—power will have to be regained by humanists. Also essential is the humanization of scientists in the manner of Norbert Wiener, who in 1947 disdained a fortune by refusing to engage in "defense" work or in the kind of work in private industry that was aimed only at the further piling up of materialistic goods in a cycle of depersonalized consumption.

It is exceedingly difficult to be optimistic that these intersecting changes in political power, in education, in the self-image of scientists will take place. But the struggle to be human does continue. What individualistic joy remains, says octogenarian Norman Thomas, is the acceptance of challenge, the refusal to regard any obstacle—even the cold thrust of the technological society as it is now—as insuperable.

Albert Camus, the most humanistic of the existentialist writers, would have agreed with Thomas. Life is absurd, he concluded, but that does not mean that when one chooses to remain alive one cannot live meaningfully. "Metaphysical pessimism," he insisted, "does not necessarily require that one should despair of man. For instance, the philosophy of the absurd does not exclude the political thought directed toward the perfection of man and deriving its optimism from the notion of relativity."

Precisely because there are no absolutes, no fixed natural laws, no fixed laws of history, no fixed laws of human nature or of the capacity for human growth, man can keep trying to create a society in which he can be free without being fearful of his freedom, in which he can be an individual but not isolated from others, in which he remains in control of himself and his machines.

Increasingly, among the activist young, there is the further conviction that even if it proves impossible on a broad scale to achieve community without conformity, individuality without *anomie,* at least the struggle itself may make life valuable and self identity possible.

"The reward," says young folk singer–composer Phil Ochs, "is the act of struggle itself, not what you win. In other words, even though you can't expect to defeat the absurdity of the world, you must make the attempt. That's morality, that's religion, that's art, that's life."

Tom Hayden, one of the founders of the Students for a Democratic Society and long an organizer of community unions in poor sections of Newark, also feels that even if "winning" isn't possible, there are alternatives to despair, alienation, passivity or conformity for those committed to a radical change in the nature of the cold society. Hayden uses the word "radicalism" not in terms of political ideology but rather to denote ways of getting at the root of man. Until *1984* does arrive, says Hayden, "the alternative might be for radicalism to make itself ordinary, patiently taking up work that has only the virtue of facing and becoming part of the realities which are society's disgrace. Radicals then would identify with all the scorned, the illegitimate and the hurt." Radicals would persistently ask the depersonalized majority, "Who *is* criminal? Who *is* representative? Who *is* delinquent?"

Radicalism—others might call it humanism—would then "give itself to, and become part of, the energy that is kept restless and active under the clamps of a paralyzed imperial society. Radicalism," Hayden concludes, "would then go beyond the concepts of pessimism and optimism as guides to work, finding itself in working despite odds. Its realism and sanity would be grounded in nothing more than the ability to face whatever comes."

If even this alternative, and other alternatives, turn out *not* to be possible, we have the vision of Jacques Ellul, the pre-eminent critic of runaway technology: "When the edifice of the technical society is completed, the stains of human passion will be lost amid the chromium gleam."

EDUCATION AND ITS DISCONTENTS

INTRODUCTION

The unique characteristic of the generation now passing through adolescence in America is that it is the first to have been born into a thoroughly technological society, where instantaneous data processing, telstar, atomic energy, moon exploration, push-button warfare, "the pill," and LSD are regarded as environmental facts and not startling innovations. The young are the first generation to experience pervasive technology and affluence as if no other human condition had ever existed. The Depression usually means nothing beyond two pages of a glossy new high school text which will be phased out in two years. Theirs is the world of planned obsolescence and unrelenting change. Because the technological era in which we now live is the only world the young have known, their values, their sensibilities, and their aspirations are distinctly different from those of their parents. Today many of our youth have only to be alive to be in radical conflict with, and alienated by, the ideas and values of an adult society which prides itself on its luxury and gluttonous consumption.

The parental generation matured in an industrial society striving for the fixed goal of a "higher standard of living," a goal which demanded nose-to-the-grindstone rigidity and strict adherence to prescribed social postures. Our young are growing up in a technolog-

"Introduction: Youth Rebellion," adapted from Barry N. Schwartz, "Youth in the Technological Era," *The Midwest Quarterly*, X, No. 3 (Spring 1969). Used by permission of the publisher.

ical society, soon to become cybernated, which creates ever greater abundance, is conducive to spontaneity, and frees individuals for new ways of thinking and behaving. Consequently, our young live within a different reality from their elders. They sincerely do not feel the sense of the "practical" which characterizes the adult world.

The value relevant to increasing numbers of young people is not what a man earns by his work, but how satisfying his work is. The current interest in nonspecialized education, the creation of interdisciplinary and general "humanities" programs, and the fact that only 12 per cent of last year's college graduates chose business careers, all reflect a shift in values. Our middle-class young constitute the first generation in history to be confronted in the mass by the problem of leisure, and they in turn are challenging society's definition of work.

The incentive implicit in the economic system of industrial capitalism is ownership. The young, however, relate to objects as they contribute to individual extension. Many urban adults, for example, take great pleasure in owning a car despite the fact that it may sit idle six days a week. As a possession it is valuable because it symbolizes status and an object achieved. The young are interested in an object as it extends the individual's powers; a car is to go, to be used, and when it is idle it has little importance. Consequently the young use objects in ways adults view as reckless or irresponsible.

Adults believe in investment; they encourage the sacrifice of an individual's time and aspiration if it promises future success, where success is usually measured in improved consumer status. While adult wage earners do what they must, the young, in large part, enjoy the privileges of a leisure class, entering the work market later and later in life. Consequently, many of the young respond to the values of leisure, not to those of work. Among many, the idea of investing oneself in an uncertain and abstract future has little currency. Indeed, many "dropouts" find it difficult to spend years of their lives in an educational system which values the degree or diploma over the act of learning. Ironically, the result of the older generation's investment makes the principle of investment untenable for its children. The new value, one made wholly practical by a technological era, is that the process itself must satisfy.

Evidence of this emergent value can be seen in the political attitudes of the young. What adult analysts have classified as mere youthful idealism, perhaps in an attempt to dismiss the activist politics of the young altogether, actually represents a philosophical view which sees all men's well-being as the measure. In the politics of the adult world what counts is the result of human activity, a result which may be achieved by lying, by hypocrisy, and by the sacrifice of personal ideals. The investment made is meaningful solely in terms of the success achieved. This concept, root and branch of a capitalist system of economics and morality, defines anything done successfully as inherently good. The politics of youth rejects the idea of investment and demands that the particular act be meaningful. The political process is validated not by the nobility of its ends, but by the authenticity of its means.

This belief in the "rightness" of the act, the demand that the activity itself be fulfilling, often leads to violation of the law. The forms of illegality may be as political as draft-card burning, draft evasion, or disruption of traffic; or as social as underage drinking and the use of drugs; or as private as abortion and sexual deviation. In all cases the law is seen as the coercive arm of the adult world, an aspect of its malignant self-righteousness. Thousands, probably millions, of young people today smoke marijuana in direct violation of laws passed by elders who exist comfortably with abundant alcohol and pep and sedative pills. Because so many young people feel that before the law is to be respected it must make sense, the unjustified rules that the adult world imposes are flouted with mass irreverence, a social phenomenon for which there can be no effective reprisals.

The dissent of the very young appears in their music. The sounds and lyrics they produce and consume feature improvisation and word combinations nearly unintelligible to adult ears, for the young dislike order and distrust words. Words are the manipulative tools used by Mom and Dad, the System, the Establishment, to herd them into the fold.

The previous generation, wishing to provide its children with everything they themselves never had, has acclimated the young to plenitude. In the material Eden they have inherited, the young are accustomed to choose what suits them and "turn off" what does not. But it is hard to turn off one's parents. The young and their elders live in the tension created by a vast difference in value systems which has never in history existed between two successive generations in the same society, and the resultant conflict has reached explosive proportions.

The young are already the main drive in our society for social change, for equality, and for democracy. It is the young who invigorate the civil rights movement, who demand educational relevance, who serve in the Peace Corps, and who provide the bodies for radical politics. Yet it is problematic whether the young will find the mechanism for directly influencing the direction of our society.

When young people enter the institutions of the adult world, they find that they must conform to succeed; their assumption of choice is antithetical to their chances of survival. Some succumb, some rebel. But institutions do not allow dissension. The power which lies in the hands of the older generation coerces obedience with subtle efficiency. The young are often expelled when they demand relevant education, outlawed for their private satisfactions, too frequently beaten and jailed for publicly supporting their convictions, and given the options of war, exile, or five years of hard labor if they are unable to avoid the draft. The encounter with the adult world is so frequent, so often severe in its consequences and hopeless in its outcome, that youth is plunged into a daily deepening crisis. Given the fact that half the population of the United States is now under twenty-six, this cleavage between the generations would be the most significant internal confrontation in the country were it not for a more overt racial conflict.

WHY THE GENERATION GAP?

Harrison Brown

I remember attending public high school a number of years ago in San Francisco at a time when many of my fellow students were sons and daughters of Orientals and Europeans who had recently immigrated to the United States. These students hardly differed from any of the rest of us either in speech or behavior. I recently checked the yearbook of my graduating class and found that their names included, among many others, Belluomini, Cicchi, Ronconi, and Simoni; Brunkhorst, Svirdoff, and Waldtenfel; Endo, Fong, Gok, Koo, and Nakagaki. Yet, in spite of their names and in spite of their parents' closeness to their "old countries," these young people were completely a part of the American culture of that time.

Their parents, by contrast, for reasons which are understandable, clung to the cultures they had left behind, often settling in colonies such as North Beach, China Town, or Japan Town. They spoke their native languages, and attempted to raise their sons and daughters in the old traditions. More often than not, these attempts were failures. The young people rebelled, recognizing often unconsciously that the world in which they were living differed greatly from the old country. Strains within families were often severe and emotions ran high. There were numerous failures of communication and understanding.

Today we call this phenomenon the "generation gap."

Harrison Brown, "Why the Generation Gap?" *Saturday Review,* July 19, 1969. Copyright © 1969, by *Saturday Review.* Reprinted by permission of the publisher and the author.

I believe that the analogy between the generation gap that existed between immigrants and their children a few decades ago and that which exists between parents and their children today is a reasonably good one. In many instances, today's adults attempt to live in the culture of the "old country," by which I mean the culture of America in their youth. They cling to that world, by now a world of dreams, which, though it existed once, can never exist again. Their children, by contrast, live in a world that differs as dramatically from the United States of a generation ago as the world of the children of immigrants differed from that of their parents.

Throughout most of human history children and their parents have lived pretty much in the same world. Change has taken place, but it has been so slow that parents have felt reasonably confident that their children and their grandchildren would live in a world much like that in which they had grown up. Until recent decades immigration from one culture to another was the only means of bringing about a truly substantial generation gap.

Today, however, so rapid is the pace of scientific and technological development and so rapidly are certain of these new developments being embraced by society, the world in which younger people now find themselves differs dramatically from that in which their parents grew up. And I suspect that like the children of immigrants, our younger people today are better able to adjust to that new environment and above all to understand it—than are their parents. Further, this is not a phenomenon confined to the United States. We see this dichotomy becoming a major force in the greater part of the world. Whether a nation is capitalist, socialist, or communist; democratic or authoritarian; Buddhist, Judeo-Christian, Muhammadan, or atheist appears to be nearly irrelevant.

Of all nations the Soviet Union has been the most successful in keeping the dissent of youth from bubbling to the surface on a substantial scale. But even there the dissent of youth is deepseated and the oldsters in power are fearful. Again, the world in which the present leaders of the U.S.S.R. grew up bears little resemblance to the real world of today. In their wildest imaginings neither Marx nor Engels, nor even Lenin, anticipated the kind of world in which we now find ourselves.

What kind of a world do most of our younger people in the United States feel they are entering as they leave our colleges and universities? In the minds of many, and for very good reasons, it is a world fraught with danger, inequity, and injustice.

They see an arms race between West and East and particularly between the U.S. and the U.S.S.R.—which has now been a way of life for a quarter of a century and which consumes a huge proportion of the available resources of the two countries.

They see massive nuclear deterrent systems sufficient to destroy both countries, and probably modern civilization as well, should either nation or a third nation rock the boat.

They see the likelihood of acceleration of the arms race through the deployment by the U.S.S.R. and the U.S. of anti-ballistic missile systems.

They know that nuclear military technology has spread from the U.S. to the U.S.S.R. to the U.K. to France to China, and they recognize that it can spread to many more nations.

They see their fellow young Americans being killed in a war in Vietnam which makes no sense, and they cannot understand the language used by older people in attempts to rationalize that war.

They see two-thirds of the human population living under horrible conditions of hunger, deprivation, and misery, while a small proportion of humanity—including a large part of the United States—lives under conditions of unprecedented affluence.

They see the gap between the rich and the poor nations widening rapidly. They recognize that while we in the rich nations are getting richer, the poor nations are either getting poorer or barely maintaining their present levels of poverty.

They see at home the racial strife, the poverty of the blacks, the gross racial discrimination, the urban decay, the rioting, and the fantastic increase in crime.

They see hunger, malnutrition, and even starvation right here in the rich United States, where there is so much food that we pay farmers well not to grow more.

They see the pollution of our atmosphere and streams, the destruction of our magnificent wilderness areas, the merging of trash heap with trash heap—a process which threatens to transform our country into a continent-wide garbage can.

They see these appalling developments and then they ask questions. They ask, for example, just what are the older persons who are supposed to be running this nation and those who are supposed to be running other nations doing about these problems?

If spending money is any real indication of effort, the nations of the world are attempting to solve their problems by maintaining large military establishments. With each passing year world-wide expenditures for military purposes have reached record heights. From $120 billion in 1962, they rose to $132 billion in 1964, to $138 billion in 1965, to $159 billion in 1966, and to more than $180 billion in 1967, and all the indications are that 1968 broke another record.

In a recent report the U.S. Arms Control and Disarmament Agency states:

> Global military expenditures take more than 7 per cent of the world's gross product. In money terms they are equivalent to the total annual income produced by the one billion people living in Latin America, South Asia, and the Near East. They are greater by 40 per cent than world-wide expenditures on education by all levels of government, and more than three times world-wide expenditures on public health.
>
> Very rough estimates indicate that since 1900 more than $4,000 billion has been spent on wars and military preparedness. If the current level of military spending should continue, this total will be doubled in only twenty years. If the recent rate of increase in military spending continues, the arms race will consume another $4,000 billion in only ten years.

Beyond our military expenditures our young people see that we are really not coming to grips with the problems of hunger or poverty either here or abroad. Our total expenditures on public education are little more than one-half our military expenditures. The problem of urban renewal has yet to be really scratched.

As for foreign technical and capital assistance, which is essential if the poorer countries are to develop both socially and economically, they see that the total effort is actually decreasing. Our expenditures for overseas assistance amounts to a mere one-half of 1 per cent of our national product and to one-fifteenth of our military expenditures. Added to this, in the face of these serious domestic and international problems which are crying for attention, our younger people see us spending billions of dollars on the space game. By the time the moon landing set for this month is completed, the cost to the Government will be just over $24 billion. They can ask with good reason why, if we are able to mobilize our science and technology so magnificently to fly to the moon, why can't we mobilize our resources equally effectively to come to grips with our problems here on Earth? Are pictures of the moon and a few pounds of lunar rocks worth more to our society than eliminating hunger and poverty? Are they worth more to society than providing adequate education for our young people? If they are worth more, and indeed there is considerable evidence that many people believe this is so, then we must face the fact that we are sick.

In short, our actions and our inactions present to younger people a picture which, to put it bluntly, is ugly. The picture is one of an insensitive and selfish people who are more concerned with themselves than with their fellow man, and who either don't attempt to solve their domestic and international problems at all or prefer to solve them by the use of force.

On the other hand, we older persons feel that we haven't exactly been inactive. We have moved from the depths of the Depression to unprecedented affluence. We have combated successfully Hitler's armies. Willy-nilly we *have* reduced poverty in the United States considerably. In less than twenty years we have reduced poverty to where fewer than one-tenth of the white families and fewer than one-third of the Negro families live below the poverty threshold. We have built the most effective mass education system the world has ever known. Never before has such a large proportion of a nation's population been given the opportunity of attending a university. We have shipped massive quantities of grain overseas to alleviate hunger. We have protected friends in Europe and elsewhere from the danger of Soviet expansion.

Are these not accomplishments of which we can reasonably feel proud? I believe they are.

But young people can say in reply that what we have done in the past has not been enough, that what we are doing today is not enough. They would be correct.

Feeling strongly about these problems young people have lashed out at the Establishment. Most of them being students they have lashed out at our colleges and universities as symbols of the Establishment. And they have lashed out in great strength. Recently George Gallup said: "Those who comfort themselves that the trouble on the college campuses of America is caused by only a 'handful of students' and that the majority is completely out of sympathy with the goals of the militant few would be disabused of this view if they were to talk to students across the nation, as seventy-five representatives of the Gallup Poll did recently." He points out that nearly a third of all students have participated in demonstrations and that although almost all students deplore violence, most students agree with the aims of campus militants. The biggest gripes range all the way from not enough say in the running of the college to the current inadequacies of society to adult and governmental authority to the Vietnam war.

The concerns about our society are reflected in the fact that more than 50 per cent of the students have done social work—a far cry from the situation in my day. Nearly one-third of the students expect to be teachers when they are forty. Do these facts make our young people appear irresponsible? I think not.

According to the Gallup survey the biggest gripes of students about their parents' generation are: "too set in their ways," "a lack of communication (they won't listen to us)," "too conservative," "indifferent," "apathetic," "materialistic," "too strict," "racial prejudice." The biggest gripes of parents about young people are: "undisciplined behavior," "lack of respect for authority," "youth are over-indulged," "just plain irresponsible," "smug," "too self-assured."

Is this not indeed a generation gap? Are we older persons not indeed immigrants from a comfortable "old country" of thirty or forty years ago?

I agree personally with about 75 per cent of the student discontent that I have seen on campus, and I have been on many campuses and have talked with many students. However, I object strongly to the use of force. I have absolutely no objection to demonstrations; I think they are healthy. But violence and the willful breaking of laws cannot be condoned. Also, the rebels lack goals. They know what they are against; in general, they really do not know what they are for. They are truly rebels with a cause, but without a program. I don't believe that it is possible to protest effectively unless one thinks through an issue to the point where concrete proposals for remedial measures can be developed.

With these reservations, we older persons should be truly grateful to the majority of our younger persons today for they are making us think seriously about problems which, if they are not solved, can lead mankind to the brink of extinction. I submit that this extinction is highly probable.

I am also convinced that we have the means for getting ourselves out of this mess. In short, our science and our technology have placed in our hands the tools to create a world in which all people can lead free and abundant lives. Starvation, hunger, misery, and poverty in the world today are absolutely inexcusable. We clearly have the power to eliminate these scourges.

Prior to the recent raising of the voices of youth we were not headed in that direction. Now perhaps the cries of youth will stimulate us to launch a frontal attack upon these basic ills.

IS THE UNIVERSITY
TO BLAME?

Henry Steele Commager

The crisis of the university today is a tribute to its importance. Within a quarter century the university has moved to the very center of American life—the center of ideas, the center of research, the center of criticism and of protest. Students who once went to the university to prepare for a career or, as we amiably say, to prepare for life, now find that the university is life. Parents who looked upon the university as a golden interlude before their children faced the hard realities of life are confronted by the fact that college years are not an interlude but the real thing and that they are not golden but iron. The public, which thought students should be protected from disturbing ideas and should provide vicarious happiness and public entertainment for those outside the university, is discovering that students are far more interested in making people unhappy than in making them happy. Student population has grown to 6 million— rather larger than the total number of farmers—and university teachers probably number half a million: a formidable phalanx. If professors ever thought of the university as an ivory tower (which may be doubted), they no longer do: they are involved in everything from advising Presidents, who rarely listen to them, to conducting seminars for businessmen, attending conferences in Asia and Africa, or mediating between capital and labor and between whites and blacks. The scientists, said Lord Snow, have the future in their bones, but it is no longer the scientists alone; it is the whole army of scholars, in all areas. The future promises no relief from this situation but rather more of the same: the university population is bound to grow, and as society and economy become increasingly complex, scholars, who stand at the levers of control of a technological society, will play an increasingly vital role.

No one bothers to attack institutions without significance or power. As long as the college was small and pastoral it could be ignored or tolerated but not taken very seriously. Now that it occupies the vital center of society it is inevitable that the winds of controversy should swirl about it, that the din of national politics and international controversies should shatter its peace, that all of its

Henry Steele Commager, "Is the University to Blame?" *The Sunday Record Call,* June 22, 1969. Syndicated by *Newsday,* Garden City, N.Y.

95

members—students, faculty, and administration—should be shaken out of their complacency and required to justify themselves.

The student protest against the university is, in a sense, a flattering gesture, though there is no doubt that most universities would gladly forgo the flattery. What students are saying, in their somewhat incoherent way, is that they no longer have any confidence in government, politics, business, industry, labor, the church, for all of these are hopelessly corrupt. Only the university is left. Clearly it is corrupt, too, but not hopelessly; it can still be saved, and if it is saved it can be made into an instrument to reform the whole of society.

Student dissent and revolt in the United States have two clear dimensions, though the students themselves are aware of only one of them. Vertically it is rooted in some two centuries of American experience with colleges and universities, experiences quite different from those of Old World nations. Horizontally it reflects the pervasive frustration, outrage and despair of the young at the Vietnam war, the draft, the armament race, the destruction of the environment, racial injustice—at all that is implied in that epithet "the establishment."

It is the heritage that largely explains why the revolt of youth against the establishment is directed against the university rather than against government, parties, the military, or Dow Chemical or Chase Manhattan or the Automobile Workers of America; it explains, too, why students who revolt against the university claim special exemption because they are part of the university and demand that it protect them and care for their every need.

The university as it emerged out of medieval Italy, France, and England and developed over the centuries, had three clear functions.

The first was to train young men for essential professions: the church, the law and medicine, and perhaps teaching.

The second was to preserve the heritage of the past and pass it on to the future generations intact.

The third—first clarified by Gottingen and her sister universities in Germany in the 18th and 19th Centuries—was to expand the boundaries of knowledge through research.

The two ancient universities of England added a fourth which was never quite clear: to train a social elite to the tasks of governance.

Because the American colonials were unable to establish genuine universities, they created instead something quite new: the college— and the college remains, to this day, a unique American institution, occupying a twilight zone between the high school and the university. As American students were very young—boys went to Harvard or

Pennsylvania or Yale at the age of 12 or 13, though a really bright lad like John Trumbull could pass the entrance examinations to Yale at the age of 7—they had to be treated as children: hence the early practice in loco parentis and its persistence through the years and even the centuries. As they came from simple middle-class households, without (for the most part) learning or sophistication, they had to be taught elementary subjects, and the plan of study had to be laid out for them with utmost circumspection. Hence the long tradition, still very much with us, that the college is a kind of extension of the high school, that students must be taught everything in formal courses, and that students were intellectually, as well as socially and morally, in statu pupillari.

These characteristics of the American college persisted into the 19th Century and when, in the 1860s, Americans created their first universities, they established them not as substitutes for the college but as continuations of the college, and adapted them, very largely, to collegiate rather than to university standards.

Just as the antecedents of the colleges had been Cambridge and Edinburgh, so the antecedents of the university were Gottingen and Berlin and Leipzig. But this could not last, or, where it did, it produced a kind of academic schizophrenia. Actually the university was bound to develop otherwise in a democratic and equalitarian society than in an aristocratic society. Because the United States did not have the scores of other institutions to carry on much of the work of science and research or even of ordinary cultural activities (as did most Old World countries), almost everything that society wanted done in these areas was handed over to the university. Thus the schools of agriculture, of engineering, of library science, of nursing, of hotel management, of business administration, of almost anything society or government wanted. Thus, too, came the multiversity, the university that did not confine itself merely to four faculties or to the traditional functions of professional training and research, but took on the most miscellaneous activities, academic and otherwise.

Thus by the 20th Century the special character of higher education in the United States was pretty well fixed. It was an education that was to be open to all, that was dominated by the collegiate idea, that inevitably took on the habits of in loco parentis. It was required to teach everything society wanted taught or special interest groups in society were strong enough to get taught; and it was expected to acquiesce in the democratic notion that all subjects were equal; it was expected to respond to all the demands of government or society, to serve these masters in every way that it could serve—as a sanctuary for the young, as a moral training ground, as a social and matrimonial agency, as a social welfare center, as an agency for entertaining the community, as a center for research in all fields, and as a handmaiden of government. Some of the private institutions escaped the most onerous of these demands, but even they fell easily into the habit of accepting them.

The pattern of the college-university worked well enough as long as almost all elements in the community agreed on the basic assumptions that were implicit in it: that the university was to reflect American life (the current formula is that its student body is supposed to be a reflection of the whole of American society), that it was to train character as well as the mind, that it was to inculcate all the going values of American life, that it was, in short, an integral part of the establishment and that the establishment itself was sound, just, and enlightened.

Now the situation is different, and the mood is different. Students no longer accept the establishment but repudiate it. They are too old and physically too mature for in loco parentis. They are not interested in the historic functions of the university, and are revolted by the dependence of the university on government or its ready response to economic interests or social demands.

They no longer believe in these traditional functions, nor do they accept these traditional objectives, but they cannot free themselves from them or from the expectations which they have encouraged. They reject the right of the university to interfere with their private lives, insisting that they be treated as adults, but they reject with equal fervor the notion that when they violate the laws or public mores they are to be treated precisely as other adults. They say, in effect, that as long as they are students, trespass isn't trespass, arson is not arson. They reject the tyranny of courses, but assume that they cannot possibly learn anything unless some professor (preferably of their own choosing) gives a course in it, and they clamor for more and more courses. They reject the connection of the university with government and with the establishment, but demand that government support the university—and its students too.

Nothing is more depressing than the gap between the evils that the young object to and the changes which they propose to the university —nothing except, perhaps, the pervasive triviality of the demands. If every academic demand student rebels have made were to be granted tomorrow, nothing would be any different—nothing, that is, that they really care about. The war would still rage, the draft would still work its injustices, the environment would still submit to ruin, the cities would still decay, racial discrimination and racial injustice would still flaunt themselves everywhere. For the students do not, on the whole, have a program, certainly not one that they have been able to make clear to the university or to society. They are passionate in protest but paralyzed when it comes to constructive achievements.

This is not to say that the demands on the university itself are inconsequential. Here the students are, for the most part, either misguided or pernicious. Consider, for example, the cri de coeur of the young, that the university be involved and that what it teach be relevant.

Consider this matter of involvement. Students assume that it means being involved in all the things that they suppose important—involved, that is, in opposition to the war, in opposition to the antiballistic missile proposals, involved in the plight of the cities and in racial discrimination and in the lawlessness of government. And so it does. But if this were all that it meant, why bother with the university? It cannot, in the nature of things, make decisions in these areas; these are the areas of government, for government.

But university involvement is something quite different. It is the duty of the university to be involved with the past and to preserve it and its contributions to civilization. It is the business of the university to be involved with the welfare of future generations, as far as imagination can reach. It is the business of the university to be involved in the welfare of the whole of mankind, not just of this local segment of it.

Suppose all the great geneticists and biologists turned away from their laboratories and went into the hospitals: they would doubtless alleviate much suffering, but we should never find the cause of cancer. Suppose all the great jurists left their legal studies and enlisted in the work of the legal aid societies: they would doubtless help many a poor wretch now the victim of racial discrimination. But we would never come to an understanding of the law, to a reassessment of the penal code, to the construction of effective system of international law. Suppose the painters and musicians turned from their easels and their pianos and devoted themselves to work with deprived children or, for that matter, to playing folk songs designed to inspire youth revolt. All very well, but would we have any Serkins or Rubensteins, any Krieslers or Elmans, any Lili Kraus or Clara Haskel in the next generation? And without these, and their equivalents in every area of art, would we have any civilization?

But it is not the business of the university to be relevant in the way that a newspaper or a television station is relevant.

Now, how does a university go about creating an atmosphere in which students can discover what is relevant to them? This is a very complicated business, one that cannot be summed up in a formula. It may do it, as Oxford and Cambridge do, by antiquity and beauty. It may do it, as Harvard and California do, by attracting great scholars and building up great libraries. It may do it as so many of our smaller colleges do, by teaching that helps students to find themselves: teaching by a Robert Frost at Amherst that made poetry relevant, teaching by a Lionel Trilling at Columbia that made criticism relevant, teaching by a David Riesman at Harvard that makes sociology part of philosophy. The university is not an institution which is, itself, relevant to any particular time or place of interest; it is an institution where students and scholars can discover what is relevant to them and find encouragement and guidance in exploring and possessing it.

One thing that should be beyond dispute is that the university is a citadel of reason; if it is not that, it is not a university. The use of force —closing buildings, assaulting or intimidating members of the faculty, setting fire to chapels or libraries—these are the very antithesis of reason and the deepest repudiation of the university

There is a sobering analogy between the use of force by students against the university and the use of force in Vietnam by President Johnson and his associates. Johnson, Dean Rusk, Walt Rostow, and others were sincerely convinced that the cause they espoused—the cause of containing Communism—was good. So too students are no doubt sincerely convinced that their own cause—the attack on the establishment—is good. The Johnson administration did not, however, whether out of prudence or out of cowardice, attack Communism at its center, China. Instead it attacked Communism on its periphery, Vietnam, which was innocent and vulnerable. So rebellious students do not attack Dow Chemical or Chase Manhattan Bank, nor do they boycott labor unions that practice discrimination; they attack the university, which is both innocent and vulnerable. Johnson and his associates were convinced that because their cause was just they were justified in disregarding international law, flouting existing agencies for the adjudication of international disputes, and using terror against the enemy. So students, sure that their cause is just and their heart pure, think it entirely proper for them to ignore the potentialities of discussion and debate—which have never been refused—to repudiate due process and to resort to force.

They hate Johnson and perhaps President Nixon too; they hate the war in which they find themselves involved. But, as so often in history, they have succumbed to what they hate, and have adopted the methods of those they reject and despise. The university is the most honorable and the least corrupt institution in American life. It is, with the church, the one institution that associates us with the past and the future, the one institution that has, through all of our history, served, or tried to serve, the interests of the whole of mankind and the interests of truth. No other institution can perform the functions which the university performs, no other can fill the place which it has for so long filled, and with such intellectual and moral affluence. If we destroy the university we shall destroy a unique institution. As the integrity of civilization depends in part on the university, we will be dealing an irreparable blow to a civilization now in moral peril.

REBELLION AS EDUCATION

Kingsley Widmer

We need not be at one with current campus rebels to give them sympathy and support. Granted, their rhetoric often comes out raspy, their tactics Pyrrhic and their programs simplex. All decent citizens decry the rebel's arrogant dogmatism, even when it matches official obtuseness; all deplore calling policemen "pigs," even if they do behave bestially; and all disapprove of erratic violence, even if provoked by systematic force. At worst, we may be evoking the style of revolt that we as a society deserve. History can judge the quality of a civilization by its rebels as well as by its official heroes, and that may shame us. Though good Americans all, our rebels might, and perhaps will, learn to do better if they continue their education in rebellion.

Among their present limitations one must include the current curriculum of insurrection, which is not altogether of their choosing. They seem to be as much chosen by, victimized by, as choosers of such basic issues as subordination to the military-industrial order, the structural exclusion of minorities, and the fatuous ideologies of autocratic elites. These academic side-washes of a competitively bureaucratic,

Kingsley Widmer, "Rebellion As Education," *The Nation,* April 28, 1969. Reprinted by permission of the publisher.

militarily aggressive and smugly unjust society rarely appear evident
to those who never touch them. One must, as do our militant students,
wade into attempts at change, or get splashed with typical American
righteousness, to realize how rough and bitter can be our social and
political waters.

But, goes the stock "liberal" retort, why should the campuses of
higher education be the scenes for these rough confrontations? Why
don't the deprived blacks assault the business and union leaders instead of the academic administrators; why don't the draftable young
men fight the government instead of the campus police, or the leftist
students attack the corporate offices instead of the university halls?
Probably they would if they could. But because academic institutions
half fraudulently claim to be sanctuaries from the worst aspects of this
society, they become especially and justifiably vulnerable. Throughout
history, revolutions have occurred more often among the half-free
than among the fully oppressed. The minorities in our universities,
including the few from the underclasses, the dissident middle-class
students and the radical-intellectual teachers, are sufficiently well
placed to revolt, though certainly not to carry out revolutionary action
in the society at large. If much of this insurgency could move from the
campuses and ghettos to the headquarters of power and the suburban
shopping centers, this would already be a quite different society. We
must understand, and critically support, dissent and protest and rebellion where we find them.

At this moment, they rightly arise in and against academic society.
Ambitious efforts at higher education long ago claimed to go beyond
antiquarianism and specialism to social pertinence. Now at last, in
insurgency and disruption, the academies do become relevant. Student revolt as education may be epitomized in the remark of a young
lady on an urban university campus: "I learned and felt more about
American society in the few days of the student strike than in four
years of taking courses." In our higher education it is an achievement
to fuse, even briefly, social role and individual intelligence and feeling.
Such responsive experience, rather than the sometimes *outré* styles
and superrevolutionary mannerisms, should be the abrasive to bring
out the grain of our responses. It takes rebellion, if not some official
beatings, to learn many of the realities of our social order and civilization.

In and of itself, today's higher education demands its troubles and
deserves its disruptions—most of which can only improve it. But even
the rebellious only reluctantly learn this lesson. They, too, are compul-

sively entrapped in the American religiosity about education. When I taught in, and attended meetings with, the student administrators of a "free university," or listened to an SDS chapter I was advising on "university reform" (now Maoistically out of fashion), or joined debates in and on the "New Student Left," or discussed polemical targets with the editors of an "underground" newspaper, or sat through interminable quasi-therapeutic sessions of a "Student-Faculty Committee for Change," or chaired protest rallies, I often cringed at what most of the rebels thought was relevant and tough criticism of the Hired Learning. Classroom habit tempted me to rush to a blackboard and list satiric novels about academic absurdity for them to read, or to quote the lovely aphorisms, from Diogenes through Veblen to Goodman, of biting contempt for official education, or to start telling personal anecdotes of the pathology of half a dozen universities. Only as the rebels literally dramatize their yearnings for more authentic education do they discover the dishonesty and intransigence of the authorities, the selfishness and cowardice of much of the faculty, and the arbitrariness and falsity of much of academic life.

Many of the rebellious poignantly suffer shock from the lack of humane sympathy for their efforts and the righteous refusal of demands for adequate changes. Hence the increasingly disenchanted and belligerent styles of campus insurrection. Their liberal professors, the students discover, all too often provide melancholy confirmation of the usual truths about sophists, mandarins, clerics, technologues and other orthodox rationalizers. Baroque professorial ways hardly obscure the primary drive of the hirelings to self-perpetuation and self-justification. In answer to student complaints about the usual mediocre teaching and mendacious programs, my colleagues fall back on one or another appeal to "our scientific and humanistic traditions." It is disingenuous and comic, for tradition in America is like instant beverage: the bland result of a little synthetic dust and a lot of hot water. Academicians sound more sincere, I suppose, when they speak of defending from disruption universities as sanctuaries for the pursuit of truth and art and dissent in a hostile and corrupting society. Logically enough, rebellious students begin to wonder why they and their supporters can't get amnesty, much less sanctuary, when the crunch comes. Rather more than the mainline faculties, the dissidents want to create autonomous places of order and joy within America's repressive fragmentation.

The aggrandizing of institutions of higher education within the past generation obscures for the rebels what restrictive places universities have been and continue to be. The real academic tradition is that of keeping out, or only tolerating, not only the poets and saints but most of the original and critical minds. Most significant intellectual and moral work remains peripheral to formalized education or in subversion of its orderings. Though academics claim large roles for their disciplines, they tend to operate as technicians of them, and even more so these days in a society that glorifies technique. To be concerned about authentic intellectual experience still, as always, includes assaulting traditional learned disciplines, accepted and honored views and official higher education.

The odds oppose most of the academic caste doing this barnyard labor. While professors currently confuse their trade with civilization itself, most vocally in the humanities, their narrow and fearful tones belie such pretensions. There is nothing mysterious about it. Academicians are the victims of one of the most elaborate processes for inculcating subservient responses: it takes about thirty years of formalized indenture, from nursery school through assistant professorship, to become a full member. Especially these days, selection is mostly by institutional conformity rather than by any autonomous achievement.

No wonder universities suffer from ornate law-and-order arbitrariness and that so many of their members feel threatened by any criticism and disruption. Next thing you know, someone will question academic hierarchy. Are most full professors (I am one) 100 to 500 per cent more competent and harder working than assistant professors? A joke! The percentages, except for salaries and similar prerogatives, usually run the other way. However, the spread in salaries has for some years been growing even faster than the excessive general increases in academic compensation. With justice, younger faculty tend resentfully to support rebellious students. And with good reason, much of the public suspects all of us of crass self-interest. The step-by-crawling fraudulence of licking and booting one's way up the crypto-military ranks—and up the crypto-theocratic path from the provincial animal farms to the "big twenty" zoos—takes a considerable human toll. Internal exploitation creates the proper atmosphere for internal rebellion.

From their captive clientele (students) through their indentured servants (teaching assistants) into their arbitrary hierarchy (professional as well as institutional) to their dubious packaging ("sciences" and "liberal" education), the universities illustrate, as much of American advertising and foreign policy illustrate, grievous mislabeling of an ideology of competitive aggrandizement. As might therefore be expected, academic hiring exhibits all the ethical delicacy of, say, real estate brokerage. Sycophantic salesmanship controls not only the acquiring of prestigious jobs, awards and publications but reaches right down to the often miserable junior colleges and their petty prerogatives. In the current expansion of higher education, the traditional elitist and paternal (master-protégé) placement system becomes a manipulation of "connections" and "professional" images. The appropriate morals and manners for all this racketeering help determine what happens in the classrooms—and, now, on the steps of the embattled administration buildings.

Behind the rhetoric of student rebels lies the awareness that when one speaks of a "power elite" or an "authoritarian bureaucracy" or "corporate liberalism," or more generally of competitive and exploitative and unjust order, one is not referring to something "out there" but to conditions right on campus. Even when the militant focus seems mainly political, as with "student power" struggles against "militarism" and "racism," it is also a protest against faculty subservience to such order. Because of decades of institutional indoctrination and corrupt recruitment and hierarchy and production, we hardly notice the lack of an autonomous community of scholars until the students rebel in its name. They teach us what we should be teaching them.

Most of us serve large, mediocre undergraduate state institutions. (Perhaps the problems presented by the "very best" colleges and universities would require a different emphasis but, having taught in several which claim such distinction, I doubt it.) In social function, these educational bureaucracies serve to indoctrinate what used to be called the lower-middle class, now relatively affluent, in the techniques and attitudes necessary for submissive service in the middle ranges of corporate and public bureaucracies. Split between the purposes and functions of the institutions and our claims to separate moral and intellectual values, we end nastily ambivalent. Only thus can one explain some of the weird and even hysterical faculty responses to rebellious demands for clear moral choices. It is hard altogether to blame dedicated little scholars, after years of institutional processing, for themselves becoming bureaucratic devices. At our best, I suppose, many of us secretly believe that we can provide some counter-education, some involvement, for example, in literature and thought, which will work against the restricted indoctrination which the students and schools officially pursue. We fall back on such wheez-

ing rationalizations of our roles as staying neutrally "Socratic," i.e.,
playing question games as a substitute for a sustained view (and as a
device to avoid class preparation). But methodological excuses only
midwife the rebelliousness which justly threatens to put us down and
out.

For most students these days, interesting educational experience
comes in inverse proportion to what passes for a "professional" or
scholarly (usually meaning a technical) emphasis. But, some of my
colleagues will reply, that is because the students came to college for
the wrong reasons. A better case might be made that their professors,
employed in one of the more lavish industries, stay in universities for
the wrong reasons. Students, of course, are drawn to campuses by all
sorts of motives: to remain adolescent a while longer, to look for sex,
to acquire a trade the slow way, to avoid the draft, to gain social status,
to play games, to join the rebellious communities, or just because they
have been drilled to believe they ought to be there. Probably many
students should not at their age be involved in higher education, at
least in the traditional scholarly and intellectual senses. A later time
of life would be much better.

The resentment of many young students, who endure years of
inappropriate academicism warps the universities into doing all sorts
of anti-scholarly things and the students into rebellions which reveal
an unpleasant anti-intellectual element. Those colleagues who piously
assume that years of submission to bureaucratic education produces
socially liberal and psychologically liberating benefits reveal themselves as quacks of educationism. College may well be a net loss for
many, including some who don't disgustedly drop out or arbitrarily get
pushed out. Students who don't develop some resistance and some
confidence in their dissatisfaction, who don't autonomously turn hip
or radical, must find the processing an anxiously competitive and
morally degrading effort to become less truly responsive and integral
human beings. Professorial self-interest has been used to deny these
students both candor and compassion.

The colleges serve partly as custodial institutions for many who
lack adequate place and role in an amorphously restrictive society.
Periodically, those treated as inmates do naturally rebel. Professors
are well paid for their institutionalization; students are not (though
they should be) and therefore feel freer to express their discontent
than do the custodians. As one finds in reading most of the apologies
for higher education, the basic ideology glorifies the custodial separa-

tion of knowing and doing, of culture and living. Campus rebellions, no matter what the immediate generous "cause," must be partly understood as defiance of that moral schizophrenia, which the students vehemently attempt to bridge by moral activism and lashing out against custodial treatment.

Whatever many of my colleagues might claim in scholarly allegiances, their devotion to busy work, to arbitrary requirements, to competitive procedures, to specialist propaganda, to punitive grading and to professional-class decorum reveals them as primarily keepers. The horrendous processing—requirements, courses, tests, majors, minors, patterns, units, grades, averages, honors, etc.—is even more stupid than vicious. Even at its best it rests on the fallacy that repetitive accumulation is learning. Students, unless they take to conning the mechanism as most of their professors did, can Schweikishly soldier or collectively disrupt. The white students' current enthusiastic support for the black students' autonomous control of ethnic studies programs goes beyond racist guilt and political principle to tell us something of their own longings. That rebellious students also display notable disrespect for our "scholarly" justifications means that they see them, too, as just more of the processing. Rightly enough.

In my own field of "literary scholar-criticism," in which I'm sufficiently published to confess rather than complain sourly, most of the production is hobbyism: the overelaborate doctoring of texts, the compulsive collection of historical trivia, and the willful interpretation of interpretations. I don't mean to attack this hobbyism as such, for it is a pleasant pastime which merits gracious support; but it should not be confused with the need for responsive teaching and critical intelligence. Turned into professionalist ideology and institutional aggrandizement, however, scholarship provides trivial and inhumane molds for much of teaching and thinking, and deserves to be broken. Nor am I arguing for the reduction of faculties to mere pedagogues and intellectual scoutmasters, which often seems to be the position of the "anti-publication" faction in academic departments. (In some institutions these people protectively align themselves with the milder student rebels.) Actively cultivated and contentious people—those with something to say—should be recognized as a good in themselves. Given the lack of other harboring institutions in this society, they should be a major part of higher education, rather more so than the sinecured scholar-researchers and the bureaucratic technicians. Sartre once commented that to be a teacher was to be an intellectual monk. I don't care for the desexed metaphor but the quality of intellectual commitment may be hard to describe in a post-religious way. Certainly it provides a proper contrast to our hired education, in which business and bureaucratic production, if not racketeering, replace true vocation. A seasoning of critical intellectuals among teacher-students and student-teachers suggests the best possibilities for a community of learning and change.

Otherwise we can expect rebellions to increase against faculties as well as officials. In past years, campus revolt aimed mostly at the administrators, especially when they asserted parental and police powers. The super-janitors who now administer most academic institutions often deserve and incite rebellions. On good Jeffersonian principles, one can agree that there should be student disruptions of power every generation (academically, every four or five years). However, the old rebellions simply wanted to dethrone the administrations and then carry on much as before, like the liberal theologians who admit that God is dead but want to keep the old show going. Those rebellions of the middle sixties brought some changes, which now look extreme only in their moderation. But other failures appeared. The changes didn't develop community and autonomy in education, partly because it wasn't really allowed and partly because American capacities for full participation have been deeply eroded, not least by years of phony play-yard democracy in schools and other institutions. Fighting the administration does not create sufficient conditions for change, both because the universities are subordinate to the state and because the faculties are loaded with mediocre bureaucrats. The demands then enlarge. The style of rebellion exacerbates until it fractions the faculty and incites government and public. The education in rebellion has now reached the intermediate level at which both new styles of insurgency and increased repression may be expected. An end to it would require major internal changes in universities as well as a move to other arenas for the drastic contentions all too necessary in this society.

As the student *enragés* keep trying to tell us, intellectual commitment can no longer be kept separate from moral passion. Modern academic humanism long ago settled, though not very successfully it becomes evident, for freedom from interference rather than freedom for innovation. We regular academicians may be justly accused of denaturing the professor, who no longer professes anything but a supposedly neutral methodology and submissive ideology for technicians. That may no longer get by. Students should rebel against us as well as against the administrators and the power forces in the larger

society. Almost any critical éclat in the academy becomes self-justify-
ing as a means to break the narcissistic routines and institutional
denaturing.(It may well be true that nothing less than disruption,
however messy, will bring most of us to the perplexity and passion of
a larger reality.)

Can the universities bear the disruption? More grandiloquently, can
our liberal humanism endure such uncouth assaults? If the institutions
are so brittle, and our culture so anemic, that they can maintain
themselves only by huddling in fearful unchange behind massed troopers, then there is little to be lost and, as the militants chant, "Shut it
down!"

No historical evidence suggests that a culture dominated by
bureaucratized intellectuals retains much vitality in the long run. We
dissident professors, also quite likely warped by decades of institutionalization and excessive engagement to official culture, must make
conscious efforts to support the rebellions. That does not mean forgo-
ing criticism: black demands sometimes contain a second-rate nationalism and chauvinism; New Leftism, especially some current trends in
SDS, desperately moves into a doctrinaire abstraction of reality and
a destructive super-militancy; such socio-cultural rebellions as hippie-
dom, though delightfully realizing in a dreary academic context what
Fourier called the "butterfly instinct," contain a mindless mystagogy
and cultism. Discrimination is our obligation, but it should be part of
a continuing radical critique to achieve the disequilibrium that allows
rebellion to surface and change to come about. Academic resistance
may, and must at times, take forms other than overt rebellion. However, professors cannot claim privileged sanctuary from the essential
struggles of the society of which they are all too obviously an exploitative part and dishonest parcel. Only when we resist do we truly teach,
turning topsy-turvy accepted values and transforming ways of life. We
cannot do this by playing professional hacks and academic custodians.
Nor do we really profess any humanism or science by mainly channel-
ing students into more bureaucratic education and corporate elites and
the nondimensional sensibility of the hired learning for a counterfeit
society. The most distasteful deceit of professors these days comes out
in those who demand intellectual and social and political change, but
always somewhere else. The overwhelming majority of liberal-radical
academicians, and not least the Neo-Marxists, have come out against
rebellions on campus. It is sheer hypocrisy. The current rebellions
should educate us, not just the students, into seeing education as
rebellion.

THE NEW REFORMATION

Paul Goodman

For a long time modern societies have been operating as if religion were a minor and moribund part of the scheme of things. But this is unlikely. Men do not do without a system of "meanings" that everybody believes and puts his hope in even if, or especially if, he doesn't know anything about it; what Freud called a "shared psychosis," meaningful because shared, and with the power that resides in deep fantasy and longing. In advanced countries, indeed, it is science and technology themselves that have gradually, and finally truiumphantly, become the system of mass faith, not disputed by various political ideologies and nationalisms that have also had religious uses.

Now this basic faith is threatened. Dissident young people are saying that science is antilife, it is a Calvinist obsession, it has been a weapon of white Europe to subjugate colored races, and scientific technology has manifestly become diabolical. Along with science, the young discredit the professions in general, and the whole notion of "disciplines" and academic learning. If these views take hold, it adds up to a crisis of belief, and the effects are incalculable. Every status and institution would be affected. Present political troubles could become endless religious wars. Here again, as in politics and morals, the worldwide youth disturbance may indicate a turning point in history and we must listen to it carefully.

In 1967 I gave a course on "Professionalism" at the New School for Social Research in New York, attended by about 25 graduate students from all departments. My bias was the traditional one: professionals are autonomous individuals beholden to the nature of things and the judgment of their peers, and bound by an explicit or implicit oath to benefit their clients and the community. To teach this, I invited seasoned professionals whom I esteemed—a physician, engineer, journalist, architect, etc. These explained to the students the obstacles that increasingly stood in the way of honest practice, and their own life experience in circumventing them.

To my surprise, the class unanimously rejected them. Heatedly and rudely they called my guests liars, finks, mystifiers, or deluded. They showed that every professional was co-opted and corrupted by the

System, all decisions were made topdown by the power structure and bureaucracy, professional peer-groups were conspiracies to make more money. All this was importantly true and had, of course, been said by the visitors. Why had the students not heard? As we explored further, we came to the deeper truth, that they did not believe in the existence of real professions at all; professions were concepts of repressive society and "linear thinking." I asked them to envisage any social order they pleased—Mao's, Castro's, some anarchist utopia— and wouldn't there be engineers who knew about materials and stresses and strains? Wouldn't people get sick and need to be treated? Wouldn't there be problems of communication? No, they insisted; it was important only to be human, and all else would follow.

Suddenly I realized that they did not really believe that there was a nature of things. Somehow all functions could be reduced to inter-personal relations and power. There was no knowledge, but only the sociology of knowledge. They had so well learned that physical and sociological research is subsidized and conducted for the benefit of the ruling class that they did not believe there was such a thing as simple truth. To be required to learn something was a trap by which the young were put down and co-opted. Then I knew that I could not get through to them. I had imagined that the worldwide student protest had to do with changing political and moral institutions, to which I was sympathetic, but I now saw that we had to do with a religious crisis of the magnitude of the Reformation in the fifteen-hundreds, when not only all institutions but all learning had been corrupted by the Whore of Babylon.

The irony was that I myself had said 10 years ago, in *Growing Up Absurd,* that these young were growing up without a world *for* them, and therefore they were "alienated," estranged from nature and other people. But I had then been thinking of juvenile delinquents and a few Beats; and a few years later I had been heartened by the Movement in Mississippi, the Free Speech protest in Berkeley, the Port Huron statement of S.D.S., the resistance to the Vietnam war, all of which made human sense and were not absurd at all. But the alienating circumstances had proved too strong after all; here were absurd gradu-ate students, most of them political "activists."

Alienation is a Lutheran concept:"God has turned His face away, things have no meaning, I am estranged in the world." By the time of Hegel the term was applied to the general condition of rational man, with his "objective" sciences and institutions divorced from his "sub-jectivity," which was therefore irrational and impulsive. In his revision of Hegel, Marx explained this as the effect of man's losing his essential nature as a cooperative producer, because centuries of exploitation, culminating in capitalism, had fragmented the community and robbed the workman of the means of production. Comte and Durkheim pointed to the weakening of social solidarity and the contradiction between law and morality, so that people lost their bearings—this was anomie, an acute form of alienation that could lead to suicide or aimless riot. By the end of the 19th century, alienation came to be used as the term for insanity, derangement of perceived reality, and psychiatrists were called alienists.

Contemporary conditions of life have certainly deprived people, and especially young people, of a meaningful world in which they can act and find themselves. Many writers and the dissenting students themselves have spelled it out. For instance, in both schools and corporations, people cannot pursue their own interests or exercise initiative. Administrators are hypocrites who sell people out for the smooth operation of the system. The budget for war has grotesquely distorted reasonable social priorities. Worst of all, the authorities who make the decisions are incompetent to cope with modern times: we are in danger of extinction, the biosphere is being destroyed, two-thirds of mankind are starving. Let me here go on to some other factors that demand a religious response.

There is a lapse of faith in science. Science has not produced the general happiness that people expected, and now it has fallen under the sway of greed and power; whatever its beneficent past, people fear that its further progress will do more harm than good. And rationality itself is discredited. Probably it is more significant than we like to think that intelligent young people dabble in astrology, witchcraft, psychedelic dreams, and whatever else is despised by science; in some sense they are not kidding. They need to control their fate, but they hate scientific explanations.

Every one of these young grew up since Hiroshima. They do not talk about atom bombs—not nearly so much as we who campaigned against the shelters and fall-out—but the bombs explode in their dreams, as Otto Butz found in his study of collegians at San Francisco State, and now George Dennison, in *The Lives of Children,* shows that it was the same with small slum children whom he taught at the First Street School in New York. Again and again students have told me that they take it for granted they will not survive the next 10 years. This is not an attitude with which to prepare for a career or to bring up a family.

Whether or not the bombs go off, human beings are becoming useless. Old people are shunted out of sight at an increasingly earlier age, young people are kept on ice till an increasingly later age. Small famers and other technologically unemployed are dispossessed or left to rot. Large numbers are put away as incompetent or deviant. Racial minorities that cannot shape up are treated as a nuisance. Together, these groups are a large majority of the population. Since labor will not be needed much longer, there is vague talk of a future society of "leisure," but there is no thought of a kind of community in which all human beings would be necessary and valued.

The institutions, technology and communications have infected even the "biological core," so that people's sexual desires are no longer genuine. This was powerfully argued by Wilhelm Reich a generation ago and it is now repeated by Herbert Marcuse. When I spoke for it in the nineteen-forties, I was condemned by the radicals, for example, C. Wright Mills, as a "bedroom revisionist."

A special aspect of biological corruption is the spreading ugliness, filth, and tension of the environment in which the young grow up. If Wordsworth was right—I think he was—that children must grow up in an environment of beauty and simple affections in order to bcome trusting, open, and magnanimous citizens, then the offspring of our ghettos, suburbs, and complicated homes have been disadvantaged, no matter how much money there is. This lack cannot be remedied by art in the curriculum, nor by vest-pocket playgrounds, nor by banning billboards from bigger highways. Cleaning the river might help, but that will be the day.

If we start from the premise that the young are in a religious crisis, that they doubt there is really a nature of things, and they are sure there is not a world for themselves, many details of their present behavior become clearer. Alienation is a powerful motivation, of unrest, fantasy and reckless action. It leads, as we shall see, to religious innovation, new sacraments to give life meaning. But it is a poor basis for politics, including revolutionary politics.

It is said that the young dissidents never offer a constructive program. And apart from the special cases of Czechoslovakia and Poland, where they confront an unusually outdated system, this is largely true. In France, China, Germany, Egypt, England, the United States, etc., most of the issues of protest have been immediate gut issues, and the tactics have been mainly disruptive, without coherent proposals for a better society. But this makes for bad politics. Unless one has a program, there is no way to persuade the other citizens, who do not have one's gut complaints, to come along. Instead one confronts them hostilely and they are turned off, even when they might be sympathetic. But the confrontation is inept too, for the alienated young cannot take other people seriously as having needs of their own; a spectacular instance was the inability of the French youth to communicate with the French working class, in May 1968. In Gandhian theory, the confronter aims at future community with the confronted; he will not let him continue a course that is bad for *him,* and so he appeals to his deeper reason. But instead of this *Satyagraha,* soul force, we have seen plenty of hate. The confronted are *not* taken as human beings, but as pigs, etc. But how can the young people think of a future community when they themselves have no present world, no profession or other job in it, and no trust in other human beings? Instead, some young radicals seem to entertain the disastrous illusion that other people can be compelled by fear. This can lead only to crushing reaction.

All the "political" activity makes sense, however, if it is understood that it is not aimed at social reconstruction at all, but is a way of desperately affirming that they are alive and want a place in the sun. "I am a revolutionary," said Cohn-Bendit, leader of the French students in 1968, "because it is the best way of living." And young Americans pathetically and truly say that there is no other way to be taken seriously. Then it is not necessary to have a program; the right method is to act, against any vulnerable point and wherever one can rally support. The purpose is not politics but to have a movement and form a community. This is exactly what Saul Alinsky prescribed to rally outcast blacks.

And such conflictful action has indeed caused social changes. In France it was conceded by the Gaullists that "nothing would ever be the same." In the United States, the changes in social attitude during the last 10 years are unthinkable without the youth action, with regard to war, the military-industrial, corporate organization and administration, the police, the blacks. When the actors have been in touch with the underlying causes of things, issues have deepened and the Movement has grown. But for the alienated, again, action easily slips into activism, and conflict is often spite and stubbornness. There is excitement and notoriety, much human suffering, and the world no better off. (New Left Notes runs a column wryly called, "We Made the News Today, O Boy!") Instead of deepening awareness and a sharpening political conflict, there occurs the polarization of mere exasperation. It often seems that the aim is just to have a shambles. Impatiently the ante of tactics is raised beyond what the "issue" warrants, and support melts away. Out on a limb, the leaders become desperate and fanatical, intolerant of criticism, dictatorial. The Movement falls to pieces. Yet it is noteworthy that when older people like myself are critical of the wrongheaded activism, we nevertheless almost invariably concede that the young are *morally* justified. For what is the use of patience and reason when meantime millions are being killed and starved, and when bombs and nerve gas are being stockpiled? Against the entrenched power responsible for these things, it might be better to do something idiotic now than something perhaps more practical in the long run. I don't know which is less demoralizing.

Maybe truth is revealed in the following conversation I had with a young hippie at a college in Massachusetts. He was dressed like an (American) Indian—buckskin fringes and a headband, red paint on his face. All his life, he said, he had tried to escape the encompassing evil of our society that was trying to destroy his soul. "But if you're always escaping," I said, "and never attentively study it, how can you make a wise judgment about society or act effectively to change it?" "You see, you don't dig!" he cried. "It's just ideas like 'wise' and 'acting effectively' that we can't stand." He was right. He was in the religious dilemma of Faith vs. Works. Where I sat, Works had some reality; but in the reign of the Devil, as he felt it, all Works are corrupted, they are part of the System; only Faith can avail. But he didn't have Faith either.

Inevitably, the alienated seem to be inconsistent in how they take the present world. Hippies attack technology and are scornful of rationality, but they buy up electronic equipment and motorcycles, and with them the whole infrastructure. Activists say that civil liberties are bourgeois and they shout down their opponents; but they clamor in court for their civil liberties. Those who say that the university is an agent of the powers that be, do not mean thereby to reassert the ideal role of the university, but to use the university for their own propaganda. Yet if I point out these apparent inconsistencies, it does not arouse shame or guilt. How is this? It is simply that they do not really understand that technology, civil law, and the university are *human* institutions, for which they too are responsible; they take them as brute given, just what's there, to be manipulated as convenient. But convenient for whom? The trouble with this attitude is that these institutions, works of spirit in history, are how Man has made himself and is. If they treat them as mere things, rather than being vigilant for them, they themselves become nothing. And nothing comes from nothing. In general, their lack of a sense of history is bewildering. It is impossible to convey to them that the deeds were done by human beings, that John Hampden confronted the King and wouldn't pay the war tax just like us, or that Beethoven too, just like a rock 'n' roll band, made up his music as he went along, from odds and ends, with energy, spontaneity and passion—how else do they think he made music? And they no longer remember their own history. A few years ago there was a commonly accepted story of mankind, beginning with the Beats, going on to the Chessman case, the HUAC bust, the Freedom Rides, and climaxing in the Berkeley Victory—"The first human event in 40,000 years," Mike Rossman, one of the innumerable spokesmen, told me. But this year I find that nothing antedates Chicago '68. Elder statesmen, like Sidney Lens and especially Staughton Lynd, have been trying with heroic effort to recall the American antecedents of present radical and libertarian slogans and tactics, but it doesn't rub off. I am often hectored to my face with formulations that I myself put in their mouths, that have become part of the oral tradition two years old, author prehistoric. Most significant of all, it has been whispered to me —but I can't check up, because I don't speak the language—that among the junior high school students, aged 12 and 13, that's really where it's at! Quite different from what goes on in the colleges that I visit.

What I do notice, however, is that dozens of Underground newspapers have a noisy style. Though each one is doing his thing, there is not much idiosyncracy in the spontaneous variety. The political radicals are, as if mesmerized, repeating the power plays, factionalism, random abuse, and tactical lies that aborted the movement in the thirties. And I have learned, to my disgust, that a major reason why the young don't trust people over 30 is that they don't understand them and are too conceited to try. Having grown up in a world too meaningless to learn anything, they know very little and are quick to resent it.

This is an unpleasant picture. Even so, the alienated young have no vital alternative except to confront the Evil, and to try to make a new way of life out of their own innards and suffering. As they are doing. It is irrelevant to point out that the System is not the monolith that they think and that the majority of people are not corrupt, just brow-beaten and confused. What is relevant is that they cannot see this, because they do not have an operable world for themselves. In such a case, the only advice I would dare to give them is that which Krishna gave Arjuna: to confront with nonattachment, to be brave and firm without hatred. (I don't here want to discuss the question of "violence," the hatred and disdain are far more important.) Also, when they are seeking a new way of life, for example when they are making a "journey inward," as Ronald Laing calls it, I find that I urge them occasionally to write a letter home.

As a citizen and father I have a right to try to prevent a shambles and to diminish the number of wrecked lives. But it is improper for us elders to keep saying, as we do, that their activity is "counterproductive." It's our business to do something more productive.

Religiously, the young have been inventive, much more than the God-is-dead theologians. They have hit on new sacraments, physical actions to get them out of their estrangement and (momentarily) break through into meaning. The terribly loud music is used sacramentally. The claim for the hallucinogenic drugs is almost never the paradisal pleasure of opium culture nor the escape from distress of heroin, but tuning in to the cosmos and communing with one another. They seem to have had flashes of success in bringing ritual participation back into theater, which for a hundred years playwrights and directors have tried to do in vain. And whatever the political purposes and results of activism, there is no doubt that shared danger for the sake of righteousness is used sacramentally as baptism of fire. Fearful moments of provocation and the poignant release of the bust bring unconscious contents to the surface, create a bond of solidarity, are "commitment."

But the most powerful magic, working in all these sacraments, is the close presence of other human beings, without competition or one-upping. The original sin is to be on an ego trip that isolates; and angry political factionalism has now also become a bad thing. What a drastic comment on the dehumanization and fragmentation of modern times that salvation can be attained simply by the "warmth of assembled animal bodies," as Kafka called it, describing his mice. At the 1967 Easter Be-In in New York's Central Park, when about 10,000 were crowded on the Sheep Meadow, a young man with a quite radiant face said to me, "Gee, human beings are legal!"—it was sufficient, to be saved, to be exempted from continual harassment by officious rules and Law and Order.

The extraordinary rock festivals at Bethel and on the Isle of Wight are evidently pilgrimages. Joan Baez, one of the hierophants, ecstatically described Bethel to me, and the gist of it was that people were nice to one another. A small group passing a joint of marijuana often behaves like a Quaker meeting waiting for the spirit, and the cigarette may be a placebo. Group therapy and sensitivity training, with Mecca at Esalen, have the same purpose. And I think this is the sense of the sexuality, which is certainly not hedonistic, nor mystical in the genre of D. H. Lawrence; nor does it have much to do with personal love, that is too threatening for these anxious youths. But it is human touch, without conquest or domination, and it obviates self-consciousness and embarrassed speech.

Around the rather pure faith there has inevitably collected a mess of eclectic liturgy and paraphernalia. Mandalas, beggars in saffron, (American) Indian beads, lectures in Zen. Obviousiy the exotic is desirable because it is not what they have grown up with. And it is true that fundamental facts of life are more acceptable if they come in fancy dress, e.g. it is good to breathe from the diaphragm and one can learn this by humming "OM," as Allen Ginsberg did for seven hours at Grant Park in Chicago. But college chaplains are also pretty busy, and they are now more likely to see the adventurous and off-beat than, as used to be the case, the staid and square.' Flowers and strobe lights are indigenous talismans.

It is hard to describe this (or any) religiosity without lapsing into condescending humor. Yet it is genuine and it will, I am convinced, survive and develop—I don't know into what. In the end it is religion that constitutes the strength of this generation, and not, as I used to think, their morality, political will, and common sense. Except for a few, like the young people of the Resistance, I am not impressed by their moral courage or even honesty. For all their eccentricity they are singularly lacking in personality. They do not have enough world to have much character. And they are not especially attractive as animals. But they keep pouring out a kind of metaphysical vitality.

Let me try to account for it. On the one hand, these young have an unusual amount of available psychic energy. They were brought up on antibiotics that minimized depressing chronic childhood diseases, and with post-Freudian freedom to act out early drives. Up to age 6 or 7, television nourished them with masses of strange images and sometimes true information—McLuhan makes a lot of sense for the kindergarten years. Long schooling would tend to make them stupid, but it has been compensated by providing the vast isolated cities of youth that the high schools and colleges essentially are, where they can incubate their own thoughts. They are sexually precocious and not inhibited by taboos. They are superficially knowledgeable. On the other hand, all this psychic energy has had little practical use. The social environment is dehumanized. It discourages romantic love and lasting friendship. They are desperately bored because the world does not promise any fulfillment. Their knowledge gives no intellectual or poetic satisfaction. In this impasse, we can expect a ferment of new religion. As in Greek plays, impasse produces gods from the machine. For a long time we did not hear of the symptoms of adolescent religious conversion, once as common in the United States as in all other places and ages. Now it seems to be recurring as a mass phenomenon.

Without doubt the religious young are in touch with something historical, but I don't think they understand what it is. Let me quote from an editorial in New Seminary News, the newsletter of dissident seminarians of the Pacific School of Religion in Berkeley: "What we confront (willingly or not we are thrust into it) is a time of disintegration of a dying civilization and the emergence of a new one." This seems to envisage something like the instant decline of the Roman Empire and they, presumably, are like the Christians about to build, rapidly, another era. But there are no signs that this is the actual situation. It would mean, for instance, that our scientific technology, civil law, professions, universities, etc., are about to vanish from the earth and be replaced by something entirely different. This is a fantasy of alienated minds. Nobody behaves as if civilization would vanish, and nobody acts as if there were a new dispensation. Nobody is waiting patiently in the catacombs and the faithful have not withdrawn into the desert. Neither the Yippies nor the New Seminarians nor any other exalted group have produced anything that is the least bit miraculous. Our civilization may well destroy itself with its atom bombs or something else, but then we do not care what will emerge, if anything.

But the actual situation is very like 1510, when Luther went to Rome, the eve of the Reformation. There is everywhere protest, revaluation, attack on the Establishment. The protest is international. There is a generation gap. (Luther himself was all of 34 when he posted his 95 theses in 1517, but Melanchthon was 20, Bucer 26, Münzer 28, Jonas 24; the Movement consisted of undergraduates and junior faculty.) And the thrust of protest is not to give up science, technology, and civil institutions, but to purge them, humanize them, decentralize them, change the priorities, and stop the drain of wealth.

These were, of course, exactly the demands of the March 4 nationwide teach-in on science, initiated by the dissenting professors of the Massachusetts Institute of Technology. This and the waves of other teach-ins, ads and demonstrations have been the voices not of the alienated, of people who have no world, but of protestants, people deep in the world who will soon refuse to continue under the present auspices because they are not viable. It is populism permeated by moral and professional unease. What the young have done is to make it finally religious, to force the grown-ups to recognize that they too are threatened with meaninglessness.

The analogy to the Reformation is even closer if we notice that the bloated universities, and the expanded school systems under them, constitute the biggest collection of monks since the time of Henry VIII. And most of this mandarinism is hocus pocus, a mass superstition. In my opinion, much of the student dissent in the colleges and especially the high schools has little to do with the excellent political and social demands that are made, but is boredom and resentment because of the phoniness of the whole academic enterprise.

Viewed as incidents of a Reformation, as attempts to purge themselves and recover a lost integrity, the various movements of the alienated young are easily recognizable as characteristic protestant sects, intensely self-conscious. The dissenting seminarians of the Pacific School of Religion do not intend to go off to primitive love feasts in a new heaven and new earth, but to form their own Free University; that is, they are Congregationalists. The shaggy hippies are not nature children as they claim, but self-conscious Adamites trying to naturalize Sausalito and the East Village. Heads are Pentecostals or children of Light. Those who spindle IBM cards and throw the dean down the stairs are Iconoclasts. Those who want Student Power, a say in the rules and curriculum, mean to deny infant baptism; they want to make up their own minds, like Henry Dunster, the first president of Harvard. Radicals who live among the poor and try to organize them are certainly intent on social change, but they are also trying to find themselves again. The support of the black revolt by white middle-class students is desperately like Anabaptism, but God grant that we can do better than the Peasants' War. These analogies are not fanciful; when authority is discredited, there is a pattern in the return of the repressed. A better scholar could make a longer list; but the reason I here spell it out is that, perhaps, some young person will suddenly remember that history was about something.

Naturally, traditional churches are themselves in transition. On college campuses and in bohemian neighborhoods, existentialist Protestants and Jews and updating Catholics have gone along with the political and social activism and, what is probably more important, they have changed their own moral, esthetic and personal tone. On many campuses, the chaplains provide the only official forum for discussions of sex, drugs and burning draft cards. Yet it seems to me that, in their zeal for relevance, they are badly failing in their chief duty to the religious young: to be professors of theology. They cannot really perform pastoral services, like giving consolation or advice, since the young believe they have the sacraments to do this for themselves. Chaplains say that the young are uninterested in dogma and untractable on this level, but I think this is simply a projection of their own distaste for the conventional theology that has gone dead for them. The young are hotly metaphysical—but alas, boringly so, because they don't know much, have no language to express their intuitions, and repeat every old fallacy. If the chaplains would stop looking in the conventional places where God is dead, and would explore the actualities where perhaps He is alive, they might learn something and have something to teach.

THE HUMANITIES AND INHUMANITIES

Louis Kampf

American higher education, like any institution, lives by myths. Still feeling threatened by the seriousness of purpose shown by students during last spring's campus rebellions, the educator's myth of the moment informs us of both the practicality and the transcendent beauty of a liberal (or humanistic) education. The same noble speech is being (or has recently been) addressed to thousands of freshmen: whether at West Point, Swarthmore, the Texas College of Mines, M.I.T. or the University of Michigan hardly seems to matter. It informs them of the primacy of a liberal—rather than a specialized, or technical—education. The humanities, the speech continues, release us from irrationally held prejudices; they open our minds; they teach us to be generalists instead of specialists. In short, a liberal education transforms the narrow career-oriented youth into a free, though of course responsible, man or woman of culture.

The underlying assumption of the speech is that four years of exposure to a balanced curriculum will produce young men and women who are objective, rational, yet not without feeling; who being

Louis Kampf, "The Humanities and Inhumanities," *The Nation,* Sept. 30, 1969. Reprinted by permission of the publisher.

free of ideological blinders will be blessed with a sense of their own autonomy. Having been made intellectually independent by their study of Homer, the Renaissance, atomic particles, Wordsworth, brain waves, Pop art and total environments, they are capable of discovering the relevant past and applying it to the problems of the moment. They are prisoners neither of history nor of the imperatives of current urgencies. Consequently they are eminently capable of dealing with the insistent pressures of change. Having absorbed the best civilization has to offer, they will be able to retain their humanity though practically engulfed by inhuman events. Briefly put, they will be liberal. Certainly, they will not resort to the barbarism of riots.

I suppose there is a grain of truth at the center of this hollow rhetoric. Certainly the motives which generate such words are often decent enough. Yet I suspect that the hearts of most academics attending freshman orientation sink as they hear the noble sentiments being piled on. There is a moment when one expects the dean of freshmen either to burst into tears, to choke on his own words, or perhaps to double up with laughter. He knows that his colleagues know his words are fake; and I suspect that most of the students see us all—teachers, deans, administrators—for the frauds we are. Is it not time we forgot about the nobility of the humanities and asked what their real function is, what social purposes they, in fact, serve?

Hardly a day passes without some representative of the industrial elite letting us know that America's corporate enterprises, not to speak of its government agencies, need managers who are not only steeped in the techniques of operations research but who are equally adept at quoting John Donne or T. S. Eliot. At M.I.T., the Sloan Fellows in Industrial Management are expected to devote a fairly substantial amount of their time to the study of literature. The exposure to literature, we are to assume, makes them better—indeed, more enlightened —managers. But who are these managers? What is their task?

> No one knows who will live in this cage in the future, or whether at the end of this tremendous development entirely new prophets will arise, or there will be a great rebirth of old ideas and ideals, or, if neither, mechanized petrification, embellished with a sort of convulsive self-importance. For the last stage of this cultural development, it might well be truly said: "Specialists without spirit, sensualists without hearts; this nullity imagines that it has attained a level of civilization never before achieved."

The melancholy words are Max Weber's. The occupants of his cage are the functionaries of the bureaucracy bequeathed us by the Protestant ethic and the spirit of capitalism. The culture he feared was one in which rationalization of the profit motive, rather than the simple urge to earn money, becomes its own end, and efficiency is pursued with religious—yet mechanical—zeal. To further such ends, traditional education is replaced by training programs for technicians and efficiency experts. M.I.T., the Harvard Business School, and their brothers and sisters were fathered by the needs of industrial capitalism.

But today such an analysis may seem naive, even simple-minded. We know that our business schools give courses in social responsibility; moreover, our industrial managers conduct seminars on the needs of the Third World and the family structure of the poor. And who would doubt that this derives from anything but the best of motives? But before we congratulate ourselves on our good luck, we might take a closer look at modern capitalism. Clearly we have moved beyond that stage of rationalization which merely involves problems in engineering. Moreover, the complexities of modern finance—the mother of industrial development—involve a subtlety of human manipulation undreamed of by Weber's contemporaries. And as the complexity insinuates itself into all areas of the social system, we reach a point where our corporations and financial institutions effectively control most public—as well as private—institutions. As Kenneth Galbraith has pointed out, in this situation the main function of the American Government is not to promote the public sector but to keep the social order stable enough for business to do its business. Its second large task is to see that America's educational institutions provide the corporate machine with enough functionaries to keep it oiled.

The function of higher education, then, is to turn out those industrial cadres, rocket engineers, researchers, planners, personnel managers and development experts needed by the economy. But not only this; our colleges and universities have also been charged with the task of shaping the more ordinary functionaries: the kind who were once not subject to a four-year grind through the educational mill. Looked at in terms of real industrial need these four years of classes, laboratories, football games, hours in the library and bull sessions seem entirely superfluous. But that is not the point. For beyond immediate mechanical requirements there are the larger social imperatives. Social order must be maintained, and the whole fabric of traditions which gives a society its continuity must be kept intact. If this proves to be impossible, then at least appearances must be kept up; patches covering up the rents must be made invisible. As ordinary mechanical tasks multiply, as more of the labor force takes on white-collar jobs and finds itself pushed into the middle-class, the process of acculturation becomes increasingly difficult. Formerly, those few who climbed the social ladder learned their manners—were educated to the proper social style—by their gradual exposure to the more or less culturally advanced. This was a slow and haphazard process; many fell by the wayside and never attained the style of life appropriate to their economic station. If the production of consumer goods is to expand, the goods must be consumed. To accomplish this, the new industrial cadres must be prepared for an "enriched"—that is, a cultured—style of life. Above all, the new class must never be allowed to feel that it constitutes a new industrial proletariat.

Let me return to Weber's metaphor: the animals in the bureaucratic cage must be civilized. Yet having consciousness, the task of civilizing tends to go beyond the development of conditioned reflexes. It must concern itself with the inescapable fact of human creativity and with the reality of man's historical memory. Both are, after all, basic components of what we call culture; they are integral to man as a species. The ordinary functionary, then, must be convinced that the rationalized task he performs—his ordinary, and inexplicable, job of work— is somehow connected to traditional culture—to all those monuments, both artistic and social, which represent our historical aspirations. What had formerly been the property of an elite now also belongs to the bureaucrat; for he, after all, has become a member of that elite. Or so he thinks. In any case, he knows he has his place in the traditions of the social system—and it is good. Consequently, there is no point in directing the anger of one's frustrations, of one's secret dissatisfactions, at the system itself, for one would be turning them against oneself—against that historic culture one has attained.

And therefore the future home economist, insurance salesman, even department store floorwalker must be made to believe that these tasks are—however mysteriously—connected to Homer, the Athenians, the Judeo-Christian tradition, and the rest of our cultural baggage. The connections may not be clear, but we feel a terrible guilt if we do not perceive them.

To perform this job of acculturation requires an expanding system of colleges and universities; to run them, a force of educational functionaries whose size seems to have no limit. The opportunities for administrators, professors, research executives, even writers, painters and composers are getting better every day. If nothing else, our colleges provide a marvelous haven for Cabinet members, mayors, Presidential advisers and generals, who are temporarily out of work. They, like their fellow humanities professors, are also students of the liberal arts. But, once more, this job of training and acculturation must proceed without upsetting our traditional notion of the university's function. The educational cadres must believe that they perform the humane tasks of scholarship. So they all write articles, and monographs, and books, and reviews of books and bibliographies of these reviews. At the highest level, in our important graduate schools, they train people like themselves to train people like themselves, to train people like themselves, to train people like themselves. . . .

Far from teaching young people to become aware of their capacities, a liberal education allows them—worst, forces them—to ignore themselves. As for the nagging reality of a world desperately in need of social change, the ordinary liberal education pretends either that the need does not exist, or that it can be taken care of painlessly, as a matter of ordinary academic routine. One thing is certain: change must do no violence to the traditional humanistic values embedded in the curriculum. These foundations of a liberal education are sacred. Thus the master task of the humanities becomes one of accommodating students to the social dislocations of industrial society by hiding their painful apprenticeship—their rite of admission to an appropriate office—behind the mask of a traditional culture. Confronted by the radical transformation of roles played by the educated, the liberal arts must assure us that the *status quo* is, after all, being maintained.

An odd development, Matthew Arnold once taught us that the object of studying the best that had been thought or said is to criticize our present mode of life, to make us see the object as it really is. Instead the study of our classics seems to provide us with ideological blinders. It mystifies—to use R. D. Laing's phrase—the very basis of our experience: our way of seeing, feeling, knowing. The humanities have been the educational system's unwitting collaborators in destroying our experience—that is, our humanity. For by blinding us to social mechanisms they have made us unconscious; they have made us the victims of a myth; they have kept us from seeing things as they really are. And, to quote Laing again, "If our experience is destroyed, our behavior will be destructive." And so it is. It is so because our culture has taught us to disguise competitive aggression as social benevolence, oppression as freedom, hate as love. These marvelous transformations have been effected not only by those who control our most powerful institutions but by our educators—our experts in acculturation. The lesson concerning the relationship of culture to aggression taught us by *Civilization and Its Discontents* seems not to have sunk in. Or perhaps it has sunk in all too well. As Freud observed, we desperately stand in need of our defense mechanisms.

But perhaps we are running out of defense mechanisms. Perhaps the contradictions liberal education creates for students are beginning to turn on us; perhaps the young will make us ask those questions we have so long refused to ask.

How so? The meaning of life is in action—whether the acts be physical or mental. Fulfilled action frees us; it makes us independent. When we can relate our thoughts, our yearnings, to activity: when our vague projections issue in conscious work—then we may rightly feel that we have our lives under a measure of control. Formerly the purpose of a traditional liberal education had been to train a cultured —and humane—elite. The act of ruling, of governing and giving guidance, was the activity which gave life its meaning; it fulfilled the objectives of the education. Clearly we still have the same goals in mind for the liberal arts today. Supposedly they teach us to be creative and to act humanely. And are these not the standards we set for our elite? But consciousness has made a fool of our objectives; for the young—or at least for some of them—the ideological fog has been cleared by the very contradictions of their education.

Precisely because we have been liberal in our education, our best students have come to understand that their deepest intellectual concerns—their very enthusiasms, their most intense involvements—cannot issue in any sort of activity which makes a claim to any social relevance beyond acculturation. And if there be no such social relevance, how can activity be fulfilling? Thus there is an almost inevitable split between thought and action. Thought may be free, but activity is controlled; stated educational objectives may be ethical, but actions immoral. The thoughts and feelings engendered by liberal education —the cultural enrichment we offer the young—become ideological masks for the politics of those who rule.

And the best of our students know this. They know that their studies are divorced from meaningful activity. They know that their courses are not intended to further their self-development: rather they become a part of the students' property, their capital. Their knowledge —technical or humanistic—makes them a product. As the material and cultural embodiments of this knowledge grow—and recall, these embodiments are products of man's self-formation, actualizations of his ideas—our practical activities, in a most ironic fashion, become ever more faintly related to our thoughts and feelings: their connection to the meaningful development of ideas and passions becomes more and more tenuous.consciousness has once more played us for the destructive fools we are. For the object of a liberal education, we tell ourselves, is the fulfillment of individual capacities, of ideas and passions. Through such fulfillment, we assume, men can become whole, sane, peaceful and free—that is, humane.

But the split we have created in the student's life has allowed him to see his education for what it is. He knows that his studies—especially those in the humanities, he is informed by our managers—make him a more valuable piece of private property. He knows that his labor in the classroom transforms him into an object; that he makes of himself a product.

Since it is the student himself who becomes the product of his own labor, he is in tension with himself; he is split. He sells those treasures which, we have taught him, best represent his humanity—that is, his civilization, his culture, his liberal education. And so he is at war with his own being, for the battle over this piece of private property is a battle over himself. For the best of our students the study of the humanities creates a more intense consciousness of this situation. Indeed, self-knowledge creates a condition which puts that very education—the act of preparing oneself for one's role—beyond endurance. What truly liberally educated human being can bear to be a commodity with consciousness?

Such are the ends of a liberal education—or at least one of the unintended ends. In their attempt to use the traditional liberal arts to gain social consent, our managers have created a situation where students must risk their sanity in order to enact the lessons of their education; or they must turn into commodities, accommodating themselves—consciously or otherwise—to the lie on which their education is based.

In seeking alternatives, the educator's first impulse is to suggest curricular reform: jiggle the mechanism a bit, make a great-books course out of freshman composition, even have them reading Norman Mailer and Mao Tse-tung. Such reforms, we assume, will effect a fundamental change in the lives of our students. I doubt it. Changes in the curriculum—though often valuable and necessary—may have the ultimate effect of making the acculturating mechanisms more efficient. They may make the beast more cultured, but will not change its objectives. To break out of Weber's cage, to face the imperatives of fundamental change without dogma—if these are the conditions to which we hope our students will aspire, we shall need a most funda-

mental critique of the very social basis and function of higher education. Much academic political science will serve as an example. Aside
from its more gross involvements with the CIA, the field's major
object is to put government *policy*—unlike the more trivial matter of
its *execution*—beyond criticism: to harden ideologies like the "national interest" into unassailable dogmas. Political science has done its
job well, for it has succeeded in putting real political inquiry beyond
the pale of academic respectability. This situation will not be changed
by curricular reforms alone. If students are once more to ask meaningful questions about the state, and if they are to meet these questions
with programs they can translate into action, the very *ends* we set for
political science will have to be changed.

The objective of a liberal education, it seems to me, should be the
harmonious reconciliation of philosophy (that is, our ways of thinking), action and nature (the world; what there is). This condition is
possible only when we do not feel estranged from the products of our
thoughts and actions, when we do not feel separated from the nature
we have helped to create. Unhappily, industrial capitalism is rooted
in these divisions, in our divided state philosophy (our principles of
education) must not be allowed to become an integral expression of
culture; it must not serve to rationalize the divisions induced by the
industrial system. It can remain philosophy, rather than ideology, only
as it is *critical*. And so for the humanities or liberal arts.

How is this criticism to be expressed? Most often, I suspect, in acts
which appear irrational, if not deranged. On October 16, 1967, while
watching nearly 300 students turning in their draft cards at Arlington
Street Church in Boston, I understood—and was saddened by that
understanding—that these young men were involved in a desperate
act of rejecting a civilization. The moral outrage required for this
heroic act is disfiguring; it warps one's sense of reality; it too makes
one's view of the world partial. Yet this seemingly mad act of rejecting
an illegitimate and immoral authority was really an attempt to relate
thought to action; to assert that the products of one's actions are one's
own; that freedom—or at least the struggle for it—is a human necessity. Saying "Hell, no, we won't go!" is one way for the student to
expose the lie of his education. Exploiting the class privilege of one's
college deferment is, after all, a moral fraud—a fraud to which higher
education not only closes its eyes but which it encourages. Ironically,
in their act of criticism, in their act of rejection in willfully separating
themselves from society these draft resisters tried to assert their
wholeness.

Yet what of the madness of this act? Recent studies of schizophren-
ics have shown that insanity may provide the morally sensitive with
the only means of staying alive in a disordered world. The ordering
principle imposed by insanity on destructive chaos keeps one from
suicide. This is one way of relating thought to action; or, more simply,
to *act*—rather than turning inward self-destructively. Yet there is an
alternative to pathology. And the students who take their education
seriously and resist the draft have pointed to that alternative. Our
ordering principle as educators must be criticism or, going further,
counteraction, resistance. This may not sound much like the detachment, the wholeness, we associate with the humanities. Indeed, we
know criticism tends to induce disorder and most of its serious practi-
tioners often act like uncivilized madmen. But consider that the only
real choice may be whether to be mad (though civilized) on society's
terms, or on one's own.

If resistance be madness, it is at least human madness, not the
rationalized lunacy of an abstract process. If our students are to retain
—or perhaps discover—their humanity, they will have to oppose the
system of acculturation and spiritual servitude which our colleges
encourage. And opposition to abstractions constantly tempts one into
irrational confrontations: the bars of the cage are beyond rationality.

Surely, the truly humanistic educator must strive to create a world
which does not demand of our students acts of madness as the price
for spiritual wholeness. Our primary need then is not for a liberal
education but for one which is actively committed to an end. If we are
to break out of the empty rhetoric of liberal educational reform, scholarship may need to become allied with activism.

Activism on what front? Not on the campus alone. For one thing,
the university is not the place where students and their teachers are
most likely to liberate themselves from the shackles of ideology. For
higher education's institutional nature has shaped it into an instrument of perpetuation for our most cherished—that is, humanistic—
ideologies: the university and most of its faculty has a vested interest
to protect. And if we are to take Richard Hofstadter's commencement
address at Columbia as an index, that vested interest will be defended
against campus activists in the name of free scholarly inquiry. For it
is the student strikers, Professor Hofstadter would have us believe,
who are the chief threat to the values of humane scholarship.

Those scholars concerned with liberating themselves from such
academic dogma and effecting fundamental change in the role played
by the liberal arts, might have to begin by forming political groupings

(such as the New University Conference) which create alliances both within and outside the university. These groupings will have to gain a sense of identity by taking clear, strong and public stances on the most important moral issues which confront our students: Vietnam, the draft, race, poverty, the nature of higher education, the uses of scholarship. Or to go deeper: American imperialism, war itself, the function of private property, sex and aggression. What is more analyses should be complemented by meaningful political action. Such activity may, in some cases, involve divisions within the faculty. But this surely must be the first step if our philosophy is to relate to our acts. Some things cannot—and must not—be smoothed over. Surely one thing our students must learn is to take their thoughts seriously.

The special urgency and occasional violence of the students' demands for university reform derive, I think, from an intuition that the liberal arts, rather than being the property of educational establishments, should embody our civilization's highest achievements. This intuition makes the integration of the liberal arts into the students' daily lives a condition toward which they (and we) desperately yearn. Yet if we are to see the object as it is, in Matthew Arnold's sense, we must look at the liberal arts within their social context. If liberal education is to perform its proper function—to help the students see things as they are, to face them humanely and freely—then that education must be placed within an appropriate social context. Creating this context becomes, consequently, the foremost task for the liberal arts.

This involves a transformation of consciousness, a transformation which must be radical—that is, it must take hold at the root. To reach this goal, the economic and social conditions which enslave our students must also be radically transformed. Is this possible inside our educational institutions? Within the imperatives of our social system? I doubt it. Yet our society is being shaken; it changes radically in spite of ourselves, and in spite of our universities. Though we have no clear answers or directives for action, we must make the attempt. For only in the attempt will our analyses unfold, our activity become consciously meaningful.

LETTER FROM A FAR FRAT

Herbert Gold

Well, the Fraternity House still exists. I almost thought it went out of fashion with Dick Powell and Jack Oakie and the great homecoming games of early MGM musicals, but by golly, the old beer-spraying, girl-harvesting, ear-splitting article can still be found on, say, the campus of the University of North Carolina at Chapel Hill, which is an excellent school with high standards. Because I was a guest in the house, I'll invent a name for the occupants. Kappa Lambda Pi.

OK, on a Saturday night the fine old lovingly demolished mansion is surrounded by MG's, Sprites, American convertibles; the lawn is covered with heartbreakingly—beautiful? well, cute—it's covered with girls, and weaving about the girls are the boys, casting their spell, making time. The band is an amplified rock group, good strong sound, tough and nonpsychedelic, out of Carrboro or the country surrounding—black, of course, and no one else is. The hospitality is immense and genuine. They are lovingly demolishing the place by hand; it's a local craft. Echo says, and echo replies: "Have a beer, have a brew. Here, have a swig. Hey, sir, have a drink of mine. Aw, come on, have fun with us, sir."

The boys of KLP are celebrating losing a game. On other nights they celebrate winning the game, or rush week, or the water shortage, or exam week, or the visit of Spiro T. Agnew to Raleigh, or it doesn't make any difference. The faucet in the kitchen is never turned off. Since there has been a prolonged drought and a crucial water shortage which threatens to shut down the school, it has seemed a fine joke to some good old boy to get out of various academic problems by doing his best to drain the lake. Some of the would-be adults in the house think this is childish behavior, he hadn't ought to do like that, but it's a matter of *esprit de corps*. It would be finking on a good buddy to interfere. When one fellow twisted the faucet shut, his good brother got red-eyed and sore, silent; but that's the limit of it. Well, it really means something to him, that water-lover. Hurtie tough-titty feelings. Anyway, they might get the emergency pipeline from Chapel Hill to Durham in time to relieve the reservoir. And in a democracy every man should be free, shouldn't

Herbert Gold, "Letter from a Far Frat," *The Atlantic Monthly,* May 1969. Reprinted by permission of the author and his agent, James Brown Associates, and the publisher. Copyright © 1969 by Herbert Gold.

131

he, to decide whether or not the town has any water? During the festivities which I attended, sex and politics were the prime subjects. So far, so good. I've heard of them. Water and studying were a distraction from real life. The future is a slightly disagreeable consequence of the present, following it by association as "liver" follows "cirrhosis of the." The smell of beer, which I thought had disappeared from campuses, is making its last stand in North Carolina. Beer was a stranger to me (I've spent a lot of time at California colleges). A tall, sandy, snub-nosed brother called Boyce explained about things: "We can't be too cool, man. We can't operate like them Ivies, you know, smoke a joint and then zap her upstairs. We got to plan and work out a three-stage campaign, not like those Ivies up north, man. I prepped at Lawrenceville, I skied in Colorado, so I had that experience, those Ivies. We got to work a three-stage campaign, not cool, man, not like those Ivies, man, sir."

"I understand," I said, almost understanding.

"First stage, we got to dance a little, get 'em a little slushed up, you know, hot, not like those Ivies. That's first stage. Love 'em up a little. Then second stage: into the car. Sir, let me explain, that's trouble, getting 'em out of here and across the parking lot into the car. Now they want it as much as we do, don't misunderstand me, sir, just like those Ivy girls, they want it, but they stumble, they make it tough crossing the parking—OK, into the car, man. Then we have these apartments in town—"

"You mean you can't take the girls upstairs?"

He looked at me, shocked at my presumption. He offered me a swig from his can. He defended Southern womanhood. "Here?" he asked. "In the house? In front of all everybody?"

"I'm sorry," I said.

"Well, we drag 'em out the door and through the parking lot. Course lots of times they yell and scream and laugh and throw up a lot, but we get 'em out, because they want to as much as we do, you know, that's human nature. So then we get 'em to our apartments in town, oh, maybe three, four of us share an apartment, and then . . . " A grin lit up his face. It was like the sun rising over Georgia. "Man, can I just tell you what I did to that little girl over there—see, that one? No, not that one, sir—you like her? Cindy?—no, the one next to Cindy."

He pointed to a little flower of Southern womanhood stubbing out her cigarette against the veneered wood atop the TV.

"You don't know her, do you? so it's all right if I tell you. But listen, sir, if you'd like to meet her . . . "

First, however, he described stage four in the three-stage plan.

I was also interested in his political views, but first we got involved about this girl.

Oh, well, I have prurient interest, too.

"Come here, honey," Boyce called to the girl (not Cindy). She came over, mussed and sulky, with a great hair-collector's mane of yellow hair, and then shot me that marvelous easeful flirty Southern smile which nice girls down there give not only their men but also girlfriends, pregnant ladies, small animals, and the short-answer questions on a nursing exam. She had liquid brown eyes, lovely, hysteric eyes, soft stalks with contact lenses perched atop the irises. "I just been telling him what we did t'other night, honey."

"Went to the movies," she said.

"No, not that night—"

"Saw *Disaster Angels,* with a revival of camp classic *Suddenly Last Summer*—"

"No, the next night, night we had the party—"

"Oh, Boyce, you're a, you're a, you're a—"

He grinned while she stuttered her failure of vocabulary. But she seemed about to cry—hysteric, remember?—so he apologized gently, saying, "Aw, honey, don't carry on like that. I didn't show him the Polaroids."

I was getting mired in interpersonal relations. It would be better all the way around, including my development as a thinking human being and a visiting writer, if I heard some of their views on wider topics.

Floyd Jones is an activist. He has been to Europe on his summer vacation. He thinks about local option and states' rights (positive). Hair and hippies mash around in his emotions (negative). In Europe he noticed the happy faces in West Berlin, the unhappy ones in East Berlin, and that settled Communism for him. It was all clear now, roger and over, and this led him straight back to American politics. "I met these German men in a bar," he told me, "good old boys, spoke good English, said why don't we kick the shit out of those hippies and draft-card burners." He had discussed everything from Vietnam to race with those happy faces, and they compacted together that Communism must be stopped.

Our conversation took place during the heat of the last political campaign, just after a Northerner, Curtis LeMay, native of my home state of Ohio, had been chosen to assist George Wallace in his mission.

"He's a good old boy," said Floyd, as the dancers flailed about us. The cigarettes were falling into the carpet, the fastidious were drinking out of plastic-foam cups, the forthright were drinking out of their cans, and the group had me backed against the color TV. The sound was turned off, but the light show flickered and spattered against the screen. I reached behind to turn it off so that the radiation wouldn't catch me behind while the vocal emanations and renditions took me afront.

Floyd is the only man I know who was overjoyed by the three major candidates for the presidency. Hubie was a good old boy, loyal to Lyndon, a virtue all in itself, and of course Wallace had the clearest and finest ideas, but he personally was voting for Mr. Nixon. It's a class thing, he felt; a duty to live up to the word "responsible"; and Mr. Nixon's speeches nearly brought tears to his eyes. They were that sincere. Also, he hoped he'd kick the shit out of those draft-card burners and long-haired hippies.

"You really like all the candidates?"

"They're loyal Americans, aren't they? That's what I ask of a man."

I offered some objections to Floyd and the others, but mainly I tried to play Socratic Method questions: Is this a happy country? Do you really think more weapons for the police are the "answers" to Law and order? What is your conception of America's role? One very tall, horn-rimmed young man, with a look of poetic angularity about him, hung on my words, and I thought I had an ally. He too seemed puzzled by America circa 1968. He suddenly burst out: "Wha yo so gol-darned negative? What is this negative bit?" Astonished by his own anger, he added: "Sir?"

A few girls had joined us. One of them was Cindy, eyes afire, that old golf club menace in them. There was some kicking and giggling going on below the level of the conversation. It was stage one and a half of the campaign, I decided, not like those Ivies.

I must have asked a question, because the sensitive-looking brother burst out, "Course I wouldn't kick the shit out of 'em! I just say that!" Then he smiled shyly. "Wouldn't want to get my shoes dirty," and nudged me. "Aw, sir, I just say that. They got the right to free speech, too, so long as they don't go tearing down this country. You're not always so negative, are you, sir?"

It was time to be their buddy, I decided. I too had done my term at Fort Bragg and elsewhere, though this was before their birth. I reminisced about Fayetteville, North Carolina, which we called Fagleberg.

"You mean Fayettenam?" Floyd asked. "When they call me there, I'm going. If they cancel my deferment, sir, I'm going. But I'm going to try to finish my education first, and get into a good position, and if the Lord is good to me, I won't have to fight. I can tell what you're thinking, sir. I got strong feelings. But like I already explained, killing's just not in the American line."

He was wearing tight maroon pants and a white button-down short-sleeve shirt with notched vents at the sleeve. One of his Hush Puppies was unlaced. He leaned on me a little, partly out of friendship and desire to be understood, saying, "Now don't get me wrong, hear? They call me, I go. I got this deferment, no gol-darned evasion."

"I'm not a pacifist either," I said.

"But I never did meet any Marine from Vietnam committed an atrocity who enjoyed it, hear? Hear me, sir? We just got to defend the American perimeter, it's as simple as that. So I'll go, I'll go, sir, soon as they call me."

When it came time to part, two of the brothers insisted on walking me home to the Carolina Inn. It had rained gleaming Burgie flip-top friendship rings on the Carolina earth. The brothers scuffed along, bumping and uneasy about the discussion. The men of the KLP house have a complex feeling about life, a minority on this campus, a majority in their own hometowns, but are they a majority in America and the world? It is no longer easy to find the tides of right and float back and forth on them. Kappa Lambda Pi is in trouble as a way of life.

There was a shy moment in the fragrant Indian summer evening, hot rods and flowering trees and sweet echo of amplified rock from the Carrboro Rhythm Ramblers. Something had been left unsaid. Some generation gap had been left ajar, some culture gap unclosed, some stony silence in the metaphysics. We all wanted to be close and warm, and yet we were not close and warm. We had kidded around, but what else? In a world of making out OK, and getting bugged by it, we had made out all right, and gotten bugged by each other, just like the Ivies; and yet there must be something more than paltry victories in love and politics. There might be, for example, real victories. Stage five. Stage six. Stage seven.

On another part of the campus the 1 A.M. showing of underground art flicks was just beginning, and the Dandelion, a head shop, was just closing and the Racial Confrontation group was continuing out under the famous Davie poplar. As we walked by, a tall black man in a denim suit, a refugee from Resurrection City, a pioneer of Freedom City, was

136

smiling and saying softly, We're sick of trickeration, we won't stand still for extermination, so we got to have communication; and an earnest young white student said, But we got to talk it all out first so's not to frighten the other people; and the man from Resurrection City said, Son, that's trickeration . . .

One of my escorts shook his head, grinning. "Man, oh, man," he said to me. Some of these jerks were beyond his comprehension.

All over the campus the gritty Indian summer smell of autumn leaves was helping lovers and celebrants and reformers and late-night scholars fix the memory in their hearts, whether they knew it or not: *This is it, this was college in my time.*

As we walked along, beer fizzing in the jiggled cans, a member of my honor guard said, "It's just, sir, we didn't want you to get the one-sided impression about this school."

"I appreciate your hospitality," I said.

We were standing near the rocking chairs on the porch of the Carolina Inn (widows, conferences, and faculty visitors). "Don't get us wrong," he said. "We have strict rules at the house. We don't always live up to them, but we try not to be litterbugs. We might be Tarheels and we got a lousy team, but we have fun, too, sir." He gazed wearily back across campus to the traditional Davie poplar, famed in song and story. Chapel Hill's little Berkeley was still strolling and consulting near that spot. "Just didn't want you to go away thinking we're all a bunch of stupid intellectuals."

COMES THE
CULTURAL REVOLUTION

James Hitchcock

From Cromwell to Robespierre, from Lenin to Castro, political revolution has carried with it the expectation of cultural revolution. In every instance, however, culture has followed upon the heels of politics; the revolution itself has been rooted in objective political and economic conditions. For a decade, now, this traditional revolutionary view has been a canon of the white radical leadership in America, but

James Hitchcock, "Comes the Cultural Revolution," *The New York Times Magazine,* July 27, 1969. Copyright © 1969, by the New York Times Company. Reprinted by permission of the publisher.

it is changing. Today there is strong evidence that the old order of priorities has given way to a conviction that a "revolution of consciousness" must be effected before the ruling institutions can be effectively undermined.

An indication of the new strategy can be found in the writings of radicals like Andrew Kopkind and Susan Sontag with their emphasis on the revolutionary uses of unconventional clothes, speech, music, sexual behavior, etc. One cannot help but suspect that there is an oblique message here: the earlier, hopeful talk of real revolution (à la the diagram of a fire bomb presented on the cover of The New York Review of Books) is no longer appropriate. The message is either a sophisticated cop-out or, what is more likely, a deepened awareness of the profound and subtle nature of the System. Even the Yippie Abbie Hoffman, the activist leader of the protest at the Democratic convention last August, now seems to be leaning toward cultural over political revolution, as in his book *Revolution for the Hell of It.*

The nature of this cultural revolution is left deliberately vague, but at a minimum it includes totally unrepressed sensuality, a contempt for the ordinary categories of rational thought and speech, rejection of organized work and support for the extreme *avant-garde* in art. In its most debased form, as every notable idea is inevitably debased, it is represented on many campuses by young people who identify the repressiveness of the System with any kind of discipline whatsoever and who regard it as a mark of revolutionary commitment to flaunt their total hedonism, their intellectual ignorance and their lack of loyalty to any institution.

If the leaders of the Movement are embarrassed by these few psychotic, semi-delinquent nihilists, they refrain from saying so publicly.

There are, in addition, some basic, practical difficulties with the cultural approach to revolution, problems that the radicals do not yet seem willing or able to face. Precisely how, for example, can their revolution succeed without a discipline and an eagerness for self-sacrifice far exceeding the demands of the System itself? Those radicals who do not make it a badge of honor to ignore complexity recognize that the System is affected in a very fundamental way when its discipline is weakened—when workers refuse the regularity of the assembly line, executives demand their evenings for themselves, students reject the diploma treadmill. They would do well to ponder the consequences of a comparable lack of discipline in their own ranks.

For faith in cultural revolution seems a form of half-play, half-magic—the revolutionary is persuaded that if he merely engages in a sufficient number of bizarre, semi-mystical and self-indulgent activities (like smoking marijuana), the revolution will automatically come. Historically, of course, revolutions can be shown to have occurred only as the result of discipline, extremely hard work, great patience and privation, and finally luck.

On its most sophisticated level the new cultural radicalism is a kind of loose amalgam of Marx and Freud, in that the roots of economic oppression are seen as organically joined with the roots of sexual repression—there can be neither kind of freedom without the other. Since the erotic instincts imply ecstasy, total freedom and true self-gratification, it is impossible to be sexually liberated and still the slave of the economic machine. Moreover, sexual liberation is seen as the precondition of ultimate wisdom, which lies beyond reason altogether; those who are free in the libido will understand the true nature of reality and can no longer be defrauded by the System's manipulative myths.

What the new radicals overlook is the fact that successful revolutionaries, beginning with the first great modern revolutionary, Cromwell himself, have usually been puritans. The discipline and single-mindedness of the puritan temper are what make possible a truly revolutionary commitment—not merely order and self-sacrifice but also what is popularly thought of as the heart of puritanism, sexual restraint. Robespierre's "reign of virtue" in the French Revolution was quite strict and old-fashioned, and many persons were disappointed when the Russian Revolution ended by turning Soviet society into perhaps the most puritanical in the world. Apparently Mao Tse-tung, Fidel Castro and other Third World revolutionaries have similar instincts. Such revolutionary leaders see sexual freedom as, if nothing else, a sign of decadent weakness and a dangerous and reactionary concern with private happiness at the expense of public duty.

One of the most curious political slogans ever coined is "Make Love, Not War," particularly when considered in its literal sense—as though the two were alternatives or even opposites. Rather than Eros and violence being enemies, they have a very intricate and intimate kinship with each other, which innumerable psychologists and novelists have delineated for us. In fact, nothing seems more conducive to the radicals' goal—the total collapse of puritanical sexual standards— than a violent milieu. The relative peace of 19th-century Europe saw the growing rigidity of middle-class attitudes towards sex, while the First World War dealt an ultimately fatal blow to this prudery. Free sex among young people did not apparently flourish on the quiet campuses of 10 years ago; one cannot but suspect that its sudden upsurge now is related to the shadow of the Vietnam conflict or, perhaps, to the hatreds and confrontations in the universities themselves.

Today's young radicals, seemingly so sure of their own standards, are profoundly ambivalent about the morals and life styles of their parents. Their favorite charge against the older generation is hypocrisy, and they fulminate like circuit preachers against their chain-smoking, gin-guzzling, bed-hopping elders, implying thereby that the puritan ethic is dead and survives as a mere facade behind which there is total moral abandon. Yet just as often, they reverse themselves and insist that their parents really are "up tight," really are puritans, really are ignorant and frightened of wordly experiences. They seem unable to decide whether they want their parents to live up to the venerable puritan ethic or whether they want to destroy it root and branch.

There is also a tendency among today's young revolutionaries to identify the kinds of restraints which traditional morality advocates with the kind of discipline demanded by modern industrialized society. A favorite analysis is the "deferred satisfactions" theory, which states that the essence of capitalism, so far as it affects men's lives directly, is that one must work hard, accept the authority of the managerial class and forgo the impulses to gratify one's desires—all in the interest of compiling substantial savings for one's old age or one's children. Hence the System is seen as necessarily anti-erotic and generally anti-sensual. If people made love on impulse, begat illegitimate children, smoked marijuana, slept in the park, went naked in public, they presumably could not fill the niches marked out for them by Wall Street.

But the System is infinitely adaptable, and human beings are infinitely complex. An instructive parallel with the present might be the 1920s in America, when it was also clear that something like a cultural revolution was taking place. Women started smoking and baring their legs, risqué jokes and forbidden words were used in polite company, some of the best people flouted the liquor laws, popular music and dancing grew wilder and wilder. Yet in retrospect it is striking how little permanent change occurred. Family structure was perhaps weakened, but it survived to enjoy the "togetherness" and "women-are-best-fulfilled-in-the-home" fads of post-World War II. The churches did not suffer massive defections, and 30 years later their membership was greater than ever. Puritan morality remained the ideal of most Americans, however much it was violated in practice. And what effect did this cultural revolution have on politics and economics? The leading cultural revolutionaries of the day, as well as those who popularized the new styles, were either apolitical or had no serious quarrel with the System as they knew it. This was true not only of the great literary radicals like Eliot, Pound and Hemingway, who were quite traditionalist in many of their views and also quite anti-democratic, but even more of the foot soldiers in those Jazz Age cultural wars. The young people who effected the "revolution of consciousness," of manners and morals, in the Roaring Twenties were, many of them, scions of wealthy capitalist families. Most apparently felt no great guilt over their inherited wealth; their wealth in fact made possible their cultural revolt. If they were anti-business, it was only because business was boring, and if they scorned Calvin Coolidge, it was only because he was colorless. In time these radical young men, so devoted to Bacchus and Eros, became tycoons and branch managers like their fathers, and their flapper girl friends fitted in well as corporate wives.

This new seriousness which they discovered did not, however, involve moral conversion. The style of business life itself changed to accommodate the new young men. John D. Rockefeller had lived puritanically and simply, and according to official doctrine this was a prerequisite for business success. But these new capitalists are men who, if we can believe what we are so often told, patronize expensive call girls as a matter of course, have innumerable affairs with secretaries and colleagues' wives and drink constantly. Their libidos are said to be as unchained as anybody's can possibly be, yet they have not discovered any hidden truths, and they have especially not found that the discipline of the corporate system is unbearable alongside their erotic freedoms.

It is now argued that marijuana and stronger drugs are the torpedoes which will finally sink the System, since they dissolve all inhibitions and thus prevent the suppressions and subserviences which the System requires. But there are obvious parallels between drugs and alcohol. In earlier days it was part of official capitalist mythology that drinking was incompatible with business success, and the Horatio Alger stories usually included reverse success stories about promising young men whose careers plummeted because of drink. In theory it could have been argued that since alcohol—like drugs—overcomes people's inhibitions, it makes impossible the kind of calculating, secretive, duplicitous, repressed attitudes which businessmen and politicians must cultivate. But as it turned out, in many industries the consumption of alcohol at business luncheons is a ritual which no respectable company would dare forgo.

Young radicals are sometimes gratified to hear that even persons within the great corporate structures—lawyers and junior executives —are secret pot-smokers, and they tend to assume that such people are preparing to defect, that the System is beginning to fall apart. It is probably more likely that for such people smoking pot is like drinking liquor—precisely that which makes the System bearable, hence that which strengthens it. Corporate America is still officially puritan, but this is not because it needs puritanical self-denial among its employes but solely because it is afraid of offending public sensibilities by being otherwise. Should pot-smoking, free love, public nudity, long hair, beads, etc., ever become respectable, there is absolutely no reason why businessmen would not be able to adopt these styles and still remain within the System.

Another key outpost of cultural revolution is thought to be popular music: the primordial, erotic rhythms of rock and soul are destroying the psychic foundations of our society. But what about jazz? Although the theory was not so well articulated, the people of 1920-40 were aware that jazz, like much of today's popular music, originated with a despised underclass (Southern blacks) with values and sensibilities quite alien to those of most Americans—a class that was in certain obvious and also hidden ways very antagonistic to the System. Yet several generations of corporate servants have grown up as jazz lovers, patronizing the movement while it was fashionable, dropping it when it ceased to be, with no discernible effect on their politics or loyalty to the System.

Those who put their faith in rock music as an agency for cultural transformation should also note some embarrassing facts about the apostles of the new sensibility, who are also its patron saints. The Beatles and the Rolling Stones, for example, are young men who have made it very big indeed in the capitalist system. They do not, however, give their money to the poor nor, so far as we know, generously support revolutionary movements; they spend their money lavishly and ostentatiously in the approved manner of successful entrepreneurs. They flout certain moral traditions like marriage, but this does not cause a drop in the stock market nor a perceptible leftward trend among the electorate.

Radicals who have any pretensions to seriousness about cultural revolution must work through the problem of distinguishing genuine subversiveness in today's *avant-garde* worlds, when virtually everything radical and new—clothes, art, films, books and drugs as well as music—has proved to be a great moneymaker, in and through the capitalist system. (Recently in St. Louis, when an association of rock bands was asked to lower its prices for teen-age dances, its spokesman refused, saying that such a move would be "contrary to the American free enterprise system.")

Whatever might be said against older liberal intellectuals they have generally been free of the corrupting influences of financial success. Few have made much money, and the magazines through which they propagate their ideas exist on subsidies and have to struggle to keep alive. Grove Press, on the other hand, specializing in erotic and other "subversive" books, is very much of a growth stock. Ramparts has a decided capitalist propensity for spending lavishly on the approved corporate accouterments. The millionaire jet-set radicals of the entertainment industry have very advanced political and cultural ideas, but their lives seem not essentially different from those of more conservative millionaires.

One of the most important logical inconsistencies of the New Left has been its identification of capitalism with puritanism and deferred satisfactions. It has looked at the relationship solely from the point of view of employees of the System (even here in a very superficial and overly ideological way) and not from the point of view of consumers, who are the same employees under a different aspect. Whatever puritanism corporate America may foster in its employees it undermines through its sales campaigns, in which every puritan restraint is thrown away; people are urged to gratify their slightest desires (even nonexistent desires) and sexual longings are shamelessly exploited. In waging war against the residual puritanism of American society the young radicals are, among other things, destroying one of the last defenses against advertising manipulation which ordinary American people still have. Hedonism can almost be defined as making oneself wholly into a consumer, without regard for any other identity, and this is the ultimate dream of Madison Avenue, to which the cultural revolutionaries help contribute.

There are other ways in which the revolutionaries are playing into the hands of the advertisers. The cult of youth, the belief that only among the unspoiled and spontaneous young is real purity and love of truth to be found, is originally a Romantic idea. Advertising is perhaps Romanticism's final vulgarization—instinctual, holding out the promise of secret and infinite fulfillments, unconcerned with the drabness and routine of life, impervious to rational criticism. Americans long felt that the old have a superior wisdom which the young must imbibe, but advertising directed its appeal unerringly to the longing for eternal youth which underlay this decorum. It was Madison Avenue which taught us that the loss of our youth is our greatest misfortune and that our money and time should be spent to prevent it. (This is true not only in obvious ways, in advertisements for cosmetics and clothes, but also in the implication that if one drives a particular car, smokes a particular cigarette or drinks a particular cola, he will remain young at heart and attractive to swingers.) Now this ideal of perpetual youth has become respectable even in intellectual circles, solemnly espoused by many persons who are a long way beyond 30.

The older generations are constantly told by the new revolutionaries that they are hopelessly out of touch with the rapidly moving times, that there is no possibility of their remaining relevant unless they follow the youth-preserving regimens of correct thought and feeling which the young set out for them, that they are in fact obsolete. In the classic words of Bob Dylan, "Come mothers and fathers throughout the land . . . / Your old road is rapidly agin'/Please get out of the way if you can't lend a hand/Oh, the times they are achangin'." Despite the alleged concern of the New Left with human values and their fierce antagonism toward the dehumanizing aspects of the System, they persist in this profoundly inhumane ideology, with its readiness to toss older people (those over 30) on the scrap heap, its refusal to allow them any voice in constructing the future (they can, if they are sufficiently docile, "lend a hand") and the unstated belief that men do not learn and mature as they grow older but merely degenerate. New Leftists accustomed to detecting hidden manipulations in the System should ask themselves whether the new cult of youth really promises revolution, coming as it does at a time when businessmen have discovered that the youth market is by far the most lucrative and promising of all. Witness the last desperate act of The Saturday Evening Post before its demise, the cutting from its subscription rolls of those who were not youthful enough to attract important advertisers.

There is yet another area in which the young radicals unconsciously give aid and comfort to the enemy. It is a commonplace among critics of the modern capitalist economy, young and old, that it is dependent upon the artificial acceleration of the demand for goods. Advertisers have found that they can best stimulate this demand by constantly overheating the atmosphere—by convincing people that they can attain happiness by reaching out for continually new and improved products and by warning them that not to reach out is to fall out of step with the times, to allow themselves to become obsolete. The great enemy of capitalist growth is consumer contentment. The young radicals are very sensitive to some of the specific debasements and vulgarizations of advertising , but they do not reflect that their own mood fits closely with the general atmosphere which Madison Avenue hopes to sustain. Admen, too, regard contentment and attachment to tradition as unthinkable. They, too, exhort us to change our ways; they, too, seek a state of bewildering and unending flux, in which men are vulnerable to the preachments for various kinds of panaceas.

In the 1950s the university was thought to be a place of civilized values—quiet, calm rationality, a striving for eternal perspective, principled loyalty to the past—while the market place was the haven of hysteria, tension, raw antagonisms, conflict as a way of life. In the 1960s, however, the young radicals have effectively brought the mood of the market place to the campus. And while the System, such as it is, continues to make the physical conditions of human life uncertain, unhappy and menacing (fine old buildings are destroyed and neighborhoods uprooted; good craftsmanship becomes almost nonexistent, air polluted, quiet nearly impossible to find, speed and movement the constant aim of all policy), the radicals help to exacerbate the nation's spiritual malaise.

The successes of the New Left in the past few years have been made possible in part by their use of the techniques of mass advertising and public relations. Ralph Goldman of San Francisco State calls this "instant equalitarianism," in which a relatively few, weak and disorganized rebels are made to seem the equal of a large, well-established and powerful institution, simply because they are given equal attention in the mass media. Some radicals exercise considerable ingenuity in devising new attention-getting ploys, and there is a great concern for symbols which will "grab" people in an immediate and emotional way, overcoming whatever resistance they may have to the basic message.

Many young rebels believe that in shouting obscenities—a not infrequently used ploy—in public they are violating one of the fundamental codes of capitalist society, but in fact advertisers probably refrain from using these words in their appeals only for fear of offending the rapidly diminishing ranks of those who still believe that there should be limits even to good salesmanship. Advertising is inherently a quite radical activity, since it recognizes no restrictions on success and seeks constantly to discover and create new realities—demands and the products to meet the demands. If advertisers find, as they probably will in a few years, that a prudent dose of obscenity is a good way to reach particular audiences, they will certainly begin using it. The extreme radicals have also joined with Madison Avenue and the Pentagon in further debasing the language of public communication, in that nuances of meaning and tone and other rhetorical devices have been thrown away; the sole method of emphasis has become volume and shock, perferably short words which, even if not literally obscene, have the impact of a fist in the stomach. There are, of course, some among the radicals with a real gift for the fresh and effective phrase and a respect for accuracy in thought and language. But these segments of the New Left seem eventually to lose out in whatever strategic wars go on behind the campus barricades. Just as on Madison Avenue, the hard sell invariably wins out when the aim is to reach the mass market. Inevitably, it is the "crazies" and other hardliners who set the style which others must follow; a more civilized approach does not bring in so many sales so quickly.

The entertainment and art merchandised by the System for the younger generation, many commentators suspect, have had important and disturbing effects upon the rebellious young. Television, for example, is in its way the most culturally iconoclastic of all the media. It has spawned no really great stars as the movies did, and even its most popular shows are likely to be dropped after a few seasons (comic books like Donald Duck and Superman survived for decades). Among other things, television teaches that nothing endures and that respect for the past is a fool's illusion.

The art and music chosen by the rebellious young are for the most part those which bombard the senses in the most direct, brutal and inescapable ways. This is a generation which admits to easy boredom and demands that all things be renewed and made constantly relevant, which often means ingeniously improved sensual assaults. Except for the hippies (now scorned by many of their political-minded fellows), the discontented young show no great inner-directedness and no great attachment to solitude and wholly private thoughts. They demand to be constantly stimulated from outside by new ideas, new experiences, new sensations; they have become politicized and radicalized partly through the conviction that reality is found wherever crowds gather and passions are high.

When Marshall McLuhan says that "the medium is the message," this is merely another way of saying that the impact of the medium is not dependent on its content and that those who seek merely the experience of being turned on can be turned on by almost any message. Hence, there is nothing inherently radical in the new media or the new art; indeed, the quest of the young for mind-blowing experiences may in time make them susceptible to the most fearsome kind of manipulation, whether revolutionary or fascist.

Today's young present an ambivalent picture with respect to manipulation, because they are at the same time acutely tuned against the shams which emanate from Washington and the dean's office and also susceptible in an extreme degree to the manipulations of certain of their own leaders and, more seriously, to certain media merchants, who have been packaged and bally-hooed as thoroughly as any detergent. (Articles now appear in serious journals explaining admiringly what fine sincere people the new millionaire pop idols are, just as similar articles still appear in lesser publications gushing over the sincerity and profundity of Pat Boone.)

The majority of discontented young people are of course not very deeply affected by the drives for cultural revolution here discussed. (This rebellious generation seems to include some of the absolute best and absolute worst people in America.) But precisely because we have seen such remarkable and unforeseen changes on the campuses in the past five years, we cannot assume that the style and attitudes of the Yippies or the Up-Against-the-Wall chapter of S.D.S. will not become dominant. Some very respected intellectuals, when they write about cultural revolution, seem to mean precisely this, and there are efforts being made to convert the moderates. But we should be on guard against a "revolution" which, while attacking various visible manifestations of the old order, has in vast, unseen, often unconscious ways been affected by the prevailing trends of our neurotic commercial society and drinks from the same hidden springs in our souls and our culture.

THE POLITICS OF
MILITARISM

INTRODUCTION

In his farewell address given in January, 1961, President Eisenhower warned: "In the councils of government we must guard against the acquisition of unwarranted influence, whether sought or unsought, by the military-industrial complex. The potential for the disastrous rise of misplaced power exists and will persist." In recognizing the dangers of this "fourth branch" of government, Eisenhower identified a new, enlarged role for the United States military in world affairs, a role which had been developing since the end of World War II.

In the late 1940s and throughout the 1950s, our government responded to an interpretation of world politics which asserted that monolithic international communism threatened the security of the United States. American military policy, previously limited to achieving specific overseas objectives and to domestic defense, turned to global military strategies designed to contain the spread of communism through either the threat or the use of military force. The commitment to these policies eventually led to American involvement in the Korean and Vietnamese wars and to numerous counterinsurgency efforts in Latin America, Africa, and other parts of Asia; to implement these efforts, Presidents Truman, Eisenhower, Kennedy, Johnson, and Nixon authorized expenditures totaling over one trillion dollars for specifically military purposes.

The visions of the Cold Warriors—in particular Secretaries of State Acheson and Dulles—showed the world on the brink of nuclear annihilation. The people, nevertheless, were encouraged to believe that

security would be guaranteed by maintaining military supremacy over
the Soviet Union, a conclusion based on the premise that the most
powerful nation was the most secure. This rationale, nourished by
fears of Russian power and cold war myths, resulted in the political
witch hunts of the early 1950s, megadeath projections, family fallout
shelters, and civil defense drills for children. While these policies and
their supporting propaganda fostered the illusion of American om-
nipotence, they failed to discern the crucial differences between the
many types of communist societies that developed after World War
II. The policy-makers also ignored or underrated the significance of
emerging nationalism in the Third World.

Throughout this period, popular criticism of the military establishment was limited to protest against nuclear weapons testing. It was not
until the American people slowly came to realize, between 1963 and
1965, that the United States was committed to a major undeclared war
in Asia that objections to the military-industrial complex became
widespread and intense. According to Anthony Hartley, the critics
began to identify the complex "as an expensive and dangerous Fran-
kenstein's monster freed from the control of its creator and crashing
through the restrictions placed on its movements by political or governmental institutions." Since the war had developed without any
significant Congressional debate, and lacked even the formal declaration required by the Constitution, the critics had little difficulty in
making a case for Senator McGovern's opinion that "the mounting
influence of the military-industrial complex is the most serious internal threat facing the United States."

In the course of the debate, some experts have come to question the
adequacy of the political process to deal with the military. "Thirty
years ago," writes Professor Hans Morgenthau, "the American people
and their elected representatives could still have a competent voice in
determining the military policy of the United States; today, Congress
passes the $70 billion budget of the Department of Defense with
essentially ritualistic scrutiny, giving the experts the benefit of the
doubt." While there are indications that recent criticism will force the
military to justify future expenditures and undertakings, the influence
exerted on a weak Congress by the nearby Pentagon and by the large
numbers of pro-military congressmen, senators, lobbyists, and businessmen makes it unlikely that controls over the system will be easily
achieved.

Of even greater danger is the possibility, also suggested by Professor Morgenthau, that the "powers that be must be tempted to deal

with our domestic problems as they are dealing with the problem of Vietnam." As a retired air force general put it recently, "Military takeover is a dirty word in this country, but if the professional politicians cannot keep law and order, it is time we do so, by devious or direct means."

If the total impact of the military on American life is beyond precise measurement, it is nevertheless obvious that the gargantuan expenditures alone drain the domestic economy of funds needed for the crises in health care, urban decay, education, pollution, and the plight of the aged. Other, more subtle effects of militarism include the legitimacy it bestows upon violence; we give war toys to our children and watch "live" warfare on television. Slowly we become less sensitive to death, more accepting of the body counts, less capable of responding to brutality.

THE NEW FORMS OF CONTROL

Herbert Marcuse

A comfortable, smooth, reasonable, democratic unfreedom prevails in advanced industrial civilization, a token of technical progress. Indeed, what could be more rational than the suppression of individuality in the mechanization of socially necessary but painful performances; the concentration of individual enterprises in more effective, more productive corporations; the regulation of free competition among unequally equipped economic subjects; the curtailment of prerogatives and national sovereignties which impede the international organization of resources. That this technological order also involves a political and intellectual coordination may be a regrettable and yet promising development.

The right and liberties which were such vital factors in the origins and earlier stages of industrial society yield to a higher stage of this society: they are losing their traditional rationale and content. Freedom of thought, speech, and conscience were—just as free enterprise, which they served to promote and protect—essentially *critical* ideas, designed to replace an obsolescent material and intellectual culture by a more productive and rational one. Once institutionalized, these rights and liberties shared the fate of the society of which they had become an integral part. The achievement cancels the premises.

To the degree to which freedom from want, the concrete substance

Herbert Marcuse, "The New Forms of Control," *One-Dimensional Man* (Boston, Mass.: Beacon Press, 1964), pp. 1–18. Reprinted by permission of the Beacon Press. Copyright © 1964, by Herbert Marcuse.

of all freedom, is becoming a real possibility, the liberties which pertain to a state of lower productivity are losing their former content. Independence of thought, autonomy, and the right to political opposition are being deprived of their basic critical function in a society which seems increasingly capable of satisfying the needs of the individuals through the way in which it is organized. Such a society may justly demand acceptance of its principles and institutions, and reduce the opposition to the discussion and promotion of alternative policies *within* the status quo. In this respect, it seems to make little difference whether the increasing satisfaction of needs is accomplished by an authoritarian or a non-authoritarian system. Under the conditions of a rising standard of living, non-conformity with the system itself appears to be socially useless, and the more so when it entails tangible economic and political disadvantages and threatens the smooth operation of the whole. Indeed, at least in so far as the necessities of life are involved, there seems to be no reason why the production and distribution of goods and services should proceed through the competitive concurrence of individual liberties.

Freedom of enterprise was from the beginning not altogether a blessing. As the liberty to work or to starve, it spelled toil, insecurity, and fear for the vast majority of the population. If the individual were no longer compelled to prove himself on the market, as a free economic subject, the disappearance of this kind of freedom would be one of the greatest achievements of civilization. The technological processes of mechanization and standardization might release individual energy into a yet uncharted realm of freedom beyond necessity. The very structure of human existence would be altered; the individual would be liberated from the work world's imposing upon him alien needs and alien possibilities. The individual would be free to exert autonomy over a life that would be his own. If the productive apparatus could be organized and directed toward the satisfaction of the vital needs, its control might well be centralized; such control would not prevent individual autonomy, but render it possible.

This is a goal within the capabilities of advanced industrial civilization, the "end" of technological rationality. In actual fact, however, the contrary trend operates: the apparatus imposes its economic and political requirements for defense and expansion on labor time and free time, on the material and intellectual culture. By virtue of the way it has organized its technological base, contemporary industrial society tends to be totalitarian. For "totalitarian" is not only a terroristic political coordination of society, but also a non-terroristic economic-technical coordination which operates through the manipulation of needs by vested interests. It thus precludes the emergence of an effective opposition against the whole. Not only a specific form of government or party rule makes for totalitarianism, but also a specific system of production and distribution which may well be compatible with a "pluralism" of parties, newspapers, "countervailing powers," etc.

Today political power asserts itself through its power over the machine process and over the technical organization of the apparatus. The government of advanced and advancing industrial societies can maintain and secure itself only when it succeeds in mobilizing, organizing, and exploiting the technical, scientific, and mechanical productivity available to industrial civilization. And this productivity mobilizes society as a whole, above and beyond any particular individual or group interests. The brute fact that the machine's physical (only physical?) power surpasses that of the individual, and of any particular group of individuals, makes the machine the most effective political instrument in any society whose basic organization is that of the machine process. But the political trend may be reversed; essentially the power of the machine is only the stored-up and projected power of man. To the extent to which the work world is conceived of as a machine and mechanized accordingly, it becomes the *potential* basis of a new freedom for man.

Contemporary industrial civilization demonstrates that it has reached the stage at which "the free society" can no longer be adequately defined in the traditional terms of economic, political, and intellectual liberties, not because these liberties have become insignificant, but because they are too significant to be confined within the traditional forms. New modes of realization are needed, corresponding to the new capabilities of society.

Such new modes can be indicated only in negative terms because they would amount to the negation of the prevailing modes. Thus economic freedom would mean freedom *from* the economy—from being controlled by economic forces and relationships; freedom from the daily struggle for existence, from earning a living. Political freedom would mean liberation of the individuals *from* politics over which they have no effective control. Similarly, intellectual freedom would mean the restoration of individual thought now absorbed by mass communication and indoctrination, abolition of "public opinion" together with its makers. The unrealistic sound of these propositions is indicative, not of their utopian character, but of the strength of the forces which prevent their realization. The most effective and enduring form of warfare against liberation is the implanting of material and intellectual needs that perpetuate obsolete forms of the struggle for existence.

The intensity, the satisfaction and even the character of human needs, beyond the biological level, have always been preconditioned. Whether or not the possibility of doing or leaving, enjoying or destroying, possessing or rejecting something is seized as a *need* depends on whether or not it can be seen as desirable and necessary for the prevailing societal institutions and interests. In this sense, human needs are historical needs and, to the extent to which the society demands the repressive development of the individual, his needs themselves and their claim for satisfaction are subject to over-riding critical standards.

We may distinguish both true and false needs. "False" are those which are superimposed upon the individual by particular social interests in his repression: the needs which perpetuate toil, aggressiveness, misery, and injustice. Their satisfaction might be most gratifying to the individual, but this happiness is not a condition which has to be maintained and protected if it serves to arrest the development of the ability (his own and others) to recognize the disease of the whole and grasp the chances of curing the diseases. The result then is euphoria in unhappiness. Most of the prevailing needs to relax, to have fun, to behave and consume in accordance with the advertisements, to love and hate what others love and hate, belong to this category of false needs.

Such needs have a societal content and function which are determined by external powers over which the individual has no control; the development and satisfaction of these needs is heteronomous. No matter how much such needs may have become the individual's own, reproduced and fortified by the conditions of his existence; no matter how much he identifies himself with them and finds himself in their satisfaction, they continue to be what they were from the beginning —products of a society whose dominant interest demands repression.

The prevalence of repressive needs is an accomplished fact, accepted in ignorance and defeat, but a fact that must be undone in the interest of the happy individual as well as all those whose misery is the price of his satisfaction. The only needs that have an unqualified claim for satisfaction are the vital ones—nourishment, clothing, lodging at the attainable level of culture. The satisfaction of these needs is the prerequisite for the realization of *all* needs, of the unsublimated as well as the sublimated ones.

For any consciousness and conscience, for any experience which does not accept the prevailing societal interest as the supreme law of thought and behavior, the established universe of needs and satisfactions is a fact to be questioned—questioned in terms of truth and falsehood. These terms are historical throughout, and their objectivity is historical. The judgment of needs and their satisfaction, under the given conditions, involves standards of *priority*—standards which refer to the optimal development of the individual, of all individuals, under the optimal utilization of the material and intellectual resources available to man. The resources are calculable. "Truth" and "falsehood" of needs designate objective conditions to the extent to which the universal satisfaction of vital needs and, beyond it, the progressive alleviation of toil and poverty, are universally valid standards. But as historical standards, they do not only vary according to area and stage of development, they also can be defined only in (greater or lesser) *contradiction* to the prevailing ones. What tribunal can possibly claim the authority of decision?

In the last analysis, the question of what are true and false needs must be answered by the individuals themselves, but only in the last analysis; that is, if and when they are free to give their own answer. As long as they are kept incapable of being autonomous, as long as they are indoctrinated and manipulated (down to their very instincts), their answer to this question cannot be taken as their own. By the same token, however, no tribunal can justly arrogate to itself the right to decide which needs should be developed and satisfied. Any such tribunal is reprehensible, although our revulsion does not do away with the question: how can the people who have been the object of effective and productive domination by themselves create the conditions of freedom?

The more rational, productive, technical, and total the repressive administration of society becomes, the more unimaginable the means and ways by which the administered individuals might break their servitude and seize their own liberation. To be sure, to impose Reason upon an entire society is a paradoxical and scandalous idea—although one might dispute the righteousness of a society which ridicules this idea while making its own population into objects of total administration. All liberation depends on the consciousness of servitude, and the emergence of this consciousness is always hampered by the predominance of needs and satisfactions which, to a great extent, have become the individual's own. The process always replaces one system of preconditioning by another; the optimal goal is the replacement of false needs by true ones, the abandonment of repressive satisfaction.

The distinguishing feature of advanced industrial society is its effective suffocation of those needs which demand liberation—liberation also from that which is tolerable and rewarding and comfortable —while it sustains and absolves the destructive power and repressive function of the affluent society. Here, the social controls exact the overwhelming need for the production and consumption of waste; the need for stupefying work where it is no longer a real necessity; the need for modes of relaxation which soothe and prolong this stupefication; the need for maintaining such deceptive liberties as free competition at administered prices, a free press which censors itself, free choice between brands and gadgets.

Under the rule of a repressive whole, liberty can be made into a powerful instrument of domination. The range of choice open to the individual is not the decisive factor in determining the degree of human freedom, but *what* can be chosen and what *is* chosen by the individual. The criterion for free choice can never be an absolute one, but neither is it entirely relative. Free election of masters does not abolish the masters or the slaves. Free choice among a wide variety of goods and services does not signify freedom if these goods and services sustain social controls over a life of toil and fear—that is, if they sustain alienation. And the spontaneous reproduction of superimposed needs by the individual does not establish autonomy; it only testifies to the efficacy of the controls.

Our insistence on the depth and efficacy of these controls is open to the objection that we overrate greatly the indoctrinating power of the "media," and that by themselves the people would feel and satisfy the needs which are now imposed upon them. The objection misses the point. The preconditioning does not start with the mass production of radio and television and with the centralization of their control. The people enter this stage as preconditioned receptacles of long standing; the decisive difference is in the flattening out of the contrast (or conflict) between the given and the possible, between the satisfied and the unsatisfied needs. Here, the so-called equalization of class distinctions reveals its ideological function. If the worker and his boss enjoy the same television program and visit the same resort places, if the typist is as attractively made up as the daughter of her employer, if the Negro owns a Cadillac, if they all read the same newspaper, then this assimilation indicates not the disappearance of classes, but the extent to which the needs and satisfactions that serve the preservation of the Establishment are shared by the underlying population. Indeed, in the most highly developed areas of contemporary society, the transplantation of social into individual needs is so effective that the difference between them seems to be purely theoretical. Can one really distinguish between the mass media as instruments of information and entertainment, and as agents of manipulation and indoctrination? Between the automobile as nuisance and as convenience? Between the horrors and the comforts of functional architecture? Between the work for national defense and the work for corporate gain? Between the private pleasure and the commercial and political utility involved in increasing the birth rate?

We are again confronted with one of the most vexing aspects of advanced industrial civilization: the rational character of its irrationality. Its productivity and efficiency, its capacity to increase and spread comforts, to turn waste into need, and destruction into construction, the extent to which this civilization transforms the object world into an extension of man's mind and body makes the very notion of alienation questionable. The people recognize themselves in their commodities; they find their soul in their automobile, hi-fi set, split-level home, kitchen equipment. The very mechanism which ties the individual to his society has changed, and social control is anchored in the new needs which it has produced.

The prevailing forms of social control are technological in a new sense. To be sure, the technical structure and efficacy of the productive and destructive apparatus has been a major instrumentality for subjecting the population to the established social division of labor throughout the modern period. Moreover, such integration has always been accompanied by more obvious forms of compulsion: loss of livelihood, the administration of justice, the police, the armed forces. It still is. But in the contemporary period, the technological controls appear to be the very embodiment of Reason for the benefit of all social groups and interests—to such an extent that all contradiction seems irrational and all counteraction impossible.

No wonder then that, in the most advanced areas of this civilization, the social controls have been introjected to the point where even individual protest is affected at its roots. The intellectual and emotional refusal "to go along" appears neurotic and impotent.

This is the socio-psychological aspect of the political event that marks the contemporary period: the passing of the historical forces which, at the preceding stage of industrial society, seemed to represent the possibility of new forms of existence.

But the term "introjection" perhaps no longer describes the way in which the individual by himself reproduces and perpetuates the external controls exercised by his society. Introjection suggests a variety of relatively spontaneous processes by which a Self (Ego) transposes the "outer" into the "inner." This introjection implies the existence of an inner dimension distinguished from and even antagonistic to the external exigencies—an individual consciousness and an individual unconscious *apart from* public opinion and behavior.[1] The idea of "inner freedom" here has its reality: it designates the private space in which man may become and remain "himself."

Today this private space has been invaded and whittled down by technological reality. Mass production and mass distribution claim the *entire* individual, and industrial psychology has long since ceased to be confined to the factory. The manifold processes of introjection seem to be ossified in almost mechanical reactions. The result is, not adjustment but *mimesis:* an immediate identification of the individual with *his* society and, through it, with the society as a whole.

This immediate, automatic identification (which may have been characteristic of primitive forms of association) reappears in high industrial civilization; its new "immediacy," however, is the product of a sophisticated, scientific management and organization. In this process, the "inner" dimension of the mind in which opposition to the status quo can take root is whittled down. The loss of this dimension, in which the power of negative thinking—the critical power of Reason —is at home, is the ideological counterpart to the very material process in which advanced industrial society silences and reconciles the opposition. The impact of progress turns Reason into submission to the facts of life, and to the dynamic capability of producing more and bigger facts of the same sort of life. The efficiency of the system blunts the individual's recognition that it contains no facts which do not communicate the repressive power of the whole. If the individuals find themselves in the things which shape their life, they do so, not by

---

[1] The change in the function of the family here plays a decisive role: its "socializing" functions are increasingly taken over by outside groups and media. See my *Eros and Civilization* (Boston: Beacon Press, 1955), p. 96ff.

giving, but by accepting the law of things—not the law of physics but the law of their society. I have suggested that the concept of alienation seems to become questionable when the individuals identify themselves with the existence which is imposed upon them and have in it their own development and satisfaction. This identification is not illusion but reality. However, the reality constitutes a more progressive stage of alienation. The latter has become entirely objective; the subject which is alienated is swallowed up by its alienated existence. There is only one dimension, and it is everywhere and in all forms. The achievements of progress defy ideological indictment as well as justification; before their tribunal, the "false consciousness" of their rationality becomes the true consciousness.

This absorption of ideology into reality does not, however, signify the "end of ideology." On the contrary, in a specific sense advanced industrial culture is *more* ideological than its predecessor, inasmuch as today the ideology is in the process of production itself. In a provocative form, this proposition reveals the political aspects of the prevailing technological rationality. The productive apparatus and the goods and services which it produces "sell" or impose the social system as a whole. The means of mass transportation and communication, the commodities of lodging, food, and clothing, the irresistible output of the entertainment and information industry carry with them prescribed attitudes and habits, certain intellectual and emotional reactions which bind the consumers more or less pleasantly to the producers and, through the latter, to the whole. The products indoctrinate and manipulate; they promote a false consciousness which is immune against its falsehood. And as these beneficial products become available to more individuals in more social classes, the indoctrination they carry ceases to be publicity; it becomes a way of life. It is a good way of life—much better than before—and as a good way of life, it militates against qualitative change. Thus emerges a pattern of *one-dimensional thought and behavior* in which ideas, aspirations, and objectives that, by their content, transcend the established universe of discourse and action are either repelled or reduced to terms of this universe. They are redefined by the rationality of the given system and of its quantitative extension.

The trend may be related to a development in scientific method: operationalism in the physical, behaviorism in the social sciences. The common feature is a total empiricism in the treatment of concepts;

their meaning is restricted to the representation of particular operations and behavior. The operational point of view is well illustrated by
P. W. Bridgman's analysis of the concept of length.[2]

We evidently know what we mean by length if we can tell what the
length of any and every object is, and for the physicist nothing more is
required. To find the length of an object, we have to perform certain
physical operations. The concept of length is therefore fixed when the
operations by which length is measured are fixed: that is, the concept
of length involves as much and nothing more than the set of operations
by which length is determined. In general, we mean by any concept
nothing more than a set of operations; *the concept is synonymous with
the corresponding set of operations.*

Bridgman has seen the wide implications of this mode of thought for
the society at large:[3]

To adopt the operational point of view involves much more than a
mere restriction of the sense in which we understand 'concept,' but
means a far-reaching change in all our habits of thought, in that we shall
no longer permit ourselves to use as tools in our thinking concepts of
which we cannot give an adequate account in terms of operations.

Bridgman's prediction has come true. The new mode of thought is
today the predominant tendency in philosophy, psychology, sociology, and other fields. Many of the most seriously troublesome concepts are being "eliminated" by showing that no adequate account of
them in terms of operations or behavior can be given. The radical
empiricist onslaught thus provides the methodological justification for
the debunking of the mind by the intellectuals—a positivism which,
in its denial of the transcending elements of Reason, forms the academic counterpart of the socially required behavior.

Outside the academic establishment, the "far-reaching change in all
our habits of thought" is more serious. It serves to coordinate ideas
and goals with those exacted by the prevailing system, to enclose them
in the system, and to repel those which are irreconcilable with the
system. The reign of such a one-dimensional reality does not mean

[2] P. W. Bridgman, *The Logic of Modern Physics* (New York: Macmillan, 1928),
p. 5. The operational doctrine has since been refined and qualified. Bridgman
himself has extended the concept of "operation" to include the "paper-and-
pencil" operations of the theorist (in Philipp J. Frank, *The Validation of Scientific Theories* [Boston: Beacon Press, 1954], Chap. II). The main impetus remains
the same: it is "desirable" that the paper-and-pencil operations "be capable of
eventual contact, although perhaps indirectly, with instrumental operations."
[3] P. W. Bridgman, *The Logic of Modern Physics, loc. cit.,* p. 31.

that materialism rules, and that the spiritual, metaphysical, and bohemian occupations are petering out. On the contrary, there is a great deal of "Worship together this week," "Why not try God," Zen, existentialism, and beat ways of life, etc. But such modes of protest and transcendence are no longer contradictory to the status quo and no longer negative. They are rather the ceremonial part of practical behaviorism, its harmless negation, and are quickly digested by the status quo as part of its healthy diet.

One-dimensional thought is systematically promoted by the makers of politics and their purveyors of mass information. Their universe of discourse is populated by self-validating hypotheses which, incessantly and monopolistically repeated, become hypnotic definitions or dictations. For example, "free" are the institutions which operate (and are operated on) in the countries of the Free World; other transcending modes of freedom are by definition either anarchism, communism, or propaganda. "Socialistic" are all encroachments on private enterprises not undertaken by private enterprise itself (or by government contracts), such as universal and comprehensive health insurance, or the protection of nature from all too sweeping commercialization, or the establishment of public services which may hurt private profit. This totalitarian logic of accomplished facts has its Eastern counterpart. There, freedom is the way of life instituted by a communist regime, and all other transcending modes of freedom are either capitalistic, or revisionist, or leftist sectarianism. In both camps, non-operational ideas are non-behavioral and subversive. The movement of thought is stopped at barriers which appear as the limits of Reason itself.

Such limitation of thought is certainly not new. Ascending modern rationalism, in its speculative as well as empirical form, shows a striking contrast between extreme critical radicalism in scientific and philosophic method on the one hand, and an uncritical quietism in the attitude toward established and functioning social institutions. Thus Descartes' *ego cogitans* was to leave the "great public bodies" untouched, and Hobbes held that "the present ought always to be preferred, maintained, and accounted best." Kant agreed with Locke in justifying revolution *if and when* it has succeeded in organizing the whole and in preventing subversion.

However, these accommodating concepts of Reason were always contradicted by the evident misery and injustice of the "great public bodies" and the effective, more or less conscious rebellion against them. Societal conditions existed which provoked and permitted real dissociation from the established state of affairs; a private as well as political dimension was present in which dissociation could develop into effective opposition, testing its strength and the validity of its objectives.

With the gradual closing of this dimension by the society, the self-limitation of thought assumes a large significance. The interrelation between scientific-philosophical and societal processes, between theoretical and practical Reason, asserts itself "behind the back" of the scientists and philosophers. The society bars a whole type of oppositional operations and behavior; consequently, the concepts pertaining to them are rendered illusory or meaningless. Historical transcendence appears as metaphysical transcendence, not acceptable to science and scientific thought. The operational and behavioral point of view, practiced as a "habit of thought" at large, becomes the view of the established universe of discourse and action, needs and aspirations. The "cunning of Reason" works, as it so often did, in the interest of the powers that be. The insistence on operational and behavioral concepts turns against the efforts to free thought and behavior *from* the given reality and *for* the suppressed alternatives. Theoretical and practical Reason, academic and social behaviorism meet on common ground: that of an advanced society which makes scientific and technical progress into an instrument of domination.

"Progress" is not a neutral term; it moves toward specific ends, and these ends are defined by the possibilities of ameliorating the human condition. Advanced industrial society is approaching the stage where continued progress would demand the radical subversion of the prevailing direction and organization of progress. This stage would be reached when material production (including the necessary services) becomes automated to the extent that all vital needs can be satisfied while necessary labor time is reduced to marginal time. From this point on, technical progress would transcend the realm of necessity, where it served as the instrument of domination and exploitation which thereby limited its rationality; technology would become subject to the free play of faculties in the struggle for the pacification of nature and of society.

Such a state is envisioned in Marx's notion of the "abolition of labor." The term "pacification of existence" seems better suited to designate the historical alternative of a world which—through an international conflict which transforms and suspends the contradictions within the established societies—advances on the brink of a global war. "Pacification of existence" means the development of man's struggle with man and with nature, under conditions where the competing needs, desires, and aspirations are no longer organized by vested interests in domination and scarcity—an organization which perpetuates the destructive forms of this struggle.

Today's fight against this historical alternative finds a firm mass basis in the underlying population, and finds its ideology in the rigid orientation of thought and behavior to the given universe of facts. Validated by the accomplishments of science and technology, justified by its growing productivity, the status quo defies all transcendence. Faced with the possibility of pacification on the grounds of its technical and intellectual achievements, the mature industrial society closes itself against this alternative. Operationalism, in theory and practice, becomes the theory and practice of *containment*. Underneath its obvious dynamics, this society is a thoroughly static system of life: self-propelling in its oppressive productivity and in its beneficial coordination. Containment of technical progress goes hand in hand with its growth in the established direction. In spite of the political fetters imposed by the status quo, the more technology appears capable of creating the conditions for pacification, the more are the minds and bodies of man organized against this alternative.

The most advanced areas of industrial society exhibit throughout these two features: a trend toward consummation of technological rationality, and intensive efforts to contain this trend within the established institutions. Here is the internal contradiction of this civilization: the irrational element in its rationality. It is the token of its achievements. The industrial society which makes technology and science its own is organized for the ever-more-effective domination of man and nature, for the ever-more-effective utilization of its resources. It becomes irrational when the success of these efforts opens new dimensions of human realization. Organization for peace is different from organization for war; the institutions which served the struggle for existence cannot serve the pacification of existence. Life as an end is qualitatively different from life as a means.

Such a qualitatively new mode of existence can never be envisaged as the mere by-product of economic and political changes, as the more or less spontaneous effect of the new institutions which constitute the necessary prerequisite. Qualitative change also involves a change in the *technical* basis on which this society rests— one which sustains the economic and political institutions through which the "second nature" of man as an aggressive object of administration is stabilized. The techniques of industrialization are political techniques; as such, they prejudge the possibilities of Reason and Freedom.

To be sure, labor must precede the reduction of labor, and industrialization must precede the development of human needs and satisfactions. But as all freedom depends on the conquest of alien necessity, the realization of freedom depends on the *techniques* of this conquest. The highest productivity of labor can be used for the perpetuation of labor, and the most efficient industrialization can serve the restriction and manipulation of needs.

When this point is reached, domination—in the guise of affluence and liberty—extends to all spheres of private and public existence, integrates all authentic opposition, absorbs all alternatives. Technological rationality reveals its political character as it becomes the great vehicle of better domination, creating a truly totalitarian universe in which society and nature, mind and body are kept in a state of permanent mobilization for the defense of this universe.

THE NEW AMERICAN MILITARISM

General David M. Shoup

America has become a militaristic and aggressive nation. Our massive and swift invasion of the Dominican Republic in 1965, concurrent with the rapid buildup of U.S. military power in Vietnam, constituted an impressive demonstration of America's readiness to execute military contingency plans and to seek military solutions to problems of political disorder and potential Communist threats in the areas of our interest.

This "military task force" type of diplomacy is in the tradition of our more primitive pre-World War II "gunboat diplomacy," in which we landed small forces of Marines to protect American lives and property from the perils of native bandits and revolutionaries. In those days the U.S. Navy and its Marine landing forces were our chief means, short of war, for showing the flag, exercising American power, and protecting U.S. interests abroad. The Navy, enjoying the freedom

General David M. Shoup, "The New American Militarism," *The Atlantic Monthly,* April 1969. Copyright © 1969 by The Atlantic Monthly Company, Boston, Mass. Reprinted by permission of the publisher. The opinions contained herein are the private ones of the author and are not to be construed as official or reflecting the views of the Navy Department or the naval service at large.

of the seas, was a visible and effective representative of the nation's sovereign power. The Marines could be employed ashore "on such other duties as the President might direct" without congressional approval or a declaration of war. The U.S. Army was not then used so freely because it was rarely ready for expeditionary service without some degree of mobilization, and its use overseas normally required a declaration of emergency or war. Now, however, we have numerous contingency plans involving large joint Air Force-Army-Navy-Marine task forces to defend U.S. interests and to safeguard our allies wherever and whenever we suspect Communist aggression. We maintain more than 1,517,000 Americans in uniform overseas in 119 countries. We have 8 treaties to help defend 48 nations if they ask us to or if we choose to intervene in their affairs. We have an immense and expensive military establishment, fueled by a gigantic defense industry, and millions of proud, patriotic, and frequently bellicose and militaristic citizens. How did this militarist culture evolve? How did this militarism steer us into the tragic military and political morass of Vietnam?

Prior to World War II, American attitudes were typically isolationist, pacifist, and generally anti-military. The regular peacetime military establishment enjoyed small prestige and limited influence upon national affairs. The public knew little about the armed forces, and only a few thousand men were attracted to military service and careers. In 1940 there were but 428,000 officers and enlisted men in the Army and Navy. The scale of the war, and the world's power relationships which resulted, created the American military giant. Today the active armed forces contain over 3.4 million men and women, with an additional 1.6 million ready reserves and National Guardsmen.

America's vastly expanded world role after World War II hinged upon military power. The voice and views of the professional military people became increasingly prominent. During the post-war period, distinguished military leaders from the war years filled many top positions in government. Generals Marshall, Eisenhower, MacArthur, Taylor, Ridgeway, LeMay, and others were not only popular heroes but respected opinion-makers. It was a time of international readjustment; military minds offered the benefits of firm views and problem-solving experience to the management of the nation's affairs. Military procedures—including the general staff system, briefings, estimates of the situation, and the organizational and operational techniques of the highly schooled, confident military professionals—spread throughout American culture.

World War II had been a long war. Millions of young American men had matured, been educated, and gained rank and stature during their years in uniform. In spite of themselves, many returned to civilian life as indoctrinated, combat-experienced military professionals. They were veterans, and for better or worse would never be the same again. America will never be the same either. We are now a nation of veterans. To the 14.9 million veterans of World War II, Korea added another 5.7 million five years later, and ever since, the large peacetime military establishment has been training and releasing draftees, enlistees, and short-term reservists by the hundreds of thousands each year. In 1968 the total living veterans of U.S. military service numbered over 23 million, or about 20 per cent of the adult population.

Today most middle-aged men, most business, government, civic, and professional leaders, have served some time in uniform. Whether they liked it or not, their military training and experience have affected them, for the creeds and attitudes of the armed forces are powerful medicine, and can become habit-forming. The military codes include all the virtues and beliefs used to motivate men of high principle: patriotism, duty and service to country, honor among fellowmen, courage in the face of danger, loyalty to organization and leaders, self-sacrifice for comrades, leadership, discipline, and physical fitness. For many veterans the military's efforts to train and indoctrinate them may well be the most impressive and influential experience they have ever had especially so for the young and less educated.

In addition, each of the armed forces has its own special doctrinal beliefs and well-catalogued customs, traditions, rituals, and folklore upon which it strives to build a fiercely loyal military character and esprit de corps. All ranks are taught that their unit and their branch of the military service are the most elite, important, efficient, or effective in the military establishment. By believing in the superiority and importance of their own service they also provide themselves a degree of personal status, pride, and self-confidence.

As they get older, many veterans seem to romanticize and exaggerate their own military experience and loyalties. The policies, attitudes, and positions of the powerful veterans' organizations such as the American Legion, Veterans of Foreign Wars, and AMVETS, totaling over 4 million men, frequently reflect this pugnacious and chauvinistic tendency. Their memberships generally favor military solutions to world problems in the pattern of their own earlier experience, and often assert that their military service and sacrifice should be repeated by the younger generations.

Closely related to the attitudes and influence of America's millions of veterans is the vast and powerful complex of the defense industries, which have been described in detail many times in the eight years since General Eisenhower first warned of the military-industrial power complex in his farewell address as President. The relationship between the defense industry and the military establishment is closer than many citizens realize. Together they form a powerful public opinion lobby. The several military service associations provide both a forum and a meeting ground for the military and its industries. The associations also provide each of the armed services with a means of fostering their respective roles, objectives, and propaganda.

Each of the four services has its own association and there are also additional military function associations, for ordnance, management, defense industry, and defense transportation, to name some of the more prominent. The Air Force Association and the Association of the U.S. Army are the largest, best organized, and most effective of the service associations. The Navy League, typical of the "silent service" traditions, is not as well coordinated in its public relations efforts, and the small Marine Corps Association is not even in the same arena with the other contenders, the Marine Association's main activity being the publication of a semi-official magazine. Actually, the service associations' respective magazines, with an estimated combined circulation of over 270,000, are the primary medium serving the several associations' purposes.

Air Force and Space Digest, to cite one example, is the magazine of the Air Force Association and the unofficial mouthpiece of the U.S. Air Force doctrine, "party line," and propaganda. It frequently promotes Air Force policy that has been officially frustrated or suppressed within the Department of Defense. It beats the tub for strength through aerospace power, interprets diplomatic, strategic, and tactical problems in terms of air power, stresses the requirements for quantities of every type of aircraft, and frequently perpetuates the extravagant fictions about the effectiveness of bombing. This, of course, is well coordinated with and supported by the multibillion-dollar aerospace industry, which thrives upon the boundless desires of the Air Force. They reciprocate with lavish and expensive ads in every issue of *Air Force.* Over 96,000 members of the Air Force Association receive the magazine. Members include active, reserve, retired personnel, and veterans of the U.S. Air Force. Additional thousands of copies go to people engaged in the defense industry. The thick mixture of advertising, propaganda, and Air Force doctrine continuously repeated in this publication provides its readers and writers with a form of intellectual hypnosis, and they are prone to believe their own propaganda because they read it in *Air Force*.

The American people have also become more and more accustomed to militarism, to uniforms, to the cult of the gun, and to the violence of combat. Whole generations have been brought up on war news and wartime propaganda; the few years of peace since 1939 have seen a steady stream of war novels, war movies, comic strips, and television programs with war or military settings. To many Americans, military training, expeditionary service, and warfare are merely extensions of the entertainment and games of childhood. Even the weaponry and hardware they use at war are similar to the highly realistic toys of their youth. Soldiering loses appeal for some of the relatively few who experience the blood, terror, and filth of battle; for many, however, including far too many senior professional officers, war and combat are an exciting adventure, a competitive game, and an escape from the dull routines of peacetime.

It is this influential nucleus of aggressive, ambitious professional military leaders who are the root of America's evolving militarism. There are over 410,000 commissioned officers on active duty in the four armed services. Of these, well over half are junior ranking reserve officers on temporary active duty. Of the 150,000 or so regular career officers only a portion are senior ranking colonels, generals, and admirals, but it is they who constitute the elite core of the military establishment. It is these few thousand top-ranking professionals who command and manage the armed forces and plan and formulate military policy and opinion. How is it, then, that in spite of civilian controls and the national desire for peace, this small group of men exert so much martial influence upon the government and life of the American people?

The military will disclaim any excess of power or influence on their part. They will point to their small numbers, low pay, and subordination to civilian masters as proof of their modest status and innocence. Nevertheless, the professional military, as a group, is probably one of the best organized and most influential of the various segments of the American scene. Three wars and six major contingencies since 1940 have forced the American people to become abnormally aware of the armed forces and their leaders. In turn the military services have produced an unending supply of distinguished, capable, articulate, and effective leaders. The sheer skill, energy, and dedication of America's military officers make them dominant in almost every government or civic organization they may inhabit, from the federal Cabinet to the local PTA.

The hard core of high-ranking professionals are, first of all, mostly service academy graduates: they had to be physically and intellectually above average among their peers just to gain entrance to an academy. Thereafter for the rest of their careers they are exposed to constant competition for selection and promotion. Attrition is high, and only the most capable survive to reach the elite senior ranks. Few other professions have such rigorous selection systems: as a result, the top military leaders are top-caliber men.

Not many industries, institutions, or civilian branches of government have the resources, techniques, or experience in training leaders such as are now employed by the armed forces in their excellent and elaborate school systems. Military leaders are taught to command large organizations and to plan big operations. They learn the techniques of influencing others. Their education is not, however, liberal or cultural. It stresses the tactics, doctrines, traditions, and codes of the military trade. It produces technicians and disciples, not philosophers.

The men who rise to the top of the military hierarchy have usually demonstrated their effectiveness as leaders, planners, and organization managers. They have perhaps performed heroically in combat, but most of all they have demonstrated their loyalty as proponents of their own service's doctrine and their dedication to the defense establishment. The paramount sense of duty to follow orders is at the root of the military professional's performance. As a result the military often operate more efficiently and effectively in the arena of defense policy planning than do their civilian counterparts in the State Department. The military planners have their doctrinal beliefs, their loyalties, their discipline—and their typical desire to compete and win. The civilians in government can scarcely play the same policy-planning game. In general the military are better organized, they work harder, they think straighter, and they keep their eyes on the objective, which is to be instantly ready to solve the problem through military action while ensuring that their respective service gets its proper mission, role, and recognition in the operation. In an emergency the military usually have a ready plan; if not, their numerous doctrinal manuals provide firm guidelines for action. Politicians, civilian appointees, and diplomats do not normally have the same confidence about how to react to threats and violence as do the military.

The motivations behind these endeavors are difficult for civilians to understand. For example, military professionals cannot measure the success of their individual efforts in terms of personal financial gain. The armed forces are not profit-making organizations, and the rewards for excellence in the military profession are acquired in less tangible forms. Thus it is that promotion and the responsibilities of higher command, with the related fringe benefits of quarters, servants, privileges, and prestige, motivate most career officers. Promotions and choice job opportunities are attained by constantly performing well, conforming to the expected patterns, and pleasing the senior officers. Promotions and awards also frequently result from heroic and distinguished performance in combat, and it takes a war to become a military hero. Civilians can scarcely understand or even believe that many ambitious military professionals truly yearn for wars and the opportunities for glory and distinction afforded only in combat. A career of peacetime duty is a dull and frustrating prospect for the normal regular officer to contemplate.

The professional military leaders of the U.S. Armed Forces have some additional motivations which influence their readiness to involve their country in military ventures. Unlike some of the civilian policymakers, the military has not been obsessed with the threat of Communism per se. Most military people know very little about Communism either as a doctrine or as a form of government. But they have been given reason enough to presume that it is bad and represents the force of evil. When they can identify "Communist aggression," however, the matter then becomes of direct concern to the armed forces. Aggressors are the enemy in the war games, the "bad guys," the "Reds." Defeating aggression is a gigantic combat-area competition rather than a crusade to save the world from Communism. In the military view, all "Communist aggression" is certain to be interpreted as a threat to the United States.

The armed forces' role in performing its part of the national security policy in addition to defense against actual direct attack on the United States and to maintaining the strategic atomic deterrent forces—is to be prepared to employ its *General Purpose Forces* in support of our collective security policy and the related treaties and alliances. To do this it deploys certain forces to forward zones in the Unified Commands, and maintains an up-to-date file of scores of detailed contingency plans which have been thrashed out and approved by the Joint Chiefs of Staff. Important features of these are the movement or deployment schedules of task forces assigned to each plan. The various details of these plans continue to create intense rivalries between the Navy-Marine sea-lift forces and the Army-Air Force team of air mobility proponents. At the senior command levels parochial pride in service, personal ambitions, and old Army-Navy game rivalry stemming back to academy loyalties can influence strategic planning far more than most civilians would care to believe. The game is to be ready for deployment sooner than the other elements of the joint task force and to be so disposed as to be the "first to fight." The danger presented by this practice is that readiness and deployment speed become ends in themselves. This was clearly revealed in the massive and rapid intervention in the Dominican Republic in 1965 when the contingency plans and interservice rivalry appeared to supersede diplomacy. Before the world realized what was happening, the momentum and velocity of the military plans propelled almost 20,000 U.S. soldiers and Marines into the small turbulent republic in an impressive race to test the respective mobility of the Army and the Marines, and to attain overall command of "U.S. Forces Dom. Rep." Only a fraction of the force deployed was needed or justified. A small 1935 model Marine landing force could probably have handled the situation. But the Army airlifted much of the 82nd Airborne Division to the scene, included a lieutenant general, and took charge of the operation.

Simultaneously, in Vietnam during 1965, the four services were racing to build up combat strength in that hapless country. This effort was ostensibly to save South Vietnam from Viet Cong and North Vietnamese aggression. It should also be noted that it was motivated in part by the same old interservice rivalry to demonstrate respective importance and combat effectiveness.

The punitive air strikes immediately following the Tonkin Gulf incident in late 1964 revealed the readiness of naval air forces to bomb North Vietnam. (It now appears that the Navy actually had attack plans ready even before the alleged incident took place!) So by early 1965 the Navy carrier people and the Air Force initiated a contest of comparative strikes, sorties, tonnages dropped, "Killed by Air" claims, and target grabbing which continued up to the 1968 bombing pause. Much of the reporting on air action has consisted of misleading data or propaganda to serve Air Force and Navy purposes. In fact, it became increasingly apparent that the U.S. bombing effort in both North and South Vietnam has been one of the most wasteful and expensive hoaxes ever to be put over on the American people. Tactical and close air support of ground operations is essential, but air power use in general has to a large degree been a contest for the operations planners, "fine experience" for young pilots, and opportunity for career officers.

The highly trained professional and aggressive career officers of the Army and Marine Corps played a similar game. Prior to the decision to send combat units to South Vietnam in early 1965, both services were striving to increase their involvement. The Army already had over 16,000 military aid personnel serving in South Vietnam in the military adviser role, in training missions, logistic services, supporting helicopter companies, and in Special Forces teams. This investment of men and matériel justified a requirement for additional U.S. combat units to provide local security and to help protect our growing commitment of aid to the South Vietnam regime.

There were also top-ranking Army officers who wanted to project Army ground combat units into the Vietnam struggle for a variety of other reasons: to test plans and new equipment, to test the new airmobile theories and tactics, to try the tactics and techniques of counterinsurgency, and to gain combat experience for young officers and noncommissioned officers. It also appeared to be a case of the military's duty to stop "Communist aggression" in Vietnam

The Marines had somewhat similar motivations, the least of which was any real concern about the political or social problems of the Vietnamese people. In early 1965, there was a shooting war going on and the Marines were being left out of it, contrary to all their traditions. The Army's military advisory people were hogging American participation except for a Marine Corps transport helicopter squadron at Danang which was helping the Army of the Republic of Vietnam. For several years young Marine officers had been going to South Vietnam from the 3rd Marine Division on Okinawa for short tours of "on-the-job training" with the small South Vietnam Marine Corps. There was a growing concern, however, among some senior Marines that the Corps should get involved on a larger scale and be the "first to fight" in keeping with the Corps's traditions. This would help justify the Corps's continued existence, which many Marines seem to consider to be in constant jeopardy.

The Corps had also spent several years exploring the theories of counterinsurgency and as early as 1961 had developed an elaborate lecture demonstration called OPERATION CORMORANT, for school and Marine Corps promotion purposes, which depicted the Marines conducting a large scale amphibious operation on the coast of Vietnam and thereby helping resolve a hypothetical aggressor-insurgency problem. As always it was important to Marine planners and doctrinaires to apply an amphibious operation to the Vietnam situation and provide justification for this special Marine functional responsibility. So Marine planners were seeking an acceptable excuse to thrust a landing force over the beaches of Vietnam when the Viet Cong attacked the U.S. Army Special Forces camp at Pleiku in February, 1965. It was considered unacceptable aggression, and the President was thereby prompted to put U.S. ground combat units into the war. Elements of the 3rd Marine Division at Okinawa were already aboard ship and eager to go, for the Marines also intended to get to Vietnam before their neighbor on Okinawa, the Army's 173rd Airborne Brigade, arrived. (Actually the initial Marine unit to deploy was an airlifted antiaircraft missile battalion which arrived to protect the Danang air base.) With these initial deployments the Army-Marine race to build forces in Vietnam began in earnest and did not slow down until both became overextended, overcommitted, and depleted at home.

For years up to 1964 the chiefs of the armed services, of whom the author was then one, deemed it unnecessary and unwise for U.S. forces to become involved in any ground war in Southeast Asia. In 1964 there were changes in the composition of the Joint Chiefs of Staff, and in a matter of a few months the Johnson Administration, encouraged by the aggressive military, hastened into what has become the quagmire of Vietnam. The intention at the time was that the war effort be kept small and "limited." But as the momentum and involvement built up, the military leaders rationalized a case that this was not a limited objective exercise, but was a proper war in defense of the United States against "Communist aggression" and in honor of our area commitments.

The battle successes and heroic exploits of America's fine young fighting men have added to the military's traditions which extol service, bravery, and sacrifice, and so it has somehow become unpatriotic to question our military strategy and tactics or the motives of military leaders. Actually, however, the military commanders have directed the war in Vietnam, they have managed the details of its conduct; and more than most civilian officials and top military planning were initially ready to become involved in Vietnam combat and have the opportunity to practice their trade. It has been popular to blame the civilian administration for the conduct and failures of the war rather than to question the motives of the military. But some of the generals and admirals are by no means without responsibility for the Vietnam miscalculations.

Some of the credibility difficulties experienced by the Johnson
Administration over its war situation reports and Vietnam policy can
also be blamed in part upon the military advisers. By its very nature
most military activity falls under various degrees of security classification. Much that the military plans or does must be kept from the
enemy. Thus the military is indoctrinated to be secretive, devious, and
misleading in its plans and operations. It does not, however, always
confine its security restrictions to purely military operations. Each of
the services and all of the major commands practice techniques of
controlling the news and the release of self-serving propaganda: in
"the interests of national defense," to make the service look good, to
cover up mistakes, to build up and publicize a distinguished military
personality, or to win a round in the continuous gamesmanship of the
interservice contest. If the Johnson Administration suffered from lack
of credibility in its reporting of the war, the truth would reveal that
much of the hocus-pocus stemmed from schemers in the military
services, both at home and abroad.

Our militaristic culture was born of the necessities of World War
II, nurtured by the Korean War, and became an accepted aspect of
American life during the years of cold war emergencies and real or
imagined threats from the Communist bloc. Both the philosophy and
the institutions of militarism grew during these years because of the
momentum of their own dynamism, the vigor of their ideas, their large
size and scope, and because of the dedicated concentration of the
emergent military leaders upon their doctrinal objectives. The dynamism of the defense establishment and its culture is also inspired and
stimulated by vast amounts of money, by the new creations of military
research and matériel development, and by the concepts of the Defense Department supported "think factories." These latter are ex-
travagantly funded civilian organizations of scientists, analysts, and
retired military strategists who feed new militaristic philosophies into
the Defense Department to help broaden to create fresh policies and
new requirements for ever larger, more expensive defense forces.

Somewhat like a religion, the basic appeals of anti-Communism,
national defense, and patriotism provide the foundation for a powerful
creed upon which the defense establishment can build, grow, and
justify its cost. More so than many large bureaucratic organizations,
the defense establishment now devotes a large share of its efforts to
self-perpetuation, to justifying its organization, to preaching its doctrines, and to self-maintenance and management. Warfare becomes an

extension of war games and field tests. War justifies the existence of the establishment, provides experience for the military novice and challenges for the senior officer. Wars and emergencies put the military and their leaders on the front pages and give status and prestige to the professionals. Wars add to the military traditions, the self-nourishment of heroic deeds, and provide a new crop of military leaders who become the rededicated disciples of the code of service and military action. Being recognized public figures in a nation always seeking folk heroes, the military leaders have been largely exempt from the criticism experienced by the more plebeian politician. Flag officers are considered "experts," and their views are often accepted by press and Congress as the gospel. In turn, the distinguished military leader feels obliged not only to perpetuate loyally the doctrine of his service but to comply with the stereotyped military characteristics by being tough, aggressive, and firm in his resistance to Communist aggression and his belief in the military solutions to world problems. Standing closely behind these leaders, encouraging and prompting them, are the rich and powerful defense industries. Standing in front, adorned with service caps, ribbons, and lapel emblems, is a nation of veterans—patriotic, belligerent, romantic, and well intentioned, finding a certain sublimation and excitement in their country's latest military venture. Militarism in America is in full bloom and promises a future of vigorous self-pollination unless the blight of Vietnam reveals that militarism is more a poisonous weed than a glorious blossom.

WHY ARE WE IN VIETNAM?

Norman Mailer

He knew the arguments for the war, and against the war—finally they bored him. The arguments in support of the war were founded on basic assumptions which had not been examined and were endlessly repeated—the arguments to withdraw never pursued the consequences.

He thought we were in the war as the culmination to a long sequence of events which had begun in some unrecorded fashion toward the end of World War II. A consensus of the most powerful middle-aged and elderly Wasps in America—statesmen, corporation executives, generals, admirals, newspaper editors, and legislators had pledged an intellectual troth: they had sworn with a faith worthy of medieval knights that Communism was the deadly foe of Christian culture. If it were not resisted in the postwar world, Christianity itself would perish. So had begun a Cold War with intervals of overt war, mixed with periods of modest collaboration. As Communist China grew in strength, and her antagonisms with the Soviet Union quickened their pace, the old troth of the Wasp knights had grown sophisticated and abstract. It was now a part of the technology of foreign affairs, a thesis to be called upon when needed. The latest focus of this thesis was of course to be found in Vietnam. The arguments presented by the parties of war suggested that if Vietnam fell to the Communists, soon then would Southeast Asia, Indonesia, the Philippines, Australia, Japan, and India fall also to the Chinese Communists. Since these Chinese Communists were in the act of developing a nuclear striking force, America would face eventually a united Asia (and Africa?) ready to engage America (and Russia?) in a suicidal atomic war which might level the earth, a condition to the advantage of the Chinese Communists, since their low level of subsistence would make it easier for them to recover from the near to unendurable privations of the post-atomic world.

Like most simple political theses, this fear of a total nuclear war was not uttered aloud by American statesmen, for the intimations of such a thesis are invariably more powerful than the thesis itself. It was sufficient that a paralysis of thought occurred in the average American at the covert question: should we therefore bomb the nuclear installations of the Chinese now? Obviously, public discussion preferred to move over to the intricate complexities of Vietnam. Of course, that was an ugly unattractive sometimes disgraceful war, murmured the superior apologists for the Hawks, perhaps the unhappiest war America had ever fought, but it was one of the most necessary, for (1) it demonstrated to China that she could not advance her guerrilla activities into Asia without paying a severe price; (2) it rallied the small Asian powers to confidence in America; (3) it underlined the depth of our promise to defend small nations; (4) it was an inexpensive means of containing a great power, far more inexpensive than fighting the power itself; and (5) it was probably superior to starting a nuclear war on China.

In answer, the debaters best armed for the Doves would reply that it was certainly an ugly disgraceful unattractive war but not necessary to our defense. If South Vietnam fell to the Vietcong, Communism would be then not 12,000 miles from our shores, but 11,000 miles. Moreover, we had not necessarily succeeded in demonstrating to China that guerrilla wars exacted too severe a price from the Communists. On the contrary, a few more guerrilla wars could certainly bankrupt America, since we now had 500,000 troops in South Vietnam to the 50,000 of the North Vietnamese, and our costs for this one small war had mounted to a figure between $25,000,000,000 and $30,000,000,000 a year, not so small an amount if one is reminded that the Second World War cost a total of $300,000,000,000 over four years, or less than three times as much on an average year as Vietnam! (Of course, there has been inflation since, but still! What incredible expense for so small a war—what scandals of procurement yet to be uncovered. How many more such inexpensive wars could the economy take?)

The Doves picked at the seed of each argument. Yes, they said, by fulfilling our commitments to South Vietnam, we have certainly inspired confidence in the other small Asian powers. But who has this confidence? Why the most reactionary profiteers of the small Asian nations now have the confidence; so the small Asian nations are polarized, for the best of their patriots, foreseeing a future plunder of Asia by Asian Capitalists under America's protection, are forced over to the Communists.

Yes, the Doves would answer, it is better to have a war in Vietnam than to bomb China, but then the war in Vietnam may serve as the only possible pretext to attack China. Besides the question of Chinese aggression has been begged. China is not, by its record, an aggressive nation, but a timid one, and suffers from internal contradictions which will leave her incapable for years of even conceiving of a major war.

This was not the least of the arguments of the Doves; they could go on to point out that North Vietnam had been occupied for centuries by China, and therefore was as hostile to China as Ireland was to England—our intervention had succeeded therefore in bringing North Vietnam and China closer together. This must eventually weaken the resistance of other small Asian powers to China.

Besides, said the Doves, part of the real damage of Vietnam takes place in America where civil rights have deteriorated into city riots, and an extraordinary number of the best and most talented students in America are exploring the frontiers of nihilism and drugs.

The Doves seemed to have arguments more powerful than the
Hawks. So the majority of people in America, while formidably patriotic were also undecided and tended to shift in their opinion like the
weather. Yet the Hawks seemed never too concerned. They held
every power securely but one, a dependable consensus of public opinion. Still this weakness left them unperturbed—their most powerful
argument remained inviolate. There, the Doves never approached.
The most powerful argument remained: what if we leave Vietnam, and
all Asia eventually goes Communist? all of SoutheastAsia, Indonesia,
the Philippines, Australia, Japan, and India?

Well, one could laugh at the thought of Australia going Communist.
The Hawks were nothing if not humorless. If Communist China had
not been able to build a navy to cross the Straits of Formosa and
capture Taiwan, one did not see them invading Australia in the next
century. No, any decent Asian Communist would probably shudder
at the thought of engaging the Anzacs, descendants of the men who
fought at Gallipoli. Yes, the Hawks were humorless, and Lyndon
Johnson was shameless. He even invoked the defense of Australia.

But could the Dove give bona fides that our withdrawal from Vietnam would produce no wave of Communism through Asia? Well, the
Dove was resourceful in answers, and gave many. The Dove talked of
the specific character of each nation, and the liberal alternatives of
supporting the most advanced liberal elements in these nations, the
Dove returned again and again to the profound weaknesses of China,
the extraordinary timidity of Chinese foreign policy since the Korean
war, spoke of the possibility of enclaves, and the resources of adroit,
well-managed economic war in Asia.

Yet the Doves, finally, had no answer to the Hawks. For the Doves
were divided. Some of them, a firm minority, secretly desired Asia to
go Communist, their sympathies were indeed with Asian peasants, not
American corporations, they wanted what was good for the peasant,
and in private they believed Communism was probably better suited
than Capitalism to introduce the technological society to the peasant.
But they did not consider it expedient to grant this point, so they
talked around it. The others, the majority of the Doves, simply refused
to face the possibility. They were liberals. To explore the dimensions
of the question, might have exploded the foundation of their liberalism, for they would have had to admit they were willing to advocate
policies which could conceivably end in major advances of Asian
Communism, and this admission might oblige them to move over to
the Hawks.

Mailer was bored with such arguments. The Hawks were smug and self-righteous, the Doves were evasive of the real question. Mailer was a Left Conservative. So he had his own point of view. To himself he would suggest that he tried to think in the style of Marx in order to attain certain values suggested by Edmund Burke. Since he was a conservative, he would begin at the root. He did not see all wars as bad. He could conceive of wars which might be noble. But the war in Vietnam was bad for America because it was a bad war, as all wars are bad if they consist of rich boys fighting poor boys when the rich boys have an advantage in the weapons. He recollected a statistic: it was droll if it was not obscene. Next to every pound of supplies the North Vietnamese brought into South Vietnam for their soldiers, the Americans brought in one thousand pounds. Yes, he would begin at the root. All wars were bad which undertook daily operations which burned and bombed large numbers of women and children; all wars were bad which relocated populations (for the root of a rich peasant lore was then destroyed) all wars were bad which had no line of battle or discernible climax (an advanced notion which supposes that wars may be in part good because they are sometimes the only way to define critical conditions rather than blur them) certainly all wars were bad which took some of the bravest young men of a nation and sent them into combat with outrageous superiority and outrageous arguments: such conditions of combat had to excite a secret passion for hunting other humans. Certainly any war was a bad war which required an inability to reason as the price of retaining one's patriotism; finally any war which offered no prospect of improving itself as a war—so complex and compromised were its roots—was a bad war. A good war, like anything else which is good, offers the possibility that further effort will produce a determinable effect upon chaos, evil, or waste. By every conservative measure (reserving to Conservatism the right to approve of wars) the war in Vietnam was an extraordinarily bad war.

Since he was also a *Left* Conservative, he believed that radical measures were sometimes necessary to save the root. The root in this case was the welfare of the nation, not the welfare of the war. So he had an answer to the Hawks. It was: pull out of Vietnam completely. Leave Asia to the Asians. What then would happen?

He did not know. Asia might go to the Communists, or it might not. He was certain no one alive knew the answer to so huge a question as that. It was only in the twentieth century, in the upper chambers of technology land (both Capitalist *and* Communist) that men began to believe there must be concrete answers to every large question. No!

So far as he had an opinion (before the vastness of this question) his opinion existed on the same order of magnitude of undiscovered ignorance as the Opinion of any Far Eastern expert. While he thought it was probable most of Asia would turn to Communism in the decade after any American withdrawal from that continent, he did not know that it really mattered. In those extraordinary World War II years when the Wasp admirals, generals, statesmen, legislators, editors, and corporation presidents had whispered to each other that the next war was going to be Christianity versus Communism, the one striking omission in their Herculean crusade was the injunction to read Marx. They had studied his ideas, of course; in single-spaced extracts on a typewritten page! but because they had not read his words, but merely mouthed the extracts, they had not had the experience of encountering a mind which taught one to reason, even to reason away from his own mind; so the old Wasps and the young Wasps in the power elite could not comprehend that Communists who read their Marx might come to reason away from the particular monoliths of Marxism which had struck the first spark of their faith. It seemed never to occur to the most powerful Wasps that one could count quite neatly on good Communists and bad Communists just as one would naturally expect good Christians and bad. In fact, just as Christianity seemed to create the most unexpected saints, artists, geniuses, and great warriors out of its profound contradictions, so Communism seemed to create great heretics and innovators and converts (Sartre and Picasso for two) out of the irreducible majesty of Marx's mind (perhaps the greatest single tool for cerebration Western man had ever produced). Or at least— and here was the kernel of Mailer's sleeping thesis—Communism would continue to produce heretics and great innovators just so long as it expanded. Whenever it ceased to expand, it would become monolithic again, mediocre, and malign. An ogre.

An explanation? A submersion of Asia in Communism was going to explode a shock into Marxism which might take a half century to digest. Between Poland and India, Prague and Bangkok, was a diversity of primitive lore which would jam every fine gear of the Marxist. There were no quick meals in Asia. Only indigestion. The real difficulty might be then to decide who would do more harm to Asia, Capitalism or Communism. In either case, the conquest would be technological, and so primitive Asian societies would be uprooted. Probably, the uprooting would be savage, the psychic carnage unspeakable. He did not like to contemplate the compensating damage to America if it chose to dominate a dozen Asian nations with its technologies and its armies while having to face their guerrilla wars. No, Asia was best left to the Asians. If the Communists absorbed those countries, and succeeded in building splendid nations who made the transition to technological culture without undue agony, one would be forced to applaud; it seemed evident on the face of the evidence in Vietnam, that America could not bring technology land to Asia without bankrupting itself in operations ill-conceived, poorly comprehended, and executed in waste. But the greater likelihood was that if the Communists prevailed in Asia they would suffer in much the same fashion. Divisions, schisms, and sects would appear. An endless number of collisions between primitive custom and Marxist dogma, a thousand daily pullulations of intrigue, a heritage of cruelty, atrocity, and betrayal would fall upon the Communists. It was not difficult to envision a time when one Communist nation in Asia might look for American aid against another Communist nation. Certainly Russia and China would be engaged in a cold war with each other for decades. Therefore, to leave Asia would be precisely to gain the balance of power. The answer then was to get out, to get out any way one could. Get out. There was nothing to fear—perhaps there never had been. For the more Communism expanded, the more monumental would become its problems, the more flaccid its preoccupations with world conquest. In the expansion of Communism, was its own containment. The only force which could ever defeat Communism, was Communism itself.

Yet there was no likelihood America would ever withdraw from Asia. Rather there was the covert and unhappy intimation that we were in Vietnam because we had to be. Such was the imbalance of the nation that war was its balance. The burning of villages by napalm might be the index of our collective instability.

Mailer had been going on for years about the diseases of America, its oncoming totalitarianism, its oppressiveness, its smog—he had written so much about the disease he had grown bored with his own voice, weary of his own petulance; the war in Vietnam offered therefore the grim pleasure of confirming his ideas. The disease he had written about existed now in open air: so he pushed further in his thoughts—the paradox of this obscene unjust war is that it provided him new energy—even as it provided new energy to the American soldiers who were fighting it.

He came at last to the saddest conclusion of them all for it went beyond the war in Vietnam. He had come to decide that the center of America might be insane. The country had been living with a controlled, even fiercely controlled, schizophrenia which had been deepening with the years. Perhaps the point had now been passed. Any man or woman who was devoutly Christian and worked for the American Corporation, had been caught in an unseen vise whose pressure could split their mind from their soul. For the center of Christianity was a mystery, a son of God, and the center of the corporation was a detestation of mystery, a worship of technology. Nothing was more intrinsically opposed to technology than the bleeding heart of Christ. The average American, striving to do his duty, drove further every day into working for Christ, and drove equally further each day in the opposite direction—into working for the absolute computer of the corporation. Yes and no, I and O. Every day the average American drove himself further into schizophrenia; the average American believed in two opposites more profoundly apart than any previous schism in the Christian soul. Christians had been able to keep some kind of sanity for centuries while countenancing love against honor, desire versus duty, even charity opposed in the same heart to the lust for power—that was difficult to balance but not impossible. The love of the Mystery of Christ, however, and the love of no Mystery whatsoever, had brought the country to a state of suppressed schizophrenia so deep that the foul brutalities of the war in Vietnam were the only temporary cure possible for the condition —since the expression of brutality offers a definite if temporary relief to the schizophrenic. So the average good Christian American secretly loved the war in Vietnam. It opened his emotions. He felt compassion for the hardships and the sufferings of the American boys in Vietnam, even the Vietnamese orphans. And his view of the war could shift a little daily as he read his paper, the war connected him to his newspaper again: connection to the outside world, and the small shift of opinions from day to day are the two nostrums of that apothecary where schizophrenia is treated. America needed the war. It would need a war so long as technology expanded on every road of communication, and the cities and corporations spread like cancer; the good Christian Americans needed the war or they would lose their Christ.

In his sleep did Mailer think of his favorite scheme, of a war which took place as a war game? Of a tract of land in the Amazon, and three divisions of Marines against three divisions of the best Chinese Communists, and real bullets, and real airplanes, real television, real deaths? It was madness. He could not present the scheme in public without exercising the audience—they were certain he had discovered the mechanism of a new and gargantuan put-on, no one could take it seriously, not even as a substitute for Vietnam. No, the most insane of wars was more sane than the most insane of games. A pity. Before he had gone to sleep, he had talked for a while with one of the guards, a mournful middle-aged Southerner with a high forehead, big jaw, long inquiring nose, and the ubiquitous silver-rimmed spectacles. The guard had been upset by the sight of so many college boys romping in the dormitory, pleasant looking boys, obviously pleased with themselves. So the guard had asked tentative questions about the war in Vietnam and how they all felt, and why they felt as they did, and Mailer tried to answer him, and thought it was hopeless. You could use every argument, but it was useless, because the guard didn't want to care. If he did, he would be at war against the cold majesty of the Corporation. The Corporation was what brought him his television and his security, the Corporation was what brought him the unspoken promise that on Judgment Day he would not be judged, for Judgement Day—so went the unspoken promise—was no worse than the empty spaces of the Tonight Show when you could not sleep.

Mailer slept. Given this portrait of his thoughts who would make book he did not snore?

THE CIRCLE OF DECEPTION

Robert Jay Lifton

It is becoming more and more apparent that the American presence in Vietnam is enclosed in a circle of deception. Distorted perceptions, false interpretations, and misguided actions have been continually reinforcing one another. During a recent re-visit to South Vietnam, I had a chance to talk at some length with both articulate Vietnamese and Americans, and their views revealed to me some of the psychological and historical dilemmas underlying our ever-deteriorating military and political involvement. And the Vietcong "Tet offensive" in late January and February has suddenly exposed this deception— reaching into every aspect of American activities in Vietnam—for all who are willing to see.

Beginning with the military situation itself, in official American evaluations I could not help noting an element of George Orwell's

Robert Jay Lifton, "The Circle of Deception," *TRANS-action Magazine* March 1968. Copyright © by TRANS-action Magazine, New Brunswick, N. J.

"Newspeak": "progress" means disintegration; and "victory" means stalemate or even defeat. American correspondents told me how, three or four times over the course of a year, they would accompany American troops through the same woods or highlands; each time be informed of the impressive number of Vietcong killed; and end up finding things the way they were, with nothing really settled, no new territory held, nothing secure. And when the Vietcong recently demonstrated their ability to mount effective attacks in cities and villages throughout the South, American spokesmen responded with dubious body counts and spoke of *our* great triumph. Indeed, the word "stalemate"—so repugnant to our President and our Secretary of State —if anything gives us the benefit of the doubt. It is difficult to estimate how much those Americans who promulgate this Newspeak really believe it, but any circle of deception does involve a good deal of self-deception.

Everybody seems to agree that a major cause of these military difficulties is the fact that the Vietnamese army won't fight. When you inquire why, Americans have a quick answer: "Lack of leadership." This explanation is put forth as though one were discussing a large machine in which a few key gears were missing, with the implication that if *we* (Americans) could only "instill leadership" in *them* (Vietnamese), they would then fight and all would be well. This *mechanistic fallacy* pervades much American thinking about Vietnam in general, and is a way of dismissing the fundamental human dimensions of the problem. (The National Liberation Front and the North do not seem to "lack leadership.") Americans are reluctant to look beyond the immediate "operation" into the chasm, preferring, wherever possible, to reinforce the circle of deception.

Symbolic Death of a Nation

The truth is that South Vietnam is a society so dislocated and fragmented that no amount of American technology or technique, military or rehabilitative, can put it together again. The dislocation goes back at least two centuries, and can be attributed to precolonial, colonial, and postcolonial social conflicts, as well as to certain "postmodern" confusions now found in all societies. The present war accelerates processes of breakdown at every level, especially in its annihilation of village life, the main source of social stability in Vietnam. And what is too often overlooked is the extension of these disintegrative tendencies into the realm of idea systems and images. There has been a breakdown not only of social institutions but of the shared symbols necessary to ordered existence—symbols defining rhythms of life and death, group loyalties, and the nature of reality. This "desymbolization" reaches deeply into individual mental lives and undermines collective efforts of all kinds, including that of fighting a war. Whatever success Communism has had as a cohesive social force in the North or the South has resulted from its ability to provide meaningful new images and symbols, or to revitalize old ones.

While all South Vietnamese are involved in this process of desymbolization, you begin to appreciate its national consequences when you observe some of the convolutions in the lives and thoughts of the country's would-be leaders.

One formerly high-ranking diplomat I spoke to had a background of diverse intellectual and political allegiances; of long and close association with Diem; and of continuing leadership in a prominent religious sect. He spoke from experience when he described the last 30 years of Vietnamese history as "nothing but explosions." But he went on to characterize all existing political systems—"so-called American democracy," European parliamentary methods, and the various kinds of communism and socialism—as inadequate for Vietnamese needs: "We have to find our own way." Somewhat vaguely he added, "These days all ideologies are a little outmoded." I was left with the impression of a man both knowledgeable and confused, in whom the pulls of old Vietnamese and contemporary international images had resulted in a facile end-of-ideology perspective that covered over a more fundamental absence of any viable ideas at all.

Another prominent public figure, after giving a strikingly uninhibited account of pervasive government corruption (including manipulation of the then-impending elections), considered the elections nonetheless hopeful—because "people are learning to play the game of the constitution." Again, I had the sense of a postmodern distrust of all thought systems—of the whole thing being a "game" or a "scenario" (perhaps a "bag") that had to be played out but was not to be taken seriously—in a man who, like his country, could construct little that was cohesive out of damaged old goods and tarnished new ones. (He did not remain hopeful when the elections were over: He condemned them as fraudulent.)

The American response to Vietnamese dislocation and anomie is more and bigger war. And this, of course, means more deception, more claims that things are getting better and that progress is being made.

I found myself reminded of two rather terrifying psychological analogies: First, the tendency of people committed to certain beliefs to refuse to surrender them when circumstances have proven their beliefs to be wrong, but instead to embrace them with renewed intensity. The second, based upon my own work relating to death imagery, is that men are most likely to kill or wish to kill when they feel themselves symbolicially dying—that is, overcome by images of stasis, meaninglessness, and separation from the larger currents of human life.

The Blind Giant

To pursue an understanding of the circle of deception, one must examine more closely the nature of the American presence in Vietnam. One is immediately confronted with the theme of the impotence of American power—of the *blind giant.* This is not to say that American men and machines count for naught, but that America-in-Vietnam, despite its vast technological and bureaucratic dimensions (one must go to Vietnam to grasp these), is incapable, *in this situation,* of doing what it says it is doing or wants to do (defend the South against Communism, help strengthen democracy, defeat the N.L.F. and the North or weaken them sufficiently to cause them to seek peace). Here the circle of deception works something like this: The giant has been called forth, fully equipped; one cannot admit that he is helpless. But the giant *is* helpless, not because he lacks strength or even intelligence, but because his vision is severely impaired. Unable to "see" the actual dimensions of the environment he finds himself in, he resorts to blind technological saturation of that environment with his destructive firepower; unable to see the enemy, he shoots blindly at elusive figures who might just as well be his wards or allies.

Yet, in another sense, the giant seems all-powerful. There is a general feeling in South Vietnam that if America does not take care of things, nothing gets done—for there is a tendency among a dislocated people, unfamiliar with Western technology, to lean on America more and more to do everything. What is becoming clear, however, is that Vietnamese passivity is not relieved but increased by the giant's presence. This is so because of the unhealthy relationship between the Vietnamese and the Americans, a relationship marked by power on one side and dependency on the other—what I call a *situation of counterfeit nurturance.* This pattern can develop in any one-sided relationship; the weak feel special need, but resent help offered because they perceive it as a confirmation of their weakness. A classical example of such a situation is colonialism. But one also finds it in

American aid to underdeveloped countries; in Negro-white relation-ships in the United States; and in virtually all programs of social welfare. The key problem is the denial of a sense of autonomy of the dependent party—indeed, the perpetuation of conditions that make autonomy impossible. I constantly came upon precisely this combination of dependency and antagonism in South Vietnamese feelings toward Americans. The sense that help received was counterfeit was aggravated by the fact that the help was accompanied by a broadening of areas of destruction. Moreover, Vietnamese hold extreme images of Americans. They see them sometimes as an omnipotent force, a hidden manipulative hand behind everything, and at other times as ineffectual innocents repeat-edly duped by a tough enemy. In such a situation of counterfeit nurtur-ance, a balanced view of Americans becomes impossible; and many aspects of the American presence, as I will point out, perpetuate this imbalanced view.

The Many Faces of America

The majority of Americans are new to the country and relate to it mainly on the basis of the war. For them there are another "two Vietnams"—one of fighting and killing, the other of healing and re-building. This "second Vietnam" is made up of physicians, agricultur-alists, and providers of various forms of social and economic relief—in short, the *humane American.* But however valuable and even heroic the humane American may be, his efforts tend to be tainted by his ultimate involvement with the first group—because he is officially sponsored; or because he must depend upon the American military (dispensers of transportation and much else in South Vietnam) to sustain himself; or simply because he is American. In these and other ways, the services offered by the humane American are likely to become imbued with the suspicion of counterfeit nurturance. Their healing efforts are, in fact, associated with a strange 20th-century moral inconsistency: on the one hand, the assuming of considerable medical and social responsibility for injured and dislocated civilians (though belated and in response to outside pressure); and on the other, the willingness to sacrifice these same civilians, and indeed entire villages, to the goals of war.

There are also many examples of the *poignant American,* a man increasingly aware of the larger contradiction surrounding his ener-getic and often compassionate reconstructive or therapeutic work. He is an entrapped idealist—entrapped by the official bureaucracy he serves and by the mission it assigns him. He tries to cope with his situation through a form of "bureaucratic idealism," but this is likely to be flawed by some version of the mechanistic fallacy mentioned before. Thus one able young foreign-service officer working in "pacification" said to me, "If I had three or four hundred good dedicated men, I could get the job done." When I asked whether he meant Americans or Vietnamese, his answer—"Of course, if they could be Vietnamese that would be fine"—made it clear that he had Americans in mind. Although well-informed about the historical complexities responsible for the absence in such a program of "three or four hundred good dedicated" Vietnamese, he chose to brush these complexities aside in favor of a characteristically American vision of the most efficient way to "get the job done." In the fashion of most Americans, he attributed the continuing success of the Vietcong (despite severe stresses) to their "organization"—and sought to equal that organization as a way of defeating it. But in Vietnam this kind of efficiency becomes inefficiency, especially when attempted by an alien force— a blind giant—whose vast resources can find no point of local integration, and whose actions, even on behalf of reconstruction, are perceived as externally imposed.

These realities were impressed upon me even more forcefully by another poignant American doing similar work. He was unusually well-trained (he spoke both French and Vietnamese) and well-regarded, and he had had extensive work in the field before assuming his current administrative position. He outlined to me the steps in the program he and his team sought to carry out—establishing security, evaluating social and economic needs, instituting necessary changes —and then admitted that the major impediment to the whole process was the simple fact that security was at best tenuous because "the Vietnamese won't fight." (The recent Vietcong offensive has demonstrated just how great an impediment this is.) He went on to describe how he and his group would seek out a village head and coax him to participate in the program, while instructing him on its procedures, then rush off to the provincial office to smooth the way for the village head's written application, then struggle with various forms of bureaucratic resistance (not to mention the resistance of villagers afraid of retaliation from the Vietcong). He defined his own role in all this as a "catalyst." But it was clear that under such conditions an American is less a catalyst than a *desperate energizer*—one who initiates and oversees a reaction that is not primarily Vietnamese—and, for that matter, is not really taking place.

The Numbed American

There are many varieties of the *numbed American*—intellectually aware of death and suffering, but emotionally desensitized. Such "psychic numbing" is a useful defense in various encounters with death, but it also permits man's most extreme inhumanity to his fellow men. One of its forms is a preoccupation with "professional" concerns. Emphasized to me repeatedly was the widespread awareness among Americans of the importance of a stint in Vietnam for professional advancement—whether for journalists ("the place where the story is"), foreign-service officers, or career military men (a record of command in Vietnam, it was said, would in the future be a prerequisite for highest military appointments). And in all three groups a large number of men conducted themselves as "professionals," in the sense of knowing their work and performing well in adversity. In Vietnam, ordinary professional numbing perpetuates the circle of deception by enabling each to think only of "doing his job." Only occasionally do you encounter men who both "do their jobs" and transcend them—doctors who combine their healing with outspoken moral revulsion toward killing, journalists who, by telling the truth, lay bare the circle of deception.

I heard much of another kind of numbed American—the official who, asked about the killing of civilians, replies, "The numbers have been exaggerated, and anyhow civilians always get hurt in war"; and when asked about the jailing of intellectuals, replies, "We haven't heard about that—after all we can't keep up with everything that goes on—and, besides, we are guests in this country." This form of numbing emerges directly from the contradiction surrounding American influence in Vietnam, as well as from the deception that we are there merely to help a worthy government in its uphill fight to create a free society.

Still other forms of numbing derive from American frustration with Vietnamese passivity. Thus a U.S. Agency for International Development representative spoke of the dreadful predicament of "unofficial refugees" who camp along the roads in order to avoid the gunfire in the villages—and a minute of two later, discussing a campaign to collect blood for needed transfusions, angrily declared, "No American should give a single pint of blood to the Vietnamese until they learn to do things for themselves." G.I.s facing similar frustrations, sometimes with life or death consequences, in a strange country that seems to offer them so little and demand so much, often characterized the

Vietnamese as "dirty," "cowardly," "not willing to do a damn thing for themselves," and "not worth fighting for." I heard extreme attitudes emerging from combinations of numbing and rage: "We should use every single weapon we have—including nuclear weapons. We used the atomic bomb in Hiroshima, didn't we?" Nor need one dwell on the brutalization of combatants, or on patterns of "military necessity" prominent on both sides: Americans firing at "anything that moves," and Vietcong killing those suspected of collaborating with Americans or those who simply possess needed equipment.

The psychological purpose of numbing is to ward off anxiety about death—and guilt about the dead and dying. In the case of Americans, both in Vietnam and at home, numbing prevents awareness of what is happening to combatants and noncombatants on all sides, but is easier to call forth with regard to an alien non-white people than to our own dead.

The closest to the *quiet American* among those I encountered were, alas, the resident social scientists. One I talked with, a man with a high academic reputation who had been supervising a series of studies under government contract, exuded an unnerving enthusiasm—about the country ("a fascinating place") and about his research ("fascinating" and "rewarding"). There was an air of unreality about this scholar's exuberance in the midst of disintegration: He discussed problems of South Vietnamese and N.L.F. "attitudes," and then the measuring of responses of villagers to the presence of TV sets provided by the Americans for experimental purposes. When I originally read the Graham Greene novel, I thought its portrait of the *quiet American* in Vietnam a bit overdrawn. But now I believe I understand more about what Greene was trying to convey: the American's misplaced decency, his altruistic commitment that is at once naive and arrogant in its ideological presuppositions, and which ends in disaster. Certainly the social scientist in Vietnam has been much less destructive than many of his fellow countrymen, but he has a special relationship to one part of the circle of deception implicit in Greene's concept—the fiction that a mixture of expert technical knowledge and dedicated anti-Communism will enable Americans to show the way toward a "solution" of the Vietnamese problem.

Finally, there was the *tired American,* emotionally drained by weeks, months, years in a deteriorating situation and by all the time having to explain, to others and to himself, its rosy possibilities. One should never underestimate the psychological work a person must do to maintain an illusion against continually impinging reality. One high-ranking official spokesman responded to my expression of doubt about our position in Vietnam with skillful openmindedness: "One *should* have doubts. Nothing is clear-cut." But his distorted version of events quickly emerged: "We have always been in favor of negotiations, but no one answers the phone." And he buttressed his interpretations with a series of "scholarly" half-truths, including an ingenious justification of the American presence: He referred to a discovery, by an American psychologist, that the Vietnamese "have a strong need for a father-figure"—a vulgarism impressive in its psychological, historical, and moral reach.

Even more revealing was his consistent technique of affirmation by negation. On the suffering of Vietnamese with fixed salaries because of spiraling prices caused by American spending: "There has been no *runaway* inflation." On the poor performance of Vietnamese troops and their tendency to desert: "There has been no defection of whole *battalions.*" On the burgeoning resentment of Americans: "There have been no all-out anti-American *riots.*" Here the circle of deception operated on the assumption that, since one could imagine (anticipate?) far worse developments, things must be quite good now. On the use of American influence to curb flagrant violations of election procedures, he wavered between decorous restraint—"It's their country"—and a sly admission that "We do, of course, talk to people." The fatigue and despair in his voice became all the more understandable when I learned that he had been among the minority of top-ranking Americans in Saigon who favored stronger support of civilian government. Now he was daily defending the course he opposed. For there are doves and hawks of sorts among resident American officials—and, as one knowledgeable journalist put it to me, "Everyone but the generals wants out." But the tired American must remain, and justify being, "in."

Unknown to most Americans, there are large numbers of Vietnamese who refuse to enter the circle of deception, who are painfully aware of the consequences of a situation of counterfeit nurturance. Vietnamese political leaders, professors, writers, and editors conveyed to me various messages of deep dissatisfaction.

. . . But the patient died

One prevailing message was: *You are curing us to death.* A prominent political candidate, who is also a physician and given to medical metaphors, referred to America as an "iron lung" being used to help "the patient" (Vietnam) to "breathe." Then he added, with considerable emotion, "But this iron lung should be for the purpose of the patient learning how to breathe by himself and becoming healthier—not to take over his breathing for him." Using a similar metaphor, a newspaper editor wrote, "The injection of a right dose—in the right place—will cure, but an overdose—injected in the wrong place—will kill." He went on: "A moderate drink . . . once in a while will improve health and morale. But too many drinks too often will poison the blood, and eventually destroy the brain and the liver. Barrels of it will drown the drinker." Here the message is: *Your "help" is poisoning (drowning) us.*

The newspaper editor elaborated that "excessive and prolonged aid" would aggravate an already harmful tendency in South Vietnam for the city to be alienated from the countryside, and make them both "dependent on the donor country" in the way that would "sap . . . physical as well as moral strength, and render [South Vietnam] power-less in the face of a threat to its social body from the inside . . . [This would be one of] the worst gifts ever made to this country, for it would mean eventual destruction . . . of its capacity to think, plan and execute, and its will to work and struggle—that is, to live." Here we encounter what is perceived as the worst form of counterfeit nurtur-ance: Help meant to be life-giving becomes deadly; in political terms, assistance meant to thwart Communism speeds its victory.

In his talk with me, the editor also lashed out at what he saw as the hypocritical nature of the American effort: "We know you are not fighting for Vietnam but against China. If you want to fight China, why not go there, to her borders, and fight?" As a Southerner, he was especially bitter about the destruction of the country ("Everyone talks about the bombing of the North, but what about the bombing of the South?"). In his writings, he referred to the "preposterous situation" in which Americans supply the military force to impose an unpopular government upon a rural population, and "even . . . carry out psycho-logical warfare and civic action to win the population over to the government side." In our talk he also brought forth what is for an Asian intellectual the most extreme kind of condemnation, referring to his country as "like a colony, but worse."

Essentially the same message was conveyed to me by a university professor, in the midst of a quiet discussion over aperitifs, when he suddenly launched into an angry denunciation of the blind giant's encroachments into intellectual spheres. He compared the modest office of his university president with the lavish suite maintained on the floor below by the resident American "adviser"; complained of

American dictation of educational policies, in ignorance of Vietnamese needs and desires; and concluded, bitterly, that "Americans always think their ways, their ideas, their teaching, their food, their way of life are the best." Like the other Vietnamese quoted above, he was by no means free of need for the Americans, but found himself humiliated, and at times paralyzed, by the form the American presence has taken.

Thus the message *You are curing us to death* readily extends itself to *Give us back our country!* Such was vividly the case with a young writer who had spent several years at an American university and now belonged to a loosely-organized group of intellectuals—highly nationalistic and vaguely socialist, with contempt for their government and respect for the N.L.F. ("We are against their terror but we understand them, and consider many of them patriots"). He spoke to me at length about America's takeover of South Vietnam, and conveyed all of his bitterness in one remark: "This is not our country." Throughout our talk he struggled with feelings of humiliation, and with the quest for renewed individual and national pride. He was contemptuous of those Vietnamese who had become French citizens; asserted, "I am Vietnamese and shall be Vietnamese until I die!"; and summed up his convictions about his country's situation as follows: "I don't care so much whether it is Communist, anti-Communist, nationalist, or imperialist [then, more slowly and pointedly] *as long as it is Vietnamese!*"

This young writer resented the Americans' collusion in what he regarded as fraudulent standards imposed upon Vietnamese intellectuals: "A friend of mine tried to publish an academic study of Marxism, but it was disapproved by the censor, so he wrote another book entitled *Sexual Response,* which was easily approved." He alluded to the helplessness of the blind giant in Vietnam by suddenly asking me the question, "Can you sleep at night?" At first I thought he was raising a problem of American conscience, but he was referring to the artillery fire one hears in Saigon every evening—his point was that it was occurring on the very outskirts of the city. Yet he in no sense gave up on America. He recalled with great affection the warm and stimulating student community he had known there, in contrast with the "other America" of generals and bureaucrats he found in Vietnam. What he seemed to be asking for was a reassertion of the libertarian spirit he had associated with America in the past. He went so far as to suggest that, since "the problem is not the North but the Chinese" (a point of view many Vietnamese nationalists share), even if the

North were to take over the country "it might want an American base in Vietnam." However one might question the accuracy of this assumption of joint interest in preventing Chinese incursion, it would seem to contain a lingering wish to remain allied to America in the struggle for national independence.

But to conclude that men with this kind of intellectual and emotional tie to the West can be counted upon to support Western—or American—political policies is to enter further into the circle of deception. Indeed, for almost a century Asian intellectuals have been emerging from their experience in the West as revolutionaries who combat Western domination. If one looks to Chou En-lai, Krishna Menon, or Ho Chi Minh, one suspects that much of the hostility ultimately felt toward the West has to do with precisely the kind of ambivalence I observed in this young writer. The strong initial attraction becomes viewed as an evil seduction that must be violently resisted in the name of individual and national integrity. And there are many ideological "Wests" to draw upon. The connection with the West is never entirely broken, but it is used mainly as a means of self-discovery.

Dependence and Resentment

Other frequent messages the Vietnamese conveyed to me about Americans were variations on *We feel that we need you but. . . .* A woman of about 30, who was the daughter of a plantation owner from the North and had lived in Paris for some time, was appalled at the generally corrupt and "Americanized" atmosphere she found upon her return to Saigon. She spoke even more bitterly about the effects of American-induced inflation upon Vietnamese civil servants and soldiers, going so far as to claim that many incidents of stealing and killing attributed to the Vietcong were actually the work of destitute members of the South Vietnamese army. Her proposed solution to these problems was a Vietnamese version of the circle of deception: a strongman running the government who would put to death a few of those indulging in graft to set examples for others; and more American soldiers "to fight the Communists." She seemed uneasy about reports of reservations on the part of Americans, and repeatedly asked me to tell her "what Americans think about the war." This kind of anxiety in the Vietnamese appeared to stem from doubts not only about American staying power, but about the validity of the demands they were making of Americans. Such uneasiness and guilt are always likely to increase resentment.

This combination of demand and resentment could take various symbolic forms. On a visit we made to a Saigon hospital, my wife distributed little dolls to children injured in the war. She had given away almost all of them when one of the parents rushed up to her, holding the head of a doll in one hand and the rest of it in the other to demonstrate that the doll had broken in half—all the while smiling with discomfort in the East Asian fashion and making it clear that she expected the broken doll to be replaced (which it was). The incident seemed to suggest several dimensions of the situation of counterfeit nurturance: the help needed and demanded is endless; the American giver will be resented for the imperfections of his gifts; and (somewhat more abstractly) Americans are expected to put severed things and people together—because they possess such great power, and because they are largely responsible for severing them in the first place.

I encountered another symbolic expression of this demand-resentment constellation in a young female dancer hospitalized at a psychiatric center in Saigon. She had lived for some time in London, and had returned to her country because of developing symptoms of mental illness. But she was convinced that "the Americans" had abducted her in London and carried her forcibly back to Saigon, and now wondered what the American psychiatrist could suggest to make her better. Again, Americans are seen as all-powerful—the ultimate source of both benevolence and suffering. The pattern is, of course, by no means unique to Vietnam: General MacArthur frequently appeared in the delusions of Japanese mental patients during the early postwar years, in this and other ways replacing the Emperor. But it is illustrative of the American-Vietnamese relationship.

The prevailing feeling one senses among Vietnamese intellectuals is that of despair and helplessness, or *immobilisme*. Similarly, the people seem in general to react neither with enthusiasm nor opposition but rather with passive resistance: general resistance to government programs; peasants' resistance to taxes; young men's (especially students') resistance to the army; and, of course, the army's resistance to fighting. The general mixture of lassitude, cynicism, and aggressive self-seeking pervading Saigon is reminiscent of accounts of the atmosphere in large cities in China just before the Communist takeover— which suggests that there is a certain style of American interplay with Asian corruption, of joint participation in the fiction that a highly unpopular and ineffectual government is a dynamic and virtuous force around which free men must rally. In truth, the most efficient and whole-hearted American-Vietnamese collaboration I encountered in

Saigon was a bar-whorehouse featuring beautiful Vietnamese girls and élite (mainly Embassy) American clientele—who had no complaints about Vietnamese "organization" or "leadership."

Since so many Vietnamese tend to reject the circle of deception, are there any authentic ideas and images to which they are capable of responding? I had the clear impression that there were three: images of *nation, social transformation,* and *peace.* To grasp the importance of these, one must remember that the human mind lives on images, absorbing and recreating them as a basis for all understanding and action. The problem in Vietnam is less a matter of "getting the bugs out of the machine," as the mechanistic fallacy would have it, than of evolving shared word-pictures that inspire and cohere. I would suggest that the unpalatable truth about the American presence in Vietnam is that it radically undermines each of the three significant images I have mentioned.

Dream of Nationhood

We have already observed the force of the *image of nations*; it has been rendered especially compelling by the very precariousness of Vietnam's historical status as a country, by old national struggles as well as by its recent dismemberment. A Vietnamese who is considered a nationalist wears a badge of honor, and much of the admiration in the South for Ho Chi Minh stems from his ability to make psychological contact with all Vietnamese through this shared image (enhanced by his creating a form of "national Communism" with considerable independence from larger Communist nations). Similarly, Vietnamese who feel threatened by the Vietcong are nonetheless willing to speak sympathetically of "nationalists" among the Vietcong.

Many Vietnamese I talked with stressed the South's need for a leader who could, like Ho, reanimate the national image—always making clear that men who have fought on the side of the French during the struggle for independence, as did most of the present military junta, would be automatically disqualified. One young political scientist with experience in government told me that the Vietnamese have been searching in the wrong places for models of leadership and economic development, and advocated someone on the order of Ayub Khan of Pakistan. Most looked to eventual reunification of their country, though differing on how this could or should be achieved. Virtually all maintained that the American presence painfully violates the image of nation, and that this violation has direct pragmatic significance: Guerillas with little military equipment can harass and outmaneuver the blind giant because he widely identified as an alien threat to their nation.

We have, of course, by now become familiar with the excesses that can surround the image of nation, with aggressive national*ism.* But this should not cause us to lose sight of the powerful integrative force exerted by a people's shared sense of geographical-racial-cultural destiny. The root of the word "nation" is the same as that of "origin" or "birth," and in our struggles to extend the concept outward from its beginnings in clan and tribe to include all of mankind, we may too readily forget that men still require it for their sense of immortalized human continuity.

Clearly, the image of nation is not something that one people can provide for another, least of all Americans for Asians. The refrain I heard from the Vietnamese was that "America must take a risk" and support leaders sufficiently independent of her to make it likely that they would question her policies. Both sides are thus presented with an excruciating paradox that the recent Vietnamese elections have by no means resolved: the American need to support opponents of American power; and the Vietnamese need to call upon American power to help them overcome it. This is part of what the editor quoted earlier meant by the "preposterous situation"—a situation that will find no solution that does not include a reassertion of Vietnamese autonomy.

The Need for Social Reform

The significance of the second general image, that of *social transformation,* is attested to by the recent use of the phrase "revolutionary development" for the American-South Vietnamese village-pacification program. The military regime's miserable record on all aspects of social transformation, especially the basic issue of land reform, renders this terminology sadly ironic. A leading legislator told me that when territory is retaken from the Vietcong, the landlords return right behind government soldiers. Yet a vision of major social reform remains fundamental to reversing the symbolic social death of South Vietnam.

While a number of the people I spoke to condemned the Communists for their "betrayal of the revolution," there was little doubt that *some* form of revolution has to take place. Thus the editor called for "a new army and a new civil service . . . [that] would have to be built up *in the field* [italics his] away from the capital and cities, around a nucleus of revolutionary men . . . living simply among the peasants."

The idea sounds familiar; its proponent readily admits that it has much in common with the successful approach of the Vietcong. Our claim that we ourselves have favored such a transformation is very much part of the circle of deception. For while we have applied pressure upon a reluctant government in the direction of reform, our relationship to that government (as well as the nature of that government itself) makes impossible the actual accomplishment of transformation from within. A related deception is the dismissal, as irrelevant or disruptive, of those groups that have most strongly articulated the widespread desire for transformation—militant Buddhists, students, and younger intellectuals. They will surely be heard from in the future.

A Strong Desire for Peace

An even greater deception has pervaded America's underestimation of the significance of the *image of peace* for the Vietnamese. The idea that the South Vietnamese are determined to continue their military struggle should have been shattered, once and for all, by the results of the recent elections. Despite the ruling generals' questionable manipulations, they drew fewer votes than the combination of three candidates who had declared themselves for peace; and the most outspoken peace candidate surprised everyone by coming in second. From all that I heard when I was in Vietnam, I would tend to agree with the opinion expressed by journalists that the dove symbol used on the ballot by the peace candidate had much to do with his impressive showing. Anyone who has talked to Vietnamese during the past few months can readily sense something close to a groundswell of peace sentiment. What symbol could appeal more to an electorate that is largely illiterate but by no means indifferent to the sufferings of war and the attractions of peace? The image of peace includes relief from a long and terrible cycle of death anxiety and death guilt, and—whatever the qualifications put forth about the kind of peace there would be—an opportunity to reverse the increasingly intolerable pattern of disintegration.

I had an encounter with a "former peace candidate" that, I believe, illustrates some of the complicated dimensions of the peace image. This man was an economist who, though still in his 30s, had been finance minister in three cabinets—and his campaign emblem was a bomb crossed out by two diagonal lines. Since the military regime had in the recent past associated peace talk with such dangerous tendencies as "neutralism" and Communism, this kind of campaign by so prominent a person was creating quite a stir. At the time Americans were divided about him—on occasion one would hear him spoken of as "unrealistic" or "put up to it by someone," and on other occasions he would be praised for his accomplishments as finance minister and described as "one of the best minds in South Vietnam." No one was very surprised when, on the day before I went to see him, he was publicly denounced by the police as having "Communist affiliations," leaving his future as a campaigner, and indeed as a free man, in doubt.

This candidate told me that he welcomed talking to me, since he too wished to stress a psychological perspective. Then he handed me a brief essay (translated from the original French) in which he had, somewhat abstractly, discussed the Vietnamese as a people caught up first in a revolution, then in opposition to revolution, and now feeling "the desire for peace" as their "most powerful psychological motivation." He insisted that the elections should give the people a chance to express this desire, stressing the urgency of proper timing—since in the past there had never been the necessary combination of war exhaustion and political climate for peace, and in the future there might be little left of the country to salvage. He spoke of a "war mechanism"—a self-perpetuating system—with no possibility of anyone's winning, but all continuing to fight "because they don't know anything else to do." (I was later reminded of this when I read John Kenneth Galbraith's contention that "War turns reason into stereotype" and freezes participants in original error.) He felt that the mechanism could be interrupted only by installing a government committed to peace through negotiations; that such a commitment would cut down the effectiveness of the Vietcong, who thrive on war and chaos; and that it would evoke a strong general response in the Vietnamese people, which would in turn impel the N.L.F. and the North to join the South in negotiations. He thought that all this would take time, and that American troops would remain in Vietnam during protracted negotiations, but that once the general undertaking had been started it would succeed in bringing peace to the country.

One could raise various points about his program, but what struck me was his serious effort not only to rally the country around the image of peace but to evolve a workable plan to bring about peace. He told me that the government was spreading false stories about him in order to prevent him from running in the election, and when I asked him why the government was determined to do this he answered, "Because the idea of peace is extremely popular." It would seem that he was right on both counts: He was officially eliminated as a candidate a short time later, and the elections provided that peace was indeed a popular idea.

But images are not so easily eliminated as candidates. Once safely established in their campaigns, a number of other office-seekers (especially the peace candidate who did so well) actively committed themselves to negotiations and the search for peace. Even the military rulers were forced to make very uncharacteristic obeisance in the same direction. Many elements seem to be converging—the influence of the "former peace candidate," an increasing American realization that there is no feasible course other than negotiations, and strong pressure from the rest of the world. But underneath everything is the tremendous power of the image of peace and its ability ultimately to break through the circle of deception.

Ever since World War II, Vietnam has been living out the painful problems besetting the world at large. Thinking back to my first visit to Saigon 13 years ago, I recall mainly scenes of ordinarily well-intentioned men—Vietnamese, French, American—arguing passionately, sometimes intelligently, apparently endlessly, about what should be done, behaving as men do when confronted by a terrible problem that, however approached, will not go away. What I have tried to suggest here is that the problem is being confounded rather than solved by the American presence—because that presence works against Vietnam's only viable psychological and historical possibilities. Is it not time for the giant to begin to see? Can he not recognize, and then step out of, the circle of deception?

TOWARD AN
AFFIRMATIVE MORALITY

John F. Wharton

"Nothing important is ever done in this world until men are ready to kill each other if it is not done."

The radiation from the Hiroshima and Nagasaki bombs was still

John F. Wharton, "Toward An Affirmative Morality," *Saturday Review,* July 12, 1969. Copyright © 1969 by Saturday Review, Inc. Reprinted by permission of the author and the publisher.

drifting away when *Saturday Review* published an editorial outlining some of the dangers and complexities of an atomic age. The editorial emphasized that change would occur at an unprecedented rate of speed. Unless modern man could deal with this change, the editorial warned, he would become obsolete.

The editorial was quite correct in its prophecies of problems to come. Unhappily, modern man has not yet shown any ability to deal with them. The leadership generation of the 1950s and 1960s—my own—is now clearly obsolete, and a cloud of obsolescence is settling down on the generations next in line. Only the young are as yet untouched.

Some hundreds of millions of words have been written by now about the students' revolt and the rebellion of the disenfranchised; I feel that I myself have read several million. One hesitates to mention the subjects again, except for the fact that nowhere have I seen anyone really facing up to certain basic causes.

One basic cause arises from the fact that the leaders of revolt see clearly something that most of their elders simply cannot admit. They see that the accepted and entrenched educational, economic, and political systems have produced a world with more warfare, bigger massacres, more powerful criminals, and more overall violence than at any other time since the Age of Englightenment began. Yet many of the leaders of these systems are still spouting platitudes which, to the young people, are patent expressions either of ignorance, self-delusion, or pure hypocrisy. Moreover, not only do these elderly folk refuse to admit any incompetence; they actually boast of the eminence that they have achieved—utterly unaware that to youth *this* is proof of incompetence. When one is part of a system that has brought a whole world to disaster, only a fool boasts that he is an *important part.* Yet these are the people, say our youth, who have the unmitigated gall to expect that we will gladly accept them as fit to train us for *any* kind of leadership.

Youth's first reaction to all of the foregoing is one of frustration, rage, and desire to destroy. The situation is similar to a man trying to learn to ride a bicycle with such crooked handle bars that he always finds himself in the ditch. He tries to fix it; he can't; no one helps him; in a rage he kicks the whole thing to pieces. He must then pick up the pieces and build a new bicycle—or perhaps a motorcycle, or even a machine never before seen. Can he do it?

The notion of rebuilding from the bottom up is by no means a new

one. More than a thousand years ago a Persian poet wrote these lines
as the climax of his poem.

Ah, Love, could you and I with Him conspire
To grasp this sorry scheme of things entire,
Would we not shatter it to bits and then
Remold it closer to our hearts' desire.

There have been a number of attempts to carry out the poet's
dream. None has been completely successful, but some have produced what most of us would call a better world.

Martin Luther I (some appellation seems necessary to prevent
confusion with the late Dr. King), backed by the armies of some
petty German princelings, almost shattered to bits the whole religious system of Western Europe. He didn't quite do it, but he did
create spots where a man who wanted freedom of religious thought
could get it without fear of torture and death at the stake. Most of us
think that, despite the wars that were fought to achieve it, Martin
Luther I made a better world. (One of the things learned in that strife
should be remembered today. The Catholics insisted that they could
not live side by side with Protestants because of the heretics' smell.
When they accepted each other, the smell mysteriously disappeared.)

In the eighteenth and nineteenth centuries the proponents of
democracy came closer to complete success in shattering the political systems of what they glibly called "the civilized world"—again,
we think, very much for the better. But, for the most part, they had
little initial impact on the economic or religious systems.

Then, in 1917, came what John Reed called *Ten Days That Shook
the World,* when the Bolsheviks shattered to bits the political, economic, and religious systems of more than 150 million people and
began rebuilding them nearer to the Bolshevik heart's desire. This
action did *not,* in the opinion of most outsiders, make a better world.

But it did scare the daylights out of what is now called the Establishment—all over the Western world.

This revolution arose because the Czarists had resolutely refused
to permit any important change. And right here is the most important of the basic causes of the ferment today. Our young people and
our disenfranchised see that the processes of change in our democracy have fallen into the control of men who are more concerned
with their own immediate well-being than with the long-term public
good. Hence, we have commissions and recommmendations, again

and again and again, but the passage of true remedial legislation is alarmingly slow or nonexistent.

For example, just about everyone today knows that air pollution is dangerous to life and health. But it is almost impossible to obtain valid remedial legislation. City legislators, in particular, want to pass laws without teeth in them. They can then pose as anti-pollution leaders, at the same time knowing that the polluters will continue to make campaign contributions. For another example, everyone knows that the narcotics trade run by organized crime takes a yearly toll of billions of dollars and millions of shattered lives. Yet, except for a brief foray by Robert Kennedy, not since Thomas Dewey's epoch-making drive in the 1930s has any political leader appeared who was ready to make a similar fight, nor is there any sign that the money to support him would be forthcoming. Instead, we hear unpleasant rumors of the Mafia's influence with city officials and legislatures (of course there is plenty of *talk* about making a fight).

The machinery for effective remedial legislation in the capitalist countries has obviously developed rust in the gears; those who sit in the seats of the mighty have become experts in proving (to themselves) that we must go slow, which usually turns out to mean never. The recommendations for alleviation of the ghettos run back *thirty years*. (In Communist countries, the gears seem to be filled with wet sand; it is even worse.)

This is the major reason why the rebel leaders quite clearly want to shatter all Establishments to bits and rebuild from the bottom up. This threat is what terrifies the "In" people, and there *is* cause for terror. Every great experiment, be it Protestantism or democracy, or anything else, carries enormous risks along with its hopes. But the willingness, nay desire, to take risks is part and parcel of every reform movement; the fear of risks will not prevent the next great reform movement from carrying on.

To digress for a moment, there is the cheerful possibility that such risk-taking will eventuate in something unimaginable at the moment—something fine, although as incomprehensible to us as the American Constitution would have been to Louis XIV of France. *If* a new world-wide type of constitution did evolve, then nuclear war might be staved off. Be it remembered that our union did not come about because of fear of intercolonial war; it came to pass because the colonies felt union would give them a more prosperous and richer life. The eighty years of interstate peace that followed were a by-product. So *might* it be with international peace. It is indeed a thin hope, a tiny gleam—but is there *any* other?

But the somber question is this: in a world completely out of control will the young people or, more likely, the economically and spiritually disenfranchised be allowed even to oil the rusty gears without first fighting the new type civil war, such as that depicted in the brilliant motion picture *The Battle of Algiers.*

Very few Westerners understand this type of war; Algiers is well worth study. Beginning with unorganized rioting in the Moslem ghetto, the Arabs formed a secret organization and *well-directed* terrorism ensued. And well-directed terrorism is something that the affluent members of our affluent society have never experienced. (The small shopkeepers and restaurateurs *have* felt the well-directed terrorism of the Mafia.)

In Algiers, Arab women walked the streets carrying large purses from which a companion terrorist could quickly extract a pistol, shoot to kill, replace it, and disappear. Time bombs were placed not only in consulates but in airports, chic dining spots, sporting arenas. Nobody's life was safe anywhere, any time.

Of course, a backlash ensued. It rose to new heights in its turn; tough paratroopers were called in. With the use of spies, they broke up the organization—for a time. Phoenix-like, it emerged again, and again, until finally the Arabs were made first-class citizens in an independent country.

Backlash in America is nothing new. More than two years ago, it defeated the proposal for a civilian review board of police action in New York City. George Wallace rode high on the backlash in the South and is still seeking new worlds to conquer. I recently met a well-educated, urbane lady from a Northern state who declared that the man responsible for our ills of today was Abraham Lincoln! (She just wished he could be made to come back and face the troubles he has caused.)

Sociologists have pointed out that there have been, in times past, phenomena very similar to the hippie and flower children movements and that these, in the absence of constructive leadership, have ended by evoking reaction and repression of the bleakest kind. On the other side of the coin, we see the black power movement, riots in the ghettos, violence everywhere in the city streets, in the country, in the suburbs. Hapless victims are mugged and murdered before crowds of onlookers; we all shrug it off and pray, "Oh, God, not me."

The dispossessed need only a magnetic, militant leader to bring about a confrontation. The backlash needs only a ruthless leader to produce a brand of American Fascism. Some of the white soldiers in Vietnam who have learned General Westmoreland's "search-and-destroy" tactics will be the perfect material for brownshirts and black-shirts. Some of the blacks returning from that war will be as ready to risk their lives for their race as they were for the country that has treated them so badly. The forces of repression will raise the cry for "law and order," by which they mean putting down violence with more violence. *The Battle of Algiers* could become the battle of New York, Chicago, Los Angeles, what you will.

Let us pray that it will not happen. Certainly it need not. Wise leadership could surely avert it. But too many of our current political leaders put their faith in violence as the means to produce peace. One might almost say that their slogan is "world peace through perpetual war." Occasionally, one of them talks in a different strain, but he is seldom forthright. The most one can say for him is what Theodore Roosevelt said of William H. Taft, "He means well feebly." And the great leader of nonviolence, Dr. Martin Luther King, lies dead. If assassination was his reward, why shouldn't the blacks turn to violent methods? What would *you* do if you were a young Negro soldier returning from Vietnam to a ghetto life?

The quotation at the beginning of this article expresses the motto of a fictional munitions-maker. Gandhi disproved it; he was assassinated. Martin Luther King tried to disprove it; he was assassinated. The mythical munitions-maker and his creator, George Bernard Shaw, must be laughing sardonically, "When will you learn?"

Of course, there are counterforces at work, but at the moment the task is frustrating. The problem is both a moral and an emotional one: can youth be made to *feel* that their elders do desire a better world; can the blacks be made to *feel* that the whites will accept them as first-class citizens; can the whites be made to *feel* that they honestly want this? Our knowledge of how to effect such changes in human behavior is almost nonexistent; we only know that groups of humans act from emotion rather than reason, and that no type of action, good or bad, is impossible. If you doubt it, read George Mackay's *Extraordinary Popular Delusions and the Madness of Crowds*.

However, there *are* men and women, many of them scientifically trained, who are studying the question of changing human behavior, and at any time a breakthrough may occur. The support of these people seems to be the world's best hope at the moment.

. . .

What is *most* needed is a leader who can inspire an affirmative morality, a morality that demands action to help others, not merely abstinence from acts that might harm one's neighbor. A few great historical figures *have* taught this and still stand out as shining landmarks. One of the most interesting is the man who founded the Franciscan order and who, incidentally, has, over the centuries, attracted more followers than the founders of the Inquisition.

We should pay more attention to St. Francis of Assisi. It would be wonderful if a campaign could be started to make every leader in politics, industry, or education say, every night, part of his famous prayer:

> Lord, make me an instrument of Thy peace. Where there is hatred, let me sow love; where there is injury, pardon; where there is doubt, faith; where there is despair, hope; where there is sadness, joy; where there is darkness, light.

Whether or not our leaders will say this prayer each night, the rest of us might be well advised to do so.

HUMAN NATURE AND
INTERNATIONAL RELATIONS

J. William Fulbright

There are three ways of considering the effects of human nature on the behavior of nations. There is the approach of the moralist or theologian who weighs behavior against moral standards, notes the discrepancy, and then prescribes certain changes in behavior. There is the approach of the behavioral scientist, who accepts the game of politics as it is played, studies the behavior of the players with a view to prediction and hopes to use the data thus derived to give "our side" the advantage in the game. Finally, there is the approach of the humanist, who weighs human behavior against human *needs,* notes the discrepancy, notes as well the irrational elements in human nature and the limitations these impose, and then tries to find ways,

J. William Fulbright, "Human Nature and International Relations." From *The Arrogance Of Power,* by J. William Fulbright, pp. 159–68. Copyright © 1966 by the author. Reprinted by permission of Random House, Inc.

within those limitations, of narrowing the gap between behavior and needs.

Civilizing the Competitive Instinct

The approach of the humanist is the one commended in this chapter, as applied to the discrepancy between man's unrestrained competitive instinct and his hope of survival at this first moment in human history when the means of violence at man's disposal have become sufficient to destroy his species. Unlike other forms of life which have faced the danger of extinction, we have had some choice in the matter, having ourselves invented the instruments that threaten us with distinction. This fact, to be sure, tells at least as much about man's folly as it does about his creative genius, but it also suggests that having created the conditions for our own collective death, we at least retain some choice about whether it is actually going to happen. Clearly, a radical change in traditional behavior is required. The question of our age is whether a change radical enough to close the gap between traditional political behavior and the requirements of survival is possible *within the limits* imposed by human nature.

It is hard to believe in the destruction of the human race. Because we have managed to avoid a holocaust since the invention of nuclear weapons only a little more than twenty years ago, the danger of its occurrence now seems remote, like Judgment Day, and references to it have become so frequent and familiar as to lose their meaning; the prospect of our disappearance from the earth has become a cliché, even something of a bore. It is a fine thing of course that the hydrogen bomb has not reduced us all to nervous wrecks, but it is not a fine thing that finding the threat incredible, we act as though it did not exist and go on conducting international relations in the traditional manner, which is to say, in a manner that does little if anything to reduce the possibility of a catastrophe.

Neither the government nor the universities are making the best possible use of their intellectual resources to deal with the problems of war and peace in the nuclear age. Both seem by and large to have accepted the idea that the avoidance of nuclear war is a matter of skillful "crisis management," as though the techniques of diplomacy and deterrence which have gotten us through the last twenty years have only to be improved upon to get us through the next twenty or a hundred or a thousand years.

The law of averages has already been more than kind to us and we have had some very close calls, notably in October 1962. We escaped a nuclear war at the time of the Cuban missile affair because of President Kennedy's skillful "crisis management" and Premier Khrushchev's prudent response to it; surely we cannot count on the indefinite survival of the human race if it must depend on an indefinite number of repetitions of that sort of encounter. Sooner or later the law of averages will turn against us; an extremist or incompetent will come to power in one major country or another, or a misjudgment will be made by some perfectly competent official, or things will just get out of hand without anyone being precisely responsible as happened in 1914. None of us, however,—professors, bureaucrats, or politicians— has yet undertaken a serious and concerted effort to put the survival of our species on some more solid foundation than an unending series of narrow escapes.

We have got somehow to try to grasp the idea of universal destruction—by some means other than actually experiencing it. We have got somehow to grasp the idea that man's competitive instinct, unalterable an element of human nature though it may be, must nonetheless be restrained, regulated or redirected in such a way that it no longer threatens to explode into universal, final violence.

The first step toward control of the competitive instinct is to acknowledge it. It is no use to declare it immoral or obsolete and to decree its abolition because, like sex, hunger, death, and taxes, it just won't go away. Nor does it make sense to accept unrestrained competitiveness as an unalterable fact of life, to resign ourselves to the game of nuclear politics as insane but inevitable and to focus our efforts on computerized war games aimed at making sure that we "get there first with the most," because even if our adversary "gets there" second and with much less, it is likely to be enough to wipe us out.

We can neither abolish nor totally accept national rivalries; we have got, somehow, to put them under some restraints, just as we have brought the rivalries of business and other groups within our own society under restraints in order to protect the community and, indeed, in order to perpetuate *competition,* which under conditions of unregulated rivalry would soon enough be ended with the elimination of the small and weak groups by the big and strong ones. In foreign politics as in domestic economics, competitive instincts are natural and, within limits, creative; but so prone are they to break out of those limits and to wreak havoc when they do that we must seek some means to confine them to their proper sphere, as the servant and not the master of civilization.

It may be that some idea as to where that sphere begins and where it ends, as to where the possibilities of human nature begin to conflict with the needs of human survival and as to whether and how the two can be reconciled, can be gotten from the study of psychology. If it be granted that the ultimate source of war and peace is human nature, then it follows that the study of politics is the study of man and that if politics is ever to acquire a new character, the change will not be wrought either in computers or in revival meetings but through a better understanding of the needs and fears of the human individual. It is a curious thing that in an era when interdisciplinary studies are favored in the universities, little has been done to apply the insights of individual and social psychology to the study of international relations.

Psychology, Ideology, and Political Behavior

Man's beliefs about how societies should be organized and related to each other are called ideologies. An understanding of the psychological roots of ideology would provide us with insight and perspective on our own political beliefs as well as those of others. To what extent, one might ask, are ideological beliefs the result of a valid and disinterested intellectual process and to what extent are they instilled in us by conditioning and inheritance? Or, to put the question another way, why exactly is it that, like Gilbert and Sullivan's Englishmen, every one of whom was miraculously born a "little Liberal" or a "little Conservative," most young Russians grow up believing in communism and most young Americans grow up believing in democracy, or, for that matter, what accounts for the coincidence that most Arabs believe in Islam and most Spaniards in Catholicism?

We must acquire some perspective about our beliefs about things. If, as psychologists suggest, the sources of ideological belief are largely accidental and irrational, the political implications are enormous. Ideologies are supposed to explain reality to people and to inspire them with political ideals for which they should be, and usually are, willing to fight and die. Yet it seems obvious that almost all of us acquire our ideological beliefs not principally as the result of an independent intellectual process but largely as the result of an accident of birth. If you happen to be born in the United States, the chances are overwhelming that you will grow up believing in democracy; if you happen to be born in Russia or China, the chances are just as great that you will grow up believing in communism. It would seem to follow that if the United States should fight a war with Russia or China, the basic issue would not be between two competing political philosophies but between two great societies made up of hundreds of millions of people, most of whom had little more choice in their ideological beliefs than in the color of their eyes and hair. It seems, to say the least, an arbitrary reason for killing hundreds of millions of people in a nuclear war.

Psychologists say that the appeal of an ideology is that it shields the individual from the painful fact that his life is a minor event in the ongoing universe. It helps us to connect our lives to some larger purpose and also helps to "organize the world for us," giving us a picture, though not necessarily an accurate picture, of reality. A person's world-view, or ideology, is said to filter the signals that come to him, giving meaning and pattern to otherwise odd bits of information. Thus, for example, when a Chinese and an American put radically different interpretations on the Vietnamese war, it is not necessarily because one or the other has chosen to propound a wicked lie but rather because each has filtered information from the real world through his ideological world-view, selecting the parts that fit, rejecting the parts that do not, and coming out with two radically different interpretations of the same events.

Ideology influences perception, perception shapes expectation, and expectation shapes behavior, making for what is called the self-fulfilling prophecy. Thus, for example, China, fearing the United States but lacking power, threatens and blusters, confirming the United States in its fears of China and causing it to arm against her, which in turn heightens Chinese fears of the United States. Professor Gordon Allport of Harvard made the point some years ago that " . . . while most people deplore war, they nonetheless *expect* it to continue. And what *people expect determines their behavior. . . .* The indispensable condition of war," wrote Professor Allport, "is that people must *expect* war and must prepare for war, before, under war-minded leadership, they make war. It is in this sense that 'wars begin in the minds of men.' "[1]

Another striking psychological phenomenon is the tendency of antagonists to dehumanize each other. To most Americans China is a strange, distant, and dangerous nation, not a society made up of more than seven hundred million individual human beings but a kind of menacing abstraction. When Chinese soldiers are described, for example, as "hordes of Chinese coolies," it is clear that they are being

---

[1]Gordon W. Allport, "The Role of Expectancy," in Hadley Cantril, ed., *Tensions That Cause Wars* (Urbana: University of Illinois Press, 1950), pp. 43, 48.

thought of not as people but as something terrifying and abstract, or as something inanimate, like the flow of lava from a volcano. Both China and America seem to think of each other as abstractions: to the Chinese we are not a society of individual people but the embodiment of an evil idea, the idea of "imperialist capitalism"; and to most of us China represents not people but an evil and frightening idea, the idea of "aggressive communism."

Obviously, this dehumanizing tendency helps to explain the savagery of war. Man's capacity for decent behavior seems to vary directly with his perception of others as individual humans with human motives and feelings, whereas his capacity for barbarous behavior seems to increase with his perception of an adversary in abstract terms. This is the only explanation I can think of for the fact that the very same good and decent citizens who would never fail to feed a hungry child or comfort a sick friend or drop a coin in the church collection basket can celebrate the number of Viet Cong killed in a particular week or battle, talk of "making a desert" of North Vietnam or of "bombing it back into the Stone Age" despite the fact that most, almost all, of the victims would be innocent peasants and workers, and can contemplate with equanimity, or even advocate, the use of nuclear weapons against the "hordes of Chinese coolies." I feel sure that this apparent insensitivity to the incineration of thousands of millions of our fellow human beings is not the result of feelings of savage inhumanity toward foreigners; it is the result of not thinking of them as humans at all but rather as the embodiment of doctrines that we consider evil.

There is a "strain toward consistency" which leads a country, once it has decided that another country is good or bad, peaceful or aggressive, to interpret every bit of information to fit that preconception, so much so that even a genuine concession offered by one is likely to be viewed by the other as a trick to gain some illicit advantage. A possible manifestation of this tendency is the North Vietnamese view of American proposals to negotiate peace as fraudulent plots. Having been betrayed after previous negotiations—by the French in 1946 and by Ngo Dinh Diem in 1955 when, with American complicity, he refused to allow the elections called for in the Geneva Accords to take place—the Hanoi government may now feel that American offers to negotiate peace, which Americans believe to be genuine, are in reality plots to trick them into yielding through diplomacy what we have been unable to make them yield by force.

The gap between perceptions of a situation by antagonists is widened by their tendency to break off communications with each other, which is caused in part by the fear of inadvertently "giving something away" and by fear of being thought disloyal at home—the Johns Hopkins psychiatrist Dr. Jerome Frank calls this the "traitor trap." The result of the breakoff of communications and the refusal to renew them is that hostile images are then the only ones available and hostility is perpetuated accordingly. Dr. Frank points out that one of the principal values of group therapy is that the individual patient cannot easily break off communication and is thus encouraged to persevere in his treatment. I wish that Dr. Frank and his colleagues could be engaged to conduct group therapy for the leaders of China and the United States.

Of and by itself, however, communication is of limited value; in a hostile atmosphere it may even make things worse. One psychologist, Muzafer Sherif, conducted an experiment in conflict and cooperation among eleven-year-old boys in an experimental camp. The boys were divided into two groups, the "Eagles" and the "Rattlers" and kept apart while they developed separate and cohesive customs, leadership, and organization. They were then brought together in a series of competitive activities in which victory for one side inevitably meant defeat for the other. These activities generated a high level of mutual hostility, with each group attributing self-glorifying qualities to itself and assigning traits to the other which warranted treating it as an enemy. In the next stage of the experiment an effort was made to restore peace simply by bringing the two groups together in social events. This did no good, however, because the boys used the social occasions to engage in accusations and recriminations. In the next step of the experiment, problems and crises were contrived in such a way as to affect both groups and to require collaboration between them. These "crises" included interruption of the camp water supply, the running of a food-carrying truck into a ditch and other situations which could only be dealt with by cooperative action between the two groups. The effect of these invoked collaborations was striking: hostilities soon diminished to a point where boys in each group were again choosing friends from the other.[2]

One cannot make major inferences for international relations from an experiment involving well-adjusted middle-class American boys. The experiment suggests, however, that there may be promise in such

[2]Muzafer Sherif et al., Intergroup Conflict and Cooperation: The Robbers Cave Experiment (Norman: University of Oklahoma Press, 1961).

enterprises as Soviet-American cooperation in the International Geo-physical Year and in a whole spectrum of possible activities (some to be suggested in Chapter 10) associated with the "building of bridges" between East and West.

Dr. Brock Chisholm suggests that "What we the people of the world need, perhaps most, is to exercise our imaginations, to develop our ability to look at things from outside our accidental area of being." Most of us, he says, "have never taken out our imaginations for any kind of run in all our lives," but rather have kept them tightly locked up within the limits of our own national, and ideological, perspective.[3]

The obvious value of liberating the imagination is that it might enable us to acquire some understanding of the world-view held by people whose past experiences and present circumstances and beliefs are radically different from our own. It might enable us to understand, for example, what it feels like to be hungry, not hungry in the way a middle-class American feels after a golf game or a fast tennis match, but hungry as an Asian might be hungry, with a hunger that has never been satisfied, with one's children having stunted limbs and swollen bellies, with a desire to change things that has little regard for due process of the law because the desire for change has an urgency and desperation about it that few Americans have ever experienced. Could we but liberate our imagination in this way, we might be able to see why so many people in the world are making revolutions; we might even be able to see why some of them are communists.

THE BATTLE OF THE ANTS

Henry David Thoreau

One day when I went out to my wood-pile, or rather my pile of stumps, I observed two large ants, the one red, the other much larger, nearly half an inch long, and black, fiercely contending with one another. Having once got hold they never let go, but struggled and wrestled and rolled on the chips incessantly. Looking farther, I was

Henry David Thoreau, "The Battle of the Ants." From "Brute Neighbors," Chapter XII of *Walden.*

[3] Brock Chisholm, *Prescription for Survival* (New York: Columbia University Press, 1957) p. 76.

surprised to find that the chips were covered with such combatants, that it was not a *duellum,* but a *bellum,* a war between two races of ants, the red always pitted against the black, and frequently two red ones to one black. The legions of these Myrmidons covered all the hills and vales in my wood-yard, and the ground was already strewn with the dead and dying, both red and black. It was the only battle which I have ever witnessed, the only battle-field I ever trod while the battle was raging; internecine war; the red republicans on the one hand, and the black imperialists on the other. On every side they were engaged in deadly combat, yet without any noise that I could hear, and human soldiers never fought so resolutely. I watched a couple that were fast locked in each other's embraces, in a little sunny valley amid the chips, now at noonday prepared to fight till the sun went down, or life went out. The smaller red champion had fastened himself like a vice to his adversary's front, and through all the tumblings on that field never for an instant ceased to gnaw at one of his feelers near the root, having already caused the other to go by the board; while the stronger black one dashed him from side to side, and, as I saw on looking nearer, had already divested him of several of his members. They fought with more pertinacity than bulldogs. Neither manifested the least disposition to retreat. It was evident that their battle-cry was "Conquer or die." In the meanwhile there came along a single red ant on the hillside of this valley, evidently full of excitement, who either had despatched his foe, or had not yet taken part in the battle; probably the latter, for he had lost none of his limbs; whose mother had charged him to return with his shield or upon it. Or perchance he was some Achilles, who had nourished his wrath apart, and had now come to avenge or rescue his Patroclus. He saw this unequal combat from afar—for the blacks were nearly twice the size of the red—he drew near with rapid pace till he stood on his guard within half an inch of the combatants; then, watching his opportunity, he sprang upon the black warrior, and commenced his operations near the root of his right fore leg, leaving the foe to select among his own members; and so there were three united for life, as if a new kind of attraction had been invented which put all other locks and cements to shame. I should not have wondered by this time to find that they had their respective musical bands stationed on some eminent chip, and playing their national airs the while, to excite the slow and cheer the dying combatants. I was myself excited somewhat even as if they had been men.

The more you think of it, the less the difference. And certainly there is not the fight recorded in Concord history, at least, if in the history of America, that will bear a moment's comparison with this, whether for the numbers engaged in it, or for the patriotism and heroism displayed. For numbers and for carnage it was an Austerlitz or Dresden. Concord Fight! Two killed on the patriots' side, and Luther Blanchard wounded! Why here every ant was a Buttrick—"Fire! for God's sake fire!"—and thousands shared the fate of Davis and Hosmer. There was not one hireling there. I have no doubt that it was a principle they fought for, as much as our ancestors, and not to avoid a three-penny tax on their tea; and the results of this battle will be as important and memorable to those whom it concerns as those of the battle of Bunker Hill, at least.

I took up the chip on which the three I have particularly described were struggling, carried into my house, and placed it under a tumbler on my window-sill, in order to see the issue. Holding a microscope to the first-mentioned red ant, I saw that, though he was assiduously gnawing at the near fore leg of his enemy, having severed his remaining feeler, his own breast was all torn away, exposing what vitals he had there to the jaws of the black warrior, whose breastplate was apparently too thick for him to pierce; and the dark carbuncles of the sufferer's eyes shone with ferocity such as war only could excite. They struggled half an hour longer under the tumbler, and when I looked again the black soldier had severed the heads of his foes from their bodies, and the still living heads were hanging on either side of him like ghastly trophies at his saddle-bow, still apparently as firmly fastened as ever, and he was endeavoring with feeble struggles, being without feelers, and with only the remnant of a leg, and I know not how many other wounds, to divest himself of them; which at length, after half an hour more, he accomplished. I raised the glass, and he went off over the window-sill in that crippled state. Whether he finally survived that combat, and spent the remainder of his days in some Hôtel des Invalides, I do not know; but I thought that his industry would not be worth much thereafter. I never learned which party was victorious, nor the cause of the war, but I felt for the rest of that day as if I had my feelings excited and harrowed by witnessing the struggle, the ferocity and carnage, of a human battle before my door.

Kirby and Spence tell us that the battles of ants have long been celebrated and the date of them recorded, though they say that Huber is the only modern author who appears to have witnessed them. "Aeneas Sylvius," say they, "after giving a very circumstantial account of one contested with great obstinacy by a great and small species on the trunk of a pear tree," adds that 'this action was fought in the pontificate of Eugenius the Fourth, in the presence of Nicholas Pistoriensis, an eminent lawyer, who related the whole history of the battle with the greatest fidelity.' A similar engagement between great and small ants is recorded by Olaus Magnus, in which the small ones, being victorious, are said to have buried the bodies of their own soldiers, but left those of their giant enemies a prey to the birds. This event happened previous to the expulsion of the tyrant Christiern the Second from Sweden." The battle which I witnessed took place in the Presidency of Polk, five years before the passage of Webster's Fugitive-Slave Bill.

RACISM: AFFLICTION
AND ORDEAL

INTRODUCTION

America, founded upon the concepts of liberty and equality for all men, self-proclaimed leader of the noncommunist world, enters the 1970s fully equipped to send troops into her own cities to quell insurrections mounted by citizens who have been denied the right to live in any way approximating the ideals to which America gives voice.

These disorders are merely the more visible signs of reaction against the long oppression which blacks have suffered in the United States since they first disembarked at Jamestown in August, 1619, a year before the Mayflower arrived at Plymouth. Three and one half centuries later, a nation shocked by civil disorder has come to realize with dramatic and frightening impact the accuracy of W. E. B. DuBois' prophetic statement, made in 1905, that racial conflict would be the major problem of the twentieth century.

Originally victims of kidnapping by English and Europeans, forced into an agricultural slave system, "emancipated" to become superfluous in an industrial society with increasingly less use for people with few technical skills, the mass of Negroes has been endlessly shunted from one hostile environment to another. As automation forced people off the land, the poor blacks of the rural south became the dispossessed inhabitants of the metropolitan slums.

"Racism: Affliction and Ordeal," adapted by permission from the introduction to *White Racism*, ed. Barry N. Schwartz and Robert Disch (Dell Publishing Company, Spring 1970). Used by permission of the publisher.

Consistently, the inevitable urban disorders have been attributed to the "Negro problem" or the "race problem," terms which mislead rather than illuminate, because the problem, according to the authoritative *Report of the National Advisory Commission on Civil Disorders,* is rooted in "race prejudice which has shaped our history decisively. . . . White racism is essentially responsible for the explosive mixture which has been accumulating in our cities since the end of World War II."

Because many whites have difficulty understanding and evaluating their responsibility for what often appears to be an inherited situation, they tend to judge the reactions of the victims to their plight. Rather than try to determine the causes of such chronic ghetto problems as drug addiction, high crime, unemployment, and school dropout rates, the white frequently falls back on racist interpretations of inherent inferiority or worthlessness. He tends to justify his reaction with the erroneous belief that in America anyone with get up and go can "make it," regardless of how dehumanizing his environment. Tragically, the emphasis is thus shifted away from the conditions which distort human growth, which prevent a child from becoming a healthy, independent adult, and, most significantly, away from the people and institutions which have the power to change those conditions. Hence the victim is ultimately identified as the cause of his own victimization.

This attitude, in turn, allows much of the white population to comprehend violence in urban ghettos as something produced by a criminal element in society directing its lawlessness against a peaceful, law-abiding citizenry. The more subtle violence practiced systematically against the Black American—by the slumlord, the white racist schoolteacher, the derogatory epithets, the "lily-white" concepts of beauty and acceptability produced by the mass media, and so on—have remained disastrously beyond the ken of white understanding or empathy. Consequently, the white community responds to "disorder" by treating symptoms rather than causes, by demanding more police with more freedom to use arms, by complaining about the taxes necessary to aid the ghettos, by harassing welfare clients with demoralizing regulations, by emasculating poverty programs, by voting against civilian boards for investigating police brutality. The Blacks, in turn, have come to expect not the amelioration of injustice, but more cops; not better job opportunities, but more exploitation and poverty; not fundamental change but promises and tokenism. While American blacks have watched African colonies gain independence from their colonial masters, they have become increasingly aware that a similar development has not yet taken place in America.

As the battle lines between the "two nations" are being drawn, the dangerous inaction of the present—ignoring causes, while turning the police and National Guard into an army of domestic occupation—can lead only to more violence. White Americans must gain greater awareness of the dimensions of the present crisis, for only understanding will lead to meaningful action. If not, the expectations of the Commission will indeed be grievously fulfilled: "In the summer of 1967, we have seen in our cities a chain reaction of racial violence. If we are heedless, we shall none of us escape the consequences."

RACISM AND
THE WHITE BACKLASH

Martin Luther King, Jr.

It is time for all of us to tell each other the truth about who and what have brought the Negro to the condition of deprivation against which he struggles today. In human relations the truth is hard to come by, because most groups are deceived about themselves. Rationalization and the incessant search for scapegoats are the psychological cataracts that blind us to our individual and collective sins. But the day has passed for bland euphemisms. He who lives with untruth lives in spiritual slavery. Freedom is still the bonus we receive for knowing the truth. "Ye shall know the truth, and the truth shall set you free."

It would be neither true nor honest to say that the Negro's status is what it is because he is innately inferior or because he is basically lazy and listless or because he has not sought to lift himself by his own bootstraps. To find the origins of the Negro problem we must turn to the white man's problem. As Earl Conrad says in a recent book, *The Invention of the Negro:* "I have sought out these new routes in the unshakable conviction that the question involved there cannot be and never could be answered merely by examining the Negro himself, his ghettos, his history, his personality, his culture. For the answer to how the Negro's status came to be what it is does not lie essentially in the world of the Negro, but in the world of the white." In short, white America must assume the guilt for the black man's inferior status.

Ever since the birth of our nation, white America has had a schizo-phrenic personality on the question of race. She has been torn between selves—a self in which she proudly professed the great principles of democracy and a self in which she sadly practiced the antithesis of democracy. This tragic duality has produced a strange indecisiveness and ambivalence toward the Negro, causing America to take a step backward simultaneously with every step forward on the question of racial justice, to be at once attracted to the Negro and repelled by him, to love and to hate him. There has never been a solid, unified and determined thrust to make justice a reality for Afro-Americans.

The step backward has a new name today. It is called the "white backlash." But the white backlash is nothing new. It is the surfacing of old prejudices, hostilities and ambivalences that have always been there. It was caused neither by the cry of Black Power nor by the unfortunate recent wave of riots in our cities. The white backlash of today is rooted in the same problem that has characterized America ever since the black man landed in chains on the shores of this nation. The white backlash is an expression of the same vacillations, the same search for rationalizations, the same lack of commitment that have always characterized white America on the question of race.

What is the source of this perennial indecision and vacillation? It lies in the "congenital deformity" of racism that has crippled the nation from its inception. The roots of racism are very deep in America. Historically it was so acceptable in the national life that today it still only lightly burdens the conscience. No one surveying the moral landscape of our nation can overlook the hideous and pathetic wreckage of commitment twisted and turned to a thousand shapes under the stress of prejudice and irrationality.

This does not imply that all white Americans are racists—far from it. Many white people have, through a deep moral compulsion, fought long and hard for racial justice. Nor does it mean that America has made no progress in her attempt to cure the body politic of the disease of racism, or that the dogma of racism has not been considerably modified in recent years. However, for the good of America, it is necessary to refute the idea that the dominant ideology in our country even today is freedom and equality while racism is just an occasional departure from the norm on the part of a few bigoted extremists.

What is racism? Dr. George Kelsey, in a profound book entitled *Racism and the Christian Understanding of Man,* states that:

> Racism is a faith. It is a form of idolatry. . . . In its early modern
> beginnings, racism was a justificatory device. It did not emerge as a

faith. It arose as an ideological justification for the constellations of political and economic power which were expressed in colonialism and slavery. But gradually the idea of the superior race was heightened and deepened in meaning and value so that it pointed beyond the historical structures of relation, in which it emerged, to human existence itself.

In her *Race: Science and Politics,* Ruth Benedict expands on the theme by defining racism as "the dogma that one ethnic group is condemned by nature to hereditary inferiority and another group is destined to hereditary superiority. It is the dogma that the hope of civilization depends upon eliminating some races and keeping others pure. It is the dogma that one race has carried progress throughout human history and can alone ensure future progress."

Since racism is based on the dogma "that the hope of civilization depends upon eliminating some races and keeping others pure," its ultimate logic is genocide. Hitler, in his mad and ruthless attempt to exterminate the Jews, carried the logic of racism to its ultimate tragic conclusions. While America has not literally sought to eliminate the Negro in this final sense, it has, through the system of segregation, substituted a subtle reduction of life by means of deprivation.

If a man asserts that another man, because of his race, is not good enough to have a job equal to his, or to eat at a lunch counter next to him, or to have access to certain hotels, or to attend school with him, or to live next door to him, he is by implication affirming that that man does not deserve to exist. He does not deserve to exist because his existence is corrupt and defective.

Racism is a philosophy based on a contempt for life. It is the arrogant assertion that one race is the center of value and object of devotion, before which other races must kneel in submission. It is the absurd dogma that one race is responsible for all the progress of history and alone can assure the progress of the future. Racism is total estrangement. It separates not only bodies, but minds and spirits. Inevitably it descends to inflicting spiritual or physical homicide upon the out-group.

Of the two dominant and contradictory strains in the American psyche, the positive one, our democratic heritage, was the later development on the American continent. Democracy, born in the eighteenth century, took from John Locke of England the theory of natural rights and the justification of revolution and imbued it with the ideal of a society governed by the people. When Jefferson wrote the Declaration of Independence, the first government of the world to be based on these principles was established on American soil. A contemporary description of Benjamin Franklin might have described the new nation: "He has torn lightning from the sky; soon he will tear their sceptres from the kings." And Thomas Paine in his enthusiasm declared, "We have the power to begin the world over again."

Yet even amid these electrifying expressions of the rights of man, racism—the myth of inferior peoples—was flourishing here to contradict and qualify the democratic ideal. Slavery was not only ignored in defining democracy, but its enlargement was tolerated in the interests of strengthening the nation.

For more than two hundred years before the Declaration of Independence, Africa had been raped and plundered by Britain and Europe, her native kingdoms disorganized, and her people and rulers demoralized. For a hundred years afterward, the infamous trade continued in America virtually without abatement, even after it had ceased to be legal on this continent.

In fact, this ghastly blood traffic was so immense and its profits were so stupendous that the economies of several European nations owed their growth and prosperity to it and New England rested heavily on it for its development. Beard declared it was fair to say of whole towns in New England and Great Britain: "The stones of your houses are cemented with the blood of African slaves." Conservatively estimated, several million Africans died in the calloused transfer of human merchandise to the New World alone.

It is important to understand that the basis for the birth, growth and development of slavery in America was primarily economic. By the beginning of the seventeenth century, the British Empire had established colonies all along the Atlantic seaboard from Massachusetts to the West Indies to serve as producers of raw materials for British manufacturing, a market for goods manufactured in Britain, and a source of staple cargoes for British shipping engaged in world trade. So the colonies had to provide an abundance of rice, sugar, cotton and tobacco. In the first few years of the various settlements along the East Coast, so-called indentured servants, mostly white, were employed on plantations. But within a generation the plantation operators were demanding outright and lifetime slavery for the Africans they imported. As a function of this new economic policy, Africans were reduced to the status of property by law, and this status was enforced by the most rigid and brutal police power of the existing governments. By 1650 slavery had been legally established as a national institution.

Since the institution of slavery was so important to the economic development of America, it had a profound impact in shaping the social-political-legal structure of the nation. Land and slaves were the chief forms of private property, property was wealth and the voice of wealth made the law and determined politics. In the service of this system, human beings were reduced to propertyless property. Black men, the creators of the wealth of the New World, were stripped of all human and civil rights. And this degradation was sanctioned and protected by institutions of government, all for one purpose: to produce commodities for sale at a profit, which in turn would be privately appropriated.

It seems to be a fact of life that human beings cannot continue to do wrong without eventually reaching out for some rationalization to clothe their acts in the garments of righteousness. And so, with the growth of slavery, men had to convince themselves that a system which was so economically profitable was morally justifiable. The attempt to give moral sanction to a profitable system gave birth to the doctrine of white supremacy.

Religion and the Bible were cited and distorted to support the status quo. It was argued that the Negro was inferior by nature because of Noah's curse upon the children of Ham. The Apostle Paul's dictum became a watchword: "Servant, be obedient to your master." In this strange way theology became a ready ally of commerce. The great Puritan divine Cotton Mather culled the Bible for passages to give comfort to the plantation owners and merchants. He went so far as to set up some "Rules for the Society of Negroes," in which, among other things, Negroes disobedient to their masters were to be rebuked and denied attendance at church meetings, and runaway slaves were to be brought back and severely punished. All of this, he reasoned, was in line with the Apostle Paul's injunction that servants should be obedient to their masters.

Logic was manipulated to give intellectual credence to the system of slavery. Someone formulated the argument for the inferiority of the Negro in the shape of a syllogism:

> All men are made in the image of God; God, as everybody knows, is not a Negro; Therefore the Negro is not a man.

Academicians eventually climbed on the bandwagon and gave their prestige to the myth of the superior race. Their contribution came through the so-called Teutonic Origins theory, a doctrine of white supremacy surrounded by the halo of academic respectability. The theorists of this concept argued that all Anglo-Saxon institutions of any worth had their historical roots in the Teutonic tribal institutions of ancient Germany, and furthermore that "only the Teutonic race had been imbued with the ability to build stable governments." Historians from the lofty academic towers of Oxford, like Bishop William Stubbs and Edward A. Freeman, expounded the Teutonic Origins theory in British intellectual circles. It leaped the Atlantic and found lodging in the mind of Herbert Baxter Adams, one of the organizers of the graduate school at Johns Hopkins University and founder of the American Historical Association. He expanded Freeman's views by asserting that the Teutonic Origins theory really had "three homes—England, Germany and the United States." Pretty soon this distorted theory dominated the thinking of American historians at leading universities like Harvard, Cornell, Wisconsin and Columbia.

Even natural science, that discipline committed to the inductive method, creative appraisal and detached objectivity, was invoked and distorted to give credence to a political position. A whole school of racial ethnologists developed using such terms as "species," "genus" and "race." It became fashionable to think of the slave as a "species of property." It was during this period that the word "race" came into fashion.

Dr. Samuel G. Morton, a Philadelphia physician, emerged with the head-size theory which affirmed that the larger the skull, the superior the individual. This theory was used by other ethnologists to prove that the large head size of Caucasians signified more intellectual capacity and more native worth. A Dr. Josiah C. Nott, in his *Collections on the Natural History of the Caucasian and Negro Races,* used pseudo-scientific evidence to prove that the black man was little above the level of an ape. A Frenchman, Count Arthur de Gobineau, in his book *The Inequality of the Human Races,* vigorously defended the theory of the inferiority of the black man and used the experience of the United States as his prime source of evidence. It was this kind of "science" that pervaded the atmosphere in the nineteenth century, and these pseudo scientists became the authoritative references for any and all seeking rationalization for the system of slavery.

Generally we think of white supremacist views as having their origins with the unlettered, underprivileged, poorer-class whites. But the social obstetricians who presided at the birth of racist views in our country were from the aristocracy: rich merchants, influential clergymen, men of medical science, historians and political scientists from some of the leading universities of the nation. With such a distinguished company of the elite working so assiduously to dis-

seminate racist views, what was there to inspire poor, illiterate, unskilled white farmers to think otherwise?

Soon the doctrine of white supremacy was imbedded in every text-
book and preached in practically every pulpit. It became a structural
part of the culture. And men then embraced this philosophy, not as
the rationalization of a lie, but as the expression of a final truth. In
1857 the system of slavery was given its ultimate legal support by the
Supreme Court of the United States in the Dred Scott decision, which
affirmed that the Negro had no rights that the white man was bound
to respect.

The greatest blasphemy of the whole ugly process was that the
white man ended up making God his partner in the exploitation of the
Negro. What greater heresy has religion known? Ethical Christianity
vanished and the moral nerve of religion was atrophied. This terrible
distortion sullied the essential nature of Christianity.

Virtually all of the Founding Fathers of our nation, even those who
rose to the heights of the Presidency, those whom we cherish as our
authentic heroes, were so enmeshed in the ethos of slavery and white
supremacy that not one ever emerged with a clear, unambiguous stand
on Negro rights. No human being is perfect. In our individual and
collective lives every expression of greatness is followed, not by a
period symbolizing completeness, but by a comma implying partial-
ness. Following every affirmation of greatness is the conjunction
"but." Naaman "was a great man," says the Old Testament, "but
. . . "—that "but" reveals something tragic and disturbing—"but he
was a leper." George Washington, Thomas Jefferson, Patrick Henry,
John Quincy Adams, John Calhoun and Abraham Lincoln were great
men, but—that "but" underscores the fact that not one of these men
had a strong, unequivocal belief in the equality of the black man.

No one doubts the valor and commitment that characterized
George Washington's life. But to the end of his days he maintained
a posture of exclusionism toward the slave. He was a fourth-genera-
tion slaveholder. He only allowed Negroes to enter the Continental
Army because His Majesty's Crown was attempting to recruit
Negroes to the British cause. Washington was not without his moments of torment, those moments of conscience when something
within told him that slavery was wrong. As he searched the future of
America one day, he wrote to his nephew: "I wish from my soul that
the legislature of this State could see the policy of gradual abolition
of slavery. It might prevent much future mischief." In spite of this,
Washington never made a public statement condemning slavery. He

could not pull away from the system. When he died he owned, or had on lease, more than 160 slaves.

Here, in the life of the father of our nation, we can see the developing dilemma of white America: the haunting ambivalence, the intellectual and moral recognition that slavery is wrong, but the emotional tie to the system so deep and pervasive that it imposes an inflexible unwillingness to root it out.

Thomas Jefferson reveals the same ambivalence. There is much in the life of Jefferson that can serve as a model for political leaders in every age; he came close to the ideal "philosopher-king" that Plato dreamed of centuries ago. But in spite of this, Jefferson was a child of his culture who had been influenced by the pseudo-scientific and philosophical thought that rationalized slavery. In his *Notes on Virginia,* Jefferson portrayed the Negro as inferior to the white man in his endowments of body, mind and imagination, although he observed that the Negro appeared to be superior at picking out tunes on the "banjar." Jefferson's majestic words, "all men are created equal," meant for him, as for many others, that all *white* men are created equal.

Yet in his heart Jefferson knew that slavery was wrong and that it degraded the white man's mind and soul. In the same *Notes on Virginia* he wrote: "For if a slave can have a country in this world, it must be any other in preference to that in which he is born to live and labor for another. . . . Indeed I tremble for my country when I reflect that God is just, that his justice cannot sleep forever . . . the Almighty has no attribute which can take sides with us in such a contest." And in 1820, six years before his death, he wrote these melancholy words: "But the momentous question [slavery] like a fire-bell in the night, awakened and filled me with terror. I considered it at once as the knell of the Union. . . . I regret that I am now to die in the belief that the useless sacrifice of themselves by the generation of 1776, to acquire self-government and happiness to their country, is to be thrown away by the unwise and unworthy passion of their sons, and that my only consolation is to be that I live not to weep over it."

This strange duality toward the Negro and slavery vexed the mind of Abraham Lincoln for years. Few men in history have anchored their lives more deeply in moral convictions than Abraham Lincoln, but on the question of slavery Lincoln's torments and vacillations were tenacious.

As early as 1837, as a State Legislator, Lincoln referred to the injustice and impracticality of slavery. Later he wrote of the physical differences between blacks and whites and made it clear that he felt whites were superior. At times he concluded that the white man could not live with the Negro. This accounted for his conviction that the only answer to the problem was to colonize the black man—send him back to Africa, or to the West Indies or some other isolated spot. This view was still in his mind toward the height of the Civil War. Delegation after delegation—the Quakers above all, great abolitionists like Charles Sumner, Horace Greeeley and William Lloyd Garrison— pleaded with Lincoln to free the slaves, but he was firm in his resistance. Frederick Douglass, a Negro of towering grandeur, sound judgment and militant initiative, sought, without success, to persuade Lincoln that slavery, not merely the preservation of the union, was at the root of the war. At the time, Lincoln could not yet see it.

A civil war raged within Lincoln's own soul, a tension between the Dr. Jekyll of freedom and the Mr. Hyde of slavery, a struggle like that of Plato's charioteer with two headstrong horses each pulling in different directions. Morally Lincoln was for black emancipation, but emotionally, like most of his white contemporaries, he was for a long time unable to act in accordance with his conscience.

But Lincoln was basically honest and willing to admit his confusions. He saw that the nation could not survive half slave and half free; and he said, "If we could first know where we are and whither we are tending, we could better judge what to do and how to do it." Fortunately for the nation, he finally came to see "whither we were tending." On January 1, 1863, he issued the Emancipation Proclamation, freeing the Negro from the bondage of chattel slavery. By this concrete act of courage his reservations of the past were overshadowed. The conclusion of his search is embodied in these words: "In giving freedom to the slave, we assure freedom to the free,—honourable alike in what we give and what we preserve."

The significance of the Emancipation Proclamation was described by Frederick Douglass in these words:

> Unquestionably, for weal or for woe, the First of January is to be the most memorable day in American Annals. The Fourth of July was great, but the First of January, when we consider it in all its relations and bearings, is incomparably greater. The one had respect to the mere political birth of a nation; the last concerns the national life and character, and is to determine whether that life and character shall be radiantly glorious with all high and noble virtues, or infamously blackened, forevermore. . . . [1]

[1] *Douglass Monthly,* Jan. 1863.

But underneath, the ambivalence of white America toward the Negro still lurked with painful persistence. With all the beautiful promise that Douglass saw in the Emancipation Proclamation, he soon found that it left the Negro with only abstract freedom. Four million newly liberated slaves found themselves with no bread to eat, no land to cultivate, no shelter to cover their heads. It was like freeing a man who had been unjustly imprisoned for years, and on discovering his innocence sending him out with no bus fare to get home, no suit to cover his body, no financial compensation to atone for his long years of incarceration and to help him get a sound footing in society; sending him out with only the assertion: "Now you are free." What greater injustice could society perpetrate? All the moral voices of the universe, all the codes of sound jurisprudence, would rise up with condemnation at such an act. Yet this is exactly what America did to the Negro. In 1863 the Negro was given abstract freedom expressed in luminous rhetoric. But in an agrarian economy he was given no land to make liberation concrete. After the war the government granted white settlers, without cost, millions of acres of land in the West, thus providing America's new white peasants from Europe with an economic floor. But at the same time its oldest peasantry, the Negro, was denied everything but a legal status he could not use, could not consolidate, could not even defend. As Frederick Douglass came to say, "Emancipation granted the Negro freedom to hunger, freedom to winter amid the rains of heaven. Emancipation was freedom and famine at the same time."

The inscription on the Statue of Liberty refers to America as the "mother of exiles." The tragedy is that while America became the mother of her white exiles, she evinced no motherly concern or love for her exiles from Africa. It is no wonder that out of despair and estrangement the Negro cries out in one of his sorrow songs: "Sometimes I feel like a motherless child." The marvel is, as Frederick Douglass once said, that Negroes are still alive.

In dealing with the ambivalence of white America, we must not overlook another form of racism that was relentlessly pursued on American shores: the physical extermination of the American Indian. The South American example of absorbing the indigenous Indian population was ignored in the United States, and systematic destruction of a whole people was undertaken. The common phrase, "The only good Indian is a dead Indian," was virtually elevated to national policy. Thus the poisoning of the American mind was accomplished not only by acts of discrimination and exploitation but by the exaltation of murder as an expression of the courage and initiative of the pioneer. Just as Southern culture was made to appear noble by ignoring the cruelty of slavery, the conquest of the Indian was depicted as an example of bravery and progress.

Thus through two centuries a continuous indoctrination of Americans has separated people according to mythically superior and inferior qualities while a democratic spirit of equality was evoked as the national ideal. These concepts of racism, and this schizophrenic duality of conduct, remain deeply rooted in American thought today. This tendency of the nation to take one step forward on the question of racial justice and then to take a step backward is still the pattern. Just as an ambivalent nation freed the slaves a century ago with no plan or program to make their freedom meaningful, the still ambivalent nation in 1954 declared school segregation unconstitutional with no plan or program to make integration real. Just as the Congress passed a civil rights bill in 1868 and refused to enforce it, the Congress passed a civil rights bill in 1964 and to this day has failed to enforce it in all its dimensions. Just as the Fifteenth Amendment in 1870 proclaimed Negro sufferage, only to permit its *de facto* withdrawal in half the nation, so in 1965 the Voting Rights Law was passed and then permitted to languish with only fractional and half-hearted implementation.

The civil rights measures of the 1960's engraved solemn rights in the legal literature. But after writing piecemeal and incomplete legislation and proclaiming its historic importance in magnificent prose, the American Government left the Negro to make the unworkable work. Against entrenched segregationist state power, with almost total dependence economically on those they had to contend with, and without political experience, the impoverished Negro was expected to usher in an era of freedom and plenty.

When the war against poverty came into being in 1964, it seemed to herald a new day of compassion. It was the bold assertion that the nation would no longer stand complacently by while millions of its citizens smothered in poverty in the midst of opulence. But it did not take long to discover that the government was only willing to appropriate such a limited budget that it could not launch a good skirmish against poverty, much less a full-scale war.

Moreover, the poverty program, which in concept elated the Negro poor, became so embroiled in political turmoil that its insufficiencies were magnified and its operations paralyzed. Big-city machines felt threatened by it and small towns, especially in the South, directed it away from Negroes. Its good intentions and limited objectives were frustrated by the skillful maneuvers of experienced politicians. The worst effect of these manipulations was to cast doubt upon the program as a whole and discredit those Negroes involved directly in its administration.

In 1965 the President presented a new plan to Congress—which it finally passed in 1966—for rebuilding entire slum neighborhoods. With other elements of the program it would, in his words, make the decaying cities of the present into "the masterpieces of our civilization." This Demonstration Cities plan is imaginative; it embodies social vision and properly defines racial discrimination as a central evil. However, the ordinary Negro, though no social or political analyst, will be skeptical. He will be skeptical, first because of the insufficient funds assigned to the program. He will be skeptical, second, because he knows how many laws exist in Northern states and cities prohibiting discrimination in housing, in education and in employment; he knows how many overlapping commissions exist to enforce the terms of these laws—and he knows how he lives. The ubiquitous discrimination in his daily life tells him that laws on paper, no matter how imposing their terms, will not guarantee that he will live in "the masterpiece of civilization."

Throughout our history, laws affirming Negro rights have consistently been circumvented by ingenious evasions which render them void in practice. Laws that affect the whole population—draft laws, income-tax laws, traffic laws—manage to work even though they may be unpopular; but laws passed for the Negro's benefit are so widely unenforced that it is a mockery to call them laws. There is a tragic gulf between civil rights laws passed and civil rights laws implemented. There is a double standard in the enforcement of law and a double standard in the respect for particular laws.

All of this tells us that the white backlash is nothing new. White America has been backlashing on the fundamental God-given and human rights of Negro Americans for more than three hundred years. With all of her dazzling achievements and stupendous material strides, America has maintained its strange ambivalence on the question of racial justice.

THE ETHICS OF LIVING JIM CROW:
AN AUTOBIOGRAPHICAL SKETCH

Richard Wright

My first lesson in how to live as a Negro came when I was quite small. We were living in Arkansas. Our house stood behind the railroad tracks. Its skimpy yard was paved with black cinders. Nothing green ever grew in that yard. The only touch of green we could see was far away, beyond the tracks, over where the white folks lived. But cinders were good enough for me and I never missed the green growing things. And anyhow cinders were fine weapons. You could always have a nice hot war with huge black cinders. All you had to do was crouch behind the brick pillars of a house with your hands full of gritty ammunition. And the first woolly black head you saw pop out from behind another row of pillars was your target. You tried your very best to knock it off. It was great fun.

I never fully realized the appalling disadvantages of a cinder environment till one day the gang to which I belonged found itself engaged in a war with the white boys who lived beyond the tracks. As usual we laid down our cinder barrage, thinking that this would wipe the white boys out. But they replied with a steady bombardment of broken bottles. We doubled our cinder barrage, but they hid behind trees, hedges, and the sloping embankments of their lawns. Having no such fortifications, we retreated to the brick pillars of our homes. During the retreat a broken milk bottle caught me behind the ear, opening a deep gash which bled profusely. The sight of blood pouring over my face completely demoralized our ranks. My fellow-combatants left me standing paralyzed in the center of the yard, and scurried for their homes. A kind neighbor saw me and rushed me to a doctor, who took three stitches in my neck.

I sat brooding on my front steps, nursing my wound and waiting for my mother to come from work, I felt that a grave injustice had been done me. It was all right to throw cinders. The greatest harm a cinder could do was leave a bruise. But broken bottles were dangerous; they left you cut, bleeding, and helpless.

When night fell, my mother came from the white folks' kitchen. I raced down the street to meet her, I could just feel in my bones that

Richard Wright, "The Ethics of Living Jim Crow" from *Uncle Tom's Children* by Richard Wright. Copyright 1937 by the author. Reprinted by permission of Harper & Row, Publishers.

she would understand. I knew she would tell me exactly what to do
next time. I grabbed her hand and babbled out the whole story. She
examined my wound, then slapped me.

"How come yuh didn't hide?" she asked me. "How come yuh
awways fightin'?"

I was outraged, and bawled. Between sobs I told her that I didn't
have any trees or hedges to hide behind. There wasn't a thing I could
have used as a trench. And you couldn't throw very far when you were
hiding behind the brick pillars of a house. She grabbed a barrel stave,
dragged me home, stripped me naked, and beat me till I had a fever
of one hundred and two. She would smack my rump with the stave,
and, while the skin was still smarting, impart to me gems of Jim Crow
wisdom. I was never to throw cinders any more. I was never to fight
any more wars. I was, never, under any conditions, to fight *white* folks
again. And they were absolutely right in clouting me with the broken
milk bottle. Didn't I know she was working hard every day in the hot
kitchens of the white folks to make money to take care of me? When
was I ever going to learn to be a good boy? She couldn't be bothered
with my fights. She finished by telling me that I ought to be thankful
to God as long as I lived that they didn't kill me.

All that night I was delirious and could not sleep. Each time I
closed my eyes I saw monstrous white faces suspended from the
ceiling, leering at me.

From that time on, the charm of my cinder yard was gone. The
green trees, the trimmed hedges, the cropped lawns grew very meaningful, became a symbol. Even today when I think of white folks, the
hard, sharp outlines of white houses surrounded by trees, lawns, and
hedges are present somewhere in the background of my mind.
Through the years they grew into an overreaching symbol of fear.

It was a long time before I came in close contact with white folks
again. We moved from Arkansas to Mississippi. Here we had the good
fortune not to live behind the railroad tracks, or close to white neighborhoods. We lived in the very heart of the local Black Belt. There
were black churches and black preachers; there were black schools
and black teachers; black groceries and black clerks. In fact, everything was so solidly black that for a long time I did not even think of
white folks, save in remote and vague terms. But this could not last
forever. As one grows older one eats more. One's clothing costs more.
When I finished grammar school I had to go to work. My mother could
no longer feed and clothe me on her cooking job.

There is but one place where a black boy who knows no trade can get a job, and that's where the houses and faces are white, where the trees, lawns, and hedges are green. My first job was with an optical company in Jackson, Mississippi. The morning I applied I stood straight and neat before the boss, answering all his questions with sharp yessirs and nosirs. I was very careful to pronounce my *sirs* distinctly, in order that he might know that I was polite, that I knew where I was, and that I knew he was a *white* man. I wanted that job badly.

He looked me over as though he were examining a prize poodle. He questioned me closely about my schooling, being particularly insistent about how much mathematics I had had. He seemed very pleased when I told him I had had two years of algebra.

"Boy, how would you like to try to learn something around here?" he asked me.

"I'd like it fine, sir," I said, happy. I had visions of "working my way up." Even Negroes have those visions.

"All right," he said. "Come on."

I followed him to the small factory.

"Pease," he said to a white man of about thirty-five, "this is Richard. He's going to work for us."

Pease looked at me and nodded.

I was then taken to a white boy of about seventeen.

"Morrie, this is Richard, who's going to work for us."

"Whut yuh sayin' there, boy!" Morrie boomed at me.

"Fine!" I answered.

The boss instructed these two to help me, teach me, give me jobs to do, and let me learn what I could in my spare time.

My wages were five dollars a week.

I worked hard, trying to please. For the first month I got along O.K. Both Pease and Morrie seemed to like me. But one thing was missing. And I kept thinking about it. I was not learning anything and nobody was volunteering to help me. Thinking they had forgotten that I was to learn something about the mechanics of grinding lenses, I asked Morrie one day to tell me about the work. He grew red.

"What yuh tryin' t' do, nigger, get smart?" he asked.

"Naw, I ain't tryin' t' git smart," I said.

"Well, don't, if yuh know whut's good for yuh!"

I was puzzled. Maybe he just doesn't want to help me, I thought. I went to Pease.

"Say, are yuh crazy, you black bastard?" Pease asked me, his gray eyes growing hard.

I spoke out, reminding him that the boss had said I was to be given a chance to learn something.

"Nigger, you think you're *white,* don't you?"

"Naw, sir!"

"Well, you're acting mighty like it!"

"But, Mr. Pease, the boss said . . . "

Pease shook his fist in my face.

"This is a *white* man's work around here, and you better watch yourself!"

From then on they changed toward me. They said good-morning no more. When I was just a bit slow in performing some duty, I was called a lazy black son-of-a-bitch.

Once I thought of reporting all this to the boss. But the mere idea of what would happen to me if Pease and Morrie should learn that I had "snitched" stopped me. And after all the boss was a white man, too. What was the use?

The climax came at noon one summer day. Pease called me to his work-bench. To get to him I had to go between two narrow benches and stand with my back against a wall.

"Yes, sir," I said.

"Richard, I want to ask you something," Pease began pleasantly, not looking up from his work.

"Yes, sir," I said again.

Morrie came over, blocking the narrow passage between the benches. He folded his arms, staring at me solemnly.

I looked from one to the other, sensing that something was coming.

"Yes, sir," I said for the third time.

Pease looked up and spoke very slowly.

"Richard, *Mr.* Morrie here tells me you called me *Pease.*"

I stiffened. A void seemed to open up in me. I knew this was the show-down.

He meant that I had failed to call him Mr. Pease. I looked at Morrie. He was gripping a steel bar in his hands. I opened my mouth to speak, to protest, to assure Pease that I had never called him simply *Pease,* and that I had never had any intentions of doing so, when Morrie grabbed me by the collar, ramming my head against the wall.

"Now, be careful, nigger!" snarled Morrie, baring his teeth. "*I* heard yuh call 'im *Pease!* 'N' if yuh say yuh didn't, yuh're callin' me a *lie,* see?" He waved the steel bar threateningly.

If I had said: No, sir, Mr. Pease, I never called you *Pease,* I would have been automatically calling Morrie a liar. And if I had said: Yes,

sir, Mr. Pease, I called you *Pease,* I would have been pleading guilty
to having uttered the worst insult that a Negro can utter to a southern
white man. I stood hesitating, trying to frame a neutral reply.

"Richard, I asked you a question!" said Pease. Anger was creeping
into his voice.

"I don't remember calling you *Pease,* Mr. Pease," I said cautiously.
"And if I did, I sure didn't mean . . . "

"You black son-of-a-bitch! You called me *Pease,* then!" he spat,
slapping me till I bent sideways over a bench. Morrie was on top of
me, demanding:

"Didn't yuh call 'im *Pease?* If yuh say yuh didn't, I'll rip yo' gut
string loose with this bar, yuh black granny dodger! Yuh can't call a
white man a lie 'n' git erway with it, you black son-of-a-bitch!"

I wilted. I begged them not to bother me. I knew what they wanted.
They wanted me to leave.

"I'll leave," I promised. "I'll leave right *now.*"

They gave me a minute to get out of the factory. I was warned not
to show up again, or tell the boss.

I went.

When I told the folks at home what had happened, they called me
a fool. They told me that I must never again attempt to exceed my
boundaries. When you are working for white folks, they said, you got
to "stay in your place" if you want to keep working.

ESAU AND JACOB: AN ALABAMA DOCTOR

Robert Coles

I first met James Butler at a medical conference in Birmingham. He
is one of the city's leading citizens as well as a doctor interested in the
quality of the city's medical and psychiatric services. That day a
number of public health officials were discussing the grossly inadequate pediatric care received by poor children, and James Butler was
there to hear what they said, to offer to do what he could.

On initial acquaintance he is a quiet, serious man. I remember his
shyness when I first met him, and his unassuming, almost deferential

Robert Coles, "Esau and Jacob: An Alabama Doctor." From *The Children Of Crisis,* by Robert
Coles, pp. 268–74. Copyright © 1964, 1965, 1966, 1967, by the author. Reprinted by permission
of Atlantic Little, Brown, and Co., Boston, Mass.

manner. In time—we talked at monthly intervals for three years—I came to appreciate how genuinely he stood in awe of people: "I grew up almost in seclusion. We lived on a large estate, and for most of my childhood the only people I knew besides my parents and my brother were the Negroes. Later I was tutored for a long while—my parents thought it the best and 'least hazardous' way to learn. What they meant by hazardous was any significant exposure to the outside world. There weren't many private schools in the South, and public school —as my mother used to put it—'meant risks.'

"She wanted us to keep our own company. We were aristocrats, I'll have to admit it, not fading but in full bloom. Our family tree is well sprinkled with governors, senators, Confederate generals, and in the beginning what we call 'tidewater Virginia names.' My father didn't sit back thinking about the past though. He was a very successful businessman and lawyer—an industrialist I guess he'd be called today in the North. We still don't use the word much down here. We've never had enough industry to make us give a special name to the owners.

"Every day my father would be driven off to work, and I recall that about the time he left the tutors would arrive for me and my brother. My brother was two years older than me, and very bright. Often his teacher and mine would combine us into a foursome for certain subjects like geography or history. Even then my brother wanted to be a teacher and a lawyer, both; only he thought a choice had to be made. Now he's a professor of law and a determined segregationist. We get along, but never discuss race.

"When we were children we loved Negroes, that's the only word that does justice to our feelings. They took care of us, and they loved us, too. I can remember every one of them the way you can with people in your childhood. Especially Ruth: she was our mother, really. I found that out when I was psychoanalyzed."

He had been psychoanalyzed when he was thirty-five, and one of the public changes in his life had to do with what he learned about his feelings toward Ruth. He became increasingly concerned with the Negro's condition in Alabama after he learned how much Ruth had meant to him as a child.

"I knew she had taken care of me. I even used to say rather casually that she brought me up. What I had to forget was how much love she had given me, and how much love I felt toward her. When I finally was able to see that, I tried to talk to my brother about it. That was a mistake. He flew into a rage. He told me I was coming out with nonsense, crazy nonsense it was. I could tell by his excitement that I had hit upon a sensitive nerve, but I also realized it was foolish of me—and maybe mean—to expect him to understand in a moment what had taken months for me finally to see and, more important, *appreciate.*"

From the beginning he told me how painfully alienated he and his brother had become, as a result of the very psychiatric treatment that had enabled him to feel closer to his brother.

"One part of my analysis helped me to relax with my brother and get over the tension and rivalry I used to feel when I was with him; but the more I began to change my racial attitudes—also because of the analysis—the worse he and I got along. For a while it was as if our old antagonism was shifting to a new level of expression, centered on race. I told the doctor that I wasn't getting over anything; I was switching the subject of the argument, not stopping the argument."

Apparently the doctor agreed with his patient's appraisal for a time, but then changed his mind.

"He said it was my brother's problem, not mine. I was trying to be as friendly as I could with my brother, but he couldn't take either that or my racial views—it's hard to know which of the two bothered him more, my new warmth toward him, or my talk about the Negro's right to vote or his need for social justice."

When I met James Butler he and his brother had already agreed upon a truce: they would be friendly to one another, but avoid any discussion of politics and race—the two being inextricably bound in the Alabama of the 1960's. It was a truce that was agreed upon before a war.

"In 1958 I wrote a letter to the Birmingham papers, saying that as a doctor I felt an obligation to *all* people, and as a citizen I could feel no different. I never once used the word Negro—here in the South there's no need for that. I said 'all people' and the message was clear. I was Birmingham's 'citizen of the year' then, and I thought it was an appropriate time to talk about the rights of citizens, all citizens, under the law.

"Frankly, I never expected what happened. You might have thought I was talking treason, the way people reacted. We were almost overwhelmed with telephone calls and letters, almost all of them telling me I was a Communist, a spy, a traitor. I was threatened with death so many times that I began to take it all as a joke, until one night someone shot into our living room. No one was hurt, but our window was shattered, and a bullet lodged in the wall, right near a portrait of my grandfather. (He fought the Klan in Alabama, but he also despised the Yankees who said we don't treat colored people right.)

"One day—I'll never forget it—the mailman came to the door because there were too many letters for our box. We had known one another for years, and liked one another, too. He looked at me as I took all those angry postcards and notes in my hands, and then he couldn't resist saying something: 'Dr. Butler, you never should have done it, never. People can't say those things you said in public. I agree with you, but I couldn't say it out loud—not even at home, I couldn't. One of my children might go repeating it, outside, and then I'd be in for it, too.'

"He was trying to console me, but he helped me in another way. I suddenly realized that it wasn't just the Negro whose freedom is unfairly restricted, but mine, and the mailman's, both of us white. I told my wife that and she agreed, but she also felt I was getting myself into more trouble than she or I or anyone else in Alabama could take. There were our three children, the rest of our family and our friends, and my work. One mistake was enough to jeopardize everything; a second one, showing that I really *meant* what I said, would ruin everything. As one of the threatening letters said: 'You may have just forgot yourself or been confused. For your sake, we hope so.'

"Actually, I never did repeat myself so openly. I had to decide how I would handle my own opposition to segregation, and for me it involved weighing a lot of things carefully, and taking each step as if I were on a tightrope—as I was. My wife agreed with my views, but worried about the children. The children were young—in 1958 they were twelve, ten and six. Of course they agree with me, but they had their friends and classmates and teacher to contend with. Then, I had my parents to worry about. They are still alive, in their eighties. My father didn't fight the Klan to achieve integration. He simply disliked violence done by whites. In Negroes he condones anything—murder, rape, robbery. He is a racist, you see, like most everybody of his generation was; and I regret to say my generation, too—in Alabama."

Since 1961 I have watched James Butler risk his comfort, his reputation, his family's security, even his life (if those who threatened him with death were to be believed) for the sake of one integrationist effort after another. Yet, at all times he was discreet enough to avoid the notoriety of outright identification as a "race mixer," a term of special condemnation reserved for more outspoken whites. Between 1960 and 1964, as Alabama increasingly had to accept at least a token of desegregation, he never signed public petitions urging compliance with federal law. Nor did he go to any interracial meetings, often enough watched by police and threatened by Klansmen.

"I wasn't afraid for my life; it was my *way* of life I tried to keep going. I did keep it going, too—until the worst was over. I took my particular stand, my risks, when it was much safer to do so; and yet I suffered more than I ever expected."

In 1965, after the Civil Rights Bill was passed, he took the lead in suggesting that the two hospitals on whose staff he served desegregate their facilities. He also publicly signed a statement of support for the new federal law—it was now the law of Congress, not the Supreme Court—and he agreed to serve on the board of a human relations council. (As he put it, "in the South that is a polite way of describing the goals of a group devoted either to desegregation or integration.")

He became ostracized. His true colors were emerging to people who had suspected them all along. Among those people he found his brother, his cousins, his friends, and most of the doctors with whom he worked every day.

"I became a radical to people hungry for one. In a way I think they were very grateful to me. It can be a relief to find a real human object for all your hates and fears. The Communists under the bed, in the shadows, up in New York and abroad stop satisfying even the most paranoid person's sense of reality after a while.

"The worst part of it was my brother's reaction. We were never exceptionally close, but neither were we unfriendly. The strangest part of all this is that I was our Negro nurse's favorite, and only realized that fact during my analysis. Our mother was very fair—impartial, really—with us, the way a mother can be when she doesn't have to sweat out the everyday tensions of her children. The nurse was really our mother, until we were sent off to school after twelve. Naturally, my brother went to school first, being older. He would come home on holidays full of jokes about niggers, how stupid they are, and animal-like. I never connected his attitude then with the fact that I was alone with Ruth, and he away from her. In his heart he must have felt the way I did when I finally did leave—homesick, and more for our nurse Ruth and handyman John than either of us dared admit to ourselves, let alone anyone else.

"When my brother became so angry at me, and started calling me a 'god-damned nigger lover,' I asked him why he was so excited, just because—in 1964, mind you—I was advocating what the United States Congress had long since proclaimed to be the law. He said I'd always been 'soft on niggers,' and I had a stubborn anti-Southern streak in me, and maybe I should go North where I seemed to belong. I couldn't get him to talk any more rationally than that, and he is a lawyer, an Ivy League-trained lawyer.

"One of the advantages of psychoanalysis is the vision into yourself and others you *keep*, not simply catch for a year or two, then forget. I'm not saying that people like my brother and me take sides on the race issue because we had different childhood experiences with Negroes. It's not as simple as that, or complicated. (What can be harder to determine than the real truth about a person's early years?) A lot of us in Alabama shout at niggers because we're afraid *not* to shout, or because it's like owning a car or a house or something: you feel you're *somebody* when you can do it, or join others who are doing it.

"But there are choices, even here, even in a closed society, and especially among the well-to-do. That's where I think individual psychology comes into the picture. Some people hate Negroes the same way they hate their parents, or their husbands and wives. There's a real intensity to their hate; it's *personal* hate, underneath. They don't just oppose Negroes in general, as a group, or oppose them because they're trying to upset the familiar ways we all grow to depend upon. They oppose because they *need* to oppose; they need an enemy.

"That's what I finally said to my brother. I wasn't going to be one of those armchair psychiatrists. I just said to him: 'Why don't you leave me and the niggers alone? That's all I ask you, leave us *all* alone, and find some other enemy.'

"That stopped him, those words. They didn't stop some kids from heckling my kids. They didn't stop some of my doctor friends from avoiding me. They stopped my brother though; and enabled me to keep my strength up. He's never said another harsh thing to me. He keeps his hate to himself and his friends, away from my ears. I can take a crank's threats, but it's too painful at my age to see old wounds still unhealed, still giving pain. I mean personal wounds, family wounds, not only the racial ones everyone knows we have here in Alabama."

THE WHITE RACE
AND ITS HEROES

Eldridge Cleaver

Right from the go, let me make one thing absolutely clear: I am not now, nor have I ever been, a white man. Nor, I hasten to add, am I now a Black Muslim—although I used to be. But I *am* an Ofay Watcher, a member of that unchartered, amorphous league which has members on all continents and the islands of the seas. Ofay Watchers Anonymous, we might be called, because we exist concealed in the shadows wherever colored people have known oppression by whites, by white enslavers, colonizers, imperialists, and neo-colonialists.

Did it irritate you, compatriot, for me to string those epithets out like that? Tolerate me. My intention was not necessarily to sprinkle salt over anyone's wounds. I did it primarily to relieve a certain pressure on my brain. Do you cop that? If not, then we're in trouble, because we Ofay Watchers have a pronounced tendency to slip into that mood. If it is bothersome to you, it is quite a task for me because not too long ago it was my way of life to preach, as ardently as I could, that the white race is a race of devils, created by their maker to do evil, and make evil appear as good; that the white race is the natural, unchangeable enemy of the black man, who is the original man, owner, maker, cream of the planet Earth; that the white race was soon to be destroyed by Allah, and that the black man would then inherit the earth, which has always, in fact, been his.

I have, so to speak, washed my hands in the blood of the martyr, Malcolm X, whose retreat from the precipice of madness created new room for others to turn about in, and I am now caught up in that tiny space, attempting a maneuver of my own. Having renounced the teachings of Elijah Muhammad, I find that a rebirth does not follow automatically, of its own accord, that a void is left in one's vision, and this void seeks constantly to obliterate itself by pulling one back to one's former outlook. I have tried a tentative compromise by adopting a select vocabulary, so that now when I see the whites of *their* eyes, instead of saying "devil" or "beast" I say "imperialist" or "colonialist," and everyone seems to be happier.

In silence, we have spent our years watching the ofays, trying to understand them, on the principle that you have a better chance coping with the known than with the unknown. Some of us have been, and some still are, interested in learning whether it is *ultimately* possible to live in the same territory with people who seem so disagreeable to live with; still others want to get as far away from ofays as possible. What we share in common is the desire to break the ofays' power over us.

At times of fundamental social change, such as the era in which we live, it is easy to be deceived by the onrush of events, beguiled by the craving for social stability into mistaking transitory phenomena for enduring reality. The strength and permanence of "white backlash" in America is just such an illusion. However much this rear-guard action might seem to grow in strength, the initiative, and the future, rest with those whites and blacks who have liberated themselves from the master/slave syndrome. And these are to be found mainly among the youth.

Over the past twelve years there has surfaced a political conflict between the generations that is deeper, even, than the struggle between the races. Its first dramatic manifestation was within the ranks of the Negro people, when college students in the South, fed up with Uncle Tom's hat-in-hand approach to revolution, threw off the yoke of the NAACP. When these students initiated the first sit-ins, their spirit spread like a raging fire across the nation, and the technique of non-violent direct action, constantly refined and honed into a sharp cutting tool, swiftly matured. The older Negro "leaders," who are now all die-hard advocates of this tactic, scolded the students for sitting-in. The students rained down contempt upon their hoary heads. In the pre-sit-in days, these conservative leaders had always succeeded in putting down insurgent elements among the Negro people. (A measure of their power, prior to the students' rebellion, is shown by their success in isolating such great black men as the late W. E. B. DuBois and Paul Robeson, when these stalwarts, refusing to bite their tongues, lost favor with the U.S. government by their unstinting efforts to link up the Negro revolution with national liberation movements around the world.)

The "Negro leaders," and the whites who depended upon them to control their people, were outraged by the impudence of the students. Calling for a moratorium on student initiative, they were greeted instead by an encore of sit-ins, and retired to their ivory towers to contemplate the new phenomenon. Others, less prudent because held on a tighter leash by the whites, had their careers brought to an abrupt end because they thought they could lead a black/white backlash against the students, only to find themselves in a kind of Bay of Pigs. Negro college presidents, who expelled students from all-Negro colleges in an attempt to quash the demonstrations, ended up losing their jobs; the victorious students would no longer allow them to preside over the campuses. The spontaneous protests on southern campuses over the repressive measures of their college administrations were an earnest of the Free Speech upheaval which years later was to shake the UC campus at Berkeley. In countless ways, the rebellion of the black students served as catalyst for the brewing revolt of the whites.

What has suddenly happened is that the white race has lost its heroes. Worse, its heroes have been revealed as villains and its greatest heroes as the arch-villains. The new generations of whites, appalled by the sanguine and despicable record carved over the face of the globe by their race in the last five hundred years, are rejecting the panoply of white heroes, whose heroism consisted in erecting the inglorious edifice of colonialism and imperialism; heroes whose careers rested on a system of foreign and domestic exploitation, rooted in the myth of white supremacy and the manifest destiny of the white race. The emerging shape of a new world order, and the requisites for survival in such a world, are fostering in young whites a new outlook. They recoil in shame from the spectacle of cowboys and pioneers—their heroic forefathers whose exploits filled earlier generations with pride—galloping across a movie screen shooting down Indians like Coke bottles. Even Winston Churchill, who is looked upon by older whites as perhaps the greatest hero of the twentieth century—even he, because of the system of which he was a creature and which he served, is an arch-villain in the eyes of the young white rebels.

At the close of World War Two, national liberation movements in the colonized world picked up new momentum and audacity, seeking to cash in on the democratic promises made by the Allies during the war. The Atlantic Charter signed by President Roosevelt and Prime Minister Churchill in 1941, affirming "the right of all people to choose the form of government under which they may live," established the principle, although it took years of postwar struggle to give this piece of rhetoric even the appearance of reality. And just as world revolution has prompted the oppressed to re-evaluate their self-image in terms of the changing conditions, to slough off the servile attitudes inculcated by long years of subordination, the same dynamics of change have prompted the white people of the world to re-evaluate their self-image as well, to disabuse themselves of the Master Race psychology developed over centuries of imperial hegemony.

It is among the white youth of the world that the greatest change is taking place. It is they who are experiencing the great psychic pain of waking into consciousness to find their inherited heroes turned by events into villains. Communication and understanding between the older and younger generations of whites has entered a crisis. The elders, who, in the tradition of privileged classes or races, genuinely do not understand the youth, trapped by old ways of thinking and blind to the future, have only just begun to be vexed—because the youth have only just begun to rebel. So thoroughgoing is the revolution in the psyches of white youth that the traditional tolerance which every older generation has found it necessary to display is quickly exhausted, leaving a gulf of fear, hostility, mutual misunderstanding, and contempt.

The rebellion of the oppressed peoples of the world, along with the Negro revolution in America, have opened the way to a new evaluation of history, a re-examination of the role played by the white race since the beginning of European expansion. The positive achievements are also there in the record, and future generations will applaud them. But there can be no applause now, not while the master still holds the whip in his hand! Not even the master's own children can find it possible to applaud him—he cannot even applaud himself! The negative rings too loudly. Slave-catchers, slaveowners, murderers, butchers, invaders, oppressors— the white heroes have acquired new names. The great white statesmen whom school children are taught to revere are revealed as the architects of systems of human exploitation and slavery. Religious leaders are exposed as condoners and justifiers of all these evil deeds. Schoolteachers and college professors are seen as a clique of brainwashers and whitewashers.

The white youth of today are coming to see, intuitively, that to escape the onus of the history their fathers made they must face and admit the moral truth concerning the works of their fathers. That such venerated figures as George Washington and Thomas Jefferson owned hundreds of black slaves, that all of the Presidents up to Lincoln presided over a slave state, and that every President since Lincoln connived politically and cynically with the issues affecting the human rights and general welfare of the broad masses of the American people —these facts weigh heavily upon the hearts of these young people.

The elders do not like to give these youngsters credit for being able to understand what is going on and what has gone on. When speaking of juvenile delinquency, or the rebellious attitude of today's youth, the elders employ a glib rhetoric. They speak of the "alienation of youth," the desire of the young to be independent, the problems of "the father image" and "the mother image" and their effect upon growing children who lack sound models upon which to pattern themselves. But they consider it bad form to connect the problems of the youth with the central event of our era—the national liberation movements abroad and the Negro revolution at home. The foundations of authority have been blasted to bits in America because the whole society has been indicted, tried, and convicted of injustice. To the youth, the elders are Ugly Americans; to the elders, the youth have gone mad.

The rebellion of the white youth has gone through four broadly discernible stages. First there was an initial recoiling away, a rejection of the conformity which America expected, and had always received, sooner or later, from its youth. The disaffected youth were refusing to participate in the system, having discovered that America, far from helping the underdog, was up to its ears in the mud trying to hold the dog down. Because of the publicity and self-advertisements of the more vocal rebels, this period has come to be known as the beatnik era, although not all of the youth affected by these changes thought of themselves as beatniks. The howl of the beatniks and their scathing, outraged denunciation of the system—characterized by Ginsberg as Moloch, a bloodthirsty Semitic deity to which the ancient tribes sacrificed their firstborn children—was a serious, irrevocable declaration of war. It is revealing that the elders looked upon the beatniks as mere obscene misfits who were too lazy to take baths and too stingy to buy a haircut.

.   .   .

The second stage arrived when these young people, having decided emphatically that the world, and particularly the U.S.A., was unacceptable to them in its present form, began an active search for roles they could play in changing the society. If many of these young people were content to lay up in their cool beat pads, smoking pot and listening to jazz in a perpetual orgy of esoteric bliss, there were others, less crushed by the system, who recognized the need for positive action. Moloch could not ask for anything more than to have its disaffected victims withdraw into safe, passive, apolitical little nonparticipatory islands, in an economy less and less able to provide jobs for

the growing pool of unemployed. If all the unemployed had followed
the lead of the beatniks, Moloch would gladly have legalized the use
of euphoric drugs and marijuana, passed out free jazz albums and
sleeping bags, to all those willing to sign affidavits promising to remain
"beat." The non-beat disenchanted white youth were attracted magnetically to the Negro revolution, which had begun to take on a mass,
insurrectionary tone. But they had difficulty understanding their relationship to the Negro, and what role "whites" could play in a "Negro
revolution." For the time being they watched the Negro activists from
afar.

The third stage, which is rapidly drawing to a close, emerged when
white youth started joining Negro demonstrations in large numbers.
The presence of whites among the demonstrators emboldened the
Negro leaders and allowed them to use tactics they never would have
been able to employ with all-black troops. The racist conscience of
America is such that murder does not register as murder, really, unless
the victim is white. And it was only when the newspapers and magazines started carrying pictures and stories of white demonstrators
being beaten and maimed by mobs and police that the public began
to protest. Negroes have become so used to this double standard that
they, too, react differently to the death of a white. When white freedom riders were brutalized along with blacks, a sigh of relief went up
from the black masses, because the blacks knew that white blood is the
coin of freedom in a land where for four hundred years black blood
has been shed unremarked and with impunity. America has never
truly been outraged by the murder of a black man, woman, or child.
White politicians may, if Negroes are aroused by a particular murder,
say with their lips what they know with their minds they should feel
with their hearts—but don't.

It is a measure of what the Negro feels that when the two white and
one black civil rights workers were murdered in Mississippi in 1964,
the event was welcomed by Negroes on a level of understanding
beyond and deeper than the grief they felt for the victims and their
families. This welcoming of violence and death to whites can almost
be heard—indeed it can be heard—in the inevitable words, oft repeated by Negroes, that those whites, and blacks, do not die in vain.
So it was with Mrs. Viola Liuzzo. And much of the anger which
Negroes felt toward Martin Luther King during the Battle of Selma
stemmed from the fact that he denied history a great moment, never
to be recaptured, when he turned tail on the Edmund Pettus Bridge
and refused to all those whites behind him what they had traveled

thousands of miles to receive. If the police had turned them back by force, all those nuns, priests, rabbis, preachers, and distinguished ladies and gentlemen old and young—as they had done the Negroes a week earlier—the violence and brutality of the system would have been ruthlessly exposed. Or if, seeing King determined to lead them on to Montgomery, the troopers had stepped aside to avoid precisely the confrontation that Washington would not have tolerated, it would have signaled the capitulation of the militant white South. As it turned out, the March on Montgomery was a show of somewhat dim luster, stage-managed by the Establishment. But by this time the young whites were already active participants in the Negro revolution. In fact they had begun to transform it into something broader, with the potential of encompassing the whole of America in a radical reordering of society.

The fourth stage, now in its infancy, sees these white youth taking the initiative, using techniques learned in the Negro struggle to attack problems in the general society. The classic example of this new energy in action was the student battle on the UC campus at Berkeley, California—the Free Speech Movement. Leading the revolt were veterans of the civil rights movement, some of whom spent time on the firing line in the wilderness of Mississippi/Alabama. Flowing from the same momentum were student demonstrations against U.S. interference in the internal affairs of Vietnam, Cuba, the Dominican Republic, and the Congo and U.S. aid to apartheid in South Africa. The students even aroused the intellectual community to actions and positions unthinkable a few years ago: witness the teach-ins. But their revolt is deeper than single-issue protest. The characteristics of the white rebels which most alarm their elders—the long hair, the new dances, their love for Negro music, their use of marijuana, their mystical attitude toward sex—are all tools of their rebellion. They have turned these tools against the totalitarian fabric of American society—and they mean to change it.

From the beginning, America has been a schizophrenic nation. Its two conflicting images of itself were never reconciled, because never before has the survival of its most cherished myths made a reconciliation mandatory. Once before, during the bitter struggle between North and South climaxed by the Civil War, the two images of America came into conflict, although whites North and South scarcely understood it. The image of America held by its most alienated citizens was advanced neither by the North nor by the South; it was perhaps best expressed by Frederick Douglass, who was born into slavery in 1817, escaped to the North, and became the greatest leader-spokesman for the blacks of his era. In words that can still, years later, arouse an audience of black Americans, Frederick Douglass delivered, in 1852, a scorching indictment in his Fourth of July oration in Rochester:

> What to the American slave is your Fourth of July? I answer: a day that reveals to him, more than all other days in the year, the gross injustice and cruelty to which he is the constant victim. To him your celebration is a sham; your boasted liberty, an unholy licence; your national greatness, swelling vanity; your sounds of rejoicing are empty and heartless; your denunciation of tyrants, brass-fronted impudence; your shouts of liberty and equality, hollow mockery; your prayers and hymns, your sermons and thanksgivings, with all your religious parade and solemnity, are, to him, more bombast, fraud, deception, impiety and hypocrisy—a thin veil to cover up crimes which would disgrace a nation of savages. . . .
>
> You boast of your love of liberty, your superior civilization, and your pure Christianity, while the whole political power of the nation (as embodied in the two great political parties) is solemnly pledged to support and perpetuate the enslavement of three millions of your countrymen. You hurl your anathemas at the crown-headed tyrants of Russia and Austria and pride yourselves on your democratic institutions, while you yourselves consent to be the mere *tools* and *bodyguards* of the tyrants of Virginia and Carolina.
>
> You invite to your shores fugitives of oppression from abroad, honor them with banquets, greet them with ovations, cheer them, toast them, salute them, protect them, and pour out your money to them like water; but the fugitive from your own land you advertise, hunt, arrest, shoot, and kill. You glory in your refinement and your universal education; yet you maintain a system as barbarous and dreadful as ever stained the character of a nation—a system begun in avarice, supported in pride, and perpetuated in cruelty.
>
> You shed tears over fallen Hungary, and make the sad story of her wrongs the theme of your poets, statesmen and orators, till your gallant sons are ready to fly to arms to vindicate her cause against the oppressor; but, in regard to the ten thousand wrongs of the American slave, you would enforce the strictest silence, and would hail him as an enemy of the nation who dares to make these wrongs the subject of public discourse!

This most alienated view of America was preached by the Abolitionists, and by Harriet Beecher Stowe in her *Uncle Tom's Cabin.* But such a view of America was too distasteful to receive wide attention, and serious debate about America's image and her reality was engaged in only on the fringes of society. Even when confronted with over-whelming evidence to the contrary, most white Americans have found it possible, after steadying their rattled nerves, to settle comfortably back into their vaunted belief that America is dedicated to the proposi-tion that all men are created equal and endowed by their Creator with certain inalienable rights—life, liberty and the pursuit of happiness. With the Constitution for a rudder and the Declaration of Indepen-dence as its guiding star, the ship of state is sailing always toward a brighter vision of freedom and justice for all.

Because there is no common ground between these two contradic-tory images of America, they had to be kept apart. But the moment the blacks were let into the white world—let out of the voiceless and faceless cages of their ghettos, singing, walking, talking, dancing, writ-ing, and orating *their* image of America and of Americans—the white world was suddenly challenged to match its practice to its preach-ments. And this is why those whites who abandon the *white* image of America and adopt the *black* are greeted with such unmitigated hos-tility by their elders.

For all these years whites have been taught to believe in the myth they preached, while Negroes have had to face the bitter reality of what America practiced. But without the lies and distortions, white Americans would not have been able to do the things they have done. When whites are forced to look honestly upon the objective proof of their deeds, the cement of mendacity holding white society together swiftly disintegrates. On the other hand, the core of the black world's vision remains intact, and in fact begins to expand and spread into the psychological territory vacated by the non-viable white lies, i.e., into the minds of young whites. It is remarkable how the system worked for so many years, how the majority of whites remained effectively unaware of any contradiction between their view of the world and that world itself. The mechanism by which this was rendered possible requires examination at this point.

Let us recall that the white man, in order to justify slavery and, later on, to justify segregation, elaborated a complex, all-pervasive myth which at one time classified the black man as a subhuman beast of burden. The myth was progressively modified, gradually elevating the blacks on the scale of evolution, following their slowly changing status, until the plateau of separate-but-equal was reached at the close of the nineteenth century. During slavery, the black was seen as a mindless Supermasculine Menial. Forced to do the backbreaking work, he was conceived in terms of his ability to do such work—"field niggers," etc. The white man administered the plantation, doing all the thinking, exercising omnipotent power over the slaves. He had little difficulty dissociating himself from the black slaves, and he could not conceive of their positions being reversed or even reversible.

Blacks and whites being conceived as mutually exclusive types, those attributes imputed to the blacks could not also be imputed to the whites—at least not in equal degree—without blurring the line separating the races. These images were based upon the social function of the two races, the work they performed. The ideal white man was one who knew how to use his head, who knew how to manage and control things and get things done. Those whites who were not in a position to perform these functions nevertheless aspired to them. The ideal black man was one who did exactly as he was told, and did it efficiently and cheerfully. "Slaves," said Frederick Douglass, "are generally expected to sing as well as to work." As the black man's position and function became more varied, the images of white and black, having become stereotypes, lagged behind.

The separate-but-equal doctrine was promulgated by the Supreme Court in 1896. It had the same purpose domestically as the Open Door Policy toward China in the international arena: to stabilize a situation and subordinate a nonwhite population so that racist exploiters could manipulate those people according to their own selfish interests. These doctrines were foisted off as *the epitome of enlightened justice, the highest expression of morality.* Sanctified by religion, justified by philosophy and legalized by the Supreme Court, separate-but-equal was enforced by day by agencies of the law, and by the KKK & Co. under cover of night. Booker T. Washington, the Martin Luther King of his day, accepted separate-but-equal in the name of all Negroes. W. E. B. DuBois denounced it.

Separate-but-equal marked the last stage of the white man's flight into cultural neurosis, and the beginning of the black man's frantic striving to assert his humanity and equalize his position with the white. Blacks ventured into all fields of endeavor to which they could gain entrance. Their goal was to present in all fields a performance that would equal or surpass that of the whites. It was long axiomatic among blacks that a black had to be twice as competent as a white in any field in order to win grudging recognition from the whites. This produced a pathological motivation in the blacks to equal or surpass the whites, and a pathological motivation in the whites to maintain a distance from the blacks. This is the rack on which black and white Americans receive their delicious torture! At first there was the color bar, flatly denying the blacks entrance to certain spheres of activity. When this no longer worked, and blacks invaded sector after sector of American life and economy, the whites evolved other methods of keeping their distance. The illusion of the Negro's inferior nature had to be maintained.

One device evolved by the whites was to tab whatever the blacks did with the prefix "Negro." We had *Negro* literature, *Negro* athletes, *Negro* music, *Negro* doctors, *Negro* politicians, *Negro* workers. The malignant ingeniousness of this device is that although it accurately describes an objective biological fact—or, at least, a sociological fact in America—it concealed the paramount psychological fact: that to the white mind, prefixing anything with "Negro" automatically consigned it to an inferior category. A well-known example of the white necessity to deny due credit to blacks is in the realm of music. White musicians were famous for going to Harlem and other Negro cultural centers literally to steal the black man's music, carrying it back across the color line into the Great White World and passing off the watered-down loot as their own original creations. Blacks, meanwhile, were ridiculed as *Negro* musicians playing inferior coon music.

The Negro revolution at home and national liberation movements abroad have unceremoniously shattered the world of fantasy in which the whites have been living. It is painful that many do not yet see that their fantasy world has been rendered uninhabitable in the last half of the twentieth century. But it is away from this world that the white youth of today are turning. The "paper tiger" hero, James Bond, offering the whites a triumphant image of themselves, is saying what many whites want desperately to hear reaffirmed; *I am still the White Man, lord of the land, licensed to kill, and the world is still an empire at my feet.* James Bond feeds on that secret little anxiety, the psychological white backlash, felt in some degree by most whites alive. It is exasperating to see little brown men and little yellow men from the mysterious Orient, and the opaque black men of Africa (to say nothing of these impudent American Negroes!) who come to the UN and talk smart to us, who are scurrying all over *our* globe in their strange modes of dress—much as if they were new, unpleasant arrivals from another planet. Many whites believe in their ulcers that it is only a matter of time before the Marines get the signal to round up these truants and put them back securely in their cages. But it is away from this fantasy world that the white youth of today are turning.

In the world revolution now under way, the initiative rests with people of color. That growing numbers of white youth are repudiating their heritage of blood and taking people of color as their heroes and models is a tribute not only to their insight but to the resilience of the human spirit. For today the heroes of the initiative are people not usually thought of as white: Fidel Castro, Che Guevara, Kwame Nkrumah, Mao Tse-tung, Gamal Abdel Nasser, Robert F. Williams, Malcolm X, Ben Bella, John Lewis, Martin Luther King, Jr., Robert Parris Moses, Ho Chi Minh, Stokeley Carmichael, W. E. B. DuBois, James Forman, Chou En-lai.

The white youth of today have begun to react to the fact that the "American Way of Life" is a fossil of history. What do they care if their old baldheaded and crew-cut elders don't dig their caveman mops? They couldn't care less about the old, stiffassed honkies who don't like their new dances: Frug, Monkey, Jerk, Swim, Watusi. All they know is that it feels good to swing to way-out body-rhythms instead of dragassing across the dance floor like zombies to the dead beat of mind-smothered Mickey Mouse music. Is it any wonder that the youth have lost all respect for their elders, for law and order, when for as long as they can remember all they've witnessed is a monumental bickering over the Negro's place in American society and the right of people around the world to be left alone by outside powers? They have witnessed the law, both domesican shores: the physical extermination of the American Indian. The South American example of absorbing the indigenous Indian population was ignored in the United States, and systematic destruction of a whole people was undertaken. The common phrase, "The only good Indian is a dead Indian," was virtually elevated to national policy. Thus the poisoning of the American mind was accomplished not only by acts of discrimination and exploitation but by the exaltation of murder as an expression of the courage and initiative of the pioneer. Just as Southern culture was made to appear noble by ignoring the cruelty of slavery, the conquest of the Indian was depicted as an example of bravery and progress.

Thus through two centuries a continuous indoctrinatiomerican Indians; he sees the civilized nations of Europe fighting in imperial depravity over the lands of other people—and over possession of the very people themselves. There seems to be no end to the ghastly deeds of which his people are guilty. *GUILTY.* The slaughter of the Jews by the Germans, the dropping of atomic bombs on the Japanese people —these deeds weigh heavily upon the prostrate souls and tumultuous consciences of the white youth. The white heroes, their hands dripping with blood, are dead.

The young whites know that the colored people of the world, Afro-Americans included, do not seek revenge for their suffering. They seek the same things the white rebel wants: an end to war and exploitation. Black and white, the young rebels are free people, free in a way that Americans have never been before in the history of their country. And they are outraged.

There is in America today a generation of white youth that is truly worthy of a black man's respect, and this is a rare event in the foul annals of American history. From the beginning of the contact between blacks and whites, there has been very little reason for a black man to respect a white, with such exceptions as John Brown and others lesser known. But respect commands itself and it can neither be given nor withheld when it is due. If a man like Malcolm X could change and repudiate racism, if I myself and other former Muslims can change, if young whites can change, then there is hope for America. It was certainly strange to find myself, while steeped in the doctrine that all whites were devils by nature, commanded by the heart to applaud and acknowledge respect for these young whites—despite the fact that they are descendants of the masters and I the descendant of slave. The sins of the fathers are visited upon the heads of the children —but only if the children continue in the evil deeds of the fathers.

OLD CON, BLACK PANTHER, BRILLIANT WRITER AND QUINTESSENTIAL AMERICAN

Harvey Swados

If Jefferson was around today, he'd be wearing love beads, reading Eldridge Cleaver and looking all over for information—Ishmael Reed.

This whimsy of a young black humorist (black in both senses) asserts a proposition that obviously cannot be proved. But Reed is unarguably on target insofar as his tribute to the Founding Fathers ("America was set up by some very groovy people. Jefferson was a

Harvey Swados, "Old Con, Black Panther, Brilliant Writer and Quintessential American," *The New York Times Magazine*, Sept. 7, 1969. Copyright © 1969 by The New York Times Company. Reprinted by permission of the publisher and the author.

releaseANTO

blind racist, but on many other matters he was very correct") points to Eldridge Cleaver as a figure at the very heart of the contemporary scene. For Cleaver, the essayist and agitator now a fugitive from the land in which a year ago he ran for the Presidency, speaks as does almost no one else to the young black community, to the white student community, and to the community of American writers who came to his defense when the California authorities were trying to throw him back into the prison in which he had already spent half of his adult life.

There are those, however, to whom Eldridge Cleaver does not speak. It is not easy to say whether they are put off because they have read reports of his tediously scabrous speeches or because they have not read his eloquent essays. In any case, there can be little doubt that a portion of the power with which he appeals to the young derives from the very fact that he frightens the old.

In what Pierre Boulez has aptly called "the blotter society," the day that Cleaver makes the cover of Time will mark the beginning of his decline; to be Man of the Yeared or New Yorkerized is to be defanged, tamed, Baldwinized. "Every fury on earth has been absorbed in time, as art, or as religion, or as authority in one form or another. The deadliest blow the enemy of the human soul can strike is to do fury honor," wrote James Agee in "Let Us Now Praise Famous Men." "Swift, Blake, Beethoven, Christ, Joyce, Kafka, name me a one who has not been thus castrated. Official acceptance is the one unmistakable symptom that salvation is beaten again. . . . "

At this point, official acceptance has not yet come to Eldridge Cleaver, nor is it likely that it will in the immediate future. And so salvation remains possible.

Eldridge Cleaver was born in Wabbaseka, Ark., in 1935 to Leroy and Thelma Cleaver, his father a pianist, his mother a grade-school teacher. When Leroy Cleaver became a waiter on the Super Chief, the family moved to Phoenix and then on to Los Angeles. But by the time Eldridge was enrolled in Abraham Lincoln Junior High, his parents had separated and he was picked up for bicycle theft and shipped off to the Fred C. Nelles School for Boys, where he learned about hustling pot. It was for this crime, these days routinely practiced by middle-class college boys for pocket money, that he was sent to the Preston School of Industry in 1953 and then to Soledad. His secondary education, begun at Belmont High School, where he had just made the football team, was completed in prison. There, too, he became an omnivorous reader and evolved a philosophical theory justifying rape as "an insurrectionary act." During 11 months of freedom, he put outrageous theory into practice, "consciously, deliberately, willfully, methodically" raping white women. When he was apprehended, he was sentenced to 2 to 14 years for assault with intent to kill.

Now Eldridge Cleaver was ready to be processed into that industrial waste which is the human product of our detention system. But he was endowed with exceptional mental equipment.

"After I returned to prison," he later wrote, "I took a long look at myself and for the first time in my life, admitted that I was wrong, that I had gone astray—astray not so much from the white man's law as from being human, civilized—for I could not approve the act of rape. Even though I had some insight into my own motivation, I did not feel justified. I lost my self-respect. My pride as a man dissolved and my whole fragile structure seemed to collapse, completely shattered. That is why I started to write. To save myself."

And he discovered the Black Muslims, whose pride, abnegation and discipline appealed to him as to thousands of other convicts across the country. During this period, he began to correspond with sympathetic attorneys on the outside. Charles R. Garry, the veteran West Coast lawyer who was subsequently to become counsel for the Black Panthers, remembers receiving letters from Cleaver in 1960 that were "typically narrow" in their sectarian religious approach to prison problems.

It was only when he came into contact with the civil-rights lawyer Beverly Axelrod that Cleaver, who had followed Malcom X in his stunning split with Elijah Muhammad, saw another path for himself. His admiration for Miss Axelrod grew into a kind of adoration even as his devotion of Malcolm paralleled the latter's growth from gangsterdom to black mysticism to a maturing racial and political consciousness. With the assassination of Malcolm, Cleaver broke definitively with the Black Muslims and began the search for a new allegiance; at the same time, the impassioned efforts of Beverly Axelrod were introducing him to the basically white literary world.

Edward Keating, the West Coast Catholic layman who was one of the founders of Ramparts, recalls meeting Miss Axelrod at an anti-Vietnam war rally in the summer of 1965. "I've got a client who's a would-be writer," she said, and she handed Keating a pile of manuscript "about an inch and a half high" to read over the weekend. He found the writing flawed but impressive, and suggested that Miss Axelrod bring her client around for an editorial discussion. "That won't be so easy," she replied. "He's in Folsom prison."

Keating, himself a lawyer and the first editor to work with Cleaver, went to Folsom to meet him. "I thought him a very powerful writer, and I was curious as to what he'd be like. This great big, black man walked up, and my very first impression was of how gentle his handshake was. We made small talk about books for a while—I'd brought him some—but he was clearly excited that I cared about his writing."

Keating cared enough to send some of it East, to Maxwell Geismar, Thomas Merton, Norman Mailer and John Howard Griffin. Their enthusiastic response was transmitted to the authorities, but it was not until November, 1966, that Cleaver was paroled. By then he had already written most of the pieces—social commentary, letters, polemics—which were to make him a national figure when gathered together in "Soul on Ice."

He had read widely if superficially, and had discovered the exhilaration that comes from the written expression of utter frankness. Searching his soul and his past, he found that he had the power to commit to paper his reflections on his early life ("Looking back, I see that I was in a frantic, wild and completely abandoned frame of mind"), on his scattered reading (the Zen Buddhism of Alan Watts, for example, reminded him "of a slick advertisement for a labor-saving device, aimed at the American housewife, out of the center page of Life magazine"), on his fascination with Malcolm X ("It was like watching a master do a dance with death on a high-strung tightrope"), on the subculture of prison life ("Negro convicts, basically, rather than see themselves as criminals and perpetrators of misdeeds, look upon themselves as prisoners of war, the victims of a vicious, dog-eat-dog social system that is so heinous as to cancel out their own malefactions").

From these elements evolved a philosophy which was to prove enormously attractive to the young and the disaffected, combining as it did an identification with the first and a commitment to the second. "It is among the white youth of the world that the greatest change is taking place," he wrote. "It is they who are experiencing the great psychic pain of waking into consciousness to find their inherited heroes turned by events into villains. . . . Their revolt is deeper than single-issue protest."

When to this Cleaver added the brew of psychosexuality as essential to an understanding of such varied phenomena as the "national-communal pagan rituals" of spectator sports, the Negro's struggle for identity, rock 'n' roll, the beatniks (derided by "the deep-frozen geeks of the Hot-Dog-and-Malted-Milk Set"), politics and literature, it was inevitable that he himself should become a culture hero, prepared to supplant Ellison and Baldwin. He was a "novelist" who had not yet written a novel, a free spirit who had spent long years in prison liberating himself.

Several of his forays into the tangled symbiosis of sexuality and the American past—"The Allegory of the Black Eunuchs" and "The Primeval Mitosis"—seem to me a mishmash of invaluable insights and half-digested Lawrencian pomposities about such capitalized entities as the Omnipotent Administrator, the Primeval Sphere, the Unitary Sexual Image, the Brute Power Function, the Supermasculine Menial, the Ultrafeminine and the Amazon. But when he focuses, in "Notes on a Native Son," upon a target that is both sharply defined and vulnerable, he draws blood.

Commencing this essay shrewdly with a warm tribute to James Baldwin—as Baldwin in his time had begun a polemic against Richard Wright with a similar tribute—Cleaver goes on to associate himself wholeheartedly with the Norman Mailer of "The White Negro" and to assault Baldwin's "total hatred of the blacks, particularly of himself, and the most shameful, fanatical, fawning, sycophantic love of the whites that one can find in the writings of any black American writer of note in our time." Baldwin's work "is the fruit of a tree with a poison root. Such succulent fruit, such a painful tree, what a malignant root!" At the end, Cleaver locates the poison in homosexuality: "I, for one, do not think homosexuality is the latest advance over heterosexuality on the scale of human evolution. Homosexuality is a sickness, just as are baby rape or wanting to become the head of General Motors."

Years later, in the spring of 1969, a member of a large audience at the University of Illinois put the question directly to James Baldwin: "Mr. Baldwin, would you react to Eldridge Cleaver's attack on you in 'Soul on Ice'?"

Baldwin refrained from observing, as he might have, that in the intervening years Cleaver had produced the wind, but not the works that might have been expected to follow such a brutal attempt to supplant him as a spokesman. Instead, he responded quietly, and with a profound effect upon his audience: "I didn't like the attack. No one likes that sort of attack. But let me say that he was using me to make a point. And if you take me out of it—he was right."

Purged of many conflicts, but obviously afflicted by many others— a hunger for the life of reason coupled with a belief that man was best whipped forward by instinct and unreason, an admiration for the cultural heritage and the ardent rebelliousness of young whites coupled with an intense belief in the political necessity of black pride and black manhood—Cleaver emerged from prision into an America moving fast toward wildness and unreason. Edward Keating asked him what was the single most striking aspect of his being a free man after all those years of confinement. Cleaver hesitated for a moment and replied: "I think it's the ability to make decisions—even small ones, like where I'm going to eat dinner, or what I'll eat." He paused, and then added: "And I like to be able to open a door for a woman."

Seemingly, the door was now open for Eldridge Cleaver's literary career, unimpeded by anything other than the tiresome necessity of reporting periodically to his parole officer. He had a book contract, an editorial job with Ramparts, a wide acquaintanceship. Together with a group of young artists, he founded Black House in San Francisco as a hangout for young people with an interest in avant-garde black culture. A young woman, at that time a college student and now active in the Panthers, remembers Black House (the name was a take-off on the White House) as a swinging place, where for 25 cents you could hear all kinds of speakers and poetry readings. Then one night in February, 1967, four young men from Oakland turned up, armed, in black berets, black leather jackets, black trousers, black shoes. As their leaders, Huey P. Newton and Bobby Seale, proceeded to distribute the Black Panther paper, she says: "It blew my mind!"

By his own account, it blew Eldridge's mind too. It was clear at once that Newton, "with a riot pump shotgun in his right hand, barrel pointed down to the floor," was to be Malcolm's successor for him. In his "Introduction to the Biography of Huey P. Newton" (included in the recently published collection "Eldridge Cleaver: Post-Prison Writings and Speeches"), Cleaver says that "you cannot help but be amazed and fascinated by his seriousness, by his willingness and readiness to lay down his life in defense of the rights of his people," and he concludes, "I find myself sharing with Bobby Seale the same attitude toward Huey—the same willingness to place my life in his hands. . . . "

Newton, unquestioned leader of the Black Panther party, is a baby-faced young man possessed of great courage and a will of iron—at this writing he is on strike against working for less than the state minimum wage in the California prison in which he is serving an indeterminate sentence for manslaugher. His lawyer, Charles Garry, whom Cleaver calls "the first White Panther" ("I'm honored by that," says Garry), characterizes Newton as much the less emotional of the two, "soft as they come but hard as nails at the same time."

In the fall of 1967, Newton had been shot and arrested in a confrontation with the Oakland police, blood enemies of the Panthers, in which a policeman died, Nearly everyone was convinced that Newton would be sentenced to the gas chamber, but the jury returned what was apparently a make-shift compromise, a manslaughter verdict, after Newton underwent three days of cross-examination throughout which, his lawyer says, "I sat back relaxed."

Starting early in 1967, Cleaver committed himself to Newton and his growing organization, and came under the scrutiny of a public considerably larger than that represented by the Adult Authority, which controls the penal system of California. In April, he was one of the featured speakers at an anti-Vietnam war rally in San Francisco's Kezar Stadium attended by 65,000 people; in May, he was picked up by the police of Sacramento when Black Panthers panicked the state legislators by turning up at a hearing on gun control armed to the teeth. The flamboyant gesture achieved the publicity the Panthers had been seeking, but it proved an embarrassment to Cleaver, whom the authorities restricted in his activities thereafter despite the fact that his "weapon" turned out to be a camera, and that he had been with the press as an accredited journalist.

Nevertheless, he, like the Panthers, was gaining increased attention almost daily. His articles were appearing in Ramparts, and he was having an impact on Americans far beyond the borders of the inflamed state of California. One of those Americans was an attractive and clever civil-rights worker named Kathleen Neal, who was working for the Student Nonviolent Coordinating Committee (now the Student National Coordinating Committee) after having been a student briefly at Oberlin and Barnard. Her background was as different from Cleaver's as one could imagine. Her father was a college professor turned diplomat. In the course of his foreign-service tours she had lived in India, the Philippines, Liberia and Sierra Leone. She organized an Easter conference for black students at Fisk University in Nashville at which Eldridge spoke; in December, 1967, they were married.

The first year of Cleaver's marriage was to be even more stunningly eventful for him and his bride than for millions of other Americans. In January, 1968, San Francisco police kicked open the door of their apartment at 3:30 in the morning after Cleaver had refused to admit them; they found nothing and did not trouble to explain the raid. In February, "Soul on Ice" was published and, with the attendant publicity, made of him a national figure. And on April 4, Martin Luther King was assassinated.

The following day, Eldridge Cleaver hurried to an Oakland junior high school threatened with destruction by furious black students. As Gene Marine recounts it in his book, "The Black Panthers," "For a half-hour he pleaded with the youths, arguing the futility of their action, the foolishness of the unorganized blindly striking out. Finally they agreed, as other knots of youth in San Francisco and Richmond, East Palo Alto and Berkeley agreed with Panthers who rushed to every threatening scene."

Nonetheless, a day later Cleaver himself was back in jail, after the Oakland police had surrounded a convoy of Panther cars and Cleaver had ducked into a cellar with Little Bobby Hutton, a teen-age Panther; a series of volleys from both sides was followed by tear gas, and as the two stumbled out to surrender blinded and wounded, the 17 year-old Hutton was shot fatally in the back.

For Cleaver, however, shocked at finding himself still alive while his young companion lay dead, this remarkable year was only beginning. In June, after he had spent two months in confinement in Vacaville, Charles Garry succeeded to everyone's astonishment in obtaining his release on a writ of habeas corpus. "There is nothing to indicate," wrote Superior Court Judge Raymond J. Sherwin, "why it was deemed necessary to cancel his parole before his trial on the pending of criminal charges of which he is presumed innocent." Judge Sherwin went on to observe: "It has to be stressed that the uncontradicted evidence presented to this court indicated that the petitioner had been a model parolee. The peril to his parole status stemmed from no failure of personal rehabilitation, but from his undue eloquence in pursuing political goals, goals which were offensive to many of his contemporaries."

The Adult Authority, of course, moved—successfully—to have Judge Sherwin's ruling reversed in the Appellate Court, a reversal sustained by the State Supreme Court. But it could not succeed in erasing one of the more luminous moments in American legal history.

Meanwhile, the Black Panther party had reached an understanding with the Peace and Freedom party which, faced with the task of persuading California voters to change their Republican or Democratic registration, had been having little luck except in campus areas. It was Cleaver who, as Minister of Information, played a substantial role in forming the alliance which led to the birth of the California Peace and Freedom party, and it was his youthful black cohorts who wove through the Oakland and Berkeley ghettoes with the Peace and Freedom registrars and were instrumental in securing the more than

100,000 voter registrations necessary to place on the ballot a party previously dominated by white anti-Vietnam war radicals of both the Old and the New Left.

"Black people," Cleaver told the founding convention of the California Peace and Freedom party, "now have control of their organizations. White people have developed several organizations in their own community that represent a real power base. . . . We see no reason for continuing this stance of isolation one from the other. . . . Let's get together and move in a common fashion against a common enemy."

Obviously both Cleaver and the Panthers were developing very swiftly. As an old West Coast socialist put it, "They were forced to become political in the full sense of the word. You could actually see it happening. They were saying that any blacks who tried to make it alone were adventurists, that political organization was the only way —and, in fact, the only way that one could find and test whites who could be trusted."

In the summer, the new party designated Eldridge Cleaver as its Presidential candidate, and in September he was invited along with the chief of police of Oakland to lecture in an experimental sociology course at the University of California. When the Board of Regents moved to prevent Cleaver from participating in the Berkeley course, he moved in on Gov. Ronald Reagan with gusto.

"I challenge Ronald Reagan to a duel," he told students at Stanford. "I challenge him to a duel to the death or until he says, 'Uncle, Eldridge.' And I give him his choice of weapons. He can use a gun, or a knife, a baseball bat or a marshmallow. And I'll beat him to death with a marshmallow. That's how I feel about him. Here is a man, a demagogue, in the negative sense. I'm a demagogue—in the positive sense. But here, here is a negative demagogue. . . . "

It is not to be wondered at that Cleaver, having captured many intellectuals with the wit and insightfulness of his prison writings, even when they were wrongheaded or overdrawn, should have gone on to captivate the student generation, even when he descended from analysis to the chanting of obscenities. His knack for the simplification of invective, his background as a "street nigger" rather than as a representative of the button-down black *bourgeoisie,* his sense of the political event as theater—all comported with the view of the world held by collegians, particularly by student radicals and those who rallied to them at moments of crisis.

Both Cleaver and the Panther party were being driven in that violent political year, to become increasingly political. Having committed themselves to an electoral alliance with white radicals, the Panthers came under attack by a whole cluster of nationalist rivals as sellouts and disguised Uncle Toms; in order to explain and defend their actions, they had to turn away from the simplistic formulas of soul-food nationalism. So did their Minister of Information. As his friend Dr. Philip Shapiro, a San Francisco psychoanalyst of the older generation, puts it: "Once Eldridge became deeply involved with the Black Panthers he became increasingly dedicated to politics and less to his own writing." He did manage to finish a long story (sold but not yet published), and his literary agent, Cyrilly Abeles, is aware of his desire to do an autobiographical novel. "But it is his more political stuff that has to come next."

As the fateful year drew to a close and the Adult Authority demonstrated its determination to lock him up as a parole violator even before his pending trial in Oakland (which both he and Garry were confident of winning), Cleaver came to know better than anyone else that his time was running out. After having experienced success, love, accomplishment and political involvement, he faced not just the possibility of years of incarceration, but of physical extinction. Nor was he alone in this belief. Edward Keating remembers clearly a conversation with the warden at the time of his first visit to Cleaver in the penitentiary: "He just looked at me, with the coldest, meanest eyes I've ever seen, and threw it at me: If Cleaver ever got out, he'd throw away the key the day he came back."

Don Cox, known to his fellow Panthers on the West Coast as D.C., puts it another way: "The purpose of prison is to break a man. Eldridge was hated because he couldn't be broken. If a thousand men stood in a chow line, all in order, all meek, Eldridge would cut off his sleeves to demonstrate his determination to remain an individual. He was a true revolutionist."

There were still moments, during his last months as a free man, when Cleaver retained the capacity to view himself with detached amusement. Sandra Levinson, a New York contributing editor of Ramparts, laughs when she remembers offering him a ride to the Peace and Freedom party headquarters late in the election campaign. "He climbed into the back seat," she says, "and I turned around and said, 'What do you think you're doing back there? I'm not your chauffeur!' 'Drive on,' he said, cocking his cigar at an angle like F.D.R.'s cigarette holder. 'You are speaking to the man who may be the next President of the United States.' "

But for the most part he became a frenetically driven man. Time, punctuality, became enormously important to him, according to the girl who served as his secretary at his home; even while he was leaving her notes that were "like little stories," he was delivering two and three speeches a day, writing articles and trying to rid his party of opportunist types. There are those who insist that he kept his cool until the last minute; others feel that he went into a tailspin as the day of his surrender to the Adult Authority approached.

There can be no question, however, that his speechmaking became increasingly erratic, oscillating wildly between the soberly descriptive and the primitive. David McReynolds, the veteran pacifist leader who was his running mate as a New York Congressional candidate on the Peace and Freedom party ticket, met him twice in the late weeks of the campaign. Their first encounter was pleasant, businesslike and characterized by an attitude of mutual respect. "I was very impressed with him as a person. A strong guy, a decent guy, someone I could trust."

But then McReynolds was asked to go out to Long Island to serve as fund raiser at a meeting being addressed by Cleaver. "I was angry at being called away from my own campaign, but that was nothing to what I felt when I had to listen to him leading a chant of four-letter words. It was irresponsible, antipolitical. I was livid, furious. I refused to participate in the session. When I told him how hurt I was, he did not get angry with me personally but shrugged it all off. He seemed to me a driven man, with his rage hardly below the surface. He was caught up in the Panthers' fascination with weapons, but I was convinced of his sincerity when he told a press conference that he disliked guns and feared violence. It's regrettable, but not too surprising that he is not consistent."

McReynolds was not the only one to be shocked by Cleaver's platform shenanigans. A white Columbia student who had been profoundly impressed by "Soul on Ice" hastened to Ferris Booth Hall to join an overflow crowd listening to a Cleaver campaign speech. "What turned me off and sent me on my way," he said later, "was the feeling that he was pandering to the most mindless of the students, giving the Barnard girls a thrill by shouting dirty words at them."

And an old-line radical who had engaged in serious political discussions with Cleaver felt that he had become somewhat brutalized during the last months of his liberty. "Earlier, in California, when a girl fell out of a tree and hurt herself, he turned up at the hospital next day with flowers. It was the sort of spontaneous thing that endeared him to people. But he wasn't behaving like that toward the end."

Gavin MacFadyen, a film-maker who made a film on Cleaver for the B.B.C. at the Peace and Freedom party's Sixth Avenue loft some six weeks before Cleaver's departure, has a somewhat different recollection. "It's true that he was over his head. But he was playing many roles—disciplinarian to the kids who looked up to him, political infighter, publicist, writer. He gave me the impression of an extremely self-disciplined, fantastically hard man, at the same time amazingly fluid. I felt that he used vulgarity consciously, and the curious thing is that he used none of it in our session. He was cool, almost distant, he spoke of the 'police' rather than of the 'pigs,' and I suspect that was one reason why the B.B.C., which had hoped for a portrait of a wild man, was dissatisfied with the film."

But MacFadyen too, like the radical politician, felt that Cleaver was —if not exactly enchanted—certainly not unmarked by the adulation he had received. "The slavish devotion of the white left impressed him. It may have had something to do with his being able to quote from the thoughts of Chairman Mao with a straight face."

In an affecting account of her life with him, Kathleen Cleaver has written of those last months: "I watched Eldridge daily grow increasingly tense, harassed and paranoid." That last adjective is one frequently resorted to by those attempting to characterize the man and his movement with some degree of precision. But it carries the implication that the persecution which one allegedly suffers is the result of a systematized delusion. Supposing, though, that the delusion itself has some basis in reality? Perhaps the matter has been put best by a radical political analyst who describes the Panthers' view of America as "seen from the bottom of the water looking up, and hence totally distorted." They have, he observes, "a hard-bitten reality orientation coupled with wild abstraction." And in Eldridge Cleaver they have a Minister of Information who is "the first autodidact I've ever met who is interested in abstraction." (He adds that Cleaver is unique in his experience, too, in that he never descended, even in the heat of argument, to the white put-down.)

Five days before he was scheduled to surrender to the authorities, Cleaver made his last public appearance at a San Francisco rally in his behalf. Shortly after he began to talk he declared: "I developed something of a social conscience. I decided to come out here and work with social problems, get involved with the Movement and make whatever contribution I possibly could. When I made that decision, I thought that the parole authorities would be tickled pink with me, because they were always telling me to do exactly that. They would tell me I was selfish. They would ask me why I didn't start relating to other people, and looking beyond the horizons of myself.

"So I did that, you know. And I just want to tell you this: I've had more trouble out of parole officers and the Department of Corrections simply because I've been relating to the Movement than I had when I was committing robberies, rapes and other things that I didn't get caught for."

And as he came to a close, he stated: "I cannot relate to spending the next four years in the penitentiary, not with madmen with supreme power in their hands. Not with Ronald Reagan the head of the Department of Corrections, as he is the head of every other state agency. Not with Dirty Red's being the warden. If they made Dr. Shapiro the warden of San Quentin, I'd go right now."

Dr. Shapiro, seated in the audience, felt everyone looking in his direction. "I was so embarrassed I wanted to hide under the chair," he says. He was uncomfortable at being the object of so much attention, and he was terribly uneasy for Cleaver, who, with "his remarkable gift for writing, qualities of leadership, sense of dedication, sensitivity to people and readiness for any sacrifice, has played a role in developing the Black Panthers against racism and in making them more sophisticated in their dealings with whites."

When Cleaver told the audience that the authorities would have to come and get him, says Dr. Shapiro, "it sent a chill through people who were devoted to him. There were visions of an apocalyptic blood bath. Unquestionably, it was romanticizing on his part. He identified with Che Guevara."

In the event, Cleaver slipped away nonviolently. Outside his house in the Fillmore district, reports his admirer the distinguished writer Kay Boyle, "college professors, college students, men and women of the black community, and C.I.A. men dressed as hippies, gathered night and day on the sidewalk. Cleaver's neighbors had hung sheets across the front steps, and across the basement windows of his house, in a sort of barricade of love. They had pinned sprays of flowers to the draped sheets, and printed in bright-colored letters words on them like: 'Eldridge, we love you.' " The authorities made no notable effort to intercept him. . . .

MOTOWN JUSTICE

Edgar Z. Friedenberg

About midnight of July 25, 1967, during the period of racial tension in Detroit usually referred to as a summer riot, three young men—Carl Cooper, Auburey Pollard, and Fred Temple, were shot to death at close range in the Algiers Motel, on Woodward Avenue—a modern place with TV, swimming pool, and room phones too plastic to seem an appropriate scene for tragedy. All three victims were, of course, Negro. They were among a group of friends who were being interrogated—if the word may be used in so broad a sense—by an aggregate of Detroit police, Michigan State Troopers, National Guardsmen, and private guards who had been directed to the scene. The commander of the National Guard detachment who had been instructed to "protect the building" of the Great Lakes Mutual Life Insurance Company a block north of the Algiers "from any kind of disturbance" had heard shots, and immediately telephoned his "high commander" that "we were being fired upon." According to two of the policemen present in the motel, their dispatcher had announced "Army under heavy fire" as he gave them their orders.

So far as any investigator has been able to discover, the shots heard were from a starting-pistol used to begin track events, which the young men were playing with, mocking the hyperactivity of the police during the early stages of the riot. Even this pistol has not been recovered; and the survivors have given conflicting testimony about its use; it would, in any case, have been incapable of firing a bullet. All it could be used for is to signal the start of an event, or series of events.

The exact circumstances of Mr. Cooper's slaying—he was the first —are still unclear; his body was found in a unit across the hall from the motel room in which Mr. Pollard and Mr. Temple died. Patrolman Ronald August was subsequently arrested and charged with the murder of Auburey Pollard. He had himself identified Pollard from a photograph as a man he had killed in a struggle over a shotgun the Patrolman had brought into the motel; and National Guard Warrant Officer Theodore Thomas, who had heard the putative sniper fire and turned in the alarm, had identified August as Pollard's killer. On rather

Edgar Z. Friedenberg, "Motown Justice," *The New York Review of Books,* Aug. 1, 1968. Reprinted with permission from *The New York Review of Books.* Copyright © 1968 The New York Review. The article reviews two books: John Hersey, *The Algiers Motel Incident* (Knopf) and Truman Nelson, *The Torture of Mothers* (Beacon).

less clear-cut evidence Patrolman Robert Paille was identified as having shot Fred Temple and was charged with his murder. The two
policemen were arraigned and taken to jail: "They held us,' Paille, who
in his time on the force had taken a good number of citizens to jail,
told me, 'for one night in the county prison. It was the most awkward
night of my life. During that time there, I tell you, it was really
something. We were confined to an area there, isolated, and—we were
both together—and jeez, it was, you know, it was almost unbreathable
in that place, it was closed and no windows or anything. It was hot
in there, it was in the summertime, you see, and all night there you
couldn't sleep, because, you know, it was just a bumpy little old
mattress and everything else there, you know. . . . Unbearable!

" 'They held us for one night in the jail, and then the next day we
went back to court, and they had looked into their logs and so forth
there and found that on previous occasions they had released prisoners for this charge, murder, that they had us on at the time, and then
they released us from that day on, on a bond, five-thousand-dollar
bond, two sureties.' "

On August 14, in Recorder's Court, where criminal complaints are
first heard in Detroit, Judge Robert E. DeMascio dismissed the complaint that had caused Patrolman Paille such an uncomfortable night.
He threw out the statements made by Paille and August when first
interrogated, on the grounds that the two police officers had not been
informed of their constitutional rights—though, as police officers, it
was of course their responsibility to inform suspects of just these rights
every day. This left no evidence on which to proceed against Paille on
the murder charge. The charge against Patrolman August was sustained, but has not yet been brought to trial. His jeopardy does not
appear to be excessive. As Judge DeMascio noted, in his statements
continuing the charge, "On the other hand, it is totally unlike defendant August."

Patrolman Paille was not wholly out of jeopardy either. The Negro
community in Detroit having responded very critically to Judge
DeMascio's handling of the complaint, Wayne County Prosecutor
William L. Cahalan brought a new charge against him, along with
Melvin Dismukes—a Negro private guard already under indictment
for taking part in the beatings that preceded the slayings at the Algiers
—and David Senak, the third Detroit policeman who had taken part
in these events, and who had not previously been charged in connection with them. The new charge, "Conspiracy to commit a legal act
in an illegal manner"—a mild enough way to refer to three slayings

and many more beatings—led to the arrest of the three defendants on August 23. On September 16, Prosecutor Cahalan also appealed Judge DeMascio's decision to dismiss the charges against Paille. The appeal went back to Recorder's Court—this time to the bench of Judge Geraldine Bledsoe Ford—a Negro, as it happens.

On December 1, the Senior Judge of Recorder's Court, Frank G. Schemanske, dismissed even the conspiracy charge for lack of evidence; Cahalan again appealed. This appeal was denied by a fourth Recorder's Court judge Gerald W. Groat, on February 20, 1968. On March 28, Judge Ford, having sat in judgment on the issue for more than six months:

> ordered Judge DeMascio to reopen the case and examine Lieutenant Hallmark, the man to whom August and Paille confessed. Such an examination would probably have the effect of causing Paille to be indicted for murder after all. [Defense] attorney Lippitt at once appealed on Paille's behalf, questioning the legality of one Recorder's Court judge's reviewing a decision of another Recorder's Court judge —a procedure to which Mr. Lippitt had naturally not objected when Groat had reviewed Schemanske and agreed with him.

There, so far as the local authorities were concerned, the matter would have rested, with only August—apparently the quietest and least aggressive of the three police officers—and Dismukes, the only Negro defendant, facing charges, at least until the constitutional issue about the Recorder's Court hearing its own appeals had been resolved. Except for pressure from Congressman John Conyers, Jr.—himself Negro—it is possible that no action at all would have been taken. There is no record that the patrolmen at the Algiers even reported to their headquarters that anyone—snipers or not—had been killed at the Algiers Motel. The bodies were found by Mr. Charles Hendrix, the Negro owner of the private guard firm retained by the Algiers Motel, who notified the morgue, which in turn notified the Homicide Bureau. The only individual implicated in the entire series of events who has yet been tried was also the only Negro. Melvin Dismukes was brought to trial on a charge of Felonious Assault on May 7, before Recorder's Court Judge Robert J. Colombo, and an all-white jury, which, perhaps appreciating his somewhat inappropriate role in the drama, deliberated thirteen minutes and acquitted him.

The Federal Government, however, finally entered the case, just as another summer was about to begin. On May 3, the United States Attorney for the Eastern District of Michigan announced that an indictment for conspiracy to deny civil rights to Auburey Pollard,

Fred Temple, Lee Forsythe, Cleveland Reed, Roderick Davis, James
Sortor, Robert Lee Greene, Julia Ann Hysell, Karen Malloy, and
Michael Clark, had been returned against August, Dismukes, Paille,
and Senak. The omission of Carl Cooper's name suggests that even the
grand jury had not been able to reconstruct a plausible hypothesis to
account for his slaying. Messrs. Forsythe, Reed, Davis, Sortor, and
Clark, friends of the slain youths, were with them at the Algiers, but
escaped being shot, though they were beaten. Miss Hysell and Miss
Malloy were guests in the Motel who, having met the young men there
earlier and come to their rooms to share a meal of hot dogs with them
because they were hungry and the curfew prevented their going out
to a café for food. Whether they shared anything more—and no evidence has been presented that they did—the invading aggregate of
enforcement officials apparently assumed that they had. Witnesses
agree that the girls were abused, their clothes torn; and then forced
to strip to their panties in order to shame them for fraternizing with
black men. The experience of Robert Lee Greene, a slightly older man
and a Vietnam war veteran who was staying in the motel when it was
attacked by the forces of law and order, as related to Assistant Wayne
County Prosecutor Jesse B. Eggleston, rather vividly conveys the tone
of the proceedings:

> "Greene was then called in and saw that Julie was bleeding about the
> forehead, a mattress on the floor was bloody, and Karen's clothing had
> been torn. Greene was questioned as to his relationship to the girls."
>
> "He started asking questions . . . and asked whether I had intercourse
> with any of the girls. I told him, 'No'. Then he asked me what I was
> doing there. I told him, 'I just got discharged. I came here looking for
> a job. I arrived here Friday.' And told him what was what, the reason
> I was there. Then he said, 'Okay,' and told me to move out. Prior to me
> going out, I noticed one of the girls' clothes was ripped. . . . This warrant
> officer, he spoke up then. I told him that I'd like to go back in the
> service. He told me, 'We don't need niggers in the Army, like you'
> . . . So I didn't say any more, and I received another blow. And I was
> struck behind the head . . . This was a rifle butt."

Then, according to an account given to Hersey by Charles Moore, a
policeman approached Greene "and began to rant at the black man
who had been discovered with two white girls in his bedroom. . . . The
officer said to Greene, 'You sure you're not one of these black-ass
nigger pimps?' "

> Greene, an ex-paratrooper, a veteran of Vietnam, reached in a
> pocket and pulled out papers warranting his honorable discharge, and

held them up for the officer to see. "I just got out of the service," he said.

The officer hit him and said, "We're going to kill all you black-ass nigger pimps and throw you in the river. We're going to fill up the Detroit River with all you pimps and whores."

The remaining individual named in the Federal indictment, accused Patrolman David Senak, who had kept calm under questioning and had not been charged with murder along with August and Paille, is by far the most interesting of the police present at the Algiers. At twenty-four, the youngest of the three—Patrolman Paille and August were about thirty—he alone could be characterized as a really zealous policeman. "I'm a police officer," Hersey quotes him as saying, "and they could fire me, and ten years from now you could ask me and I'd still be a police officer, whether I'm fired or not. But August I don't think is. I think he's just a nice family-type fellow. . . . Just a general nice guy."

Senak, surely, cannot be dismissed so blandly. He has won two special citations in three years on the force. As Hersey describes him, he sounds attractive—perhaps fascinating would be a better word:

. . . a boyish pink complexion that flushes and pales markedly in response to the ebb and flow of emotion; with an attractive smile which pushes deep dimples into his cheeks; called by some Dave but also the bearer of two other nicknames, of which he tells with a humorous sparkle in his eyes, the first an anagram of his name, Snake, and the other given him by an aunt, Inda, which means snake poison in Slovak —sat at his desk in his den at home, under the snarling fangs of the stuffed head of a wolf shot by an uncle of his, beside a carefully kept file of his exploits on the force ("I like to look back and see what I've done").

What Senak has done, at this point, is not exactly clear and under the terms of the May 3 indictment is for the courts to decide. On July 24, 1967, the second day of the riots, he and two other patrolmen had, in the course of duty, slain an apparent looter, Joseph Chandler, as he fled over a fence. On Friday, July 28, in an incident held by Prosecutor Cahalan to be not riot-connected, he shot and killed another Negro suspect, Palmer Gray, Jr. According to the police report:

Patrolman Senak ordered the deceased to raise his hands. Instead, the deceased ran back down the stairs towards the officer and reached into his pocket as if to draw a gun. The officer, being previously apprized by witnesses at 570 E. Kirby that the man had threatened them with a small dark-colored hand gun, feared the deceased was about to draw his gun, and fired one shot from his revolver, fatally wounding the deceased as described. No hand gun or other weapon was found on the deceased's person or in the immediate area at this time.

There can be no doubt of David Senak's commitment to the police force and sense of high vocation. It is in his blood, and that of at least two other persons as well. But having, with his two colleagues, been suspended since the Algiers Motel incident, he has become aware that his career is in jeopardy and is responding with what, by Hersey's account, is not only commendable maturity but an unusual degree of insight into social alternatives that may promise him much continued satisfaction:

> At the beginning I wasn't too logical about the thing. I figured there was no way of them firing me for what I did, but now you see all this bad publicity and stuff, and the Police Department can fire you for just about anything. So I'm looking toward the future. I was planning to get my education in police administration, even before the riots, but now it would be sort of ridiculous for me to go into police administration, at this moment, because if I'm fired from the Police Department, obviously I can't go into that field.
>
> So what I'm doing is going into education. Liberal-arts education major. And plan on, if they fire me from the Department, going into teaching.

I have stressed the frustrating legal processes to which the Algiers Motel Incident has given rise because they bear on what seems to me the most immediate issue in the case: whether it is realistic, or just a cop-out, to demand that the most aggrieved members of the commonwealth continue to appeal to due process rather than direct confrontation for a redress of their grievances. In doing so, I have done scant justice to the richness and detail of John Hersey's account; much less to his courage and sense of social responsibility in undertaking to write it, and the consummate skill with which he has accomplished what I find an almost unimaginably difficult task.

In writing *The Algiers Motel Incident* he was obliged to unravel a mass of conflicting testimony about a brutal and obscene series of events whose participants had strong reasons—and in many cases official authority—to obscure and falsify their own roles. He had to win the confidence of persons who had become lethal adversaries of one another, and without the conventional cloak of neutrality; since his feelings of outrage are not only clear in the document but supported by the mass of evidence he presents. Most of this I have not dealt with here at all; the mutilation of the corpses of the three young

Negro victims, the official harassment of the survivors who had
become involved in the complaint against the authorities—Prosecutor
Cahalan even filed suit to have the Algiers Motel itself padlocked—
and, perhaps the most hopeful consequence, the organization of the
Negro community to strengthen its demands for decent treatment and
redress. "In the third week in August," Hersey reports, "a coalition
of militant black leadership in Detroit was formed; it called itself the
Citywide Citizens Action Committee. . . . The group chose as its
chairman the pastor of the Central United Church of Christ, the Rev.
Albert Cleage, Jr. . . . The CCAC voted to hold a people's tribunal on
August 30, 1967, at which the events at the motel and the response
of the Negro community to them could be more fully aired. When the
theater at which the tribunal had been scheduled canceled the event
it was held at the Reverend Cleage's church."

> "I was there," [Eddie Temple told Hersey], "as a witness, actually
> as the person who identified my brother at the morgue. It had a tremen-
> dous value, in that it exposed to a large number of people what had
> happened there, what these people had to go through, the beatings, the
> fear. . . . It was a Negro audience, primarily middle class. It was a large
> number of people, it was packed, and they had it outside, and they had
> another annex type of place where they had speakers. This place was
> really packed. People were interested in it."

Mr. Hersey's book, in effect, extends this impact to a much larger and
possibly more influential group of persons; it tells more about what
happened, in greater depth and more permanent form; and by telling
it more coolly is harder for the educated middle classes, committed
to pure tolerance, to dismiss. Yet its greatest value lies, I think, in its
implications for the American social system itself: particularly the
questions it raises about American democracy. Despite its innumerable proved instances of infidelity and gross cruelty, we remain faithful
to our social system; though lately we have begun to ask more frequently whether our society isn't terribly sick. But *The Algiers Motel
Incident* makes it very clear that, though what happened may be sick,
it wasn't really abnormal. Similar events, some on a smaller scale, and
one or two on a larger one, have happened and continue to happen;
it isn't much better in Buffalo; and in Oakland, it's worse. What made
the difference in Detroit was not the particular viciousness of its
political system, as American urban politics go, but the courage and
tenacity of its Negro leadership, which had already acquired a political
operating base.

Even with courage, determination, and a certain amount of political power, can those groups which American society at present victimizes hope to wrest from it a reasonable degree of justice and personal security? The question is broader than that of racism, which in any case rather misstates the issue. "I think the police force is prejudiced —against people altogether," Mrs. Auburey Pollard, Sr. commented to Hersey; and she is right, not only about the police force in Detroit but wherever, internally or externally, we seek to police the world.

But policemanship is American public policy: and, against it, the Detroit Negro community does not seem to be winning any very signal victories. The hearts of civil libertarians everywhere are, no doubt, uplifted, and their minds set at ease, when the Federal government returns an indictment for conspiring to "deny civil rights." But does not the very obliqueness of this action attest to the fact that the incidents at the Algiers Motel, if they do not reflect public policy, do not greatly offend public interest either? What is unfolding seems, despite its gruesome content, a rather conventional piece of American political brokerage, in which the unexpectedly strong and persistent demands of a newly entrenched ethnic group are being met by legal ingenuity which avoids explicit indictment of either the actions taken by their attackers or the social forces those actions express. It is those forces that, being regular and recurrent themselves, produce the effect of the conspiracy: while, in fact, they make it unnecessary and the charge basically meaningless.

Hersey's extremely careful and cogent account of *The Algiers Motel Incident* does not suggest that August, Dismukes, Paille, and Senak conspired to do anything; and it makes it extremely implausible that the three patrolmen could have conspired with Dismukes under any circumstances. It suggests strongly the contrary: that they were doing what came naturally to them, and doing it with great gusto. It also suggests that what they did was, except for the manner of execution, consistent with their social role though not, to be sure, a regular part of it. There were, after all, other revealing riot-connected killings. Hersey summarizes a full account of them published after five weeks of research by the Detroit *Free Press* on September 3, 1967. Sixteen persons—excluding those who died at the Algiers Motel—were killed by Detroit police; fourteen as looters, including the aforementioned Joseph Chandler; one a suspected arsonist, and one—and only one— a genuine but drunken and apparently crazed sniper, though earlier the *Free Press* had headlined the question: "Are Sniper Attacks Part of a Nationwide Plot?" One policeman, Jerome Olshove, had been killed, and one fireman—the latter perhaps by a stray National

Guardsman's bullet. "At least six of the forty-three victims were killed by the National Guard," Hersey observes, "five of them, according to the [*Free Press* reporting] team, 'innocent, the victims of what now seem to be tragic accidents.' Five other deaths were caused by bullets that might have been fired by either police or National Guardsmen; four of these victims were clearly innocent. Two looters were shot by storeowners; three others were killed by private citizens, two of whom were promptly charged with murder."

In view of this, the phrase used in the earlier indictment "to commit a legal act in an illegal manner," seems poetically precise; for Detroit clearly tends to regard killing by policemen as legal. Nor does David Senak seem quite so insensitive in observing that "I figured there was no way of them firing me for what I did." It is not, after all, customary to fire a dedicated officer for zeal beyond the call of duty; and, certainly, not for volunteering to participate, at some danger to himself, in a civic pageant designed to act out the fantasies of the populace. The problem is those fantasies; and it lies with the populace itself.

Law enforcement in the United States does not serve primarily the function of maintaining order. In times of crisis, particularly, it is more often, as in Detroit, the major source of disorder. It serves another function more fundamental to keeping American society going. It expresses, under conditions of impunity, the rage and aggression of a disappointed *lumpenbourgeoisie* against any style of life that seems either more privileged or more authentic. In his book, Hersey stresses his conclusion that the underlying basis of white racism is probably sexual, reasoning from the mutilation of the Algiers Motel corpses, the language of the police and National Guardsmen, and the fact that the most violent of the police seem also to be those who have served most enthusiastically on the vice-squad and been most ingenious in entrapping whores, pimps, and queers. He is right, I think, as far as his reasoning goes; but it does not go far enough. For sexuality, though surely the greatest triumph of the senses and hence the key to the most profound authenticity—or betrayal—is only one channel of spontaneous self-expression, and the *lumpenbourgeoisie* is against all of them. And the language and attitude of the police and of much of the working class generally toward hippies, pot-blowers, and other creatures who strike them as obscenely subjective is much the same. "COP KILL A CREEP! pow pow pow," The Mothers of Invention justly observe.

Law enforcement, I stated earlier, is public policy. Enforcement officers are hired to do what they do; and what they do when they blow their cool isn't all that different from what they do normally, and what is expected of them. The fraternal spirit of law-enforcement officials as a cadre is manifest throughout *The Algiers Motel Incident,* and is responsible for the one event that most distressed Hersey: the decision of the *State* Police, who were included in the party that descended on the motel, to withdraw rather than interfere with or witness the actions of their municipal colleagues:

> Of all the chapters in this narrative, this may have been the most inglorious. Law-enforcement officers of the State of Michigan, having seen actions by policemen of the City of Detroit that were "out of control," were evacuated by a commander "as he didn't like what he had seen there." Faced with the evident need for strong measures to prevent the crimes of that scene from being carried further, the state troopers simply washed their hands of the whole nasty business and walked out.

As might have been predicted from the most elementary role-theory. Professional actors do not take it upon themselves to disrupt a performance simply because they come upon atrocious examples of miscasting among their colleagues. And the drama that Hersey has recounted here plays a very important part in mass democracy. It asserts the superiority of the mass to elitist legal constraints and fancy constitutional safeguards. These atavisms are tolerated in American society on the tacit condition that their invocation will not too seriously impinge on the activities of daily life.

For liberal intellectuals and perhaps the upper middle classes generally law enforcement serves a rather different function than for the *lumpenbourgeoisie.* In the not-quite-Fascist state, law enforcement seeks to provide much the same kind of protection against the onset of ultimate violence that inoculation used to provide against smallpox. Inoculation is *not* vaccination; and the practice was abandoned as soon as Jenner's inventiveness made vaccination possible. In prophylactic inoculation the virulent discharge from true smallpox is administered; and true smallpox is transmitted. The advantage to the victim is that the conditions of his illness are to some degree controlled; he picks his time instead of falling ill precisely when he is weakened. Of course, many of those inoculated, being not quite so strong as they thought they were, died.

Middle-class enthusiasts for police action apparently believe the violence they support—though they deplore each successive incident as it occurs—can be expected ordinarily to take a benign and self-limiting form, uncomfortable to be sure, but too attenuated to threaten the body politic it is designed to protect from more malignant outbreak. They deceive themselves. Police action is driven by precisely the social forces and expresses the same attitude it is supposed to contain and it does so with the added power of legitimacy. In Detroit last summer law enforcement got rather out of hand. Whether any substantial immunity was conferred on the surviving community, this summer may yet tell.

RACISM: THE CANCER THAT IS DESTROYING AMERICA

Malcolm X

1 I am not a racist, and I do not subscribe to any of the tenets of racism. But the seed of racism has been firmly planted in the hearts of most American whites ever since the beginning of that country. This seed of racism has rooted itself so deeply in the subconsciousness of many American whites that they themselves ofttimes are not even aware of its existence, but it can be easily detected in their thoughts, their words, and in their deeds.

2 In the past I permitted myself to be used by Elijah Muhammad, the leader of the sect known as the Black Muslims, to make sweeping indictments of all white people, the entire white race, and these generalizations have caused injuries to some whites who perhaps did not deserve to be hurt. Because of the spiritual enlightenment which I was blessed to receive as the result of my recent pilgrimage to the Holy City of Mecca, I no longer subscribe to sweeping indictments of any one race.

3 My religious pilgrimage (hajj) to Mecca has given me a new insight into the true brotherhood of Islam, which encompasses all the races of mankind. The pilgrimage broadened my scope, my mind, my outlook, and made me more flexible in approaching life's many complexities and in my reactions to its paradoxes.

4 At Mecca I saw the spirit of unity and true brotherhood displayed

Malcolm X, "Racism: The Cancer that is Destroying America." From *Malcolm X: The Man and His Times*, ed. J. H. Clarke, pp. 302–306. Reprinted with permission of The Macmillan Company. Copyright © 1969 by John Henrik Clarke, Earl Grant and A. Peter Bailey. (Written for the *Egyptian Gazette*, Aug. 25, 1964.)

by tens of thousands of people from all over the world, from blue-eyed blonds to black-skinned Africans. This served to convince me that perhaps some American whites can also be cured of the rampant racism which is consuming them and about to destroy that country.

5 I am now striving to live the life of a true Suni Muslim. In the future I intend to be careful not to sentence anyone who has not first been proven guilty. I must repeat that I am not a racist nor do I subscribe to the tenets of racism. I can state in all sincerity that I wish nothing but freedom, justice, and equality, life, liberty, and the pursuit of happiness for all people.

6 However, the first law of nature is self-preservation, so my first concern is with the oppressed group of people to which I belong, the 22 million Afro-Americans, for we, more than any other people on earth today, are deprived of these inalienable *human rights*.

7 But time is running out for America. The 22 million Afro-Americans are not yet filled with hate or a desire for revenge, as the propaganda of the segregationists would have people believe. The universal law of justice is sufficient to bring judgment upon the American whites who are guilty of racism. The same law will also punish those who have benefited from the racist practices of their forefathers and have done nothing to atone for the "sins of their fathers." Just look around on this earth today and see the increasing troubles this generation of American whites is having. The "sins of their fathers" are definitely being visited upon the heads of this present generation. Most intelligent American whites will admit freely today without hesitation that their present generation is already being punished and plagued for the evil deeds their forefathers committed when they enslaved millions of Afro-Americans in that country.

8 But it is not necessary for their victim—the Afro-American—to seek revenge. The very conditions the American whites created are already plaguing them into insanity and death. They are reaping what their forefathers have sown. "Their chickens are coming home to roost." And we, the 22 million Afro-Americans—their victims—need only to spend more time removing the "scars of slavery" from the backs and the mind of our own people, physical and mental scars left by four hundred years of inhuman treatment there in America at the hands of white racists.

9 The key to our success lies in *united action*. Lack of unity among the various Afro-American groups involved in our struggle has always been the reason we have failed to win concrete gains in our war against America's oppression, exploitation, discrimination, segregation, deg-

radation, and humiliation. Before the miserable condition of the 22 million "second-class citizens" can be corrected, all the groups in the Afro-American community must form a united front. Only through united efforts can our problems there be solved.

10How can we get the unity of the Afro-American community? Ignorance of each other is what has made unity impossible in the past. Therefore we need enlightenment. We need more light about each other. Light creates understanding, understanding creates love, love creates patience, and patience creates unity. Once we have more knowledge (light) about each other we will stop condemning each other and a *united front* will be brought about.

11All 22 million Afro-Americans have the same basic objective. We want freedom, justice, and equality, we want recognition and respect as *human beings.* We are not divided over objectives, but we have allowed our racist enemies to divide us over the *methods* of attaining these common objectives. Our enemy has magnified our minor points of difference, then maneuvered us into wasting our time debating and fighting each other over insignificant and irrelevant issues.

12 The common goal of 22 million Afro-Americans is respect as *human beings,* the God-given right to be a *human being.* Our common goal is to obtain the *human rights* that America has been denying us. We can never get civil rights in America until our *human rights* are first restored. We will never be recognized as citizens there until we are first recognized as *humans.*

13The present American "system" can never produce freedom for the black man. A chicken cannot lay a duck egg because the chicken's "system" is not designed or equipped to produce a duck egg. The system of the chicken was produced by a chicken egg and can therefore reproduce only that which produced it.

14The American "system" (political, economic, and social) was produced from the enslavement of the black man, and this present "system" is capable only of perpetuating that enslavement.

15In order for a chicken to produce a duck egg its system would have to undergo a drastic and painful revolutionary change ... or *REVOLUTION.* So be it with America's enslaving system.

16In the past the civil rights groups in America have been foolishly attempting to obtain constitutional rights from the same Government that has conspired against us to deny our people these rights. Only a world body *(a world court)* can be instrumental in obtaining those rights which belong to a human being by dint of his being a member of the human family.

17 As long as the freedom struggle of the 22 million Afro-Americans is labeled a civil rights issue it remains a domestic problem under the jurisdiction of the United States, and as such, bars the intervention and support of our brothers and sisters in Africa, Asia, Latin America, as well as that of the well-meaning whites of Europe. But once our struggle is lifted from the confining civil rights label to the level of *human rights,* our freedom struggle has then become *internationalized.*

18 Just as the violation of *human rights* of our brothers and sisters in South Africa and Angola is an international issue and has brought the racists of South Africa and Portugal under attack from all other independent governments at the United Nations, once the miserable plight of the 22 million Afro-Americans is also lifted to the level of *human rights* our struggle then becomes an international issue, and the direct concern of all other civilized governments. We can then take the racist American Government before the World Court and have the racists in it exposed and condemned as the criminals that they are.

19 Why should it be necessary to go before a world court in order to solve America's race problem? One hundred years ago a civil war was fought supposedly to free us from the Southern racists. We are still the victims of their racism. Lincoln's Emancipation Proclamation was supposedly to free us. We are still crying for freedom. The politicians fought for amendments to the Constitution supposedly to make us first-class citizens. We are still second-class citizens.

20 In 1954, the U.S. Supreme Court itself issued a historic decision outlawing the segregated school system, and ten years have passed and this law is yet to be enforced even in the Northern states.

21 If white America doesn't think the Afro-American, especially the upcoming generation, is capable of adopting the guerrilla tactics now being used by oppressed people elsewhere on this earth, she is making a drastic mistake. She is underestimating the force that can do her the most harm.

22 A real honest effort to remove the just grievances of the 22 million Afro-Americans must be made immediately or in a short time it will be too late.

THE ECOLOGICAL
DISASTER

INTRODUCTION

A highly sophisticated achievement of millions of years of evolutionary process, man has come to inhabit several environments simultaneously. As well as existing physically in the world, he also lives in psychic, religious, emotional, social, and mythological environments. Yet, that the specifically physical environment necessarily precedes all others is a fact men have often failed to respect. The very evolutionary processes which included man among myriad forms of life were dependent upon a delicate balance of physical states and ecological conditions. It is therefore surprising to find that this unique phenomenon of evolution, capable of reason, language, and love, is so destructively interfering with his physical surroundings as to cause many experts to predict that he will shortly return to the oblivion from which he emerged.

Throughout history, men from different cultures and periods have held strikingly different attitudes toward their relationship with the physical environment. At one extreme we find the pious reverence of a Saint Francis, who taught that flowers, rocks, rivers, and meadows all reflect the divine spirit and demand worship and respect. Because he loved all of creation, Saint Francis preached to the birds and made a point to walk gently over stones, out of respect for their unique existence. An early conservationist, he argued against cutting down a tree whole, insisting that some living part of it be allowed to remain. Contrasting with this attitude is the popular view well expressed by an American businessman, who said that "the rivers are one of our great natural resources; they can be used to carry industrial wastes to the ocean." More recently, Ronald Reagan, the Governor of California, observed that if you have seen one redwood tree, you have seen them all, possibly a prophetic statement in the light of the depletion rate of American forest lands.

Unfortunately, in modern times, it is the businessman and not the conservationist whose views have held sway in the Western world. The advent of capitalism, the rapid development of technology, and the work ethic of Protestantism promoted the attitude that the natural environment was fertile ground to be exploited for profit. This dangerous rationale was greatly enhanced by the discovery of the New World, which seemed to contain such an abundance of resources that no matter what man did he would be able to utilize only a small fraction of what was available.

Consequently, the early settlers in North America were rarely concerned with protecting the great natural wonders they expropriated from the Indian. The potential danger in man's abuse of the physical environment had scarcely become noticeable before the turn of this century. Even those who watched the massacre of the buffalo herds found it difficult to convince others that this was a question worthy of debate. Since then, as a result of the use of the earth, air, seas, and rivers as vast garbage disposal systems, we enter the 1970s with a crisis of the physical environment.

Ironically, the ecological problems arose from popular goals, among them the struggle to increase standards of living, the desire for lower production costs, the fight against disease, the search for new products and greater profits. In short, the crisis grew out of activities which most societies consider to be in pursuit of legitimate objectives. Throughout the last two centuries and without concern for other than immediate, visible social or economic gain, the Western nations have introduced a barrage of new technologies. Recently, students of technology have shown that it is practically impossible to determine the ultimate effects of any important technological innovation before it is utilized, and that innovations which appear to have very beneficial effects (such as irrigation, steam power, internal combustion, atomic energy) in the immediate present can have disastrous long-term consequences which may remain latent for decades or even centuries. Because the industrial revolution is less than two centuries old, we are just now beginning to study and understand the severity of the impact of massive environmental pollution on man's mental and physical health.

Despite our technical knowledge, the problem is sufficiently complicated to prevent evaluation of the effects of our present levels of pollution or assign a precise degree of severity to it, although most experts agree that the situation is accurately described as a crisis. We do know that the industrial revolution brought with it a staggering increase in the use of fuels and processes which contribute dangerous pollutants to the environment. We also know that once a method of production, power generation, or waste disposal is widely accepted, it becomes very difficult for society to alter such methods or to dispense with the resulting products and services. Frequently, the society awakes to discover that what had formerly been a luxury for the rich or the dream of an inventor is now an absolute necessity for the entire population.

For example, if Americans were suddenly warned that the automobile presents a dangerous threat to health, would we react by abandoning automobiles and resorting to less destructive forms of transportation? Would we be willing to make the necessary social, economic, and psychological adjustments suggested by the diagnosis? In the case of the automobile, almost every major city in the country will soon have to begin answering these questions.

Western man in general, and Americans in particular, will soon be faced with the need to make crucial decisions, not only in the touchy area of lethal consumer items like the automobile, but in the entire range of processes and production methods, marketing techniques, waste disposal, and transportation systems which are ravaging the environment.

On the international level, environmental pollution raises serious questions of human cooperation. Since pollutants do not distinguish communists from capitalists, blacks from whites, Greeks from Turks, human survival will demand that very divergent groups suspend their hostilities to join in the solution of common problems. Secondarily, environmental pollution raises questions of morality, because pollution, not observing national boundaries, subjects the undeveloped countries to the consequences of the West's high level of pollution. The impoverished nations are thus granted the misfortune of living in the international garbage dump but are denied the benefits of the high standard of living which results from advanced technology.

Assigning responsibility for the present disaster is of value only insofar as it will help us to deal with the future. Certainly it is obvious that universities without courses in ecology, especially for engineers and business majors, are irresponsible; that industry has been greedy and selfish in its unconscionable exploitation of nature for profit; that governments have been lax and needlessly timid in not enforcing existing legislation, appropriating funds for improved pollution control, or taking the drastic steps necessary to reverse the present chaotic situation. Ultimately, responsibility rests with those who know better but refuse to act.

A FABLE FOR TOMORROW

Rachel Carson

There was once a town in the heart of America where all life seemed to live in harmony with its surroundings. The town lay in the midst of a checkerboard of prosperous farms, with fields of grain and hillsides of orchards where, in spring, white clouds of bloom drifted above the green fields. In autumn, oak and maple and birch set up a blaze of color that flamed and flickered across a backdrop of pines. Then foxes barked in the hills and deer silently crossed the fields, half hidden in the mists of the fall mornings.

Along the roads, laurel, viburnum and alder, great ferns and wild-flowers delighted the traveler's eye through much of the year. Even in winter the roadsides were places of beauty, where countless birds came to feed on the berries and on the seed heads of the dried weeds rising above the snow. The countryside was, in fact, famous for the abundance and variety of its bird life, and when the flood of migrants was pouring through in spring and fall people traveled from great distances to observe them. Others came to fish the streams which flowed clear and cold out of the hills and contained shady pools where trout lay. So it had been from the days many years ago when the first settlers raised their houses, sank their wells, and built their barns.

Then a strange blight crept over the area and everything began to change. Some evil spell had settled on the community: mysterious

Rachel Carson, "A Fable for Tomorrow." From *The Silent Spring* (Boston: Houghton Mifflin, 1962), pp. 1–3. Reprinted by permission of the publisher.

maladies swept the flocks of chickens; the cattle and sheep sickened and died. Everywhere was a shadow of death. The farmers spoke of much illness among their families. In the town the doctors had become more and more puzzled by new kinds of sickness appearing among their patients. There had been several sudden and unexplained deaths, not only among adults but even among children, who would be stricken suddenly while at play and die within a few hours.

There was a strange stillness. The birds, for example—where had they gone? Many people spoke of them, puzzled and disturbed. The feeding stations in the backyards were deserted. The few birds seen anywhere were moribund; they trembled violently and could not fly. It was a spring without voices. On the mornings that had once throbbed with the dawn chorus of robins, catbirds, doves, jays, wrens, and scores of other bird voices there was now no sound; only silence lay over the fields and woods and marsh.

On the farms the hens brooded, but no chicks hatched. The farmers complained that they were unable to raise any pigs—the litters were small and the young survived only a few days. The apple trees were coming into bloom but no bees droned among the blossoms, so there was no pollination and there would be no fruit.

The roadsides, once so attractive, were now lined with browned and withered vegetation as though swept by fire. These, too, were silent, deserted by all living things. Even the streams were now lifeless. Anglers no longer visited them, for all the fish had died.

In the gutters under the eaves and between the shingles of the roofs, a white granular powder still showed a few patches; some weeks before it had fallen like snow upon the roofs and the lawns, the fields and streams.

No witchcraft, no enemy action had silenced the rebirth of new life in this stricken world. The people had done it themselves.

This town does not actually exist, but it might easily have a thousand counterparts in America or elsewhere in the world. I know of no community that has experienced all the misfortunes I describe. Yet every one of these disasters has actually happened somewhere, and many real communities have already suffered a substantial number of them. A grim specter has crept upon us almost unnoticed, and this imagined tragedy may easily become a stark reality we all shall know.

What has already silenced the voices of spring in countless towns in America?

CAN THE WORLD
BE SAVED?

La Mont C. Cole

In recent years, we have heard much discussion of distinct and nearly independent cultures within our society that fail to communicate with each other—natural scientists and social scientists, for example. The particular failure of communication I am concerned with here is that between ecologists on the one hand and, on the other, those who consider that continuous growth is desirable—growth of population, industry, trade and agriculture. Put another way, it is the dichotomy between the thinkers and the doers—those who insist that man should try to know the consequences of his actions before he takes them versus those who want to get on with the building of dams and canals, the straightening of river channels, the firing of nuclear explosives and the industrialization of backward countries.

The message that the ecologists—the "thinkers," if you will—seek to impart could hardly be more urgent or important. It is that man, in the process of seeking a "better way of life," is destroying the natural environment that is essential to any kind of human life at all; that, during his time on earth, man has made giant strides in the direction of ruining the arable land upon which his food supply depends, fouling the air he must breathe and the water he must drink and upsetting the delicate chemical and climatic balances upon which his very existence depends. And there is all too little indication that man has any intention of mending his ways.

The aspect of this threat to human life that has received the least public attention, but which is, I believe, the most serious is the manner in which we are altering the biological, geological and chemical cycles upon which life depends.

When you burn a ton of petroleum hydrocarbon, you obtain as by-products about one and a third tons of water and about twice this amount of carbon dioxide. A Boeing 707 in flight accomplishes this feat about every 10 minutes. I read in the papers that 10,000 airplanes per week land in New York City alone, not including military aircraft. If we assume very crudely that the 707 is typical of these airplanes, and that its average flight takes four hours, this amounts to an annual release into the atmosphere of about 36 million tons of carbon dioxide. And not all flights have a terminus in New York.

Thus the amount of carbon dioxide put into the atmosphere is rising at an ever-rising rate. At the same time, we are removing vast tracts of land from the cycle of photosynthetic production—in this country alone, nearly a million acres of green plants are paved under each year. The loss of these plants is drastically reducing the rate at which oxygen enters the atmosphere. And we do not even know to what extent we are inhibiting photosynthesis through pollution of fresh-water and marine environments.

The carbon-oxygen balance is tipping. When, and if, we reach the point at which the rate of combustion exceeds the rate of photosynthesis, we shall start running out of oxygen. If this occurred gradually, its effect would be approximately the same as moving everyone to a mountaintop—a change that might help to alleviate the population crisis by raising death rates. However, the late Lloyd Berkner, director of the Graduate Research Center of the Southwest, thought that atmospheric depletion might occur suddenly.

The increase in the proportion of carbon dioxide in the atmosphere will have other effects. Carbon dioxide and water vapor are more transparent to shortwave solar radiation than to the longwave heat radiation from the earth to space. Thus the increased proportion of these substances in the atmosphere tends to bring about a rise in the earth's surface temperature, the so-called greenhouse effect, altering climates in ways that are still highly controversial in the scientific community but that everyone agrees are undesirable.

One school holds that the increase in temperature will melt the icecaps of Greenland and the Antarctic, raising the sea level by as much as 300 feet and thereby obliterating most of the major cities of the world. Another school believes that higher temperatures will bring about an increase in evaporation and with it a sharp rise in precipitation; the additional snow falling upon the icecaps will start the glaciers moving again, and another Ice Age will be upon us.

And these represent only the lesser-known effects of combustion on the world. They do not include the direct hazards from air pollution —on man's lungs, for example, or on vegetation near some kinds of industrial plants. Nor do they include the possibility, suggested by some scientists, that we will put enough smoke particles into the air to block solar radiation, causing a dangerous decrease in the earth's temperature. Just to indicate the complexity and uncertainty of what we are doing to the earth's climates, I should mention that the smoke-caused decrease in temperatures would most likely be offset by the carbon dioxide-caused greenhouse effect.

In any case, if we don't destroy ourselves first, we are eventually going to run out of fossil fuels—a prospect surely not many generations away. Then, presumably, we shall turn to atomic energy (although, like the fossil fuels, it represents a non-renewable resource; one would think that its present custodians could find better things to do with it than create explosions). And then we will face a different breed of environmental pollution.

I am aware that reactors to produce electricity are already in use or under development, but I am apprehensive of what I know of the present generation of reactors and those proposed for the future.

The uranium fuel used in present reactors has to be reprocessed periodically to keep the chain reaction going. The reprocessing yields long-lived and biologically hazardous isotopes such as [90] Strontium and [137] Cesium that should be stored where they cannot contaminate the environment for at least 1,000 years; yet a goodly number of the storage tanks employed for this purpose are already leaking. At least these products of reprocessing can be chemically trapped and stored; another product, [85] Krypton, cannot be so trapped—it is sent into the atmosphere to add to the radiation exposure of the earth's biota, including man, and I don't think that anyone knows a practicable way to prevent this.

To soothe our concern about the pollution of the environment involved in fission reactors, we are glibly offered the prospect of "clean" fusion bombs and reactors. They do not require reprocessing and thus would not produce the Strontium, Cesium and Krypton isotopes. But to the best of my knowledge, no one knows how this new generation of reactors is to be built. And even if development is successful, fusion reactors will produce new contaminants. One such is tritium ([3] Hydrogen) which would become a constituent of water— and that water with its long-lived radioactivity would contaminate all environments and living things. The danger of tritium was underlined in an official publication of the Atomic Energy Commission in which it was suggested that for certain mining operations it might be better to use fission (i.e. "dirty") devices rather than fusion (i.e. "clean") devices "to avoid ground water contamination."

A prime example of what irresponsible use of atomic power could bring about is provided by the proposal to use nuclear explosives to dig a sea-level canal across Central America. The argument in its favor is that it is evidently the most economical way to accomplish the task.

Yet consider the effects upon our environment. If 170 megatons of nuclear charges will do the job, as has been estimated by the Corps of Engineers which apparently wants to do it, and if the fission explosions take place in average materials of the earth's crust, enough [137] Cesium would be produced to give every person on earth a radioactive dosage 26.5 times the permissible exposure level. Cesium behaves as a gas in such a cratering explosion, and prevailing winds in the region are from east to west, so the Pacific area would presumably be contaminated first. And Cesium moves right up through biological food chains, so we could anticipate its rapid dissemination among living things.

So much of the danger to man is summed up in that simple phrase, "We don't know." For example, consider the nitrogen cycle, which provides that element all organisms require for the building of proteins. Nitrogen is released into the atmosphere, along with ammonia, as a gas when plants and animals decay; live plants use both elements to build their proteins, but they cannot use nitrogen in gaseous form—that task is accomplished by certain bacteria and primitive algae in the soil and the roots of some plants. Animals build their proteins from the constituents of plant proteins. As in the case of oxygen, the rates of use and return of nitrogen have reached a balance so that the percentage of nitrogen in the atmosphere remains constant.

If any one of these numerous steps in the nitrogen cycle were to be disrupted, disaster would ensue for life on earth. Depending upon which step broke down, the nitrogen in the atmosphere might disappear, it might be replaced by poisonous ammonia or it might remain unused in the atmosphere because the plants could not absorb it in gaseous form.

Are any of these possibilities at hand? Has man's interference with natural processes begun to have a serious effect on the nitrogen cycle? The point is, we don't know—and we should, before we do too much more interfering.

We are dumping vast quantities of pollutants into the oceans. According to one estimate by the United States Food and Drug Administration, these include a half-million substances; many are of recent origin, including biologically active materials such as pesticides, radioisotopes and detergents to which the ocean's living forms have never before had to try to adapt. No more than a minute fraction of these substances or the combinations of them have been tested for toxicity to life—to the diatoms, the microscopic marine plants that produce most of the earth's oxygen, or to the bacteria and microorganisms involved in the nitrogen cycle.

If the tanker Torrey Canyon had been carrying a concentrated herbicide instead of petroleum, could photosynthesis in the North Sea have been stopped? Again, we don't know, but Berkmer is said to have believed that a very few instances of herbicide pollution, occurring in certain areas of the ocean that are high in photosynthetic activity, might cause the ultimate disaster.

The interference with delicately balanced cycles is not, however, the only instance of man's misuse of his natural heritage. He has also succeeded in rendering useless huge tracts of the earth's arable land.

We hear a lot today about "underdeveloped" and "developing" nations, but many of them might more accurately be called "overdeveloped." The valleys of the Tigris and Euphrates Rivers, for example, were supporting the Sumerian civilization in 3500 B.C. By the year 2000 B.C., a great irrigation complex based on these rivers had turned the area into the granary of the great Babylonian Empire (Pliny says that the Babylonians harvested two crops of grain each year and grazed sheep on the land between crops). But today less than 20 per cent of the land in Iraq is cultivated; more than half of the nation's income is from oil. The landscape is dotted with mounds, the remains of forgotten towns; the ancient irrigation works are filled with silt, the end product of soil erosion, and the ancient seaport of Ur is now 150 miles from the sea, its buildings buried under as much as 35 feet of silt.

The valley of the Nile was another cradle of civilization. Every year the river overflowed its banks at a predictable time, bringing water to the land and depositing a layer of soil rich in mineral nutrients for plants. Crops could be grown for seven months of the year.

Extensive irrigation systems were established in the valley before 2000 B.C. The land was the granary of the Roman Empire, and continued to flourish for another 2,000 years. But in modern times, economic considerations have inspired governments to divert the land from food to cash crops such as cotton in spite of the desperate need for more foodstuffs to feed a growing population. In 1902 a dam was built at Aswan to prevent the spring flood and to make possible year-round irrigation, and since then the soils have deteriorated through salinization and productivity in the valley has decreased.

Salinization is a typical phenomenon of arid regions where evaporation is greater than precipitation. Rainwater soaks into the earth, dissolving salts as it goes; when the sun appears, evaporation at the earth's surface draws this salty water upward by capillary action; and when this water in turn evaporates, it leaves a deposit of salts on the surface. The essential condition for salinization to take place is a net upward movement of water.

Irrigation in arid areas, though it may have short-range benefits, can also be fraught with long-range dangers. The large quantities of water used in irrigation are added to the water table, raising it to the level of the irrigation ditch bottom—that is to say, the ground below that point is saturated with water. Otherwise, of course, the water in the ditches would soak right down into the earth immediately below, rather than spreading outward to nourish land on either side. But this results in a sideward and then upward movement of the irrigation water toward the surface. And when the saltladen water reaches the surface and evaporates, salinization occurs. Unless great care is taken, irrigation can thus eventually ruin land—and it has often done so. The new Aswan high dam is designed to bring another million acres of land under irrigation, and it may well prove to be the ultimate disaster for Egypt.

Such sorry stories, could be told for country after country. The glories of ancient Mali and Ghana in West Africa were legends in medieval Europe. Ancient Greece had forested hills, ample water and productive soil. In the land that once exported the cedars of Lebanon to Egypt, the erosion-proof old Roman roads now stand several feet above a rock desert. In China and India ancient irrigation systems stand abandoned and filled with silt.

When the British assumed the rule of India two centuries ago, the population was about 60 million. Today it is about 500 million, and most of the nation's land problems have been created in the past century by deforestation and plowing and the resulting erosion and siltation, all stemming from efforts to support this fantastic population growth.

Overdevelopment is not confined to the Old World. Archaeologists have long wondered how the Mayas managed to support what was obviously a high civilization on the now unproductive soils of Guatemala and Yucatan. Evidently they exploited their land as intensively as possible until its fertility was exhausted and their civilization collapsed.

So this is the heritage of man's past—an impoverished land, a threat to the biogeochemical cycles. And what are we doing about it?

I don't want to comment on the advertising executive who asserts that billboards are "the art gallery of the public" or on the industry spokesman who says that "the ability of a river to absorb sewage is one

of our great natural resources and should be utilized to the utmost."
In the face of such self-serving statements, the efforts of those who try
to promote conservation on esthetic grounds seem inevitably doomed.
It makes one wonder, are we selecting for genotypes who can satisfy
all their esthetic needs in our congested cities? Are the Davy Crock-
etts and Kit Carsons who are born today destined for asylums, jail or
suicide?

POLLUTING THE ENVIRONMENT

Lord Ritchie-Calder

To hell with posterity! After all, what have the unborn ever done
for us? Nothing. Did they, with sweat and misery, make the Industrial
Revolution possible? Did they go down into the carboniferous forests
of millions of years ago to bring up coal to make wealth and see
nine-tenths of the carbon belched out as chimney soot? Did they drive
the plows that broke the plains to release the dust that the buffalo had
trampled and fertilized for centuries? Did they have to broil in steel
plants to make the machines and see the pickling acids poured into the
sweet waters of rivers and lakes? Did they have to labor to cut down
the tall timbers to make homesteads and provide newsprint for the
Sunday comics and the celluloid for Hollywood spectaculars, leaving
the hills naked to the eroding rains and winds? Did they have the
ingenuity to drill down into the Paleozoic seas to bring up the oil to
feed the internal-combustion engines so that their exhausts could
create smog? Did they have the guts to man rigs out at sea so that
boreholes could probe for oil in the offshore fissures of the San An-
dreas Fault? Did they endure the agony and the odium of the atom
bomb and spray the biosphere with radioactive fallout? All that the
people yet unborn have done is to wait and let us make the mistakes.
To hell with posterity! That, too, can be arranged. As Shelley wrote:
"Hell is a city much like London, a populous and smoky city."

At a conference held at Princeton, New Jersey, at the end of 1968,
Professor Kingsley Davis, one of the greatest authorities on urban
development, took the role of hell's realtor. The prospectus he offered

Lord Ritchie-Calder, "Polluting the Environment," *The Center Magazine,* a publication of The
Center for the Study of Democratic Institutions (May 1969). Reprinted by permission of the
publisher and author.

from his latest survey of world cities was hair-raising. He showed that thirty-eight per cent of the world's population is already living in what are defined as "urban places." Over one-fifth of the world's population is living in cities of a hundred thousand or more. Over 375,000,000 people are living in cities of a million and over. On present trends it will take only fifteen years for half the world's population to be living in cities, and in fifty-five years everyone will be urbanized.

Davis foresaw that within the lifetime of a child born today, on present rates of population increase, there will be fifteen billion people to be fed and housed—over four times as many as now. The whole human species will be living in cities of a million and over and the biggest city will have 1,300,000,000 inhabitants. Yes, 1.3 billion. That is 186 times as many as there are in Greater London today.

In his forebodings of Dystopia (with a "y" as in dyspepsia, but it could just as properly be "Dis," after the ruler of the Underworld), Doxiades has warned about the disorderly growth of cities, oozing into each other like confluent ulcers. He has given us Ecumenopolis— World City. The East Side of Ecumenopolis would have as its Main Street the Eurasian Highway, stretching from Glasgow to Bangkok, with the Channel tunnel as an underpass and a built-up area all the way. West Side, divided not by railroad tracks but by the Atlantic, is already emerging (or, rather, merging) in the United States. There is talk, and evidence, of "Boswash," the urban development of a built-up area from Boston to Washington. On the Pacific Coast, with Los Angeles already sprawling into the desert, the realtor's garden cities, briskly reënforced by industrial estates, are slurring into one another and presently will stretch all the way from San Diego to San Francisco. The Main Street of Sansan will be Route 101. This is insanity. We do not need a crystal ball to foresee what Davis and Doxiades are predicting—we can see it through smog-colored spectacles; we can smell it seventy years away because it is in our nostrils today; a blind man can see what is coming.

Are these trends inevitable? They are unless we do something about them. I have given up predicting and have taken to prognosis. There is a very important difference. Prediction is based on the projection of trends. Experts plan for the trends and thus confirm them. They regard warnings as instructions. For example, while I was lecturing in that horror city of Calcutta, where three-quarters of the population live in shacks without running water or sewage disposal, and, in the monsoon season, wade through their own floating excrement, I warned that within twenty-five years there would be in India at least five cities, each with populations of over sixty million, ten times bigger than Calcutta. I was warning against the drift into the great conurbations now going on, which has been encouraged by ill-conceived policies of industrialization. I was warning against imitating the German Ruhr, the British Black Country, and America's Pittsburgh. I was arguing for "population dams," for decentralized development based on the villages, which make up the traditional cultural and social pattern of India. These "dams" would prevent the flash floods of population into overpopulated areas. I was *warning,* but they accepted the prediction and ignored the warning. Soon thereafter I learned that an American university had been given a contract to make a feasibility study for a city of sixty million people north of Bombay. When enthusiasts get busy on a feasibility study, they invariably find that it is feasible. When they get to their drawing boards they have a whale of a time. They design skyscrapers above ground and subterranean tenements below ground. They work out minimal requirements of air and hence how much breathing space a family can survive in. They design "living-units," hutches for battery-fed people who are stacked together like kindergarten blocks. They provide water and regulate the sewage on the now well-established cost-efficiency principles of factory-farming. And then they finish up convinced that this is the most economical way of housing people. I thought I had scotched the idea by making representations through influential Indian friends. I asked them, among other things, how many mental hospitals they were planning to take care of the millions who would surely go mad under such conditions. But I have heard rumors that the planners are so slide-rule happy they are planning a city for six hundred million.

Prognosis is something else again. An intelligent doctor, having diagnosed the symptoms and examined the patient's condition, does not say (except in soap operas): "You have six months to live." He says: "Frankly, your condtion is serious. Unless you do so-and-so, and unless I do so-and-so, it is bound to deteriorate." The operative phrase is "do so-and-so." One does not have to plan *for* trends; if they are socially undesirable our duty is to plan *away* from them, and treat the symptoms before they become malignant.

A multiplying population multiplies the problems. The prospect of a world of fifteen billion people is intimidating. Three-quarters of the world's present population is inadequately fed—hundreds of millions are not getting the food necessary for well-being. So it is not just a question of quadrupling the present food supply; it means six to eight times that to take care of present deficiencies. It is not a matter of numbers, either; it is the *rate* of increase that mops up any improvements. Nor is it just a question of housing but of clothing and material satisfactions—automobiles, televisions, and the rest. That means greater inroads on natural resources, the steady destruction of amenities, and the conflict of interest between those who want oil and those who want oil-free beaches, or between those who want to get from here to there on wider and wider roads and those whose homes are going to collapse in mud slides because of the making of those roads. Lewis Mumford has suggested that civilization really began with the making of containers—cans, non-returnable bottles, cartons, plastic bags, none of which can be redigested by nature. Every sneeze accounts for a personal tissue. Multiply that by fifteen billion.

Environmental pollution is partly rapacity and partly a conflict of interest between the individual, multimillions of individuals, and the commonweal; but largely, in our generation, it is the exaggerated effects of specialization with no sense of ecology, i.e. the balance of nature. Claude Bernard, the French physiologist, admonished his colleagues over a century ago: "True science teaches us to doubt and in ignorance to refrain." Ecologists feel their way with a detector through a minefield of doubts. Specialists, cocksure of their own facts, push ahead, regardless of others.

Behind the sky-high fences of military secrecy, the physicists produced the atomic bomb—just a bigger explosion—without taking into account the biological effects of radiation. Prime Minister Attlee, who consented to the dropping of the bomb on Hiroshima, later said that no one, not Churchill, nor members of the British Cabinet, nor he himself, knew of the possible genetic effects of the blast. "If the scientists knew, they never told us." Twenty years before, Hermann Muller had shown the genetic effects of radiation and had been awarded the Nobel Prize, but he was a biologist and security treated this weapon as a physicist's bomb. In the peacetime bomb-testing, when everyone was alerted to the biological risks, we were told that the fallout of radioactive materials could be localized in the testing grounds. The radioactive dust on The Lucky Dragon, which was fishing well beyond the proscribed area, disproved that. Nevertheless, when it was decided to explode the H-bomb the assurance about localization was blandly repeated. The H-bomb would punch a hole into the stratosphere and the radioactive gases would dissipate. One of those gases is radioactive krypton, which decays into radioactive strontium, a particulate. Somebody must have known that but nobody worried unduly because it would happen above the troposphere, which might be described as the roof of the weather system. What was definitely overlooked was the fact that the troposphere is not continuous. There is the equatorial troposphere and the polar troposphere and they overlap. The radioactive strontium came back through the transom and was spread all over the world by the climatic jet streams to be deposited as rain. The result is that there is radiostrontium (which did not exist in nature) in the bones of every young person who was growing up during the bomb-testing—every young person, everywhere in the world. It may be medically insignificant but it is the brandmark of the Atomic Age generation and a reminder of the mistakes of their elders.

When the mad professor of fiction blows up his laboratory and then himself, that's O.K., but when scientists and decision-makers act out of ignorance and pretend it is knowledge, they are using the biosphere, the living space, as an experimental laboratory. The whole world is put in hazard. And they do it even when they are told not to. During the International Geophysical Year, the Van Allen Belt was discovered. The Van Allen Belt is a region of magnetic phenomena. Immediately the bright boys decided to carry out an experiment and explode a hydrogen bomb in the Belt to see if they could produce an artificial aurora. The colorful draperies, the luminous skirts of the aurora, are caused by drawing cosmic particles magnetically through the rare gases of the upper atmosphere. It is called ionization and is like passing electrons through the vacuum tubes of our familiar neon lighting. It was called the Rainbow Bomb. Every responsible scientist in cosmology, radio-astronomy, and physics of the atmosphere protested against this tampering with a system we did not understand. They exploded their bomb. They got their pyrotechnics. We still do not know the price we may have to pay for this artificial magnetic disturbance.

We could blame the freakish weather on the Rainbow Bomb but, in our ignorance, we could not sustain the indictment. Anyway, there are so many other things happening that could be responsible. We can look with misgiving on the tracks in the sky—the white tails of the jet aircraft and the exhausts of space rockets. These are introducing into the climatic system new factors, the effects of which are immensurable. The triggering of rain clouds depends upon the water vapor having a toehold, a nucleus, on which to form. That is how artificial precipitation, so-called rainmaking, is produced. So the jets, crisscrossing the weather system, playing tic-tac-toe, can produce a man-made change of climate.

On the longer term, we can see even more drastic effects from the many activities of *Homo insapiens,* Unthinking Man. In 1963, at the United Nations Science and Technology Conference, we took stock of the several effects of industrialization on the total environment. The atmosphere is not only the air which humans, animals, and plants breathe; it is the envelope which protects living things from harmful radiation from the sun and outer space. It is also the medium of climate, the winds and the rain. These are inseparable from the hydrosphere, including the oceans, which cover seven-tenths of the earth's surface with their currents and evaporation; and from the biosphere, with the vegetation and its transpiration and photosynthesis; and from the lithosphere, with its minerals, extracted for man's increasing needs. Millions of years ago the sun encouraged the growth of the primeval forests, which became our coal, and the life-growth in the Paleozoic seas, which became our oil. Those fossil-fuels, locked in the vaults through eons of time, are brought out by modern man and put back into the atmosphere from the chimney stacks and exhaust pipes of modern engineering.

This is an overplus on the natural carbon. About six billion tons of primeval carbon are mixed with the atmosphere every year. During the past century, in the process of industrialization, with its burning of fossil-fuels, more than four hundred billion tons of carbon have been artificially introduced into the atmosphere. The concentration in the air we breathe has been increased by approximately ten per cent; if all the known reserves of coal and oil were burned the concentration would be ten times greater.

This is something more than a public-health problem, more than a question of what goes into the lungs of the individual, more than a question of smog. The carbon cycle in nature is a self-adjusting mechanism. One school of scientific thought stresses that carbon monoxide can reduce solar radiation. Another school points out that an increase in carbon dioxide raises the temperature at the earth's surface. They are both right. Carbon dioxide, of course, is indispensable for plants and hence for the food cycle of creatures, including humans. It is the source of life. But a balance is maintained by excess carbon being absorbed by the seas. The excess is now taxing this absorption, and the effect on the heat balance of the earth can be significant because of what is known as "the greenhouse effect." A greenhouse lets in the sun's rays and retains the heat. Similarly, carbon dioxide, as a transparent diffusion, does likewise; it admits the radiant heat and keeps the convection heat close to the surface. It has been estimated that at the present rate of increase (those six billion tons a year) the mean annual temperature all over the world might increase by 5.8° F. in the next forty to fifty years.

Experts may argue about the time factor or about the effects, but certain things are observable not only in the industrialized Northern Hemisphere but also in the Southern Hemisphere. The ice of the north polar seas is thinning and shrinking. The seas, with their blanket of carbon dioxide, are changing their temperatures with the result that marine life is increasing and transpiring more carbon dioxide. With this combination, fish are migrating, even changing their latitudes. On land, glaciers are melting and the snow line is retreating. In Scandinavia, land which was perennially under snow and ice is thawing. Arrowheads of a thousand years ago, when the black earth was last exposed and when Eric the Red's Greenland was probably still green, have been found there. In the North American sub-Arctic a similar process is observable. Black earth has been exposed and retains the summer heat longer so that each year the effect moves farther north. The melting of the sea ice will not affect the sea level because the volume of floating ice is the same as the water it displaces, but the melting of the land's ice caps and glaciers, in which water is locked up, will introduce additional water to the oceans and raise the sea level. Rivers originating in glaciers and permanent snowfields (in the Himalayas, for instance) will increase their flow, and if the ice dams break the effects could be catastrophic. In this process, the patterns of rainfall will change, with increased precipitation in areas now arid and aridity in places now fertile. I am advising all my friends not to take ninety-nine-year leases on properties at present sea level.

The pollution of sweet-water lakes and rivers has increased so during the past twenty-five years that a Freedom from Thirst campaign is becoming as necessary as a Freedom from Hunger campaign. Again it is a conflict of motives and a conspiracy of ignorance. We can look at the obvious—the unprocessed urban sewage and the influx of industrial effluents. No one could possibly have believed that the Great Lakes in their immensity could ever be overwhelmed, or that Niagara Falls could lose its pristine clearness and fume like brown smoke, or that Lake Erie could become a cesspool. It did its best to oxidize the wastes from the steel plants by giving up its free oxygen until at last it surrendered and the anaerobic microörganisms took over. Of course, one can say that the mortuary smells of Lake Erie are not due to the pickling acids but to the dead fish.

The conflict of interests amounts to a dilemma. To insure that people shall be fed we apply our ingenuity in the form of artificial fertilizers, herbicides, pesticides, and insecticides. The runoff from the lands gets into the streams and rivers and distant oceans. DDT from the rivers of the United States has been found in the fauna of the Antarctic, where no DDT has ever been allowed. The dilemma becomes agonizing in places like India, with its hungry millions. It is now believed that the new strains of Mexican grain and I.R.C. (International Rice Center in the Philippines) rice, with their high yields, will provide enough food for them, belly-filling if not nutritionally balanced. These strains, however, need plenty of water, constant irrigation, plenty of fertilizers to sustain the yields, and tons of pesticides because standardized pedigree plants are highly vulnerable to disease. This means that the production will be concentrated in the river systems, like the Gangeatic Plains, and the chemicals will drain into the rivers.

The glib answer to this sort of thing is "atomic energy." If there is enough energy and it is cheap enough, you can afford to turn rivers into sewers and lakes into cesspools. You can desalinate the seas. But, for the foreseeable future, that energy will come from atomic fission, from the breaking down of the nucleus. The alternative, promised but undelivered, is thermonuclear energy—putting the H-bomb into dungarees by controlling the fusion of hydrogen. Fusion does not produce waste products, fission does. And the more peaceful atomic reactors there are, the more radioactive waste there will be to dispose of. The really dangerous material has to be buried. The biggest disposal area in the world is at Hanford, Washington. It encloses a stretch of the Columbia River and a tract of country covering 650 square miles. There, a twentieth-century Giza, it has cost much more to bury live atoms than it cost to entomb all the mummies of all the Pyramid Kings of Egypt.

At Hanford, the live atoms are kept in tanks constructed of carbon steel, resting in a steel saucer to catch any leakage. These are enclosed in a reënforced concrete structure and the whole construction is buried in the ground with only the vents showing. In the steel sepulchers, each with a million-gallon capacity, the atoms are very much alive. Their radioactivity keeps the acids in the witches' brew boiling. In the bottom of the tanks the temperature is well above the boiling point of water. There has to be a cooling system, therefore, and it must be continuously maintained. In addition, the vapors generated in the tanks have to be condensed and scrubbed, otherwise a radioactive miasma would escape from the vents. Some of the elements in those high-level wastes will remain radioactive for at least 250,000 years. It is most unlikely that the tanks will endure as long as the Egyptian pyramids.

Radioactive wastes from atomic processing stations have to be transported to such burial grounds. By the year 2000, if the present practices continue, the number of six-ton tankers in transit at any given time would be well over three thousand and the amount of radioactive products in them would be 980,000,000 curies—that is a mighty number of curies to be roaming around in a populated country.

There are other ways of disposing of radioactive waste and there are safeguards against the hazards, but those safeguards have to be enforced and constant vigilance maintained. There are already those who say that the safety precautions in the atomic industry are excessive.

Polluting the environment has been sufficiently dramatized by events in recent years to show the price we have to pay for our recklessness. It is not just the destruction of natural beauty or the sacrifice of recreational amenities, which are crimes in themselves, but interference with the whole ecology—with the balance of nature on which persistence of life on this planet depends. We are so fascinated by the gimmicks and gadgetry of science and technology and are in such a hurry to exploit them that we do not count the consequences.

We have plenty of scientific knowledge but knowledge is not wisdom: wisdom is knowledge tempered by judgment. At the moment, the scientists, technologists, and industrialists are the judge and jury in their own assize. Statesmen, politicians, and administrators are ill-equipped to make judgments about the true values of discoveries or developments. On the contrary, they tend to encourage the crash programs to get quick answers—like the Manhattan Project, which turned the laboratory discovery of uranium fission into a cataclysmic bomb in six years; the Computer/Automation Revolution; the Space Program; and now the Bio-engineering Revolution, with its possibilities not only of spare-organ plumbing but of changing the nature of living things by gene manipulation. They blunder into a minefield of undetected ignorance, masquerading as science.

The present younger generation has an unhappy awareness of such matters. They were born into the Atomic Age, programmed into the Computer Age, rocketed into the Space Age, and are poised on the threshold of the Bio-engineering Age. They take all these marvels for granted, but they are also aware that the advances have reduced the world to a neighborhood and that we are all involved one with another in the risks as well as the opportunities. They see the mistakes writ large. They see their elders mucking about with *their* world and *their* future. That accounts for their profound unease, whatever forms their complaints may take. They are the spokesmen for posterity and are justified in their protest. But they do not have the explicit answers, either.

Somehow science and technology must conform to some kind of social responsibility. Together, they form the social and economic dynamic of our times. They are the pacesetters for politics and it is in the political frame of reference that answers must be found. There can never be any question of restraining or repressing natural curiosity, which is true science, but there is ample justification for evaluating and judging developmental science. The common good requires nothing less.

THE NATIONAL POLLUTION SCANDAL

Gaylord Nelson

The natural environment of America—the woods and waters and wildlife, the clear air and blue sky, the fertile soil and the scenic landscape—is threatened with destruction. Our growing population and expanding industries, the explosion of scientific knowledge, the vast increase in income levels, leisure time, and mobility—all of these powerful trends are exerting such pressure on our natural resources that many of them could be effectively ruined over the next ten or fifteen years. Our overcrowded parks are becoming slums. Our birds and wildlife are being driven away or killed outright. Scenic rural areas are blighted by junkyards and billboards, and neon blight soils the outskirts of most cities. In our orgy of expansion, we are bulldozing away the natural landscape and building a cold new world of concrete and aluminum. Strip miners' shovels are tearing away whole mountains and spreading ugly wastes for miles around. America the affluent is well on the way to destroying America the beautiful. Of all these developments, the most tragic and the most costly is the rapidly mounting pollution of our lakes and streams.

Perhaps the pain is more intense for a Senator from a state like

Gaylord Nelson, "The National Pollution Scandal," *The Progressive,* February 1967. Reprinted by permission of the publisher.

Wisconsin, bordered on three sides by the Great Lakes and the Mississippi, blessed with 8,000 inland lakes and hundreds of rivers and trout streams. Actually, our state seems rather fortunate at the moment. A yachtsman on Lake Superior can raise a bucket of water still crystal-clear and cold enough to drink with delight. Canoeists on the St. Croix or Wolf Rivers still shoot through frothing rapids of sparkling water, and catch fish in the deep, swirling pools.

But the bell is tolling for Wisconsin just as for all the nation. A recent survey of twelve major river basins in southeastern Wisconsin found not a single one fit even for the partial body contact involved in fishing or wading. A competent governmental agency concluded that 754 miles of rivers in this region had been turned into open sewers. Beaches along Lake Michigan, a vast blue sea with seemingly limitless quantities of fresh water, are being closed to swimmers. A sordid ocean of pollution is pouring into the Mississippi from the Minneapolis-St. Paul urban complex. The first serious signs of pollution are soiling Lake Superior, and our small inland lakes are, one by one, becoming murky and smelly and choked with algae.

Elsewhere, all across the nation, the same tragedy is being enacted, although in many areas the curtain already has come down. The waters are already ruined. Every major river system in America is seriously polluted, from the Androscoggin in Maine to the Columbia in the far Northwest. The rivers once celebrated in poetry and song —the Monongahela, the Cumberland, the Ohio, the Hudson, the Delaware, the Rio Grande—have been blackened with sewage, chemicals, oil, and trash. They are sewers of filth and disease. The Monogahela, which drains the mining and industrial areas of West Virginia and Pennsylvania, empties the equivalent of 200,000 tons of sulfuric acid each year into the Ohio River—which in turn is the water supply for millions of people who use and re-use Ohio River water many times over.

National attention has been centered on once beautiful Lake Erie, the great lake which is the recreational front yard of Buffalo, Cleveland, Toledo and Detroit, and which supplies water for ten million Americans. A Public Health Service survey of Lake Erie made the shocking discovery that, in the 2,600 square mile heart of the lake, there was no dissolved oxygen at all in the water. The lake in this vast area could support no desirable aquatic life, only lowly creatures such as bloodworms, sludgeworms, sowbugs, and bloodsuckers.

Along with the germs and industrial acids which pour into Lake Erie are millions of pounds of phosphates, a major ingredient in detergents. Each pound of phosphate will propagate 700 pounds of algae. Beneath the waters of this great lake, largely hidden from sight, a hideous cancer-like growth of algae is forming. As algae blooms and dies, it becomes a pollutant itself. It robs the lake of still more oxygen —and it releases the phosphate to grow another crop of algae. Lake Erie is a product of its tributaries. A Public Health Service study of these American sewers is horrifying to read.

The Maumee River flows from Fort Wayne, Indiana, through Defiance and Napoleon, Ohio, and on to Toledo, where it joins the lake. Even as far upstream as Fort Wayne, the river has insufficient oxygen to support anything but trash fish and lower organisms, and as it flows toward Lake Erie conditions get steadily worse. The count of coliform bacteria runs as high as 24,000 times the allowable maximum under Federal drinking water standards. The concentration of carbolic acid, a byproduct of steelmaking, runs up to 137 times the allowable maximum. A packing company dumps 136 pounds of oil per day into the Maumee River. A plating company dumps thirty-eight pounds of cyanide per day. Defiance, Ohio, closes its sewage plant entirely for one or two months each year, and all its raw sewage goes directly into the Maumee. Below Defiance, a foundry dumps cinders and ashes into the river. The Maumee is joined by the Auglaize River, which is even more polluted than the Maumee, and is especially rich in ammonia compounds. At Napoleon, Ohio, the city draws its drinking water from the sordid Maumee, and a soup company draws off ten million gallons a day for soup processing. (The firm assures me that its modern water treatment plant, complete with carbon filters, can "polish the water to a high quality.") Below Napoleon, things get really bad. Forty per cent of samples taken by the Public Health Service showed presence of salmonella, an intestinal bacteria that can cause severe illness. As the Maumee flows into Lake Erie at Toledo, it gets its final dose of pollution—the effluent from the Toledo sewage plant and what the Public Health Service describes as "oil, scum, metallic deposits, and toxic materials."

Another Lake Erie tributary—the Cuyahoga—which flows into the lake at Cleveland, is described by the Public Health Service as "debris-filled, oil-slicked, and dirty-looking throughout." It is loaded with coliform bacteria and salmonella. It is so polluted with oil that it frequently catches fire. Structures known as "fire breaks" have been built out into the river to fight these blazes. In the Cleveland harbor, the Public Health Service could find virtually no conventional aquatic life. However, the sludgeworms which thrive on organic matter were well represented—400,000 per square meter on the harbor bottom.

That is the story of Lake Erie, and although it is so shocking and disgusting as to deserve urgent national attention, it is not unique. Southern Lake Michigan, ringed with oil refineries, steel mills, and municipal sewage outfalls, may be even worse. Scientists estimate that it would take 100 years to replace the polluted water of southern Lake Michigan, and some consider the pollution in this area irreversible.

We have our own Wisconsin pollution scandal in Green Bay, a magnificent recreational body of water in northeastern Wisconsin, widely known as a yachtsman's paradise and site of a multimillion dollar resort industry. This "Cape Cod of Wisconsin" is threatened with ruin by a tide of pollution which is moving up the bay at the rate of more than one mile per year. The pollution comes from rivers such as the Fox, the Peshtigo, the Oconto, and the Menominee, which drain large areas of Wisconsin and northern Michigan.

The experience in Lake Erie, Lake Michigan, and Green Bay has convinced many experts of this chilling fact: It is a definite possibility that the Great Lakes—the greatest single source of fresh water in the world—could be effectively destroyed by pollution in the years ahead. If this were to happen, it would be the greatest natural resource disaster in modern history.

That is the outline of this new American tragedy. The obvious question now is, what can be done about it? First, I think we must learn what a complex and widespread problem we face in water pollution. Like crime, like death on the highway, pollution is a social problem which extends throughout our society. There is no single villain, and there is no simple answer. It must be attacked for what it is—a sinister byproduct of the prosperous, urbanized, industrialized world in which we live. We must take care not to ride off in pursuit of just one villain —such as city sewage, or industrial waste, or detergents, or toilet wastes from boats; this is a battle which must be fought with skill and courage on many different fronts. Nor should we be fooled by the strategy of many polluters, who argue, in effect: "The pollution which we cause is minor compared to the big, nation-wide problem. Why not leave us alone and go after the big offenders?" Even some of the lesser offenders in the pollution crisis could ruin us in time.

The primary sources of pollution are these:

Municipal Sewage. Despite heroic efforts and heavy investments by many cities, our municipal sewage treatment plants are woefully inadequate. Some cities have no treatment at all; others remove only part of the pollutants found in sewage. As a result, the effluent discharged by our cities today (treated and untreated) is equivalent to the *untreated* sewage from a nation of seventy-five million people.

Industrial Pollution. This is roughly twice as big a problem as municipal sewage. Despite tremendous investments in research and treatment plant construction by some industries, the overall record is terrible. Some industries feel they cannot remain competitive if they spend heavily for treatment plants. Communities and states are reluctant to push them too far. As a result, industrial wastes (treated and untreated) now discharged into our waters are presently equal to the *untreated* sewage of a nation of 165 million people.

Septic Tanks. Vast sections of the nation have no sewer collection or treatment system at all. In such areas, underground septic tanks, often poorly made and undersized, are expected to distribute wastes into the soil. They overflow into natural watercourses, they leak bacteria and detergents into underground wells, and they are destroying lakes by filling them with nutrients that foster heavy growths of algae.

Ships and Marine Terminals. In selected areas, the discharge of toilet wastes, oil, garbage, and rubbish from ships and shoreline installations is a major problem. For some reason, this form of pollution is widely tolerated and enforcement of laws forbidding it is virtually nonexistent.

Pesticides. The terrifying prospect of spreading poison all over the globe confronts us. We now use more than 700 million pounds a year of synthetic pesticides and agricultural chemicals of 45,000 varities. This volume is expected to increase tenfold in the next twenty years. Many of these poisons persist forever in the environment, and their concentration builds up geometrically as they progress through the food chain (water, seaweed, fish, birds, mammals). DDT residue has been discovered in penguins in Antarctica, in reindeer in Alaska, in seals, and in fish caught in remote areas of the Pacific Ocean. One part of DDT in one billion parts of water will kill blue crabs in eight days.

Silt. One of the most serious pollutants all over the world is the dirt which washes into our waters from off the land. This somewhat natural problem is disastrously aggravated by contemporary trends—widespread clearing of land for subdivisions and shopping centers; construction of highways and parking lots (which cause rapid runoff) and the intensive development of lakeshores and riverbanks. Controlling surface runoff and the silation which it causes is complicated by our patchwork of political boundaries and the lack of coordinated government planning.

Detergents, Fertilizers, and Other Chemicals. Some of these commonly used substances pass through even good waste treatment systems and become persistent pollutants. Such pollution can be eliminated only by changing the composition of such substances, regulating their use, or devising new removal techniques.

Obviously, any nationwide problem made up of so many elements is extremely difficult to attack. Yet I believe that the rapidly accelerating destruction of our natural resources is our number one domestic problem, and the greatest of all our resource problems is water pollution. If we are to meet this pollution threat, if we are to save the waters of America and preserve this most indispensable part of our natural environment, we must make the war on pollution a high priority matter at every level of government—local, state and Federal—and we must insist that private industry do likewise. Baffling and complicated as the pollution problem is, it is not insoluble. There is no reason in the world why a great and prosperous nation, with the money and knowhow to shoot man to the moon, cannot prevent its lakes and rivers from being destroyed and its life-giving water supplies endangered. Just as there is no single cause of pollution, so is there no single solution to the problem.

Consider the question of what to do about municipal sewage and industrial wastes. Why do we tolerate a situation where these two sources alone pour into our waters each year the equivalent of the completely untreated sewage of a nation of 240 million persons? Here it is largely a matter of lack of money, aggravated in some cases by a shocking lack of public concern. There are now more than 1300 communities which have sewer systems but discharge their wastes into the waters without any treatment at all. These communities have a population of more than eleven million people. How such a condition could exist in the year 1966—when it is generally illegal to throw a gum wrapper out of a car window—is inconceivable.

We have another 1300 communities—with almost seventeen million population—which treat their wastes but in a completely inadequate manner. In most cases, these are communities which use what is known as "primary" treatment. They screen their sewage and let the solids settle out, but they do not remove dissolved solids, salts, chemicals, bacteria, and special problems such as detergents. Every community should have what is known as "secondary" treatment, under which sewage—after primary treatment—is held in holding tanks, brought into contact with air and biologically active sludge, so that bacteria have a chance to consume the pollutants.

The Conference of State Sanitary Engineers estimates that it would cost $1.8 billion to provide adequate sewage collection and treatment for these communities which now have no treatment or completely inadequate treatment. But even this would still leave us with a massive municipal pollution problem. Even good secondary treatment removes only eighty per cent to ninety per cent of the pollutants. Chicago, for instance, with a good secondary treatment plant, discharges treated effluent which is equivalent to the untreated, raw sewage of one million people. It dumps 1,800 tons of solids per day into the Illinois waterway. At the rate the pollution load is increasing it is estimated that even if all communities have secondary treatment plants by 1980, the total amount of pollutants reaching watercourses would still be the same as today. Obviously, we need a massive program to build highly effective city sewage treatment plants.

It is also obvious that local property taxes cannot support such a gigantic investment, and that if we wait for communities to do this on their own, it will never be done. Most state budgets also are severely strained, so much of this burden is going to have to be borne by the Federal government—if we want the job done early enough to be effective. The Senate Air and Water Pollution subcommittee estimates that it will cost $20 billion to provide secondary treatment in plants serving eighty per cent of the population and more advanced treatment in plants serving the other twenty per cent. We have had a Federal program to assist communities in building such treatment plants for the past ten years, but it has been inadequate. It has recently been greatly improved, but it is still inadequate. In the past it has provided grants of up to thirty per cent within the limits of available funds. The most recent act—the Clean Waters Restoration Act of 1966—authorizes a total of about $3.6 billion over the next five years ($150 million in 1967, $450 million in 1968, $700 million in 1969, $1 billion in 1970, and $1.25 billion in 1971). A community can get a grant for up to fifty per cent of the cost of a project, provided the state pays twenty-five per cent and provided water quality standards have been established.

New York needs an estimated $1.7 billion for new sewage plants. The new law would give it a total of only $307 million. Ohio needs $1 billion and would get $180 million. Wisconsin needs $286 million and would get $75 million. If we are serious about the Federal government paying fifty per cent of the cost of eliminating municipal pollution, then Washington must provide $10 billion—not $3.6 billion—and even then we will be expecting our hard-pressed states and communities to come up with another $10 billion. Personally, I think it is unrealistic to expect the states and localities to assume a burden of this size. And I do not think the nation can sit by and wait while its communities struggle to build up the financial resources and the political courage needed to do the job. I think we should get sewage treatment plants built the way we are getting interstate highways built—by offering ninety per cent Federal financing. I have introduced legislation which would establish such a program.

The municipal sewage problem is complicated by another problem —combined storm and sanitary sewers. By combining storm water and human wastes in one sewer system, many cities build up such a tremendous load during rainstorms that their sewage treatment plants cannot handle it. They have had to install automatic devices which divert the combined sewer load directly into lakes or streams whenever it gets above a certain level. In this manner, sixty-five billion gallons of raw, untreated sewage goes into our lakes and rivers each year. Most cities are separating storm and sanitary sewers in new subdivisions, but the task of separating the sewers in the older areas is a staggering one. Complete separation would cost an estimated $30 billion. It would cost $160 per resident in Washington, D.C., $215 in Milwaukee, $280 in Concord, New Hampshire. It would cost Wisconsin an estimated $186 million, Indiana $496 million, Michigan $970 million, New York and Illinois about $1.12 billion each. These are only general estimates of the direct costs and they do not take into account the disruption of traffic and the local economy caused by ripping up miles of underground sewers. In the hope of avoiding such costs, the Federal government has underwritten several research projects to see if this problem cannot be met in some othe way—through temporary underground storage of sewer overflows, for instance, or by building smaller sanitary sewer pipes inside existing storm sewers.

The staggering problem of *industrial* pollution is virtually untouched today by our Federal anti-pollution programs, even though industry contributes twice as much pollution to our waters as do municipalities. If we do not step up our industrial waste treatment plant construction, the pollution effect of industrial wastes alone by 1970 will be equal to the untreated, raw sewage from our entire population. Industries are widely criticized for dumping wastes into our waters, and this criticism is often justified. They are pressured by local, state, and Federal officials. But some industries are able to avoid a serious crackdown against them by threatening to move. Most industries argue—sometimes effectively—that they cannot be expected to make massive investments in treatment plants if their competitors—often in different parts of the country—are not forced to do so.

I have come to the conclusion that the threat of enforcement alone is not going to solve our industrial pollution problem. We must provide direct financial assistance to see to it that the plants are built. I have introduced legislation to provide both loans and grants of up to fifty per cent to industries whose size and economic circumstances prevent them from assuming the full burden of providing their own facilities. I think such assistance should be carefully limited and should be for a short period, but I do not think we can avoid it. We are going to pay the cost of industrial pollution in one way or another—in the cost of the manufactured product, in taxes, or in ruined water resources.

But massive construction programs alone are not going to solve our municipal and industrial pollution problems. We need a tremendous expansion of Federally supported research to find completely new answers. Our whole waste disposal system, from the household toilet to the municipal sewage treatment plant, is a holdover from another era. The system should be studied and redesigned, using the latest scientific techniques, and fitted into a coordinated, nationwide system of waste disposal. Research grants should be made to private industry and universities to develop new methods and devices to refine, use, neutralize, or destroy pollutants. We should compute what our present waste disposal systems are costing us—including the loss in natural resources destroyed—and what alternative systems would cost.

Compared with municipal and industrial pollution, the other pollution problems I have mentioned are statistically small. For that reason, they are often ignored. But we cannot safely do that. Even if we managed to contain the flood of municipal and industrial pollution, the other sources could do fatal damage to our environment. Septic tanks must be controlled at the state and local level, and in many areas I think we must forbid new installations and work to replace existing ones with sewer systems. For instance, once an inland lake is ringed with cottages with septic tanks, it is doomed. Septic tanks must drain somewhere and in most lakeshore settings the natural drainage flow is into the lake. At the very least, this drainage will fertilize the lake, cause the rapid growth of algae, and turn the lake into a murky, foul-smelling mess.

Ship pollution is certainly serious enough to justify Federal action, even though such suggestions cause howls of protest from those who insist it "isn't practical." Why is it practical to install retention facilities on buses, house trailers, and aircraft but not on boats and ships? Obviously, we are willing to allow wastes to be dumped into our water supplies which we would never tolerate being dumped onto the land. We need Federal laws to require suitable facilities on all vessels using our navigable waters, and we need a better enforcement system to crack down on such disgraceful practices as dumping oil and pumping out oily ballast tanks on the Great Lakes and in our rivers.

The siltation problem can be controlled only through strict zoning and land use controls. We have got to prevent intensive development of our shorelines if we are to save our waters. Once a large portion of the natural vegetative cover is destroyed, the water resource is in danger. I believe that the Federal government should provide financial assistance to those willing to carry out soil conservation practices along our lakes and streams on a scale large enough to be meaningful:

Pesticides, detergents, and exotic new chemicals will plague us for years to come. New treatment systems may offer some hope for removing these substances, but I think they must be controlled directly. Those which cannot be removed safely in normal treatment processes, and those which have chemical structures which cause them to persist in our environment and to threaten fish, wildlife, and human health, should be banned or their use strictly regulated.

In speeches in some twenty-three states in the past four years, I have called for an emergency, crash program to fight water polution. I have offered my estimate of the cost of conquering water pollution as $50 to $100 billion over the next decade. It now appears I may have been conservative. The Public Health Service now estimates that it will cost some $20 billion to clean up the Great Lakes alone, and the total national cost is now estimated at $100 billion. But everywhere I have gone I have found the public willing to pay this cost to save their waters. In fact, I think the public is far ahead of local, state, and Federal officials in facing up to this crisis. I think that citizens in most communities would support a sharp crackdown on local polluters of every variety. I think they want their states to establish high water quality standards, and then enforce them. I think they can be shown the need for bold regional action to deal with those vast interstate pollution problems (such as on the Mississippi and the Great Lakes) which obviously are too big for any community or any state to handle. And I think that the citizens of America now recognize that the destruction of the major river networks of the nation, the threatened destruction of the Great Lakes, and the slow ruination of our treasured inland lakes and trout streams is a calamity of such gigantic proportions as to deserve the urgent attention of all citizens and prompt action by the national government.

ECO-CATASTROPHE!

Paul Ehrlich

The end of the ocean came late in the summer of 1979, and it came even more rapidly than the biologists had expected. There had been signs for more than a decade, commencing with the discovery in 1968 that DDT slows down photosynthesis in marine plant life. It was announced in a short paper in the technical journal, Science, but to ecologists it smacked of doomsday. They knew that all life in the sea depends on photosynthesis, the chemical process by which green plants bind the sun's energy and make it available to living things. And they knew that DDT and similar chlorinated hydrocarbons had polluted the entire surface of the earth, including the sea.

But that was only the first of many signs. There had been the final gasp of the whaling industry in 1973, and the end of the Peruvian anchovy fishery in 1975. Indeed, a score of other fisheries had disappeared quietly from over-exploitation and various eco-catastrophes by 1977. The term "eco-catastrophe" was coined by a California ecologist in 1969 to describe the most spectacular of man's attacks on the systems which sustain his life. He drew his inspiration from the Santa Barbara offshore oil disaster of that year, and from the news which spread among naturalists that virtually all of the Golden State's seashore bird life was doomed because of chlorinated hydrocarbon interference with its reproduction. Eco-catastrophes in the sea became

Dr. Paul Ehrlich, "Eco-Catastrophe!" *Ramparts*, Sept. 1969. Copyright Ramparts Magazine, Inc., 1969. By permission of the Author and the Editors.

increasingly common in the early 1970's. Mysterious "blooms" of previously rare micro-organisms began to appear in offshore waters. Red tides—killer outbreaks of a minute single-celled plant—returned to the Florida Gulf coast and were sometimes accompanied by tides of other exotic hues.

It was clear by 1975 that the entire ecology of the ocean was changing. A few types of phytoplankton were becoming resistant to chlorinated hydrocarbons and were gaining the upper hand. Changes in the phytoplankton community led inevitably to changes in the community of zooplankton, the tiny animals which eat the phytoplankton. These changes were passed on up the chains of life in the ocean to the herring, plaice, cod and tuna. As the diversity of life in the ocean diminished, its stability also decreased.

Other changes had taken place by 1975. Most ocean fishes that returned to fresh water to breed, like the salmon, had become extinct, their breeding streams so dammed up and polluted that their powerful homing instinct only resulted in suicide. Many fishes and shellfishes that bred in restricted areas along the coasts followed them as onshore pollution escalated.

By 1977 the annual yield of fish from the sea was down to 30 million metric tons, less than one-half the per capita catch of a decade earlier. This helped malnutrition to escalate sharply in a world where an estimated 50 million people per year were already dying of starvation. The United Nations attempted to get all chlorinated hydrocarbon insecticides banned on a worldwide basis, but the move was defeated by the United States. This opposition was generated primarily by the American petrochemical industry, operating hand in glove with its subsidiary, the United States Department of Agriculture. Together they persuaded the government to oppose the U.N. move—which was not difficult since most Americans believed that Russia and China were more in need of fish products than was the United States. The United Nations also attempted to get fishing nations to adopt strict and enforced catch limits to preserve dwindling stocks. This move was blocked by Russia, who, with the most modern electronic equipment, was in the best position to glean what was left in the sea. It was, curiously, on the very day in 1977 when the Soviet Union announced its refusal that another ominous article appeared in Science. It announced that incident solar radiation had been so reduced by worldwide air pollution that serious effects on the world's vegetation could be expected.

Apparently it was a combination of ecosystem destabilization, sunlight reduction, and a rapid escalation in chlorinated hydrocarbon pollution from massive Thanodrin applications which triggered the ultimate catastrophe. Seventeen huge Soviet-financed Thanodrin plants were operating in underdeveloped countries by 1978. They had been part of a massive Russian "aid offensive" designed to fill the gap caused by the collapse of America's ballyhooed "Green Revolution."

It became apparent in the early '70s that the "Green Revolution" was more talk than substance. Distribution of high yield "miracle" grain seeds had caused temporary local spurts in agricultural production. Simultaneously, excellent weather had produced record harvests. The combination permitted bureaucrats, especially in the United States Department of Agriculture and the Agency for International Development (AID), to reverse their previous pessimism and indulge in an outburst of optimistic propaganda about staving off famine. They raved about the approaching transformation of agriculture in the underdeveloped countries (UDCs). The reason for the propaganda reversal was never made clear. Most historians agree that a combination of utter ignorance of ecology, a desire to justify past errors, and pressure from agro-industry (which was eager to sell pesticides, fertilizers, and farm machinery to the UDCs and agencies helping the UDCs) was behind the campaign. Whatever the motivation, the results were clear. Many concerned people, lacking the expertise to see through the Green Revolution drivel, relaxed. The population-food crisis was "solved."

But reality was not long in showing itself. Local famine persisted in northern India even after good weather, brought an end to the ghastly Bihar famine of the mid-'60s. East Pakistan was next, followed by a resurgence of general famine in northern India. Other foci of famine rapidly developed in Indonesia, the Philippines, Malawi, the Congo, Egypt, Colombia, Ecuador, Honduras, the Dominican Republic, and Mexico.

Everywhere hard realities destroyed the illusion of the Green Revolution. Yields dropped as the progressive farmers who had first accepted the new seeds found that their higher yields brought lower prices—effective demand (hunger plus cash) was not sufficient in poor countries to keep prices up. Less progressive farmers, observing this, refused to make the extra effort required to cultivate the "miracle" grains. Transport systems proved inadequate to bring the necessary fertilizer to the fields where the new and extremely fertilizer-sensitive grains were being grown. The same systems were also inadequate to move produce to markets. Fertilizer plants were not built fast enough, and most of the underdeveloped countries could not scrape together funds to purchase supplies, even on concessional terms. Finally, the inevitable happened, and pests began to reduce yields in even the most carefully cultivated fields. Among the first were the famous "miracle rats" which invaded Philippine "miracle rice" fields early in 1969. They were quickly followed by many insects and viruses, thriving on the relatively pest-susceptible new grains, encouraged by the vast and dense plantings, and rapidly acquiring resistance to the chemicals used against them. As chaos spread until even the most obtuse agriculturists and economists realized that the Green Revolution had turned brown, the Russians stepped in.

In retrospect it seems incredible that the Russians, with the American mistakes known to them, could launch an even more incompetent program of aid to the underdeveloped world. Indeed, in the early 1970's there were cynics in the United States who claimed that outdoing the stupidity of American foreign aid would be physically impossible. Those critics were, however, obviously unaware that the Russians had been busily destroying their own environment for many years. The virtual disappearance of sturgeon from Russian rivers caused a great shortage of caviar by 1970. A standard joke among Russian scientists at that time was that they had created an artificial caviar which was indistinguishable from the real thing—except by taste. At any rate the Soviet Union, observing with interest the progressive deterioration of relations between the UDCs and the United States, came up with a solution. It had recently developed what it claimed was the ideal insecticide, a highly lethal chlorinated hydrocarbon complexed with a special agent for penetrating the external skeletal armor of insects. Announcing that the new pesticide, called Thanodrin, would truly produce a Green Revolution, the Soviets entered into negotiations with various UDCs for the construction of massive Thanodrin factories. The USSR would bear all the costs; all it wanted in return were certain trade and military concessions.

It is interesting now, with the perspective of years, to examine in some detail the reasons why the UDCs welcomed the Thanodrin plan with such open arms. Government officials in these countries ignored the protests of their own scientists that Thanodrin would not solve the problems which plagued them. The governments now knew that the basic cause of their problems was overpopulation, and that these problems had been exacerbated by the dullness, daydreaming, and cupidity endemic to all governments. They knew that only population control and limited development aimed primarily at agriculture could have spared them the horrors they now faced. They knew it, but they were not about to admit it. How much easier it was simply to accuse the Americans of failing to give them proper aid; how much simpler to accept the Russian panacea.

And then there was the general worsening of relations between the United States and the UDCs. Many things had contributed to this. The situation in America in the first half of the 1970's deserves our close scrutiny. Being more dependent on imports for raw materials than the Soviet Union, the United States had, in the early 1970's, adopted more and more heavy-handed policies in order to insure continuing supplies. Military adventures in Asia and Latin America had further lessened the international credibility of the United States as a great defender of freedom—an image which had begun to deteriorate rapidly during the pointless and fruitless Viet-Nam conflict. At home, acceptance of the carefully manufactured image lessened dramatically, as even the more romantic and chauvinistic citizens began to understand the role of the military and the industrial system in what John Kenneth Galbraith had aptly named "The New Industrial State."

At home in the USA the early '70s were traumatic times. Racial violence grew and the habitability of the cities diminished, as nothing substantial was done to ameliorate either racial inequities or urban blight. Welfare rolls grew as automation and general technological progress forced more and more people into the category of "unemployable." Simultaneously a taxpayers' revolt occurred. Although there was not enough money to build the schools, roads, water systems, sewage systems, jails, hospitals, urban transit lines, and all the other amenities needed to support a burgeoning population, Americans refused to tax themselves more heavily. Starting in Youngstown, Ohio in 1969 and followed closely by Richmond, California, community after community was forced to close its schools or curtail educational operations for lack of funds. Water supplies, already marginal in quality and quantity in many places by 1970, deteriorated quickly. Water rationing occurred in 1723 municipalities in the summer of 1974, and hepatitis and epidemic dysentery rates climbed about 500 per cent between 1970–1974.

Air pollution continued to be the most obvious manifestation of environmental deterioration. It was, by 1972, quite literally in the eyes of all Americans. The year 1973 saw not only the New York and Los

Angeles smog disasters, but also the publication of the Surgeon General's massive report on air pollution and health. The public had been partially prepared for the worst by the publicity given to the U.N. pollution conference held in 1972. Deaths in the late '60s caused by smog were well known to scientists, but the public had ignored them because they mostly involved the early demise of the old and sick rather than people dropping dead on the freeways. But suddenly our citizens were faced with nearly 200,000 corpses and massive documentation that they could be the next to die from respiratory disease. They were not ready for that scale of disaster. After all, the U.N. conference had not predicted that accumulated air pollution would make the planet uninhabitable until almost 1990. The population was terrorized as TV screens became filled with scenes of horror from the disaster areas. Especially vivid was NBC's coverage of hundreds of unattended people choking out their lives outside of New York's hospitals. Terms like nitrogen oxide, acute bronchitis and cardiac arrest began to have real meaning for most Americans.

The ultimate horror was the announcement that chlorinated hydrocarbons were now a major constituent of air pollution in all American cities. Autopsies of smog disaster victims revealed an average chlorinated hydrocarbon load in fatty tissue equivalent to 26 parts per million of DDT. In October, 1973, the Department of Health, Education and Welfare announced studies which showed unequivocally that increasing death rates from hypertension, cirrhosis of the liver, liver cancer and a series of other diseases had resulted from the chlorinated hydrocarbon load. They estimated that Americans born since 1946 (when DDT usage began) now had a life expectancy of only 49 years, and predicted that if current patterns continued, this expectancy would reach 42 years by 1980, when it might level out. Plunging insurance stocks triggered a stock market panic. The president of Velsicol, Inc., a major pesticide producer, went on television to "publicly eat a teaspoonful of DDT" (it was really powdered milk) and announce that HEW had been infiltrated by Communists. Other giants of the petrochemical industry, attempting to dispute the indisputable evidence, launched a massive pressure campaign on Congress to force HEW to "get out of agriculture's business." They were aided by the agro-chemical journals, which had decades of experience in misleading the public about the benefits and dangers of pesticides. But by now the public realized that it had been duped. The Nobel Prize for medicine and physiology was given to Drs. J. L. Radomski and W. B. Deichmann, who in the late 1960's had pioneered in the documentation of the long-term lethal effects of chlorinated hydrocarbons. A Presidential Commission with unimpeachable credentials directly accused the agro-chemical complex of "condemning many millions of Americans to an early death." The year 1973 was the year in which Americans finally came to understand the direct threat to their existence posed by environmental deterioration.

And 1973 was also the year in which most people finally comprehended the indirect threat. Even the president of Union Oil Company and several other industrialists publicly stated their concern over the reduction of bird populations which had resulted from pollution by DDT and other chlorinated hydrocarbons. Insect populations boomed because they were resistant to most pesticides and had been freed, by the incompetent use of those pesticides, from most of their natural enemies. Rodents swarmed over crops, multiplying rapidly in the absence of predatory birds. The effect of pests on the wheat crop was especially disastrous in the summer of 1973, since that was also the year of the great drought. Most of us can remember the shock which greeted the announcement by atmospheric physicists that the shift of the jet stream which had caused the drought was probably permanent. It signalled the birth of the Midwestern desert. Man's air-polluting activities had by then caused gross changes in climatic patterns. The news, of course, played hell with commodity and stock markets. Food prices skyrocketed, as savings were poured into hoarded canned goods. Official assurances that food supplies would remain ample fell on deaf ears, and even the government showed signs of nervousness when California migrant field workers went out on strike again in protest against the continued use of pesticides by growers. The strike burgeoned into farm burning and riots. The workers, calling themselves "The Walking Dead," demanded immediate compensation for their shortened lives, and crash research programs to attempt to lengthen them.

It was in the same speech in which President Edward Kennedy, after much delay, finally declared a national emergency and called out the National Guard to harvest California's crops, that the first mention of population control was made. Kennedy pointed out that the United States would no longer be able to offer any food aid to other nations and was likely to suffer food shortages herself. He suggested that, in view of the manifest failure of the Green Revolution, the only hope of the UDCs lay in population control. His statement, you will recall, created an uproar in the underdeveloped countries. Newspaper editorials accused the United States of wishing to prevent small countries from becoming large nations and thus threatening American hegemony. Politicians asserted that President Kennedy was a "creature of the giant drug combine" that wished to shove its pills down every woman's throat.

Among Americans, religious opposition to population control was very slight. Industry in general also backed the idea. Increasing poverty in the UDCs was both destroying markets and threatening supplies of raw materials. The seriousness of the raw material situation had been brought home during the Congressional Hard Resources hearings in 1971. The exposure of the ignorance of the cornucopian economists had been quite a spectacle—a spectacle brought into virtually every American's home in living color. Few would forget the distinguished geologist from the University of California who suggested that economists be legally required to learn at least the most elementary facts of geology. Fewer still would forget that an equally distinguished Harvard economist added that they might be required to learn some economics, too. The overall message was clear: America's resource situation was bad and bound to get worse. The hearings had led to a bill requiring the Departments of State, Interior, and Commerce to set up a joint resource procurement council with the express purpose of "insuring that proper consideration of American resource needs be an integral part of American foreign policy."

Suddenly the United States discovered that it had a national consensus: population control was the only possible salvation of the underdeveloped world. But that same consensus led to heated debate. How could the UDCs be persuaded to limit their populations, and should not the United States lead the way by limiting its own? Members of the intellectual community wanted America to set an example. They pointed out that the United States was in the midst of a new baby boom: her birth rate, well over 20 per thousand per year, and her growth rate of over one per cent per annum were among the very highest of the developed countries. They detailed the deterioration of the American physical and psychic environments, the growing health threats, the impending food shortages, and the insufficiency of funds for desperately needed public works. They contended that the nation was clearly unable or unwilling to properly care for the people it already had. What possible reason could there be, they queried, for adding any more? Besides, who would listen to requests by the United States for population control when that nation did not control her own profligate reproduction?

Those who opposed population controls for the U.S. were equally vociferous. The military-industrial complex, with its all-too-human mixture of ignorance and avarice, still saw strength and prosperity in numbers. Baby food magnates, already worried by the growing nitrate pollution of their products, saw their market disappearing. Steel manufacturers saw a decrease in aggregate demand and slippage for that holy of holies, the Gross National Product. And military men saw, in the growing population-food-environment crisis, a serious threat to their carefully nurtured Cold War. In the end, of course, economic arguments held sway, and the "inalienable right of every American couple to determine the size of its family," a freedom invented for the occasion in the early '70s, was not compromised.

The population control bill, which was passed by Congress early in 1974, was quite a document, nevertheless. On the domestic front, it authorized an increase from 100 to 150 million dollars in funds for "family planning" activities. This was made possible by a general feeling in the country that the growing army on welfare needed family planning. But the gist of the bill was a series of measures designed to impress the need for population control on the UDCs. All American aid to countries with overpopulation problems was required by law to consist in part of population control assistance. In order to receive any assistance each nation was required not only to accept the population control aid, but also to match it according to a complex formula. "Overpopulation" itself was defined by a formula based on U.N. statistics, and the UDCs were required not only to accept aid, but also to show progress in reducing birth rates. Every five years the status of the aid program for each nation was to be re-evaluated.

The reaction to the announcement of this program dwarfed the response to President Kennedy's speech. A coalition of UDCs attempted to get the U.N. General Assembly to condemn the United States as a "genetic aggressor." Most damaging of all to the American cause was the famous "25 Indians and a dog" speech by Mr. Shankarnarayan, Indian Ambassador to the U.N. Shankarnarayan pointed out that for several decades the United States, with less than six per cent of the people of the world had consumed roughly 50 per cent of the raw materials used every year. He described vividly America's contribution to worldwide environmental deterioration, and he scathingly denounced the miserly record of United States foreign aid as "unworthy of a fourth-rate power, let alone the most powerful nation on earth."

It was the climax of his speech, however, which most historians claim once and for all destroyed the image of the United States. Shankarnarayan informed the assembly that the average American family dog was fed more animal protein per week than the average Indian got in a month. "How do you justify taking fish from protein-starved Peruvians and feeding them to your animals?" he asked. "I contend," he concluded, "that the birth of an American baby is a greater disaster for the world than that of 25 Indian babies." When the applause had died away, Mr. Sorensen, the American representative, made a speech which said essentially that "other countries look after their own self-interest, too." When the vote came, the United States was condemned.

This condemnation set the tone of U.S.-UDC relations at the time the Russian Thanodrin proposal was made. The proposal seemed to offer the masses in the UDCs an opportunity to save themselves and humiliate the United States at the same time; and in human affairs, as we all know, biological realities could never interfere with such an opportunity. The scientists were silenced, the politicians said yes, the Thanodrin plants were built, and the results were what any beginning ecology student could have predicted. At first Thanodrin seemed to offer excellent control of many pests. True, there was a rash of human fatalities from improper use of the lethal chemical, but, as Russian technical advisors were prone to note, these were more than compensated for by increased yields. Thanodrin use skyrocketed throughout the underdeveloped world. The Mikoyan design group developed a dependable, cheap agricultural aircraft which the Soviets donated to the effort in large numbers. MIG sprayers became even more common in UDCs than MIG interceptors.

Then the troubles began. Insect strains with cuticles resistant to Thanodrin penetration began to appear. And as streams, rivers, fish culture ponds and onshore waters became rich in Thanodrin, more fisheries began to disappear. Bird populations were decimated. The sequence of events was standard for broadcast use of a synthetic pesticide: great success at first, followed by removal of natural enemies and development of resistance by the pest. Populations of crop-eating insects in areas treated with Thanodrin made steady comebacks and soon became more abundant than ever. Yields plunged, while farmers in their desperation increased the Thanodrin dose and shortened the time between treatments. Death from Thanodrin poisoning became common. The first violent incident occurred in the Canete Valley of Peru, where farmers had suffered a similar chlorinated hydrocarbon disaster in the mid-'50s. A Russian advisor serving as an agricultural pilot was assaulted and killed by a mob of enraged farmers in January, 1978. Trouble spread rapidly during 1978, especially after the word got out that two years earlier Russia herself had banned the use of Thanodrin at home because of its serious effects on ecological systems. Suddenly Russia, and not the United States, was the *bête noire* in the UDCs. "Thanodrin parties" became epidemic, with farmers, in their ignorance, dumping carloads of Thanodrin concentrate into the sea. Russian advisors fled, and four of the Thanodrin plants were leveled to the ground. Destruction of the plants in Rio and Calcutta led to hundreds of thousands of gallons of Thanodrin concentrate being dumped directly into the sea.

Mr. Shankarnarayan again rose to address the U.N., but this time it was Mr. Potemkin, representative of the Soviet Union, who was on the hot seat. Mr. Potemkin heard his nation described as the greatest mass killer of all time as Shankarnarayan predicted at least 30 million deaths from crop failures due to overdependence on Thanodrin. Russia was accused of "chemical aggression," and the General Assembly, after a weak reply by Potemkin, passed a vote of censure.

It was in January, 1979, that huge blooms of a previously unknown variety of diatom were reported off the coast of Peru. The blooms were accompanied by a massive die-off of sea life and of the pathetic remainder of the birds which had once feasted on the anchovies of the area. Almost immediately another huge bloom was reported in the Indian ocean, centering around the Seychelles, and then a third in the South Atlantic off the African coast. Both of these were accompanied by spectacular die-offs of marine animals. Even more ominous were growing reports of fish and bird kills at oceanic points where there were no spectacular blooms. Biologists were soon able to explain the phenomena: the diatom had evolved an enzyme which broke down Thanodrin; that enzyme also produced a breakdown product which interfered with the transmission of nerve impulses, and was therefore lethal to animals. Unfortunately, the biologists could suggest no way of repressing the poisonous diatom bloom in time. By September, 1979, all important animal life in the sea was extinct. Large areas of coastline had to be evacuated, as windrows of dead fish created a monumental stench.

But stench was the least of man's problems. Japan and China were faced with almost instant starvation from a total loss of the seafood on which they were so dependent. Both blamed Russia for their situation and demanded immediate mass shipments of food. Russia had none to send. On October 13, Chinese armies attacked Russia on a broad front. . . .

A pretty grim scenario. Unfortunately, we're a long way into it already. Everything mentioned as happening before 1970 has actually occurred; much of the rest is based on projections of trends already appearing. Evidence that pesticides have long-term lethal effects on human beings has started to accumulate, and recently Robert Finch, Secretary of the Department of Health, Education and Welfare expressed his extreme apprehension about the pesticide situation. Simultaneously, the petrochemical industry continues its unconscionable poison-peddling. For instance, Shell Chemical has been carrying on a high-pressure campaign to sell the insecticide Azodrin to farmers as a killer of cotton pests. They continue their program even though they know that Azodrin is not only ineffective, but often *increases* the pest density. They've covered themselves nicely in an advertisement which states, "Even if an overpowering migration [sic] develops, the flexibility of Azodrin lets you regain control fast. Just increase the dosage according to label recommendations." It's a great game—get people to apply the poison and kill the natural enemies of the pests. Then blame the increased pests on "migration" and sell even more pesticide!

Right now fisheries are being wiped out by over-exploitation, made easy by modern electronic equipment. The companies producing the equipment know this. They even boast in advertising that only their equipment will keep fishermen in business until the final kill. Profits must obviously be maximized in the short run. Indeed, Western society is in the process of completing the rape and murder of the planet for economic gain. And, sadly, most of the rest of the world is eager for the opportunity to emulate our behavior. But the underdeveloped peoples will be denied that opportunity—the days of plunder are drawing inexorably to a close.

Most of the people who are going to die in the greatest cataclysm in the history of man have already been born. More than three and a half billion people already populate our moribund globe, and about half of them are hungry. Some 10 to 20 million will starve to death *this year.* In spite of this, the population of the earth will increase by 70 million souls in 1969. For mankind has artificially lowered the death rate of the human population, while in general birth rates have remained high. With the input side of the population system in high gear and the output side slowed down, our fragile planet has filled with people at an incredible rate. It took several million years for the population to reach a total of two billion people in 1930, while a *second two billion will have been added by 1975!* By that time some experts feel that food shortages will have escalated the present level of world hunger and starvation into famines of unbelievable proportions. Other experts, more optimistic, think the ultimate food-population collision will not occur until the decade of the 1980's. Of course more massive famine may be avoided if other events cause a prior rise in the human death rate.

Both worldwide plague and thermonuclear war are made more probable as population growth continues. These, along with famine, make up the trio of potential "death rate solutions" to the population problem—solutions in which the birth rate-death rate imbalance is redressed by a rise in the death rate rather than by a lowering of the birth rate. Make no mistake about it, *the imbalance will be redressed.* The shape of the population growth curve is one familiar to the biologist. It is the outbreak part of an outbreak-crash sequence. A population grows rapidly in the presence of abundant resources, finally runs out of food or some other necessity, and crashes to a low level or extinction. Man is not only running out of food, he is also destroying the life support systems of the Spaceship Earth. The situation was recently summarized very succinctly: "It is the top of the ninth inning. Man, always a threat at the plate, has been hitting Nature hard. It is important to remember, however, that NATURE BATS LAST."

DEATH IN OUR AIR

Ben H. Bagdikian

At one o'clock in the morning about a month ago, Peter Briola, a tough and spirited lawyer, sat up in bed with a familiar agony. He was alone in his white clapboard house in Lincoln, a town of 3,600 people in the middle of Maine. The typical New England homestead, among rolling and forested hills near the banks of the Penobscot River, looks like a romantic painting of an idyllic scene of peace and purity, of an unspoiled America.

"It was like all the other times, as though someone had you by the

Ben H. Bagdikian, "Death in Our Air," *The Saturday Evening Post,* October 8, 1966. Reprinted with permission of *The Saturday Evening Post* © 1966. The Curtis Publishing Company.

throat, trying to choke you. There was that terrible smell, like rotting dead stuff. You begin to cough and gasp. Your eyes run. You shut the windows, but it doesn't do any good. Nothing does any good."

Here among the ancient spruce of the deep woods a paper mill is pouring filth upon Peter Briola and his fellow townsmen. They suffer from a contamination that has now infested every city in the United States and not a few small towns. Today, polluted air threatens the health of most Americans, corrodes their property, obscures or obliterates their scenery and insults their peace of mind.

Mrs. Peter Rose, a housewife on a major thoroughfare in Denver, "The Mile-High City," says: "Twenty years ago when we moved into this bungalow it was a delight. The yard had nice green grass and beautiful roses. The whole neighborhood was clean. The house needed only one good cleaning a week, and the curtains and drapes I used to clean twice a year. From the neighborhood you could see the mountains clearly most of the time, with snowcaps visible through that wonderful purple. But in the last few years, since they made the road one-way and started the traffic growing the way it has—well, about six years ago my husband began having eye trouble, irritation and watering. A short time later my eyes did the same thing. We both began getting frequent inflammations like sinus trouble. The doctor has us use eyewashes every day now. The roses all shriveled and died. The lawn began to go. Half the time you can't see the mountains anymore. I have to clean the house every day, and it's still gritty and greasy. Curtains and drapes can stand cleaning every week. I've got forty-five windows in the house, and they need a cleaning every week instead of twice a year. It's the same house and the neighborhood is still a nice residential one, but the air has become dirty, uncomfortable and expensive."

Dr. La Rele Stephens, a physician in Moscow, Idaho, says he can almost tell by the barometer and the direction of the wind when he will begin getting calls from patients in Lewiston, a town of 13,000 that is 29 miles away: "When the wind blows the mill fumes over the town or there is a dead calm, the patients begin to come in with respiratory troubles, nasal congestion, allergies, difficulty in breathing, lots of sneezing. I'm convinced we get some deaths, too, because when the fumes make the natural fogs thicker, which you can tell by the smell, we get more automobile accidents."

Donald McLean, of Polk County, Fla., told a Senate committee that since phosphate plants began putting seven tons of fluorides a day into the air he has had to sell his cattle and his citrus groves because the cattle sickened and died, crops that used to mature in 80 days now take 200, barbed wire that used to last 20 years rots in 4, and he doesn't dare grow vegetables for his family for fear they will pick up the same chemicals that fall onto his pastures and groves. "It eats up the paint and etches glass, it kills trees, it kills cattle. It is an irritant to mucous membrane, and we have sore throats, tears run out of our eyes, we sneeze, we have nosebleeds. Gentlemen, am I a fool to assume that that stuff [is] injurious to humans?"

There is evidence that Mr. McLean is no fool.

Damage to health and property from unclean air is increasing. Some places, like Lincoln, Maine, and Polk County, Fla., have special and dramatic problems. But every American city of more than 50,000 population has air pollution serious enough to worry about, whether or not its citizens see or smell it. Smoky industry and dark motor exhausts provide extra doses, but masses of atmospheric poisons come from smokeless chimneys and from perfectly tuned engines. Four-fifths of all pollution is invisible, most of it odorless.

Three years ago, when open fires, incinerators, chimneys, smoke-stacks and tail pipes were putting 125 million tons of chemical junk into the American air, the threat was already serious. But the burden has risen relentlessly until this year it is 145 million tons and headed still higher.

There is a vast ocean of clean air around the earth, enough for 2.5 million tons for each human being. Yet people become uncomfortable and sick for lack of each man's requirement of 30 pounds of clean air a day. The 2.5 million tons elsewhere does a man no good if what is under his nose is dirty and dangerous, if he cannot get his 30 daily pounds where he lives and works.

It was not until after World War II, when city air became loaded with the wastes of the new prosperity, that Americans began to notice that they don't always have access to the air they can see above them. For there is a lid, usually invisible from the ground, that regularly cuts off whole communities from the upper air and traps the accumulated poisons of smokestack and tail pipe at the lower levels, where men breathe. Now that men recognize the container that periodically locks in communities with their aerial wastes, they also realize, with justified uneasiness, that clean air is man's most urgent demand upon his environment. He can do without water for days and without food for weeks. But he cannot hold his breath for more than a minute or two. Then he must breathe, even if it kills him. As it sometimes does.

"There is no doubt," John Gardner, the Secretary of Health, Education and Welfare, said recently, "that air pollution is a contributing factor to the rising incidence of chronic respiratory diseases—lung cancer, emphysema, bronchitis and asthma."

In four days of 1948 polluted air sickened 43 percent of the population of Donora, Pa., and killed 20; in four days of 1952 it killed 4,000 people in London; in 15 days of 1963 it killed 400 people in New York City. Polluted air undoubtedly kills many people in many other places, but they are not counted because the death certificates never read "air pollution," and few cities ever analyze how many "extra" deaths they get during a siege of severe pollution.

Yet few Americans are aware of the alarming growth of respiratory disease—doubling every five years in the United States. Few suspect that foul air is most probably a factor in the rise in allergic-like reactions, or that it may contribute to the common cold. Emphysema, a fast-growing disease of the lung and almost surely the result of air pollution, has no public reputation. Emphysema creeps up in the form of increasing colds, chest congestion, breathlessness; and then, usually after age 50, there is a definite diagnosis and ultimately death. California has recorded an astounding 300 percent increase in cases since 1955. About seven percent of all Social Security disability payments, $80 million a year, is paid for emphysema victims, who are second in number only to those with arteriosclerotic heart disease.

Even when unclean air does not kill people or hurt their health, it often makes their lives miserable. It stings their eyes, dries out their throat tissues. It envelops their cities in a thick smog that blanks out the scenery. It sends offensive smells into their homes and produces an estimated $11 billion damage a year to property, such as paint and metal and masonry.

In every urban area of the country it has reduced vegetation of all kinds, from petunias to mighty oaks, by 10 to 20 percent. It kills some plants, blights new shoots, damages leaves to cut off nourishment and produces premature old age. Perennials are now harder to grow because of the peculiar atmospheric soup that comes out of automobile tail pipes. Dr. C. Stafford Brandt, chief of the agricultural section of the U.S. Public Health Service's Air Pollution Division, says, "From Washington to Boston and inland for a hundred miles there is not a square mile that is free from air-pollution injury. I don't see how anyone can look at our evidence and not become gravely concerned with the effect on our vegetation." Sometimes the evidence is obvious: One night of heavy industrial output killed $10,000 worth of commercially grown flowers on Staten Island, N.Y. Most of it is more subtle:

Fruit trees grown in normal city air are 10 percent smaller and produce 10 percent less fruit than trees in clean air.

Air pollution is mainly the result of things burning—gasoline in cars, coal and oil in factories and homes, trash and garbage in incinerators and dumps. The curve of dirty air follows fairly closely the curve of national wealth—more cars to put out exhaust, more power plants to make electricity, more factories to turn out goods, more trash to burn. This is why air pollution has reached serious levels in the 1960's. The biggest single source of air contamination, gasoline consumption in motor vehicles, doubled in the 20 years before 1945 but almost quadrupled in the 20 years since then. Starting in 1968, the auto industry will install antipollution devices in all new cars. Still, in the next decade the air is going to get even thicker—urban population, motor vehicles, electricity production and trash will greatly increase.

Another factor aggravating the situation is that the nature of aerial wastes is changing. For example, when the plastics now common in households are burned, some of them yield phosgene, a poison gas used in World War I. A report of the National Academy of Sciences-National Research Council says: "Chemical poisons are being produced in new forms so fast that the toxicologists cannot keep up with them."

Bad air once was a problem of the poor. "The wrong side of the tracks" as an expression for the lower-class section of town came from the days of coal-burning locomotives. Neighborhoods downwind of the cinders and smoke were so unpleasant that those who could afford it bought homes upwind. But the postwar population explosion in people and the even greater one in tail pipes and smokestacks have begun to end the delicate class distinction in breathing. It is still generally true that the farther from industrial centers one can get, the cleaner his air; but, expensive suburbia is no guarantee of pure air. For one thing, the high-speed highway carries a growing burden of exhaust to the suburbs. For another, the atmospheric lids that keep pollution near the ground frequently cover large areas, often thousands of square miles, and the quantities of aerial poisons that the modern metropolis puts into the air quickly raise the level of pollution over the entire area, not just in the neighborhoods around the smokestacks. It is more and more common that everyone, rich and poor, breathes polluted air. Fewer and fewer of us are immune to the problem.

Of the total of 145 million tons of junk Americans put into their air every year, it is estimated that 52 percent is the colorless and invisible gas called carbon monoxide. That remarkable equipment of natural man—the dime-sized tissue at the top of the nasal passage that can detect some odors better than any device made by man—is useless when it comes to this deadly gas.

It is recognized that at 1,000 parts of monoxide per million parts of air, the gas kills quickly. At 100 parts it produces bad headaches and dizziness. At present, 50 parts is considered the danger point. But as we learn more, we are less sure. California found that 30 parts per million for eight hours seriously affects people who already have poor blood circulation. Since monoxide sickens and kills by capturing the oxygen carriers in the blood, people with heart disease, arteriosclerosis, asthma or emphysema, as well as heavy smokers, are unusually vulnerable.

The U.S. Public Health Service sampled air in six cities—Cincinnati, St. Louis, Philadelphia, Denver, Chicago and Washington, D.C. —during periods of heavy traffic. It found carbon monoxide at 30 parts per million in 10 percent of the tests; the average levels inside passenger cars during rush-hour range from 21 to 29 parts per million, and there were concentrations higher than 100 parts inside tunnels and garages.

The effects of monoxide at these "low," everyday levels may be profound, even on healthy people. In the Public Health Service's Taft Center in Cincinnati, Dr. Charles Xintaras studied the brain waves of rats. When his rats breathed monoxide in rush-hour concentrations, almost at once the "intellectually alert" pattern of the brain waves disappeared and was replaced by one typical of a dream state: The brain kept receiving impressions from the outside but did nothing about them.

Many researchers believe that "turnpike fatigue," the lassitude that comes with long drives in cars without air conditioning, may be mild monoxide poisoning and may produce more accidents than supposed. One speculation is that, except for the results of new anti-pollution controls, increasing monoxide from increasing traffic could reduce alertness not just among motorists but in whole sections of the population.

The next heaviest portion of poison in the American air, 18 percent, is the sulfur oxides, which come mostly from the burning coal and oil in power plants, factories and homes. They have been the chief villain of every recent pollution disaster, like Donora, New York and London. They paralyze the tiny hairlike tissues that ordinarily protect sensitive lung tissues from dangerous invaders. They irritate the throat and damage the lungs. Their presence makes lung and heart work harder. In Nashville a study of 9,313 people showed that cardiovascular disease in people over 55 was twice as common in areas of the city with high sulfur readings.

The most recent studies show that quite ordinary sulfur-dioxide levels in the air do human and property damage. With an annual average of 0.01 to 0.02 parts per million in the air, there is increased cardiovascular illness, noticeable impairment of breathing among otherwise healthy people, and significant mental corrosion. At 0.02 to 0.03 levels for a year the death rate from respiratory disease begins to go up, and perennial flowers become chronically damaged. It is therefore alarming to note that the 1964 sulfur-dioxide mean in the following cities was: Chicao, 0.18; Cincinnati, 0.04; Los Angeles, 0.01; Philadelphia, 0.08; San Francisco, 0.02; St. Louis, 0.06; and Washington, 0.05. Vernon MacKenzie, chief of the Division of Air Pollution of the Public Health Service, says, "The sulfur-pollution problem in some sections of the country in our opinion has reached virtually a critical stage."

The next most common contaminators in urban air are the hydrocarbons, a large group of compounds coming mainly from escaped, unburned fuel, mostly invisible and mostly from cars.

They are known to cause cancer, though it takes higher concentrations than usually found in the air. Worse yet, sunlight causes hydrocarbons to combine insidiously with still another pollutant— the oxides of nitrogen—to produce photochemical smog (also called oxidant), the bourbon-colored haze that regularly blurs most modern cities. In photochemical smog, people breathe harder but get less oxygen. Very high concentrations for a few hours can produce impaired breathing and general malaise for days afterward.

A car pollutes the air in four ways: from its gas tank, from its carburetor (both give off evaporated gasoline), from its crankcase vent and from its tail pipe. Of the hydrocarbons, mostly evaporated or unburned fuel, 10 percent come from gas tank and carburetor, 30 percent from the crankcase vent and 60 percent from tail pipe, out of which also come all of the carbon monoxide and oxides of nitrogen.

Elimination of the 30 percent of hydrocarbons from the crankcase is relatively simple. A pipe can refeed the raw gas back to the intake manifold. Redesign of engines can reduce carbon monoxide by 50 percent and hydrocarbons by 65 percent. California required the automobile industry to produce such cars in that state beginning with 1966 models, and the result has been a marked improvement. The Federal Government followed suit for all cars, and the auto industry has applied its skills and money to achieving a solution.

Slowly the Federal Government has taken measures to try to reverse the upward curve of dirty air. It started in 1955 with an appropriation of $186,000. Thanks largely to Sen. Edmund S. Muskie of Maine, there is now a growing national program, begun in earnest with the Clean Air Act of 1963.

In accord with this program, the automobile industry is installing antipollution controls on all new 1968 cars sold in this country. Communities polluted by sources across a state line now can call for federal aid, as can any local government that says its own problem is beyond its capacity to handle. And the national government is developing techniques for controlling pollution and programs for training technicians so desperately needed in cities and states. It will double any money that localities put up to cleanse their own air.

Nevertheless, the national atmosphere continues to get worse. The country has more gasoline, more fuel oil, more trash to burn every year, more people to do it, more of them congregated in cities already polluted, but no more air than before. A third of the states have no one concerned with their air, and most of the remainder have only a token employee. It is estimated that a good local air-pollution program costs 40 to 50 cents per capita a year, but most places spend nothing.

A total program that with present knowledge could *reduce* the pollution levels would cost three billion dollars a year. Such a program might even stem the appalling growth of respiratory disease among urban Americans.

When President Johnson signed the Clean Air Act Amendment last October, he quoted author Rachel Carson: "In biological history, no organism has survived long if its environment became in some way unfit for it, but no organism before man has deliberately polluted its own environment."

OIL IN THE VELVET PLAYGROUND

Harvey Molotch

Santa Barbara seems worlds apart both from the sprawling Los Angeles metropolis a hundred miles further south on the coast highway and from the avant-garde San Francisco Bay Area to the north. It has always been calm, clean and orderly. Of the city's 70,000 residents, a large number are upper and upper-middle class. They are people who have a wide choice of places in the world to live, but they have chosen Santa Barbara because of its ideal climate, gentle beauty and sophistication. Hard-rock Republicans, they vote for any GOP candidate who comes along, including Ronald Reagan and Max Rafferty, California's right-wing Superintendent of Public Education.

Under normal circumstances, Santa Barbarans are not the sort of people who are accustomed to experiencing stark threats to their survival, or arbitrary, contemptuous handling of their wishes. They are an unlikely group to be forced to confront brutal realities about how the "normal channels" in America can become hopelessly clogged and unresponsive. Yet this is exactly what happened when the Union Oil Company's well erupted in the Santa Barbara Channel last January, causing an unparalleled ecological disaster, the effects of which are still washing up on the local beaches.

In the ensuing months it became clear that more than petroleum had leaked out from Union Oil's drilling platform. Some basic truths about power in America had spilled out along with it. The oil disaster was more than simply another omen for an increasingly "accident-prone" civilization. Precisely because it was an accident—a sudden intrusion into an extremely orderly social process—it provided Santa Barbarans with sharp insights into the way our society is governed and into the power relationships that dictate its functions.

Across the political spectrum in Santa Barbara, the response has been much the same: fury. Some, including persons who never before had made a political move in their lives, were led from petition campaigns to the picket line and demonstrations, to the sit-down, and even to the sail-in. The position they finally came to occupy shows that radicalism is not, as experts like Bruno Bettelheim have implied, a subtle form of mental imbalance caused by rapid technological change or by the increasing impersonality of the modern world; radicals are

Harvey Molotch, "Oil in the Velvet Playground," *Ramparts,* Nov. 1969. Reprinted with permission of the Editors.

334

not "immature," "undisciplined" or "anti-intellectual." Quite the contrary. They are persons who live in conditions where injustice is apparent, and who have access to more complete information about their plight than the average man, giving them a perspective that allows them to become angry in a socially meaningful way. . . .

Optimistic Indignation: Government by the People

For over fifteen years, Santa Barbara's political leaders attempted to prevent the despoilation of their coastline by oil drilling in adjacent federal waters. Although they were unsuccessful in blocking the leasing of *federal* waters beyond the three-mile limit, they were able to establish a sanctuary within *state* waters (thus foregoing the extraordinary revenues which leases in such areas bring to adjacent localities). It was therefore a great irony that the one city which had voluntarily exchanged revenue for a pure environment should find itself faced, in January of 1969, with a massive eruption which was ultimately to cover the entire city coastline with a thick coat of crude oil. The air was soured for many hundreds of feet inland, and tourism —the traditional economic base of the region—was severely threatened. After ten days, the runaway well was brought under control, only to erupt again in February. This fissure was closed in March, but was followed by a sustained "seepage" of oil—a leakage which continues today to pollute the sea, the air and the famed local beaches. The oil companies had paid a record $603 million for their lease rights, and neither they nor the federal government bore any significant legal responsibility toward the localities which those lease rights might endanger.

The response of Santa Barbarans to this pollution of their near-perfect environment was immediate. A community organization called "GOO" (Get Oil Out!) was established under the leadership of a former state senator and a local corporate executive. GOO took a strong stand against any and all oil activity in the Channel and circulated a petition to that effect which eventually gained 110,000 signatures and was sent to President Nixon. The stodgy Santa Barbara News-Press (oldest daily newspaper in Southern California, its masthead proclaims) inaugurated a series of editorials, unique in their uncompromising stridency and indicative of the angry mood of the community. "The people of the Santa Barbara area can never be repaid for the hurt that has been done to them and their environment," said a front-page editorial. "They are angry—and this is not the time for them to lose their anger. This is the time for them to fight for action that will guarantee absolutely and permanently that there will be no recurrence of the nightmare of the last two weeks. . . ."

The same theme emerged in the hundreds of letters published by the News-Press in the weeks that followed and in the positions taken by virtually every local civic and government body. Rallies were held at the beach, and GOO petitions were circulated at local shopping centers and sent to sympathizers around the country. Local artists, playwrights, advertising men, retired executives and academic specialists from the local campus of the University of California executed special projects appropriate to the areas of expertise.

A GOO strategy emerged for an attack on two fronts. Local indignation, producing the petition to the President and thousands of letters to key members of Congress and the executive, would lead to appropriate legislation. Legal action against the oil companies and the federal government would have the double effect of recouping some of the financial losses certain to be suffered by the local tourist and fishing industries while at the same time serving notice that drilling in the Channel would become a much less profitable operation. Legislation to ban drilling was introduced by Senator Alan Cranston in the U.S. Senate and Representative Charles Teague in the House of Representatives. Joint suits for $1 billion in damages were filed against the oil companies and the federal government by the city and county of Santa Barbara (later joined by the State of California).

All of these activities—petitions, rallies, court action and legislative lobbying—expressed their proponents' basic faith in "the system." There was a muckraking tone to the Santa Barbara protest: the profit-mad executives of Union Oil were ruining the coastline, but once national and state leaders became aware of what was going on and were provided with the "facts" of the case, justice would be done.

Indeed, there was good reason for hope. The quick and enthusiastic responses of the right-wing Teague and the liberal Cranston represented a consensus of men otherwise polar opposites in their political behavior. But from other important quarters there was silence. Santa Barbara's representatives in the state legislature either said nothing or (in later stages) offered only minimal support. Most disappointing of all to Santa Barbarans, Governor Ronald Reagan withheld support for proposals which would end the drilling.

As subsequent events unfolded, the seemingly inexplicable silence of most of the democratically-elected representatives began to fall into place as part of a more general pattern. Santa Barbarans began to see

American democracy as a very complicated affair—not simply a system in which governmental officials carry out the desires of their constituents once those desires become known. Instead, increasing recognition came to be given to the "all-powerful Oil lobby"; to legislators "in the pockets of Oil"; to academicians "bought" by Oil and to regulatory agencies that lobby for those they are supposed to regulate. In other words, Santa Barbarans became increasingly ideological, increasingly sociological and, in the words of some observers, increasingly "radical." Writing from his lodgings in the Santa Barbara Biltmore, the city's most exclusive residence hotel, an irate citizen penned these words in a letter published in the local paper: "We the People can protest and protest and it means nothing because the industrial and military junta are the country. They tell us, the People, what is good for the oil companies is good for the People. To that I say, Like Hell! . . . Profit is their language and the proof of all this is their history."

Disillusionment: Government by Oil

From the start, Secretary of Interior Walter Hickel was regarded with suspicion, and his publicized association with Alaskan oil interests did little to improve his image in Santa Barbara. When he called a halt to drilling immediately after the initial eruption, some Santa Barbarans began to believe that he would back them up. But even the most optimistic were quite soon forced to recognize that government policy would indeed confirm their worst fears. For, only one day later, Secretary Hickel ordered a resumption of drilling and production— even as the oil continued to gush into the Channel.

Within 48 hours Hickel reversed his position and ordered another halt to the drilling. But this time his action was seen as a direct response to the massive nationwide media play then being given to the Santa Barbara plight and to the citizens' mass outcry just then beginning to reach Washington. Santa Barbarans were further disenchanted with Hickel and the executive branch both because the Interior Department failed to back any legislation to halt drilling and because it consistently attempted to downplay the entire affair—minimizing the extent of the damages and hinting at possible "compromises" which were seen locally as near-total capitulation to the oil companies.

One question on which government officials systematically erred on the side of Oil was that of the *volume* of oil spilling into the Channel. The U.S. Geological Survey (administered by the Department of the Interior), when queried by reporters, produced estimates which Santa Barbarans could only view as incredible. Located in Santa Barbara is a technological establishment among the most sophisticated in the country—the General Research Corporation, a research and development firm with experience in marine technology. Several officials of the corporation made their own study of the oil outflow and announced findings of pollution volume at a minimum of *ten-fold* that of the government's estimate. The methods which General Research used to prepare its estimates were made public. The Geological Survey and the oil interests, however, continued to blithely issue their own lower figures, refusing to provide any substantiating arguments.

Another point of contention was the effect of the oil on the beaches. The oil companies, through various public relations officials, constantly minimized the actual amount of damage and maximized the effect of Union Oil's cleanup activities; and the Department of the Interior seemed determined to support Union Oil's claims. Thus Hickel referred at a press conference to the "recent" oil spill, providing the impression that the oil spill was over at a time when freshly erupting oil was continuing to stain local beaches. When President Nixon appeared locally to "inspect" the damage to beaches, Interior arranged for him to land his helicopter on a city beach which had been thoroughly cleaned in the days just before, thus sparing him a close-up of much of the rest of the county shoreline, which continued to be covered with a thick coat of crude oil. (The beach visited by Nixon has been oil-stained on many occasions subsequent to the President's departure.) Secret servicemen kept the placards and shouts of several hundred demonstrators at a safe distance from the President.

The damage to the "ecological chain," while still of unknown proportions, was treated in a similarly deceptive way. A great many birds died from oil which they had ingested while trying to preen their oil-soaked feathers—a process Santa Barbarans saw in abundant examples. In what local and national authorities called a hopeless task, two bird-cleaning centers were established (with help from oil company money) to cleanse feathers and otherwise minister to injured wildfowl. Spokesmen from both Oil and the federal government then adopted these centers as sources of "data" on the extent of damage to the bird life. Thus, the number of birds killed by oil pollution was computed on the basis of the number of fatalities at the wildfowl centers. It was a preposterous method and was recognized as such. Clearly, the dying birds in the area were provided with inefficient means of propelling themselves to these designated centers.

At least those birds in the hands of local ornithologists could be confirmed as dead, and this fact could not be disputed by either Oil or Interior. This was not so, however, with species whose corpses are more dificult to produce on command. Several official observers at the Channel Islands, a national wildlife preserve containing one of the country's largest colonies of sea animals, reported sighting unusually large numbers of dead sea lion pups on the oil-stained shores of one of the islands. Statement and counter-statement followed, with Oil's defenders (including the Department of the Navy) arguing that the animals were not dead at all, but only appeared inert because they were sleeping. In a similar case, the dramatic beaching in Northern California of an unusually large number of dead whales—whales which had just completed their migration through the Santa Barbara Channel—was acknowledged, but held not to be caused by oil pollution.

In the end, it was not simply the Interior Department, its U.S. Geological Survey and the President who either supported or tacitly accepted Oil's public relations tactics. The regulatory agencies at both national and state levels, by action, inaction and implication, effectively defended Oil at virtually every turn. In a letter to complaining citizens, for instance, N. B. Livermore, Jr. of the Resources Agency of California referred to the continuing oil spill as "minor seepage" with "no major long term effect on the marine ecology." The letter adopted the perspective of Interior and Oil, even though the state was in no way being held culpable for the spill. This tendency was so blatant that it led the State Deputy Attorney General, Charles O' Brien, to charge the state conservation boards with "industry domination." Thomas Gaines, a Union Oil executive, actually sits on the state agency board most directly connected with the control of pollution in Channel waters.

Understandably enough, Secretary Hickel's announcement that the Interior Department was generating new "tough" regulations to control off-shore drilling was met with considerable skepticism. The Santa Barbara County Board of Supervisors was invited to "review" these new regulations and refused to do so in the belief that such participation would be used to provide a false impression of democratic responsiveness.

In previous years when they were fighting against the leasing of the Channel, the Supervisors had been assured of technological safeguards; now, as the emergency continued, they could witness for themselves the absence of any method for ending the leakage in the Channel. They also had heard the testimony of Donald Solanas, a regional supervisor of Interior's U.S. Geological Survey, who said about the Union platform eruption: "I could have had an engineer on that platform 24 hours a day, seven days a week and he couldn't have prevented the accident." His explanation of the cause of the "accident"? "Mother earth broke down on us." Given these facts, Santa Barbarans saw Interior's proposed regulations—and the invitation to the County to participate in making them—as only a ruse to preface a resumption of drilling.

Their suspicions were confirmed when the Interior Department announced a selective resumption of drilling "to relieve pressures." The new "tough" regulations were themselves seriously flawed by the fact that most of their provisions specified measures (such as buoyant booms around platforms, use of chemical dispersants, etc.) which had proven almost totally useless in the current emergency.

The new regulations did specify that oil companies would henceforth be financially responsible for damages resulting from pollution mishaps. Several of the oil companies have now entered suit (supported by the ACLU) against the federal government, complaining that the arbitrary changing of lease conditions deprives them of rights of due process.

Irritations with Interior were paralleled by frustrations encountered in dealing with the congressional committee which had the responsibility of holding hearings on ameliorative legislation. A delegation of Santa Barbarans was scheduled to testify in Washington on the Cranston bill to ban drilling. From the questions which congressmen asked them, and the manner in which they were "handled," the delegates could only conclude that the committee was "in the pockets of Oil." As one of the returning delegates put it, the presentation bespoke of "total futility."

At this writing, six months after their introduction, both the Cranston and Teague bills, though significantly softened, lie buried in committee with little prospect of surfacing.

Disillusionment: Power is Knowledge

The American Dream is a dream of progress, of the efficacy of know-how and technology; science is seen as both servant and savior. From the start, part of the shock of the oil spill was that such a thing could happen in a country having such a sophisticated technology. The much overworked phrase "If we can send a man to the moon . . . " took on special meaning in Santa Barbara. When, in years previous, Santa Barbara's elected officials had attempted to halt the original sale of leases, "assurances" were given by Interior that such an "accident" could not occur, given the highly developed state of the industry. Not only did it occur, but the original gusher of oil spewed forth completely out of control for ten days, and the continual "seepage" which followed it remains uncontrolled to the present moment —seven months later. That the government would embark upon so massive a drilling program with such unsophisticated technology was shocking indeed.

Further, not only was the technology inadequate and the plans for stopping a leak, should one occur, nonexistent, but the area in which the drilling took place was known from the outset to be extremely hazardous. That is, drilling was occuring on an ocean bottom known for its extraordinary geological circumstances—porous sand lacking a bedrock "ceiling" capable of restraining uncontrollably seeping oil. Thus, the continuing leakage through the sands at various points above the oil reservoir cannot be stopped, and this could have been predicted from the data known to all parties involved.

Another peculiarity of the Channel that had been known to the experts is the fact that it is located in the heart of earthquake activity in a region which is among the most earthquake prone in the country. Santa Barbarans are now asking what might occur during an earthquake; if pipes on the ocean floor and casings through the ocean bottom should be sheared, the damage done by the Channel's thousands of potential producing wells would devastate the entire coast of Southern California. The striking contrast between the sophistication of the means used to locate and extract oil and the primitiveness of the means to control and clean its spillage became extremely clear in Santa Barbara.

Recurrent attempts have been made to ameliorate the continuing seep by placing floating booms around an area of leakage and then sending workboats to skim off the leakage from within the demarcated area. Chemical dispersants of various kinds have also been tried. But the oil bounces over the booms in the choppy waters, the workboats suck up only a drop in the bucket, and the dispersants are effective only when used in quantities which constitute a graver pollution threat than the oil they are designed to eliminate. Cement is poured into suspected fissures in an attempt to seal them up. Oil on the beaches is periodically cleaned by dumping straw over the sands and then raking it up along with the oil which it has absorbed. The common sight of men throwing straw on miles of beaches, within view of complex drilling rigs capable of exploiting resources thousands of feet below the ocean's surface, became a clear symbol to Santa Barbarans. They gradually began to see the oil disaster as the product of a system that promotes research and development in areas which lead to strategic profitability—without regard for social utility.

This kind of subordination of science to profit came out more directly in the workings of the Presidential committee of "distinguished" scientists and engineers (the DuBridge Panel) which was to recommend means of eliminating the seepage under Platform A. When the panel was appointed, hopes were raised that at last the scientific establishment of the nation would come forth with a technologically sophisticated solution to the problem. Instead, the panel—after a two-day session and after hearing no testimony from anyone not connected with either Oil or the Interior Department—recommended the "solution" of drilling an additional 50 wells under Platform A in order to pump the area dry as quickly as possible. One member of the panel estimated that the process would take from 10 to 20 years. Despite an immediate local clamor, Interior refused to make public the data or the reasoning behind the recommendations. The information on Channel geological conditions had been provided by the oil companies (the Geological Survey routinely depends upon the oil industry for the data upon which it makes its "regulatory" decisions). The data, being private property, thus could not be released —or so the government claimed. For Union Oil itself has given a clearance to the public release of the data. In this way both parties are neatly protected, while Santa Barbara's local experts remain thwarted by the counter-arguments of Oil/Interior that "if you had the information we have, you would agree with us."

Science played a similarly partisan role in other areas of the fight that Santa Barbarans were waging against the oil companies. The Chief Deputy Attorney General of California, for example, complained that the oil industry "is preventing oil drilling experts from aiding the Attorney General's office in its lawsuits over the Santa Barbara oil spill." Noting that his office had been unable to get assistance from petroleum experts at California universities, the Deputy Attorney General stated: "The university experts all seem to be working on grants from the oil industry. There is an atmosphere of fear. The experts are afraid that if they assist us in our case on behalf on the people of California, they will lose their oil industry grants."

At the Santa Barbara campus of the University, there is little oil money in evidence and few, if any, faculty members have entered into proprietory research arrangements with Oil. Petroleum geology and engineering is simply not a local specialty. Yet it is a fact that oil interests did contact several Santa Barbara faculty members with offers of funds for studies on the ecological effects of the oil spill, with publication rights stipulated by Oil. It is also the case that the Federal Water Pollution Control Administration explicitly requested a U.C. Santa Barbara botanist to withhold the findings of his study, funded by that agency, on the ecological effects of the spill.

Most of these revelations received no publicity outside of Santa Barbara. The Attorney's allegation, however, did become something of a state-wide issue when a professor at the Berkeley campus, in his attempt to refute the charge, actually confirmed it. Wilbur H. Somerton, professor of petroleum engineering, indicated he could not testify against Oil "because my work depends on good relations with the petroleum industry. My interest is serving the petroleum industry. I view my obligation to the community as supplying it with well-trained petroleum engineers. We train the industry's engineers and they help us."

Santa Barbara's leaders were incredulous about the whole affair. The question—one which is asked more often by the downtrodden sectors of the society than by the privileged—was posed: "Whose university is this, anyway?" A local executive and GOO leader asked, "If the truth isn't in the universities, where is it?" A conservative member of the state legislature, in a move reminiscent of SDS demands, went so far as to demand an end to all faculty "moonlighting" for industry. In Santa Barbara, the only place where all of this publicity was appearing, there was thus an opportunity for insight into the linkages between knowledge, the university, government and oil—and into the resultant non-neutrality of science. The backgrounds of many members of the DuBridge Panel were linked publicly to the oil industry. DuBridge himself, as a past president of Cal Tech, served under a board of trustees which included the president of Union Oil and which accepted substantial Union Oil donations.

While "academic truth" was being called into question, some truths not usually dwelt on by Oil's experts were gaining public attention. In another of its front-page editorials, the News-Press set forth a number of revealing facts about the oil industry. The combination of output restrictions, extraordinary tax write-off privileges for drilling expenses, the import quota, and the 27½ per cent depletion allowance creates an artifically high price for U.S. oil—a price almost double the world market price for a comparable product delivered to comparable U.S. destinations. The combination of available incentives creates a situation where some oil companies pay no taxes whatsoever during extraordinarily profitable years. In the years 1962–1966, Standard Oil of New Jersey paid less than four per cent of its profits in taxes, Standard of California less than three per cent, and 22 of the other largest oil companies paid slightly more than six per cent. It was pointed out again and again to Santa Barbarans that it was this system of subsidy which made the relatively high cost deep-sea exploration and drilling in the Channel profitable in the first place. Thus the citizens of Santa Barbara, as federal taxpayers and fleeced consumers, were subsidizing their own eco-catastrophe.

The Mechanisms of Deception

The way in which federal officials and the oil industry frustrated the democratic process and thwarted popular dissent in Santa Barbara is hardly unfamiliar. But the upper-middle-class nature of the community, and the sharp features of an event which was a sudden disruption of normality, make it an ideal case for illustrating some of the techniques by which the powers that be maintain the status quo.

The first of these has been described by Daniel Boorstin as the technique of the "pseudo-event." A pseudo-event occurs when men arrange conditions to simulate a particular kind of event so that certain prearranged consequences follow as though the actual event had taken place. Several pseudo-events took place in Santa Barbara. From the outset, it was obvious that national actions concerning oil were aimed at freezing out any local participation in decisions affecting the Channel. Thus, when the federal government first called for bids on a Channel lease in 1968, local officials were not even informed. Further, local officials were not notified by any government agency in the case of the original oil spill, nor (except after the spill was already widely known) in the case of any of the previous or subsequent more "minor" spills. The thrust of the federal government's colonialist attitude toward the local community was contained in an Interior Department engineer's memo released by Senator Cranston's office. Written to the Assistant Secretary of the Interior to explain the policy of refusing to hold public hearings prior to drilling, it said: "We preferred not to stir up the natives any more than possible."

The Santa Barbara County Board of Supervisors turned down the call for "participation" in drawing up new "tougher" drilling regulations precisely because they knew the government had no intention of creating "safe" drilling regulations. They refused to utilize "normal channels," refusing thereby to take part in the pseudo-event and thus to let the consequences (in this case the appearance of democratic decision-making and local assent) of a non-event occur.

There were other attempts to stage pseudo-events. Nixon's "inspection" of the Santa Barbara beachfront was an obvious one. Another series of such events were the congressional hearings set up by legislators who were, in the words of a well-to-do lady leader of GOO, "kept men." The locals were allowed to blow off steam at the hearings, but their arguments, however cogent, failed to bring about legislation appropriate to the pollution crisis. Many Santa Barbarans had a similar impression of the court hearings regarding the various legal maneuvers against oil drilling.

Another technique for diffusing and minimizing popular protest evidenced in the Santa Barbara affair might be called the "creeping event." A creeping event is, in a sense, the opposite of a pseudo-event. It occurs when something *is* actually taking place, but when the manifestations of the event are arranged to occur at an inconspicuously gradual and piecemeal pace, thus avoiding some of the consequences which would follow from the event if it were immediately perceived to be occurring.

The major creeping event in Santa Barbara was the piecemeal resumption of production and drilling after Hickel's second moratorium. Authorization to resume *production* at different specific groups of wells occurred on various dates throughout February and early March. Authorization to resume *drilling* of various groups of new wells was announced by Interior on dates from April 1 through August. Each resumption was announced as a particular safety precaution to relieve pressures, until finally on the most recent resumption date, the word "deplete" was used for the first time in explaining the granting of permission to drill. There is thus no *specific* point in time at which production and drilling were re-authorized for the Channel —and full resumption still has not been officially authorized.

A creeping event has the consequence of diffusing resistance by withholding what journalists call a "time peg" on which to hang the story. By the time it becomes quite clear that "something *is* going on," the sponsors of the creeping event (and the aggrieved themselves) can ask why there should be any protest "now" when there was none before, in the face of the very same kind of provocation. In this way, the aggrieved has resort only to frustration and the gnawing feeling that events are sweeping by him.

A third way of minimizing legitimate protest is by use of the alleged "neutrality" of science and the knowledge producers. I have discussed

the "experts" and the University. After learning of the collusion between government and Oil and the use of secret science as a prop to
that collusion, Santa Barbarans found themselves in the unenviable
position of having to demonstrate that science and knowledge were
not, in fact, neutral arbiters. They had to prove, *by themselves,* that
continued drilling was not safe; that the "experts" who said it was safe
were the hirelings, directly or indirectly, of oil interests; and that the
report of the DuBridge Panel recommending massive drilling was a
fraudulent document. They had to show that the university petroleum
geologists themselves were in league with the oil companies and that
information unfavorable to the oil interests was systematically withheld by virtue of the very structure of the knowledge industry. This
is no small task. It is a long and complicated story, and one which pits
lay persons (and a few academic renegades) against an entire profession and the patrons of that profession. An illustration of the difficulties involved may be drawn from very recent history. Seventeen Santa
Barbara plaintiffs, represented by the ACLU, sought a temporary injunction against additional Channel drilling at least until the information utilized by the DuBridge Panel was made public and a hearing
could be held. The injunction was not granted, and in the end the
presiding federal judge ruled in favor of what he termed the "expert"
opinions available to the Secretary of the Interior. Due to limited time
for rebuttal, the disorienting confusions of courtroom procedures, and
also perhaps the desire not to offend the Court, the ACLU lawyer
could not make his subtle, complex and highly controversial case that
the "experts" were partisans and that their scientific "findings" followed from that partisanship.

A fourth obstacle was placed in the way of dissenters by the communications media. Just as the courtroom setting was not amenable
to a full reproduction of the facts supporting the ACLU case, so the
media in general—due to restrictions of time and style—prevented a
full airing of the details of the case. A more cynical analysis of the
media's inability to make known the Santa Barbara "problem" in its
full fidelity might hinge on an allegation that the media were constrained by fear of "pressures" from Oil and its allies. Metromedia, for
example, sent to Santa Barbara a team which spent several days docu-
menting, interviewing and filming for an hour-long program—only to
suddenly drop the project entirely due to what is reported by locals
in touch with the network to have been "pressures" from Oil. Even
without such blatant interventions, however, the full reproduction of
the Santa Barbara "news" would remain problematic.

News media are notorious for the anecdotal nature of their reporting; even so-called "think pieces" rarely go beyond a stringing together of proximate events. There are no analyses of the "mobilization of bias" or linkages of men's actions with their pecuniary interests. Science and learning are assumed to be neutral; regulatory agencies are assumed to function as "watchdogs" for the public. Information contradicting these assumptions is treated as an exotic exception.

The complexity of the situations to be reported and the wealth of details needed to support such analyses require more time and effort than journalists have at their command. Their recitation would produce long stories not consistent with space limitations and make-up preferences of newspapers, or with analogous requirements within the other media. A full telling of the story would tax the reader/viewer and would risk boring him. The rather extensive media coverage of the oil spill centered on a few dramatic moments in its history (e.g., the initial gusher of oil) and a few simple-to-tell "human interest" stories such as the pathetic deaths of the sea birds struggling along the oil-covered sands. With increasing temporal and geographical distance from the initial spill, national coverage became increasingly rare and sloppy. Interior Department statements on the state of the "crisis" were reported without local rejoinders as the newsmen who might have gathered them began leaving the scene. While the Santa Barbara spill received extraordinarily extensive national coverage relative to other controversial events, this coverage nevertheless failed to adequately inform the American public about a situation which Santa Barbarans knew from first-hand experience.

Finally, perhaps the most pernicious technique of all because of the damage it does to the social conscience, is the routinization of evil. Pollution of the Santa Barbara Channel is now routine; the issue is not whether or not the Channel is polluted, but *how much* it is polluted. A recent oil slick discovered off a Phillips Oil platform in the Channel was dismissed by an oil company official as a "routine" drilling by-product which was not viewed as "obnoxious." That about half of the oil currently seeping into the Channel is allegedly being recovered is taken as an improvement sufficient to preclude the "outrage" that a big national story would require.

Similarly, the pollution of the moral environment becomes routine; it is accepted as natural that politicans are "on the take," "in the pockets of Oil." The depletion allowance remains a question of percentages (20 per cent or 27½ per cent), rather than a focus for questioning the very legitimacy of such special benefits. "Compromises" emerge, such as the 24 per cent depletion allowance and the new "tough" drilling regulations, which are already being hailed as "victories" for the reformers. Like the oil spill itself, the depletion allowance debate becomes buried in its own disorienting detail, in its pseudo-events and in the triviality of the "solutions" which ultimately come to be considered as the "real" options. Evil is both banal and complicated, and each of these attributes contributes to its durability.

The Mechanism of change

What the citizens of Santa Barbara learned through their experience was that the parties competing to shape decision-making on oil in Santa Barbara do not have equal access to the means of "mobilizing bias." The Oil/Government combine had, from the start, an extraordinary number of advantages. Lacking ready access to media, the ability to stage events at will, and a well-integrated system of arrangements for achieving their goals (at least in comparison to their adversaries), Santa Barbara's citizens have met with repeated frustrations.

Their response to their relative powerlessness has been analogous to that of other groups and individuals who, from a similar vantage point, come to see the system up close. They become willing to expand their repertoire of means of influence as their cynicism and bitterness increase. Letter writing gives way to demonstrations, demonstrations to civil disobedience. People refuse to participate in "democratic procedures" which are a part of the opposition's event-management strategy. Confrontation politics arises as means of countering official events with "events" of one's own, thus providing the media with stories which can be simply and energetically told.

Thus, in Santa Barbara, rallies were held at local beaches; congressmen and state and national officials were greeted by demonstrations. (Fred Hartley of Union Oil inadvertently landed his plane in the middle of one such demonstration, causing a rather ugly name-calling scene to ensue.) A "sail-in" was held one Sunday with a flotilla of local pleasure boats forming a circle around Platform A, each craft bearing large anti-Oil banners. City hall meetings were packed with citizens reciting demands for immediate and forceful local action.

A City Council election held during the crisis resulted in a landslide for the Council's bitterest critic and the defeat of a veteran councilman suspected of having "oil interests." In a rare action, the News-Press condemned the local Chamber of Commerce for accepting oil money for a fraudulent tourist advertising campaign which touted Santa Barbara (including its beaches) as completely restored to its former beauty.

One possible grand strategy for Santa Barbara was outlined by a local public relations man and GOO worker, who said, "We've got to run the oil men out. The city owns the wharf and the harbor that the company has to use. The city has got to deny its facilities to oil traffic, service boats, cranes and the like. If the city contravenes some federal navigation laws [which such actions would unquestionably involve], to hell with it. The only hope to save Santa Barbara is to awaken the nation to the ravishment. That will take public officials who are willing to block oil traffic with their bodies and with police hoses, if necessary. Then federal marshals or federal troops would have to come in. This would pull in the national news media."

This scenario has thus far not occurred in Santa Barbara, although the continued use of the wharf by the oil industries has led to certain militant actions. A picket was maintained at the wharf for two weeks to protest the conversion of the pier from a recreation and tourist facility into an industrial plant for the use of the oil companies. A boycott of other wharf businesses (e.g., two restaurants) was urged. The picket line was led by white, middle-class adults—one of whom was a local businessman who, two years earlier, was a close runner-up in the Santa Barbara mayoralty race.

Prior to the picketing, a dramatic Easter Sunday confrontation (involving approximately 500 persons) took place between demonstrators and city police. Just as a wharf rally was breaking up, an oil service truck began driving up the pier to make a delivery of casing supplies for oil drilling. There was a spontaneous sit-down in front of the truck. For the first time since the Ku Klux Klan folded in the '30s, a group of (heavily) middle-class Santa Barbarans was publicly taking the law into its own hands. After much lengthy discussion between police, the truck driver and the demonstrators, the truck was ordered away and the demonstrators remained to rejoice over their victory. The following day's News-Press editorial, while not supportive of such tactics, was quite sympathetic, which was noteworthy given the paper's longstanding bitter opposition to similar tactics when exercised by dissident Northern blacks or student radicals. . . .

It would be difficult to predict what forms Santa Barbara's resistance will take in the future. A veteran News-Press reporter who covered the important oil stories has publicly stated that if the government fails to eliminate both the pollution and its causes, "there will, at best, be civil disobedience in Santa Barbara and at worst, violence."

In fact, talk of "blowing up" the ugly platforms has been recurrent—
and it is heard in all social circles.

But just as this kind of talk is not entirely serious, it is difficult to
know the degree to which the other militant statements are meaningful. Despite frequent observations about the "radicalization" of Santa
Barbara, it is difficult to determine the extent to which the authentic
grievances against Oil have been generalized into a radical analysis of
American society. Certainly an SDS membership campaign among
Santa Barbara adults would be a dismal failure. But that is too severe
a test. People, particularly basically contented people, change their
world-view very slowly, if at all. Most Santa Barbarans still go about
their comfortable lives in the ways they always have; they may even
help Ronald Reagan win another term in the state house. But I do
conclude that large numbers of persons have been moved, and that
they have been moved in the direction of the radical left. They have
gained insights into the structure of power in America not possessed
by similarly situated persons in other parts of the country. It can be
a revealing shock to experience an event first-hand and then to hear
it described, and distorted, by the press and the government. People
extrapolate from such experiences to the possibility that official de-
scriptions of other events may be similarly biased and misleading. And
when these questions arise, deeper ones follow. As a consequence
some Santa Barbarans, especially those with the most interest in and
information about the oil spill, while still surrounded by comfort and
certainty, have nevertheless come to view power in America more
intellectually, more analytically, more sociologically—more radically
—than they did before.

WASTELAND

Marya Mannes

Cans. Beer cans. Glinting on the verges of a million miles of roadways, lying in scrub, grass, dirt, leaves, sand, mud, but never hidden.
Piel's, Rheingold, Ballantine, Schaefer, Schlitz, shining in the sun or
picked by moon or the beams of headlights at night; washed by rain

or flattened by wheels, but never dulled, never buried, never destroyed. Here is the mark of savages, the testament of wasters, the stain of prosperity.

Who are these men who defile the grassy borders of our roads and lanes, who pollute our ponds, who spoil the purity of our ocean beaches with the empty vessels of their thirst? Who are the men who make these vessels in millions and then say, "Drink—and discard"? What society is this that can afford to cast away a million tons of metal and to make of wild and fruitful land a garbage heap?

What manner of men and women need thirty feet of steel and two hundred horsepower to take them, singly, to their small destinations? Who demand that what they eat is wrapped so that forests are cut down to make the paper that is thrown away, and what they smoke and chew is sealed so that the sealers can be tossed in gutters and caught in twigs and grass?

What kind of men can afford to make the streets of their towns and cities hideous with neon at night, and their roadways hideous with signs by day, wasting beauty; who leave the carcasses of cars to rot in heaps; who spill their trash into ravines and make smoking mountains of refuse for the town's rats? What manner of men choke off the life in rivers, streams and lakes with the waste of their produce, making poison of water?

Who is as rich as that? Slowly the wasters and despoilers are impoverishing our land, our nature, and our beauty, so that there will not be one beach, one hill, one lane, one meadow, one forest free from the debris of man and the stigma of his improvidence.

Who is so rich that he can squander forever the wealth of earth and water for the trivial needs of vanity or the compulsive demands of greed; or so prosperous in land that he can sacrifice nature for unnatural desires? The earth we abuse and the living things we kill will, in the end, take their revenge; for in exploiting their presence we are diminishing our future.

And what will we leave behind us when we are long dead? Temples? Amphora? Sunken treasure?

Or mountains of twisted, rusted steel, canyons of plastic containers, and a million miles of shores garlanded, not with the lovely wrack of the sea, but with the cans and bottles and light-bulbs and boxes of a people who conserved their convenience at the expense of their heritage, and whose ephemeral prosperity was built on waste.

VALUES AND
THE PERSONAL CHOICE

INTRODUCTION

Those who concern themselves with the present state of civilization tend to agree that the Western nations are currently experiencing a crisis of values, belief, and personal choice which may threaten the very characteristics that identify the "human" animal. While it is difficult to make enlightening comparisons with older societies, one cannot avoid observing the consequences of the loss of those systems of value and belief which have structured—for better or worse—the psychic, social, religious, and emotional life of the individual.

It is obvious, for example, that modern technological man, laboring in depersonalized bureaucracies, living in sterile megalopolises, incessantly bombarded by thousands of media communications daily, lacks a gratifying involvement with the physical environment. Instead of feeling a sense of relationship to nature, he watches the eclipse of the moon on television, perhaps because air pollution blocks his view or perhaps because he has lost the capacity to believe in the possibility of experiencing directly without an intervening "explanation" from the electronic programmers.

While children previously absorbed their values and beliefs from the elders of their family, clan, or community, they now acquire much of their world outlook from the thousands of hours of television they "experience" before they enter first grade. Many of their grandparents, euphemistically labeled "senior citizens" or "pioneers," having lost cultural and economic usefulness, are exiled to "homes" where, cut off from the young, they wait for death. In an era in which values are so transient and the knowledge required for living so impermanent, only the young or the highly imaginative are able to "keep up." At this point death becomes an inconvenient obscenity, momentarily interrupting the meaningless flux of contemporary existence.

Having banished its elders and lost touch with its children, the family is suffering from increasing threats to its stripped down nuclear existence. Under attack by psychologists such as Bruno Bettelheim, the family is alleged to be the source of permanent emotional and psychic injury to children. Even the sacred mystique of motherhood is questioned by social scientists who argue that many of the anxieties and insecurities of the present derive from a pathological relationship between mother and child. Without attempting to decide these difficult questions, we can safely conclude that the family, as a stable source of values, direction, and definition for human existence, is in a state of crisis.

Also, the values which our school textbooks still identify as being specifically and uniquely American—those associated with the Protestant work ethic, Benjamin Franklin, log cabin Presidents, Horatio Alger, in short, the American Dream, in which hard work and strict ethical standards lead to salvation through economics—are rejected, often *in toto*. The privileged white middle-class children of those who have "made it" have found often salvation instead of affluent boredom. The critics point to an America where two-fifths of the people remain chronically poor, where twenty-five million people are denied full participation in American life on racial or ethnic grounds, and where the previously sacred cow of flag-waving patriotism is identified as a symbol of aggressive war.

If many Americans continue to participate in organized religion and family life and to envision gratifying careers within corporate bureaucracies, many others find no future in these institutions, forsaking them to attempt to define new ways of life based on entirely different attitudes toward work, child-rearing, education, politics, and sex. Inevitably, those who feel the absence of values in the traditional institutions, or who believe that the values of those institutions are corrupt, invalid, or insufficient to live by, will attempt to construct their own values and create their own visions of a new society. These efforts will load a great burden upon the individual, who must either find the courage to define himself through choice or succumb to the confusion and chaos of the present. Lacking the moral and ethical absolutes that helped guide, define, and identify him in the past, man is now, as Sartre has written, "condemned to be free."

THE DECLINE OF RELIGION

William Barrett

The central fact of modern history in the West—by which we mean
the long period from the end of the Middle Ages to the present—is
unquestionably the decline of religion. No doubt, the Churches are
still very powerful organizations; there are millions of churchgoers all
over the world; and even the purely intellectual possibilities of religious belief look better to churchmen now than in the bleak days of
self-confident nineteenth-century materialism. A few years ago there
was even considerable talk about a "religious revival," and some popular and patriotic periodicals such as *Life* magazine gave a great deal
of space to it; but the talk has by now pretty much died down, the
movement, if any, subsided, and the American public buys more automobiles and television sets than ever before. When *Life* magazine
promotes a revival of religion, one is only too painfully aware from the
nature of this publication that religion is considered as being in the
national interest; one could scarcely have a clearer indication of the
broader historical fact that in the modern world the nation-state, a
thoroughly secular institution, outranks any church.

The decline of religion in modern times means simply that religion
is no longer the uncontested center and ruler of man's life, and that
the Church is no longer the final and unquestioned home and asylum
of his being. The deepest significance of this change does not even

appear principally at the purely intellectual level, in loss of belief, though this loss due to the critical inroads of science has been a major historical cause of the decline. The waning of religion is a much more concrete and complex fact than a mere change in conscious outlook; it penetrates the deepest strata of man's total psychic life. It is indeed one of the major stages in man's psychic evolution—as Nietzsche, almost alone among nineteenth-century philosophers, was to see. Religion to medieval man was not so much a theological system as a solid psychological matrix surrounding the individual's life from birth to death, sanctifying and enclosing all its ordinary and extraordinary occasions in sacrament and ritual. The loss of the Church was the loss of a whole system of symbols, images, dogmas, and rites which had the psychological validity of immediate experience, and within which hitherto the whole psychic life of Western man had been safely contained. In losing religion, man lost the concrete connection with a transcendent realm of being; he was set free to deal with this world in all its brute objectivity. But he was bound to feel homeless in such a world, which no longer answered the needs of his spirit. A home is the accepted framework which habitually contains our life. To lose one's psychic container is to be cast adrift, to become a wanderer upon the face of the earth. Henceforth, in seeking his own human completeness man would have to do for himself what he once had done for him, unconsciously, by the Church, through the medium of its sacramental life. Naturally enough, man's feeling of homelessness did not make itself felt for some time; the Renaissance man was still enthralled by a new and powerful vision of mastery over the whole earth.

No believer, no matter how sincere, could possibly write the *Divine Comedy* today, even if he possessed a talent equal to Dante's. Visions and symbols do not have the immediate and overwhelming reality for us that they had for the medieval poet. In the *Divine Comedy* the whole of nature is merely a canvas upon which the religious symbol and image are painted. Western man has spent more than five hundred years—half a millennium—in stripping nature of these projections and turning it into a realm of neutral objects which his science may control. Thus it could hardly be expected that the religious image would have the same force for us as it did for Dante. This is simply a psychic fact within human history; psychic facts have just as much historical validity as the facts that we now, unlike the man of Dante's time, travel in airplanes and work in factories regulated by computing machines. A great work of art can never be repeated—the history of art shows us time and again that literal imitation leads to pastiche—

because it springs from the human soul, which evolves like everything else in nature. This point must be insisted upon, contrary to the view of some of our more enthusiastic medievalists who picture the psychic containment of medieval man as a situation of human completeness to which we must return. History has never allowed man to return to the past in any total sense. And our psychological problems cannot be solved by a regression to a past state in which they had not yet been brought into being. On the other hand, enlightened and progressive thinkers are equally blind when they fail to recognize that every major step forward by mankind entails some loss, the sacrifice of an older security and the creation and heightening of new tensions. (We should bear this in mind against some of the criticisms of Existentialism as a philosophy that has unbearably heightened human tensions: it did not create those tensions, which were already at work in the soul of modern man, but simply sought to give them philosophic expression, rather than evading them by pretending they were not there.)

It is far from true that the passage from the Middle Ages to modern times is the substitution of a rational for a religious outlook; on the contrary, the whole of medieval philosophy—as Whitehead has very aptly remarked—is one of "unbounded rationalism" in comparison with modern thought. Certainly, the difference between a St. Thomas Aquinas in the thirteenth century and a Kant at the end of the eighteenth century is conclusive on this point: For Aquinas the whole natural world, and particularly this natural world as it opens toward God as First Cause, was transparently accessible to human reason; while to Kant, writing at the bitter end of the century of Enlightenment, the limits of human reason had very radically shrunk. (Indeed, as we shall see later, the very meaning of human reason became altered in Kant.) But this "unbounded rationalism" of the medieval philosopher is altogether different from the untrammeled use later thinkers made of human reason, applying it like an acid solvent to all things human or divine. The rationalism of the medieval philosophers was contained by the mysteries of faith and dogma, which were altogether beyond the grasp of human reason, but were nevertheless powerfully real and meaningful to man as symbols that kept the vital circuit open between reason and emotion, between the rational and non-rational in the human psyche. Hence, this rationalism of the medieval philosophers does not end with the attenuated, bleak, or grim picture of man we find in the modern rationalists. Here, once again, the condition under which the philosopher creates his philosophy, like that under which the poet creates his poetry, has to do with deeper levels of his being—deeper than the merely conscious level of having or not having a rational point of view. We could not expect to produce a St. Thomas Aquinas, any more than a Dante, today. The total psychic condition of man—of which after all thinking is one of the manifestations—has evolved too radically. Which may be why present-day Thomists have on the whole remained singularly unconvincing to their contemporaries.

At the gateway that leads from the Middle Ages into the modern world stand Science (which later became the spirit of the Enlightenment), Protestantism, and Capitalism. At first glance, the spirit of Protestantism would seem to have very little to do with that of the New Science, since in matters religious Protestantism placed all the weight of its emphasis upon the irrational datum of faith, as against the imposing rational structures of medieval theology, and there is Luther's famous curse upon "the whore, Reason." In secular matters, however—and particularly in its relation toward nature—Protestantism fitted in very well with the New Science. By stripping away the wealth of images and symbols from medieval Christianity, Protestantism unveiled nature as a realm of objects hostile to the spirit and to be conquered by puritan zeal and industry. Thus Protestantism, like science, helped carry forward that immense project of modern man: the despiritualization of nature, the emptying of it of all the symbolic images projected upon it by the human psyche. With Protestantism begins that long modern struggle, which reaches its culmination in the twentieth century, to strip man naked. To be sure, in all of this the aim was progress, and Protestantism did succeed in raising the religious consciousness to a higher level of individual sincerity, soul-searching, strenuous inwardness. Man was impoverished in order to come face to face with his God and the severe and inexplicable demands of his faith; but in the process he was stripped of all the mediating rites and dogmas that could make this confrontation less dangerous to his psychic balance. Protestantism achieved a heightening of the religious consciousness, but at the same time severed this consciousness from the deep unconscious life of our total human nature. In this respect, its historical thrust runs parallel to that of the New Science and capitalism, since science was making the mythical and symbolic picture of nature disappear before the success of its own rational explanations, and capitalism was opening up the whole world as a field of operations for rationally planned enterprise.

Faith, for Protestantism, is nevertheless the irrational and numinous center of religion; Luther was saturated with the feeling of St.

Paul that man of himself can do nothing and only God working in us can bring salvation. Here the inflation of human consciousness is radically denied, and the conscious mind is recognized as the mere instrument and plaything of a much greater unconscious force. Faith is an abyss that engulfs the rational nature of man. The Protestant doctrine of Original Sin is in all its severity a kind of compensatory recognition of those depths below the level of consciousness where the earnest soul demands to interrogate itself—except that those depths are cast into the outer darkness of depravity. So long as faith retained its intensity, however, the irrational elements of human nature were accorded recognition and a central place in the total human economy. But as the modern world moves onward, it becomes more and more secularized in every department of life; faith consequently becomes attenuated, and Protestant man begins to look more and more like a gaunt skeleton, a sculpture by Giacometti. A secular civilization leaves him more starkly naked than the iconoclasm of the Reformation had ever dreamed. The more severely he struggles to hold on to the primal face-to-face relation with God, the more tenuous this becomes, until in the end the relation to God Himself threatens to become a relation to Nothingness. In this sense Kierkegaard, in the middle of the nineteenth century, was the reckoning point of the whole Protestant Reformation that began three centuries earlier: He sees faith for the uncompromising and desperate wager it is, if one takes it in all its Protestant strictness; and he cannot say, like his Catholic counterpart Pascal, "Stupefy yourself, take holy water, receive the sacraments, and in the end all shall be well"—for Protestant man has forsworn the sacraments and natural symbols of the soul as the snares and pomp of the devil. Some of Kierkegaard's books as *The Sickness Unto Death* and *The Concept of Dread,* are still frightening to our contemporaries and so are excused or merely passed over as the personal outpourings of a very melancholy temperament; yet they are the truthful record of what the Protestant soul must experience on the brink of the great Void. Protestant man is the beginning of the West's fateful encounter with Nothingness—an encounter that was long overdue and is perhaps only now in the twentieth century reaching its culmination.

THE REVOLT OF THE DIMINISHED MAN

Archibald MacLeish

Robert Frost had the universe, not the university, in mind when he wrote his laconic couplet about the secret in the middle, but the image fits the academic world in crisis as well as the mysteries of space.

We dance around in a ring and
suppose
But the secret sits in the middle and
knows.

Indeed, we do. Faculty committees, state legislatures, alumni associations, police departments, and all the rest of us whirl in a circle with our favorite suppositions—which increasingly tend to roll up into one supposition: that the crisis in the university is really only a student crisis, or, more precisely, a crisis precipitated by a small minority of students, which would go away if the students would stop doing whatever it is they are doing or whatever they plan to do next.

Which, needless to say, is not a wholly irrational supposition. Those who have seen a purposeful task force of Harvard students take over University Hall, carry out reluctant deans, break into files, shout down professors are within their logical rights when they conclude that the occupying students were the cause of the crisis thus created. But the supposition remains a supposition notwithstanding for it does not follow—did not follow at Harvard certainly—that the crisis is a student crisis in the critical sense that it can be ended merely by suppressing the students involved. When the students involved were suppressed at Harvard, the crisis (as at other universities) was not reduced but enlarged. Which suggests, if it suggests anything, that the actual crisis is larger than its particular incidents or their perpetrators.

And there are other familiar facts which look in the same direction; as, for example, the fact that it is only when the general opinion of an entire student generation supports, or at least condones, minority disruptions that they can hope to succeed. The notion that the activist tail wags the huge, indifferent student dog is an illusion. Had a minority of the kind involved at Harvard attempted to bring the University to that famous "grinding halt" in the Forties or the Fifties it would have had its trouble for its pains no matter how forceful the police. It succeeded in the Sixties for one reason and for one reason only—because the climate of student opinion as a whole had changed in the Sixties; because there has been a change in the underlying beliefs, the accepted ideas, of an entire academic generation, or the greater part of it.

To look for the cause of crisis, therefore, is to examine, not the demands of the much discussed minorities but something larger—the changes in belief of the generation to which they belong. And there at once a paradox appears. The most striking of these changes far from disturbing the academic world should and does encourage it. There are, of course, romantics in the new generation who talk of destroying the university as a symbol of a defunct civilization, but the great mass of their contemporaries, however little they sometimes seem to understand the nature of the university—the vulnerability, fragility even, of that free and open community of minds which a university is—are nevertheless profoundly concerned with the university's well-being and, specifically, its relation to the world and to themselves.

This is a new thing under the academic sun—and, in itself, a hopeful thing. Down to the decade now closing, demands by any considerable number of American undergraduates for changes in the substance or manner or method or purpose of their instruction were rare indeed. In my day at Yale, back before the First World War, no one concerned himself less with matters of curriculum and teaching and the like than a college undergraduate. We were not, as undergraduates, indifferent to our education, but it never occurred to any of us to think of the curriculum of Yale College as a matter within our concern, or the policies of the university as decisions about which we—we of all creatures living—were entitled to an opinion. Some of my college classmates protested compulsory chapel (largely because of its interference with breakfast), but no one to my knowledge ever protested, even in a letter to the *News,* the pedantic teaching of Shakespeare, from which the college then suffered, or the non-teaching of Karl Marx, who was then on the point of changing the history of the world.

And the same thing was true of the relation between the university and the world outside. We in the class of 1915 spent our senior year in a Yale totally surrounded by the First World War, but we were "inside" and all the rest were "outside," and it was not for us to put the two together—not even for those of us who were to go from New Haven to die on the Marne or in the Argonne under extremely unpleasant circumstances in the most murderous, hypocritical, unneccessary, and generally nasty of all recorded wars, the present one included. Our deaths, as we came to know would be our own but not their reasons. When I myself was asked by a corporal in my battery what we were there for—"there" being the second battle of the Marne —I quoted President Wilson: "to make the world safe for democracy." It was not my war. President Wilson was running it.

And the generation which fought the next war twenty years later saw things in much the same way. They too were in a sense observers —observers, in their case, of their own heroism. When the war came they fought it with magnificent courage: no citizen army in history ever fought better than theirs after that brutal North African initiation. But until the war came, while it was still in the agonizing process of becoming, it was somebody else's war—President Roosevelt's, as the Chicago *Tribune* kept insinuating, or Winston Churchill's "America First" was, in part, a campus movement but the terrible question posed by Adolf Hitler—a question of life or death for thousands of young Americans and very possibly for the Republic itself— was little argued by the undergraduates of 1941. The political aspects of fascism they left to their elders at home and the moral agony to their contemporaries in the French Resistance. They themselves merely fought the war and won it—fought it with a kind of gallant indifference, an almost ironic gallantry, which was, and still remains, the hallmark of that incredible generation and its improbable triumph.

It is in this perspective and against this background that the attitudes of the undergraduates of the Sixties must be seen. Here, suddenly and almost without warning, is a generation of undergraduates that reverses everything that has gone before, rejects the traditional undergraduate isolation, refuses the conventional segregation of the university from the troubled world, and not only accepts for itself but demands for itself a measure of responsibility for both—for university *and* world, for life as well as for education.

And the question, if we wish to understand this famous crisis of ours, is: Why? Why has this transformation of ideas—metamorphosis more precisely—taken place? Why does the generation of the Sixties make itself morally responsible for the war in Vietnam, while the generation of 1917 stood on the Marne quoting Woodrow Wilson and the generation of 1941 smashed the invincible Nazi armor from Normandy to the Rhine without a quotation from anybody? Why, for the first time in the remembered history of this Republic, do its college and university students assert a responsibility for their own education, demand a part in the process? Are we really to believe with some of our legislators, that the whole thing is the result of a mysterious, country-wide conspiracy among the hairier of the young directed perhaps by a sinister professor somewhere? Or is it open to us to consider that the crisis in the university may actually be what we call it: a crisis *in* the university—a crisis in education itself precipitated by a revolution in ideas, a revolution in the ideas of a new generation of mankind?

There are those who believe we must find the answer to that question where we find the question: in the decade in which we live. Franklin Ford, dean of the Faculty of Arts and Sciences at Harvard and one of the ablest and most admired of university administrators, attributes this change mentality in great part to the particular malaise of the Sixties. "Undertaking to explain to his colleagues his view of what we have come to call "student unrest," Dean Ford defined it in terms of concentric circles, the most important of which would include students who had been profoundly hurt by the anguish of these recent years: "The thought-benumbing blows of successive assassinations, the equally tragic though more comprehensible crisis of the cities, the growing bitterness of the poor amid the self-congratulations of affluence, the even greater bitterness of black Americans, rich or poor . . . all these torments of our day have hit thoughtful young people with peculiar force. . . . Youth is a time of extreme vulnerability to grief and frustration, as well as a time of impatient, generous sympathy." And to all this, Dean Ford continues, must be added the war in Vietnam, which he sees as poisoning and exacerbating everything else, contributing "what can only be described as (a sense) of horror."

Most of us—perhaps I should qualify that by saying most of those with whom I talk—would agree. We would agree, that is to say, that the war in Vietnam has poisoned the American mind. We would agree that the affluent society—more precisely the affluent half-society—has turned out to be a sick society, for the affluent half as well as for the other. We would agree that the cancer of the cities, the animal hatred of the races, the bursting pustule of violence has hurt us all and particularly those of us who are young and they in particular *because* they are young, because, being young, they are generous, because, being young and generous, they are vulnerable. We would agree to all this, and we would agree in consequence that there is a relationship between the malaise in the universities and Dean Ford's "particular malaise of the Sixties."

But would we agree, reflecting on those considerations and this conclusion, that it is the tragic events of the decade which, alone, are the root cause—the effective cause—of the unrest of which Dean Ford is speaking? If the bitterness, the brutality, the suffering of the last few years were the effective cause, would the *university* be the principal target of resentment? If Vietnam were the heart of the trouble, would the university curriculum be attacked—the methods of teaching, the teachers themselves? Would the reaction not have expressed itself, as indeed it once did, at the Pentagon?

What is resented, clearly, is not only the present state of the Republic, the present state of the world, but some relation or lack of relation between the state of the Republic, the state of the world, and the process of education—the process of education at its most meaningful point—the process of education in the university.

But what relation or lack of relation? A direct, a one to one, relationship? is the university blamed *because* the war is being fought, *because* the ghettos exist, *because* the affluent society is the vulgar, dull, unbeautiful society we see in our more ostentatious cities? Is the demand of the young a demand that the university should alter its instruction and its practices so as to put an end to this ugliness, these evils—reshape this society?

There are some undergraduates, certainly, who take this position. There are some who would like to bring the weight and influence of the university to bear directly on the solution of economic and social problems through the management of the university's real estate and endowments. There are others who would direct its instruction toward specific evils by establishing courses in African affairs and urban studies. Both attitudes are familiar: they are standard demands of student political organizations. They are also reasonable—reasonable at least in purpose if not always in form. But do they go to the heart of the matter? Is this direct relationship of specific instruction to specific need—of specific land-use program to specific land-use evil—the relation undergraduates have in mind when they complain, as they do, over and over, that their courses are not "relevant," that their education does not "respond to their needs," "preach to their condition"? Is it only "applicability," only immediate pertinence, the generation of the young demands of us? Is the deep, almost undefinable restlessness of the student generation—the dark unhappiness of which Senator Muskie spoke in that unforgettable speech at Chicago—an unhappiness which Centers of Urban Studies, however neccessary, can cure?

I do not think so and neither, if you will forgive me for saying it, do you. The distress, the very real and generous suffering and distress of an entire generation of young men and young women is related certainly to the miseries of the Sixties, but it is not founded in them and it will not disappear when they vanish—when, if ever, the war ends and the hot summers find cool shade and the assassinations cease. The "relevance" these students speak of is not relevance to the *Huntley-Brinkley Report*. It is relevance to their own lives, to the living of their lives, to themselves as men and women living. And their resentment, their very real resentment and distress, rises not only from the tragedies and mischances of the last ten years but from a human situation, a total human situation involving human life as human life, which has been three generations in the making, and which this new generation now revolts against—rejects.

At the time of the Sorbonne riots a year ago a French politician spoke in terms of apocalypse: We had come to a point in time like the fall of Rome when civilizations collapse because belief is dead. What was actually happening in Paris and elsewhere was, of course, the precise opposite. Belief, passionate belief, had come alive for the first time in the century and with it rage and violence.The long diminishment, the progressive diminution, of value put upon man, upon the idea of man, in modern society had met the revulsion of a generation of the young who condemned it in all its aspects, left as well as right, Communist as well as capitalist, the indifference of the Marxist bureaucracies as well as the bureaucratic industrial indifference of the West.

This diminishment of the idea of man has been a long time in progress. I will not claim for my generation that we witnessed its beginning, I will assert only that we were the first to record it where alone it could be recorded. The arts with us became aware of a flatness in human life, a loss of depth as though a dimension had somehow dropped from the world—as though our human shadows had deserted us. The great metaphor of the journey of mankind—Ulysses among the mysteries and monsters—reduced itself in our youth to that other Ulysses among the privies and the pubs of Dublin, Ireland. Cleopatra on her flowery barge floated through a Saturday night in the Bloomsbury Twenties. Even death itself was lessened: the multitudes of Dante's damned crossed T. S. Eliot's London Bridge, commuters in the morning fog. Nothing was left remarkable beneath the visiting moon.

And in the next generation—the generation, as we are now beginning to see, of Joyce's secretary and disciple, Samuel Beckett—the testimony of the arts went on. The banality of the age turned to impotence and numbness and paralysis, a total anesthesia of the soul.

Leopold Bloom no longer maundered through the musty Dublin streets. He was incapable even of maundering, incapable of motion. He sat to his neck in sand, like a head of rotting celery in a autumn garden, and waited, or did not even wait—just sat there. While as for Cleopatra—Cleopatra was an old man's youthful memory played back upon a worn-out tape.

The arts are honest witnesses in these matters. Pound was right enough, for all the well-known plethora of language, when he wrote in praise of Joyce's *Ulysses* that "it is a summary of pre-war Europe, the blackness and mess and muddle of a 'civilization,' " and that "Bloom very much *is* the mess." The arts, moreover, are honest witnesses in such matters not only when they achieve works of art as with Joyce and Eliot and frequently with Beckett. They testify even when they fail. The unpoem, the nonpainting of our era, the play that does not play, all bear their penny's worth of witness. The naked, half-embarrassed boy displaying his pudenda on an off Off-Broadway stage is not an actor nor is his shivering gesture a dramatic act, but still he testifies. He is the last, sad, lost reincarnation of L. Bloom, the resurrection of the head of celery. Odysseus on his lonely raft in the god-infested sea has come to this.

What was imagined in Greece, reimagined in the Renaissance, carried to a passion of pride in Europe of the Enlightenment and to a passion of hope in the Republic of the New World—John Adams's hope as well as Jefferson's and Whitman's; Lincoln's that he called "the last, best hope"—all this grimaces in pitiful derision of itself in that nude, sad, shivering figure. And we see it or we hear about it and protest. But protest *what*? The nakedness! The morals of the playwright! Undoubtedly the playwright needs correction in his morals and above all in the practice of his art, but in his *vision*? His *perception*! Is he the first to see this? On the contrary, his most obvious failure as playwright is precisely the fact that he is merely one of thousands in a thronging, long contemporary line—a follower of fashion. He testifies as hundreds of his betters have been testifying now for years—for generations—near a century.

Why have they so testified? They cannot tell you. The artist's business is to see and to show, not answer why: to see as no one else can see, and to show as nothing else can show, but not to explain. He knows no more of explanation than another. And yet *we* cannot help but wonder why—why the belief in man has foundered; why it has foundered *now*—precisely *now*—now at the moment of our greatest intellectual triumphs, our never equaled technological mastery, our electronic miracles. Why was man a wonder to the Greeks—to Sophocles of all the Greeks—when he could do little more than work a ship to windward, ride a horse, and plow the earth, while now that he knows the whole of modern science he is a wonder to no one—certainly not to Sophocles' successors and least of all, in any case, to himself?

There is no easy answer, though thoughtful men are beginning to suggest that an answer may be found and that, when it is, it may very well relate precisely to this vast new knowledge. George W. Morgan states the position in his *The Human Predicament.* "The sheer weight of accumulated but uncontrolled knowledge and information, of print, views, discoveries, and interpretations, of methods and techniques, inflicts a paralyzing sense of impotence. The mind is overwhelmed by a constant fear of its ignorance. . . . The individual man, feeling unable to gain a valid perspective of the world and of himself, is forced to regard both as consisting of innumerable isolated parts to be relinquished, for knowledge and control, to a legion of experts." All this, says Mr. Morgan, diminishes human understanding in the very process of augmenting human knowledge. It also, I should wish to add, diminishes something else. It diminishes man. For man, as the whole of science as well as the whole of poetry, will demonstrate, is not what he thinks he knows, but what he thinks he *can* know, can become.

But however much or little we comprehend of the cause of our paradoxical diminishment in our own eyes at the moment of our greatest technological triumphs, we cannot help but understand a little of its consequences and particularly its relation to the crisis in the university. Without the belief in man, the university is a contradiction in terms. The business of the university is education at its highest possible level, and the business of education at its highest possible level is the relation of men to their lives. But how is the university to concern itself with the relation of men to their lives, to the living of their lives, to the world in which their lives are lived, without the bold assumption, the brave, improbable hypothesis, that these lives matter, that these men count—that Odysseus on his battered, drifting raft still stands for a reality we take for real?

And how can a generation of the young, born into the world of the diminished man and in revolt against it—in revolt against its indifference to humanity in its cities and in its wars and in the weapons of its wars—how can a generation of the young help but demand some teaching from the universities which will interpret all this horror and make cause against it?

Centuries ago in a world of gods and mysteries and monsters when man's creativity, his immense creative powers, had been, as Berdyaev put it. "paralyzed by the Middle Ages"—when men had been diminished in their own eyes by the demeaning dogma of the Fall—centuries ago the university conceived an intellectual and spiritual position which released mankind into a new beginning, a rebirth, a Renaissance. What is demanded of us now in a new age of gods and mysteries and monsters, not without dogmas and superstitions of its own, is a second humanism that will free us from our new paralysis of soul as the earlier humanism freed us from that other. If it was human significance which was destroyed by the Middle Ages, it is human significance which we ourselves are now destroying. We are witnessing, as the British critic F.R. Leavis phrases it, the elimination of that "day-by-day creativity of human response which manifests itself in the significances and values without which there is no reality—nothing but emptiness that has to be filled with drink, sex, eating, background music, and . . . the papers and the telly."

Mr. Leavis, not the most optimistic of dons on any occasion, believes that something might be done to revive "the creative human response that maintains cultural continuity" and that gives human life a meaning. I, with fewer qualifications to speak, would go much further. I would say that a conscious and determined effort to conceive a new humanism which would do for our darkness what that earlier humanism did for the darkness of the Middle Ages is not only a present dream but a present possibility, and that it is a present possibility not despite the generation of the young—the generation of the Sixties—but because of it.

That generation is not perhaps as sophisticated politically as it—or its activist spokesmen—would have us think. Its moral superiority to earlier generations may not, in every instance, be as great as it apparently believes. But one virtue it does possess to a degree not equaled by any generation in this century: It believes in man.

It is an angry generation, yes but its resentment is not the disgust of the generation for which Beckett speaks. Its resentment is not a resentment *of* our human life but a resentment *on behalf* of human life; not an indignation that we exist on the Earth but that we *permit* ourselves to exist in a selfishness and wretchedness and squalor which we have the means to abolish. Resentment of this kind is founded, can only be founded, on belief in man. And belief in man—a return to a belief in man—is the reality on which a new age can be built.

Thus far, that new belief has been used by the young largely as a weapon—as a justification of an indictment of earlier generations for their exploitation and debasement of human life and earth. When it is allowed to become itself—when the belief in man becomes an affirmative effort to re-create the life of man—the crisis in the university may well become the triumph of the university.

For it is only the university in this technological age which can save us from ourselves. And the university, as we now know, can only function effectively when it functions as a common labor of all its generations dedicated to the highest purpose of them all.

FREEDOM AND RESPONSIBILITY

Jean-Paul Sartre

... Absolute responsibility is not resignation; it is simply the logical requirement of the consequences of our freedom. What happens to me happens through me, and I can neither affect myself with it nor revolt against it nor resign myself to it. Moreover everything which happens to me is *mine*. By this we must understand first of all that I am always equal to what happens to me *qua* man, for what happens to a man through other men and through himself can be only human. The most terrible situations of war, the worst tortures do not create a non-human state of things; there is no non-human situation. It is only through fear, flight, and recourse to magical types of conduct that I shall decide on the non-human, but this decision is human, and I shall carry the entire responsibility for it. But in addition the situation is *mine* because it is the image of my free choice of myself, and everything which it presents to me is *mine* in that this represents me and symbolizes me. Is it not I who decide the coefficient of adversity in things and even their unpredictability by deciding myself?

Thus there are no *accidents* in a life; a community event which suddenly bursts forth and involves me in it does not come from the outside. If I am mobilized in a war, this war is *my* war; it is in my image and I deserve it. I deserve it first because I could always get out of it by suicide or by desertion; these ultimate possibles are those which must always be present for us when there is a question of envisaging a situation. For lack of getting out of it, I have *chosen* it. This can be

Jean-Paul Sartre, "Freedom and Responsibility" from *Being And Nothingness* (1957), pp. 53–59. Reprinted by permission of the Philosophical Library, Inc.

due to inertia, to cowardice in the face of public opinion, or because I prefer certain other values to the value of the refusal to join in the war (the good opinion of my relatives, the honor of my family, *etc.*). Anyway you look at it, it is a matter of a choice. This choice will be repeated later on again and again without a break until the end of the war. Therefore we must agree with the statement by J. Romains, "In war there are no innocent victims." If therefore I have preferred war to death or to dishonor, everything takes place as if I bore the entire responsibility for this war. Of course others have declared it, and one might be tempted perhaps to consider me as a simple accomplice. But this notion of complicity has only a juridical sense, and it does not hold here. For it depended on me that for me and by me this war should not exist, and I have decided that it does exist. There was no compulsion here, for the compulsion could have got no hold on a freedom. I did not have any excuse; for as we have said repeatedly in this book, the peculiar character of human-reality is that it is without excuse. Therefore it remains for me only to lay claim to this war.

But in addition the war is *mine* because by the sole fact that it arises in a situation which I cause to be and that I can discover it there only by engaging myself for or against it, I can no longer distinguish at present the choice which I make of myself from the choice which I make of the war. To live this war is to choose myself through it and to choose it through my choice of myself. There can be no question of considering it as "four years of vacation" or as a "reprieve," as a "recess," the essential part of my responsibilities being elsewhere in my married, family, or professional life. In this war which I have chosen I choose myself from day to day, and I make it mine by making myself. If it is going to be four empty years, then it is I who bear the responsibility for this.

Finally, as we pointed out earlier, each person is an absolute choice of self from the standpoint of a world of knowledges and of techniques which this choice both assumes and illumines; each person is an absolute upsurge at an absolute date and is perfectly unthinkable at another date. It is therefore a waste of time to ask what I should have been if this war had not broken out, for I have chosen myself as one of the possible meanings of the epoch which imperceptibly led to war. I am not distinct from this same epoch; I could not be transported to another epoch without contradiction. Thus *I am* this war which restricts and limits and makes comprehensible the period which preceded it. In this sense we may define more precisely the responsibility of the for-itself if to the earlier quoted statement, "There are no innocent victims," we add the words, "We have the war we deserve." Thus, totally free, undistinguishable from the period for which I have chosen to be the meaning, as profoundly responsible for the war as if I had myself declared it, unable to live without integrating it in *my* situation, engaging myself in it wholly and stamping it with my seal, I must be without remorse or regrets as I am without excuse; for from the instant of my upsurge into being, I carry the weight of the world by myself alone without anything or any person being able to lighten it.

Yet this responsibility is of a very particular type. Someone will say, "I did not ask to be born." This is a naive way of throwing greater emphasis on our facticity. I am responsible for everything, in fact, except for my very responsibility, for I am not the foundation of my being. Therefore everything takes place as if I were compelled to be responsible. I am *abandoned* in the world, not in the sense that I might remain abandoned and passive in a hostile universe like a board floating on the water, but rather in the sense that I find myself suddenly alone and without help, engaged in a world for which I bear the whole responsibility without being able, whatever I do, to tear myself away from this responsibility for an instant. For I am responsible for my very desire of fleeing responsibilities. To make myself passive in the world, to refuse to act upon things and upon Others is still to choose myself, and suicide is one mode among others of being-in-the-world. Yet I find an absolute responsibility for the fact that my facticity (here the fact of my birth) is directly inapprehensible and even inconceivable, for this fact of my birth never appears as a brute fact but always across a projective reconstruction of my for-itself. I am ashamed of being born or I am astonished at it or I rejoice over it, or in attempting to get rid of my life I affirm that I live and I assume this life as bad. Thus in a certain sense I *choose* being born. This choice itself is integrally affected with facticity since I am not able not to choose, but this facticity in turn will appear only in so far as I surpass it toward my ends. Thus facticity is everywhere but inapprehensible; I never encounter anything except my responsibility. That is why I can not ask, "*Why* was I born?" or curse the day of my birth or declare that I did not ask to be born, for these various attitudes toward my birth —i.e., toward the *fact* that I realize a presence in the world—are absolutely nothing else but ways of assuming this birth in full responsibility and of making it *mine.* Here again I encounter only myself and my projects so that finally my abandonment—*i.e.,* my facticity—consists simply in the fact that I am condemned to be wholly responsible for myself. I am the being which *is* in such a way that in its being its being is in question. And this "is" of my being *is* as present and inapprehensible.

Under these conditions since every event in the world can be revealed to me only as an *opportunity* (an opportunity made use of, lacked, neglected, *etc.*), or better yet since everything which happens to us can be considered as a *chance* (*i.e.,* can appear to us only as a way of realizing this being which is in question in our being) and since others as transcendences-transcended are themselves only *opportunities* and *chances,* the responsibility of the for-itself extends to the entire world as a peopled-world. It is precisely thus that the for-itself apprehends itself in anguish; that is, as a being which is neither the foundation of its own being nor of the Other's being nor of the in-itselfs which form the world, but a being which is compelled to decide the meaning of being—within it and everywhere outside of it. The one who realizes in anguish his condition as *being* thrown into a responsibility which extends to his very abandonment has no longer either remorse or regret or excuse; he is no longer anything but a freedom which perfectly reveals itself and whose being resides in this very revelation. But as we pointed out at the beginning of this work, most of the time we flee anguish in bad faith.

CRAP DETECTING

Neil Postman and Charles Weingartner

"In 1492, Columbus discovered America. . . . " Starting from this disputed fact, each one of us will describe the history of this country in a somewhat different way. Nonetheless, it is reasonable to assume that most of us would include something about what is called the "democratic process," and how Americans have valued it, or at least have said they valued it. Therein lies a problem: one of the tenets of a democratic society is that men be allowed to think and express themselves freely on any subject, even to the point of speaking out against the idea of a democratic society. To the extent that our schools

Neil Postman and Charles Weingartner, "Crap Detecting," *Teaching As A Subversive Activity* (N.Y.: Delacorte Press, 1969), Chap. 1. Reprinted by permission of the publisher.

are instruments of such a society, they must develop in the young not only an awareness of this freedom but a will to exercise it, and the intellectual power and perspective to do so effectively. This is necessary so that the society may continue to change and modify itself to meet unforeseen threats, problems, and opportunities. Thus, we can achieve what John Gardner calls an "ever-renewing society."

So goes the theory.

In practice, we mostly get a different story. In our society, as in others, we find that there are influential men at the head of important institutions who cannot afford to be found wrong, who find change inconvenient, perhaps intolerable, and who have financial or political interests they must conserve at any cost. Such men are, therefore, threatened in many respects by the theory of the democratic process and the concept of an ever-renewing society. Moreover, we find that there are obscure men who do *not* head important institutions who are similarly threatened because they have identified themselves with certain ideas and institutions which they wish to keep free from either criticism or change.

Such men as these would much prefer that the schools do little or nothing to encourage youth to question, doubt, or challenge any part of the society in which they live, especially those parts which are most vulnerable. "After all," say the practical men, "they are *our* schools, and they ought to promote *our* interests, and *that* is part of the democratic process, too." True enough; and here we have a serious point of conflict. Whose schools are they, anyway, and whose interests should they be designed to serve? We realize that these are questions about which any self-respecting professor of education could write several books, each one beginning with a reminder that the problem is not black or white, either/or, yes or no. But if you have read our introduction, you will not expect us to be either professorial or prudent. We are, after all, trying to suggest strategies for survival as they may be developed in our schools, and the situation requires emphatic responses. We believe that the schools must serve as the principal medium for developing in youth the attitudes and skills of social, political, and cultural criticism. No. That is not emphatic enough. Try this: In the early 1960s, an interviewer was trying to get Ernest Hemingway to identify the characteristics required for a person to be a "great writer." As the interviewer offered a list of various possibilities, Hemingway disparaged each in sequence. Finally, frustrated, the interviewer asked, "Isn't there any one essential ingredient that you can identify?" Hemingway replied, "Yes, there is.

In order to be a great writer a person must have a built-in, shock-proof crap detector."

It seems to us that, in his response, Hemingway identified an essential survival strategy and the essential function of the schools in today's world. One way of looking at the history of the human group is that it has been a continuing struggle against the veneration of "crap." Our intellectual history is a chronicle of the anguish and suffering of men who tried to help their contemporaries see that some part of their fondest beliefs were misconceptions, faulty assumptions, superstitions, and even outright lies. The mileposts along the road of our intellectual development signal those points at which some person developed a new perspective, a new meaning, or a new metaphor. We have in mind a new education that would set out to cultivate just such people—experts at "crap detecting."

There are many ways of describing this function of the schools, and many men who have. David Riesman, for example, calls this the "counter-cyclical" approach to education, meaning that schools should stress values that are not stressed by other major institutions in the culture. Norbert Wiener insisted that the schools now must function as "anti-entropic feedback systems," "entropy" being the word used to denote a general and unmistakable tendency of all systems—natural and man-made—in the universe to "run down," to reduce to chaos and uselessness. This is a process that cannot be reversed but that can be slowed down and partly controlled. One way to control it is through "maintenance." This is Eric Hoffer's term, and he believes that the quality of maintenance is one of the best indices of the quality of life in a culture. But Wiener uses a different metaphor to get at the same idea. He says that in order for there to be an anti-entropic force, we must have adequate feedback. In other words, we must have instruments to tell us when we are running down, when maintenance is required. For Wiener, such instruments would be people who have been educated to recognize change, to be sensitive to problems caused by change, and who have the motivation and courage to sound alarms when entropy accelerates to a dangerous degree. This is what we mean by "crap detecting." It is also what John Gardner means by the "ever-renewing society," and what Kenneth Boulding means by "social self-consciousness." We are talking about the schools' cultivating in the young that most "subversive" intellectual instrument—the anthropological perspective. This perspective allows one to be part of his own culture and, at the same time, to be out of it. One views the activities of his own group as would an anthropologist, observing its tribal rituals, its fears, its conceits, its ethnocentrism. In this way, one is able to recognize when reality begins to drift too far away from the grasp of the tribe.

We need hardly say that achieving such a perspective is extremely difficult, requiring, among other things, considerable courage. We are, after all, talking about achieving a high degree of freedom from the intellectual and social constraints of one's tribe. For example, it is generally assumed that people of other tribes have been victimized by indoctrination from which our tribe has remained free. Our own outlook seems "natural" to us, and we wonder that other men can perversely persist in believing nonsense. Yet, it is undoubtedly true that, for most people, the acceptance of a particular doctrine is largely attributable to the accident of birth. They might be said to be "ideologically interchangeable," which means that they would have accepted any set of doctrines that happened to be valued by the tribe to which they were born. Each of us, whether from the American tribe, Russian tribe, or Hopi tribe, is born into a symbolic environment as well as a physical one. We become accustomed very early to a "natural" way of talking, and being talked to, about "truth." Quite arbitrarily, one's perception of what is "true" or real is shaped by the symbols and symbol-manipulating institutions of his tribe. Most men, in time, learn to respond with fervor and obedience to a set of verbal abstractions which they feel provides them with an ideological identity. One word for this, of course, is "prejudice." None of us is free of it, but it is the sign of a competent "crap detector" that he is not completely captivated by the arbitrary abstractions of the community in which he happened to grow up.

In our own society, if one grows up in a language environment which includes and approves such a concept as "white supremacy," one can quite "morally" engage in the process of murdering civil-rights workers. Similarly, if one is living in a language environment where the term "black power" crystalizes an ideological identity, one can engage, again quite "morally," in acts of violence against any nonblack persons or their property. An insensitivity to the unconscious effects of our "natural" metaphors condemns us to highly constricted perceptions of how things are and, therefore, to highly limited alternative modes of behavior.

Those who *are* sensitive to the verbally built-in biases of their "natural" environment seem "subversive" to those who are not. There is probably nothing more dangerous to the prejudices of the latter than a man in the process of discovering that the language of his group is limited, misleading, or one-sided. Such a man is dangerous because he is not easily enlisted on the side of one ideology or another, because he sees beyond the words to the processes which give an ideology its reality. In his *May Man Prevail?*, Erich Fromm gives us an example of a man (himself) in the process of doing just that:

> The Russians believe that they represent socialism because they talk in terms of Marxist ideology, and they do not recognize how similar their system is to the most developed form of capitalism. We in the West believe that we represent the system of individualism, private initiative, and humanistic ethics, because we hold on to *our* ideology, and we do not see that our institutions have, in fact, in many ways become more and more similar to the hated system of communism.

Religious indoctrination is still another example of this point. As Alan Watts has noted: "Irrevocable commitment to any religion is not only intellectual suicide; it is positive unfaith because it closes the mind to any new vision of the world. Faith is, above all, openness—an act of trust in the unknown." And so "crap detecting" requires a perspective on what Watts calls "the standard-brand religions." That perspective can also be applied to knowledge. If you substitute the phrase "set of facts" for the word "religion" in the quotation above, the statement is equally important and accurate.

The need for this kind of perspective has always been urgent but never so urgent as now. We will not take you again through that painful catalogue of twentieth-century problems we cited in our Introduction. There are, however, three particular problems which force us to conclude that the schools must consciously remake themselves into training centers for "subversion." In one sense, they are all one problem but for purposes of focus may be distinguished from each other.

The first goes under the name of the "communications revolution," or media change. As Father John Culkin of Fordham University likes to say, a lot of things have happened in this century and most of them plug into walls. To get some perspective on the electronic plug, imagine that your home and all the other homes and buildings in your neighborhood have been cordoned off, and from them will be removed all the electric and electronic inventions that have appeared in the last 50 years. The media will be subtracted in reverse order, with the most recent going first. The first thing to leave your house, then, is the television set—and everybody will stand there as if they are attending the funeral of a friend, wondering, "What are we going to do tonight?" After rearranging the furniture so that it is no longer aimed at a blank space in the room, you suggest going to the movies. But there won't be any. Nor will there be LP records, tapes, radio, telephone, or telegraph. If you are thinking that the absence of the media would only affect your entertainment and information, remember that, at some point, your electric lights would be removed, and your refrigerator, and your heating system, and your air conditioner. In short, you would have to be a totally different person from what you are in order to survive for more than a day. The chances are slim that you could modify yourself and your patterns of living and believing fast enough to save yourself. As you were expiring, you would at least know something about how it was before the electric plug. Or perhaps you wouldn't. In any case, if you had energy and interest enough to hear him, any good ecologist could inform you of the logic of your problem: a change in an environment is rarely only additive or linear. You seldom, if ever, have an old environment *plus* a new element, such as a printing press or an electric plug. *What you have is a totally new environment requiring a whole new repertoire of survival strategies.* In no case is this more certain than when the new elements are technological. Then, in no case will the new environment be more radically different from the old than in political and social forms of life. When you plug something into a wall, someone is getting plugged into you. Which means you need new patterns of defense, perception, understanding, evaluation. You need a new kind of education.

It was George Counts who observed that technology repealed the Bill of Rights. In the eighteenth century, a pamphlet could influence an entire nation. Today all the ideas of the Noam Chomskys, Paul Goodmans, Edgar Friedenbergs, I. F. Stones, and even the William Buckleys, cannot command as much attention as a 30-minute broadcast by Walter Cronkite. Unless, of course, one of them were given a prime-time network program, in which case he would most likely come out more like Walter Cronkite than himself. Even Marshall McLuhan, who is leading the field in understanding media, is having his ideas transformed and truncated by the forms of the media to fit present media functions. (One requirement, for example, is that an idea or a man must be "sensational" in order to get a hearing; thus, McLuhan comes out not as a scholar studying media but as the "Apostle of the Electronic Age.")

We trust it is clear that we are not making the typical, whimpering academic attack on the media. We are not "against" the media. Any more, incidentally, than McLuhan is "for" the media. You cannot reverse technological change. Things that plug in are here to stay. But you can study media, with a view toward discovering what they are doing to you. As McLuhan has said, there is no inevitability so long as there is a willingness to contemplate what is happening.

Very few of us have contemplated more rigorously what is happening through media change than Jacques Ellul, who has sounded some chilling alarms. Without mass media, Ellul insists, there can be no effective propaganda. With them, there is almost nothing but. "Only through concentration of a large number of media in a few hands can one attain a true orchestration, a continuity, and an application of scientific methods of influencing individuals." That such concentration is occurring daily, Ellul says, is an established fact, and its results may well be an almost total homogenization of thought among those the media reach. We cannot afford to ignore Norbert Wiener's observation of a paradox that results from our increasing technological capability in electronic communication: as the number of messages increases, the amount of information carried decreases. We have more media to communicate fewer significant ideas.

Still another way of saying this is that, while there has been a tremendous increase in media, there has been, at the same time, a decrease in available and viable "democratic" channels of communication. For example, as a means of affecting public policy, the town meeting is dead. Significant community action (without violence) is increasingly rare. A small printing press in one's home, as an instrument of social change, is absurd. Traditional forms of dissent and protest seem impractical, e.g., letters to the editor, street-corner speeches, etc. No one can reach many people unless he has access to the mass media. As this is written, for example, there is no operational two-way communication possible with respect to United States policies and procedures in Vietnam. The communication is virtually all one way: from the top down, via the mass media, especially TV. The pressure on everyone is to subscribe without question to policies formulated in the Pentagon. The President appears on TV and clearly makes the point that anyone who does not accept "our policy" can be viewed only as lending aid and comfort to the enemy. The position has been elaborately developed in all media that "peaceniks" are failing in the obligation to "support our boys overseas." The effect of this process on all of us is to leave no alternative but to accept policy, act on orders from above, and implement the policy without question or dialogue. This is what Edgar Friedenberg calls "creeping Eichmannism," a sort of spiritless, mechanical, abstract functioning which does not allow much room for individual thought and action.

As Paul Goodman has pointed out, there are many forms of censorship, and one of them is to deny access to "loudspeakers" to those with dissident ideas, or even *any* ideas. This is easy to do (and not necessarily conspiratorial) when the loudspeakers are owned and operated by mammoth corporations with enormous investments in their proprietorship. What we get is an entirely new politics, including the possibility that a major requirement for the holding of political office be prior success as a show-business personality. Goodman writes in *Like a Conquered Province:*

> The traditional American sentiment is that a decent society cannot be built by dominant official policy anyway, but only by grassroots resistance, community cooperation, individual enterprise, and citizenly vigilance to protect liberty. . . . *The question is whether or not our beautiful libertarian, pluralist, and populist experiment is viable in modern conditions.* If it's not, I don't know any other acceptable politics, and I am a man without a country.

Is it possible that there are millions becoming men without a country? Men who are increasingly removed from the sources of power? Men who have fewer and fewer ideas available to them, and fewer and fewer ways of expressing themselves meaningfully and effectively? Might the frustration thus engendered be one of the causes of the increasing use of violence as a form of statement?

We come then to a second problem which makes necessary a "subversive" role for the schools. This one may appropriately be called the "Change Revolution." In order to illustrate what this means, we will use the media again and the metaphor of a clock face. Imagine a clock face with 60 minutes on it. Let the clock stand for the time men have had access to writing systems. Our clock would thus represent something like 3,000 years, and each minute on our clock 50 years. On this scale, there were no significant media changes until about nine minutes ago. At that time, the printing press came into use in Western culture. About three minutes ago, the telegraph, photograph, and locomotive arrived. Two minutes ago: the telephone, rotary press, motion pictures, automobile, airplane, and radio. One minute ago, the talking picture. Television has appeared in the last ten seconds, the computer in the last five, and communications satellites in the last second. The laser beam—perhaps the most potent medium of communication of all—appeared only a fraction of a second ago.

It would be possible to place almost any area of life on our clock face and get roughly the same measurements. For example, in medicine, you would have almost no significant changes until about one minute ago. In fact, until one minute ago, as Jerome Frank has said, almost the whole history of medicine is the history of the placebo effect. About a minute ago, antibiotics arrived. About ten seconds ago, open-heart surgery. In fact, within the past ten seconds there probably have been more changes in medicine than is represented by all the rest of the time on our clock. This is what some people call the "knowledge explosion." It is happening in every field of knowledge susceptible to scientific inquiry.

The standard reply to any comment about change (for example, from many educators) is that change isn't new and that it is easy to exaggerate its meaning. To such replies, Norbert Wiener had a useful answer: the difference between a fatal and a therapeutic dose of strychnine is "only a matter of degree." In other words, change isn't new; what is new is the *degree of change*. As our clock-face metaphor was intended to suggest, about three minutes ago there developed a qualitative difference in the character of change. Change changed.

This is really quite a new problem. For example, up until the last generation it was possible to be born, grow up, and spend a life in the United States without moving more than 50 miles from home, without ever confronting serious questions about one's basic values, beliefs, and patterns of behavior. Indeed, without ever confronting serious challenges to anything one knew. Stability and consequent predictability—within "natural cycles"—was the characteristic mode. But now, in just the last minute, we've reached the stage where change occurs so rapidly that each of us in the course of our lives has continuously to work out a set of values, beliefs, and patterns of behavior that are viable, or *seem* viable, to each of us personally. And just when we have identified a workable system, it turns out to be irrelevant because so much has changed while we were doing it.

Of course, this frustrating state of affairs applies to our education as well. If you are over twenty-five years of age, the mathematics you were taught in school is "old"; the grammar you were taught is obsolete and in disrepute; the biology, completely out of date, and the history, open to serious question. The best that can be said of you, assuming that you *remember* most of what you were told and read, is that you are a walking encyclopedia of outdated information. As Alfred North Whitehead pointed out in *The Adventure of Ideas:*

> Our sociological theories, our political philosophy, our practical maxims of business, our political economy, and our doctrines of education are derived from an unbroken tradition of great thinkers and of practical examples from the age of Plato . . . to the end of the last century. The whole of this tradition is warped by the vicious assumption

that each generation will substantially live amid the conditions governing the lives of its fathers and will transmit those conditions to mould
with equal force the lives of its children. *We are living in the first period
of human history for which this assumption is false.*

All of which brings us to the third problem: the "burgeoning bureaucracy." We are brought there because bureaucracies, in spite of
their seeming indispensability, are by their nature highly resistant to
change. The motto of most bureaucracies is, "Carry On, Regardless."
There is an essential mindlessness about them which causes them, in
most circumstances, to accelerate entropy rather than to impede it.
Bureaucracies rarely ask themselves Why?, but only How? John Gardner, who as President of the Carnegie Corporation and (as of this
writing) Secretary of Health, Education, and Welfare has learned
about bureaucracies at first hand, has explained them very well:

> To accomplish renewal, we need to understand what prevents it.
> When we talk about revitalizing a society, we tend to put exclusive
> emphasis on finding new ideas. But there is usually no shortage of new
> ideas; the problem is to get a hearing for them. And that means breaking
> through the crusty rigidity and stubborn complacency of the *status quo.*
> The aging society develops elaborate defenses against new ideas—
> "mind-forged manacles," in William Blake's vivid phrase. . . . As a
> society becomes more concerned with precedent and custom, it comes
> to care more about how things are done and less about whether they
> are done. The man who wins acclaim is not the one who "gets things
> done" but the one who has an ingrained knowledge of the rules and
> accepted practices. Whether he accomplishes anything is less important
> than whether he conducts himself in an "appropriate" manner.
>   The body of custom, convention, and "reputable" standards exer-
> cises such an oppressive effect on creative minds that new developments
> in a field often originate outside the area of respectable practice.

In other words, bureaucracies are the repositories of conventional
assumptions and standard practices—two of the greatest accelerators
of entropy.

We could put before you a volume of other quotations—from Ma-
chiavelli to Paul Goodman—describing how bureaucratic structures
retard the development and application of new survival strategies. But
in doing so, we would risk creating the impression that we stand with
Goodman in yearning for some anarchistic Utopia in which the Army,
the Police, General Motors, the U. S. Office of Education, the Post
Office, et al. do not exist. We are not "against" bureaucracies, any
more than we are "for" them. They are like electric plugs. They will

probably not go away, but they do need to be controlled if the prerogatives of a democratic society are to remain visible and usable. This is
why we ask that the schools be "subversive," that they serve as a kind
of antibureaucracy bureaucracy, providing the young with a "What is
it good for?" perspective on its own society. Certainly, it is unrealistic
to expect those who control the media to perform that function. Nor
the generals and the politicians. Nor is it reasonable to expect the
"intellectuals" to do it for they do not have access to the majority of
youth. But schoolteachers do, and so the primary responsibility rests
with them.

The trouble is that most teachers have the idea that they are in some
other sort of business. Some believe, for example, that they are in the
"information dissemination" business. This was a reasonable business
up to about a minute or two ago on our clock. (But then, so was the
horseshoe business and the candle-snuffer business.) The signs that
their business is failing are abundant, but they keep at it all the more
diligently. Santayana told us that a fanatic is someone who redoubles
his efforts when he has forgotten his aim. In this case, even if the aim
has not been forgotten, it is simply irrelevant. But the effort has been
redoubled anyway.

There are some teachers who think they are in the "transmission
of our cultural heritage" business, which is not an unreasonable business if you are concerned with the whole clock and not just its first
57 minutes. The trouble is that most teachers find the last three minutes too distressing to deal with, which is exactly why they are in the
wrong business. Their students find the last three minutes distressing
—and confusing—too, especially the last 30 seconds, and they need
help. While they have to live with TV, film, the LP record, communication satellites, and the laser beam, their teachers are still talking as
if the only medium on the scene is Gutenberg's printing press. While
they have to understand psychology and psychedelics, anthopology
and anthropomorphism, birth control and biochemistry, their teachers
are teaching "subjects" that mostly don't exist anymore. While they
need to find new roles for themselves as social, political, and religious
organisms, their teachers (as Edgar Friedenberg has documented so
painfully) are acting almost entirely as shills for corporate interests,
shaping them up to be functionaries in one bureaucracy or another.

Unless our schools can switch to the right business, their clientele
will either go elsewhere (as many are doing) or go into a severe case
of "future shock," to use a relatively new phrase. Future shock occurs
when you are confronted by the fact that the world you were educated

to believe in doesn't exist. Your images of reality are apparitions that disappear on contact. There are several ways of responding to such a condition, one of which is to withdraw and allow oneself to be overcome by a sense of impotence. More commonly, one continues to act *as if* his apparitions were substantial, relentlessly pursuing a course of action that he knows will fail him. You may have noticed that there are scores of political, social, and religious leaders who are clearly suffering from advanced cases of future shock. They repeat over and over again the words that are supposed to represent the world about them. But nothing seems to work out. And then they repeat the words again and again. Alfred Korzybski used a somewhat different metaphor to describe what we have been calling "future shock." He likened one's language to a map. The map is intended to describe the territory that we call "reality," i.e., the world outside of our skins. When there is a close correspondence between map and territory, there tends to be a high degree of effective functioning, especially where it relates to survival. When there is little correspondence between map and territory, there is a strong tendency for entropy to make substantial gains. In this context, the terrifying question What did you learn in school today? assumes immense importance for all of us. We just may not surve another generation of inadvertent entropy helpers. . . . What is the necessary business of the schools? To create eager consumers? To transmit the dead ideas, values, metaphors, and information of three minutes ago? To create smoothly functioning bureaucrats? *These* aims are truly subversive since they undermine our chances of surviving as a viable, democratic society. And they do their work in the name of convention and standard practice. We would like to see the schools go into the anti-entropy business. Now, that is subversive, too. But the purpose is to subvert attitudes, beliefs, and assumptions that foster chaos and uselessness.

THEM AND US:
ARE PEACE PROTESTS
SELF-THERAPY?

Nat Hentoff

On a Sunday morning toward the end of January, twenty-three people rose during a high mass at St. Patrick's Cathedral in New York. They unfurled posters showing a maimed Vietnamese child. They and their posters were bundled up so quickly by forewarned police that only a few of the worshipers in the Cathedral knew what was going on. Many later found out, of course, through the extensive newspaper and television coverage.

Had the demonstrators not been rushed out by the police, their intent had been to leave anyway in protest against Cardinal Spellman's Christmas declaration that "the war in Vietnam is a war for civilization."

I knew about the planned interruption of the mass some days before. In characteristically liberal fashion, I sent a few dollars for the bail fund. But the event continued to trouble me as I began to wonder whether this kind of demonstration—and many other kinds involving various sectors of the peace movement—did not actually increase divisions between "them" and "us." Whom were the demonstrators talking to? If to the Catholics in the Cathedral, what less effective way is there to persuade them of their complicity in what is happening in Vietnam than by interrupting an occasion that is sacred to them? The context is hardly one for rational dialogue. If the intent was to speak to all those who would see or read about the demonstration, what actually was the effect on *them*? In all likelihood, their reaction was one of resentment and anger. Instead of the issue being focused on Vietnam, attention had been directed to the demonstrators and their manner of demonstration.

With all respect for, and some envy of the particular qualities of courage which enabled the twenty-three to do what they did, I would suggest that their act's essential effect was to make *them* feel relevant, to make *them* feel that some of their guilt as Americans had been atoned for by this witness. I am all for self-therapy, but if that's what it is, let us call it that.

The conviction used to be—and still is in some areas of the peace and post-civil-rights movements—that demonstrations have to exacerbate because only in that way can full attention be drawn to injustice. Dead rats were thrown in front of city halls. Rush hour traffic was stalled. Young people chained themselves to pillars in front of court buildings. And nothing very much happened as a result. Nothing happened because those demonstrations made it easier for the bystander—the *moyen* citizen—to separate himself from the activists and their concerns. The idea was to speak truth to power. But the mayors and the governors and the legislators, seeing no real counterpower behind the few demonstrators, ignored them. And the *moyen* citizen, who also feels himself impotent to affect change even if he wanted to, regarded the activists as so different in kind from him that the thought of ever possibly allying himself with them was inconceivable. (Even if such a thought could have stirred in any case.)

These days, there is a thrust among black people to mount more of their demonstrations in their own neighborhoods as a means not only of underlining injustices—bad ghetto schools, for instance, which are not accountable to the parents—but also of using the demonstrations to mobilize other black people. That direction makes sense. If there is ever to be sufficient counter-power from the ghettos, there has to be recruitment and organization, and demonstrations can be one way to mobilize. If, however, there are not further plans to keep up the pressure and to construct feasible alternatives—ways of real community participation in the schools, for example—the initial impetus to get together is quickly lost.

But what of those of us who do want to speak to, to persuade, the citizenry at large to end the war in Vietnam? What of those who want to amass sufficient political pressure so that this country's resources can be directed at the cities, at creating new jobs, at establishing a guaranteed annual income? Simply demonstrating in the old ways—peacefully or abrasively—won't do it. The twenty-three at St. Patrick's Cathedral did not, I expect, make many converts. Nor did the members of the San Francisco Mime Troupe a few years ago when they suddenly put on a free anti-war performance in a San Francisco public park. Lenny Bruce, observing the occasion, shook his head. "The people in the park," he said, "didn't *ask* for this. They didn't come here for this. And so they're turned off, not on."

I would suggest that one reason the old ways of demonstrating continue to be held onto is that most of "us" have never tried role reversal, have never tried to imagine being one of "them," have no idea of what worries them, motivates them. We see them as a homo-geneous, passive mass that can be moved, if at all, the way one would move clay. Or rather, the way one would mold clay. We want to shape them, direct them. The I-thou relationship of Buber doesn't enter at all. And so we few continue to stand on one side of the divide, and all of "them" are on the other. We are encapsulated, and they are encapsulated.

Consider, for instance, how naturally and inevitably we of more or less similar goals congregate together. I don't know, I literally don't know, a single political conservative, let alone a member of the John Birch Society. And, in fact, if I were not a journalist, I would know very few different kinds of people. I would be limited, as most people are, to the peripheral relationships of an office or institution and to a few after-hours friends of roughly consonant tastes and values. Of course, we huddle together for comfort. And there are some who make their islands as small as possible, sometimes consisting only of a wife and children.

How to break through? First, there has to be the desire to, and then the opportunity. And before the desire, there has to be the recognition that there are individuals making up that passive mass of "them." To begin that recognition, I would suggest a remarkable book, Studs Terkel's *Division Street: America* (Pantheon). The book consists of conversations by Terkel with some seventy people in and around Chicago. A more diversified range of people than most of us ever get a chance to know. They are of a wide variety of backgrounds, voca-tions, temperaments. Most are "ordinary," as we might regard them, but each is, of course, unique. (How seldom we who want to change society and mankind ever really consider the uniqueness of everyone in the society to be changed. We too have our categorical assumptions about the poor, the cops, the right-wingers, the administrators of the power structure, the politicians, the Midwesterners, the general. And they of us. And so there *cannot* be any communication. Categories do not communicate.)

Wisely, Terkel eliminated from the book clergymen, college profes-sors, journalists, and writers of any kind. "I felt," he explained, "that their articulateness and literacy offered them other forums. They had created their own books; my transcribing their attitudes would be nothing more than self-indulgence. It was the man of inchoate thought I was seeking rather than the consciously articulate."

I will not try to summarize seventy different lives and life styles, but *Division Street: America* does make clear how deep the sense of loss of community is among many otherwise widely different members of "them." It makes clear how powerless *they* feel. Or most of them. It reveals in all kinds of people a yearning to communicate, to relate, to be an organic part of a neighborhood, a city. But they don't know how.

In the *New York Times,* Tom Wicker distilled how most of "us" feel. Intellectuals, for example, protesting against the war in Vietnam. We suffer, he says, "the malaise beyond dissent." And that is "the fear that dissent does not matter any more; that only action counts; but that no one really knows what action to take. More and more, twentieth-century man crouches like an old woman on her stoop, pointing her rusty shotgun at the oncoming expressway, knowing all the time that in the end the bulldozer will go through."

And "they" feel that way too. A thirty-five-old mother of six, a Catholic, says in *Division Street: America:* "This morning when I went to work there was a red brick building. When I came home, the building wasn't there. It was flattened. I can't decide whether it's all for the good. All I know is there's a feeling of loss, a lot of things leaving us."

A seventy-five-year old widow: "I can't understand, and never will, what gives the few men the right to hold all our lives in the palm of their hand? What right have they got, what God-given right have they got? Just to press the button and say you've had it. And you think of your own son, who's just starting to live, and all these kids. Is it really freedom for them they're seeking?"

As if in answer, a middle-aged woman who owns a tavern: "Most that disturbs me today is when I talk to some of my neighbors, none of them, they don't like this Vietnam going on, but here's where they say, 'What's the use? Who are we? We can't say nothing. We have no word. We got the President. We elected him. We got congressmen in there. They're responsible. Let them worry. Why should I worry about it?' It's already pounded into them, you're just a little guy, you vote and you're through, it won't do no good anyhow."

"There is a coldness to our time," says an architect. A woman in her sixties, living in a public housing project: "I don't like all this steel and glass that's going up straight. It don't look very warm or homey. I know they are inside, but they just don't look that way from the outside. It makes the city look cold, I think. People are moving to get away from people. I don't like the way we're going."

Some, of course, have accepted the coldness. A swinger and part-owner of a bar: "I don't bother anybody and I don't like anybody to bother me. If I were walkin' down the street and they were robbin' a

bank, the guy would walk out and say, 'Hi Gene, how are you?' And
if I knew him or didn't know him, I'd say, 'Hi, how are you?' And as
long as he didn't step on my foot while I was walkin' by the bank, let
him do what he wants to do. It's none of my goddamn business
. . . I'm pleasant, get along, courteous."

And that reminded me of a letter I received from a girl at Pembroke
College, a New Left activist: "There are in fact few real ogres on the
scene. One sees the world being killed off by nice, generous, courteous,
kind people."

And yet there are many more throughout the book who, though
resigned to the coldness, have not accepted it. Impotent, they dream
of community. A thirty-five-year-old housewife, with no political
ideology, in an "ordinary" neighborhood: "The greatest day of my life
was the day I went to see a Pete Seeger concert. I think he's good. But
to me the greatest thrill that I got was the fact that there were that
many people together that felt a certain way. And I've never been in
a crowd where everybody felt that way. And yet at the same time, how
come. . . . You could read in the paper that so many people felt like
you do, yet you could never yourself meet anybody that feels the same
way."

A John Bircher: "I've lived in a wilderness all my life." A nineteen-
year-old, a loner, who works in a supermarket while going to college:
"I love life. I only wish some of it would come my way." A girl, who
has been drinking since she was twelve and is a frequent user of
marijuana, ends a poem: "If I am for myself alone/ What am I?" A
fifty-three-year-old cop: "I'd like to take up something else if I can.
Be able to enter—this sounds sort of corny—more of a community life,
in a smaller community where you participated more, you know. *In
doing something.*"

My point in all this is that because we do not know "them," we do
not recognize how great a sense of waste of life, of spirit, does exist
beyond our own islands. There are many who could be activated to
work for change in their neighborhoods, in their cities, if they felt a
possibility of enough others coming together with them. And there are
more than the polls reveal who are deeply disquieted by the war but
feel isolated as well as impotent. I do not want to sound ingenuous.
Many of "them" have dropped out and make it as best they can in
isolation. But others who are isolated do not want to be.

How can they begin to feel that their lives can have greater dimension, that they can have a say in what happens to them and their
neighborhood and their city? Not by us parading among them. One

way, as yet a very small beginning of a way, is being discovered by the young community organizers who live among the people for whom they're trying to be catalysts. One is in this book, a member of JOIN (Jobs or Income Now), a subsidiary of Students for a Democratic Society, which works among poor Appalachians transplanted to Chicago. The young woman in JOIN says: "We've recently discovered we're not getting anywhere with the door-to-door technique. . . . Somehow this is not working because we're not friends with these people, we're not part of their lives; as one guy put it, maybe getting drunk with these guys on Saturday night (would help).

"Now," she continues, talking of her child, "I just take Sarah on my arm and just go up and have coffee with the lady down the block and talk about her son, who she's afraid is going to be a delinquent. And I just have coffee with another lady and we talk about what it's like back home. Not just gripes they have, something wholly unrelated, personal. At meetings, we have country music."

And in Newark, a member of the SDS-initiated Newark Community Union became a teacher there, in the neighborhood in which he lives. His methods—trying to overturn the school dictum of substituting discipline for interest—drew him into conflict with the bureaucracy, and he has been fired. Now he and some parents are working on their own school, which will be certified by the state as a private school. He has found an organic way of relating to that community.

And in other cities throughout the country, there are young teachers—hardly enough of them yet—who are trying to give children and their parents a sense of themselves and a sense of the possibility of community. And not only in poor neighborhoods.

Meanwhile there are peace activists who are beginning to realize that if there is to be an end to this country's militarism, large *ad hoc* parades and demonstrations are not going to be nearly effective enough. Instead, roots have to be grown in as wide a variety of neighborhoods as possible. My own feeling is that there's a wide scope of potentiality for young peace activists, not yet anchored to a job or a particular neighborhood of those like themselves. Their role in "the movement" could be to become part of different kinds of neighborhoods, get to know as many of their neighbors as they can, and like the young woman from JOIN, find out who each of them is—as individuals, not as manipulatable subjects for proselytization.

I don't expect those of "us" in our thirties and forties and beyond to spread out and live among "them," but the young can, and I hope a sizable number will. Meanwhile there are other ways of bridging the divide between "them" and "us." In New York City last year, the Committee of the Professions started an experimental community action project based on meetings in apartments throughout the city for which the Committee provided speakers. Several thouand people, most of whom had never taken part in a demonstration, or even thought of the possibility, became involved in over a hundred meetings. From those meetings, block clubs and community organizations were formed which began work on other issues besides peace. Now the Committee of the Professions is trying to establish "a network of neighborhood political groups that would span the city and which could provide the basis for concerted political and educational activity." And most of these neighborhoods, it should be emphasized, are largely populated by "them."

There must be other ways of bridging the division, and I'd welcome any ideas readers of this article have. In the meantime, of course, there will be need for demonstrations. If, for instance, the draft-resistance movement among college students grows to the point at which sizable numbers of them are arrested, they will need support; and demonstrations—if large enough—can be part of that support. And if only to keep a sense of community alive among those already converted to an end to militarism, massive demonstrations. . . . are important.

But if we are ever to break through our own encapsulation and if "they" are to release themselves from *their* isolation, the I-thou relationship will have to become the normative principle of more and more movements for change. At this very late time in this administered society, afflicted by "the malaise beyond dissent," the only way out—simplistic and corny as it may sound—is the individual. An architect in *Division Street: America* notes that "the doctrine of the announced idea" won't make it. No matter how many placards proclaim MAKE LOVE, NOT WAR. The only thing that will make it is: "man must listen to man himself talking."

The late A. J. Muste was, as usual, prescient when he wrote in 1952: "Precisely on that day when the individual appears to be utterly hopeless, to 'have no choice,' when the aim of the 'system' is to convince him that he is helpless as an individual and that the only way to meet regimentation is by regimentation, there is absolutely no hope save in going back to the beginning. The human being . . . must exercise the choice which is no longer accorded him by society. (It is a choice) which, 'naked, weaponless, armourless, without shield or spear, but only with naked hands and open eyes,' he must create again.

He must understand that this naked human being is the one *real* thing in the face of the machines and the mechanized institutions of our age."

He must also understand that there are other naked human beings who would like a chance to believe they can exercise that choice. And that they are to be found in places not yet familiar to the peace agitators and those others who want to stop and then redirect the machinery. And that it makes much more sense to talk to them in their bars or schools than to rise up in isolated protest in the middle of St. Patrick's Cathedral.

WHY WOMEN'S LIBERATION?

Marlene Dixon

The 1960s has been a decade of liberation; women have been swept up by that ferment along with blacks, Latins, American Indians and poor whites—the whole soft underbelly of this society. As each oppressed group in turn discovered the nature of its oppression in American society, so women have discovered that they too thirst for free and fully human lives. The result has been the growth of a new women's movement, whose base encompasses poor black and poor white women on relief, working women exploited in the labor force, middle class women incarcerated in the split level dream house, college girls awakening to the fact that sexiness is not the crowning achievement in life, and movement women who have discovered that in a freedom movement they themselves are not free. In less than four years women have created a variety of organizations, from the nationally-based middle class National Organization of Women (NOW) to local radical and radical feminist groups in every major city in North America. The new movement includes caucuses within nearly every New Left group and within most professional associations in the social sciences. Ranging in politics from reform to revolution, it has produced critiques of almost every segment of American society and constructed an ideology that rejects every hallowed cultural assumption about the nature and role of women.

As is typical of a young movement, much of its growth has been

Marlene Dixon, "Why Women's Liberation?" *Ramparts Magazine,* Dec. 1969. Reprinted by permission of the Editors.

underground. The papers and manifestos written and circulated would
surely comprise two very large volumes if published, but this literature
is almost unknown outside of women's liberation. Nevertheless, where
even a year ago organizing was slow and painful, with small cells of
six or ten women, high turnover, and an uphill struggle against fear
and resistance, in 1969 all that has changed. Groups are growing up
everywhere with women eager to hear a hard line, to articulate and
express their own rage and bitterness. Moving about the country, I
have found an electric atmosphere of excitement and responsiveness.
Everywhere there are doubts, stirrings, a desire to listen, to find out
what it's all about. The extent to which groups have become politically
radical is astounding. A year ago the movement stressed male chauvinism and psychological oppression; now the emphasis is on understanding the economic and social roots of women's oppression, and
the analyses range from social democracy to Marxism. But the most
striking change of all in the last year has been the loss of fear. Women
are no longer afraid that their rebellion will threaten their very identity
as women. They are not frightened by their own militancy, but liberated by it. Women's Liberation is an idea whose time has come.

The old women's movement burned itself out in the frantic decade
of the 1920s. After a hundred years of struggle, women won a battle,
only to lose the campaign: the vote was obtained, but the new millennium did not arrive. Women got the vote and achieved a measure of
legal emancipation, but the real social and cultural barriers to full
equality for women remained untouched.

For over 30 years the movement remained buried in its own ashes.
Women were born and grew to maturity virtually ignorant of their
own history of rebellion, aware only of a caricature of blue stockings
and suffragettes. Even as increasing numbers of women were being
driven into the labor force by the brutal conditions of the 1930s and
by the massive drain of men into the military in the 1940s, the old
ideal remained: a woman's place was in the home and behind her
man. As the war ended and men returned to resume their jobs in
factories and offices, women were forced back to the kitchen and
nursery with a vengeance. This story has been repeated after each
war and the reason is clear: women form a flexible, cheap labor pool
which is essential to a capitalist system. When labor is scarce, they
are forced onto the labor market. When labor is plentiful, they are
forced out. Women and blacks have provided a reserve army of
unemployed workers, benefiting capitalists and the stable male white
working class alike. Yet the system imposes untold suffering on the

victims, blacks and women, through low wages and chronic unemployment.

With the end of the war the average age at marriage declined, the average size of families went up, and the suburban migration began in earnest. The political conservatism of the '50s was echoed in a social conservatism which stressed a Victorian ideal of the woman's life: a full womb and selfless devotion to husband and children.

As the bleak decade played itself out, however, three important social developments emerged which were to make a rebirth of the women's struggle inevitable. First, women came to make up more than a third of the labor force, the number of working women being twice the prewar figure. Yet the marked increase in female employment did nothing to better the position of women, who were more occupationally disadvantaged in the 1960s than they had been 25 years earlier. Rather than moving equally into all sectors of the occupational structure, they were being forced into the low paying service, clerical and semi-skilled categories. In 1940, women had held 45 per cent of all professional and technical positions; in 1967, they held only 37 per cent. The proportion of women in service jobs meanwhile rose from 50 to 55 per cent.

Second, the intoxicating wine of marriage and suburban life was turning sour; a generation of women woke up to find their children grown and life (roughly 30 more productive years) of housework and bridge parties stretching out before them like a wasteland. For many younger women, the empty drudgery they saw in the suburban life was a sobering contradiction to adolescent dreams of romantic love and the fulfilling role of woman as wife and mother.

Third, a growing civil rights movement was sweeping thousands of young men and women into a moral crusade—a crusade which harsh political experience was to transmute into the New Left. The American Dream was riven and tattered in Mississippi and finally napalmed in Viet-Nam. Young Americans were drawn not to Levittown, but to Berkeley, the Haight-Ashbury and the East Village. Traditional political ideologies and cultural myths, sexual mores and sex roles with them, began to disintegrate in an explosion of rebellion and protest.

The three major groups which make up the new women's movement—working women, middle class married women and students—bring very different kinds of interests and objectives to women's liberation. Working women are most concerned with the economic issues of guaranteed employment, fair wages, job discrimination and child care. Their most immediate oppression is rooted in industrial capitalism and felt directly through the vicissitudes of an exploitative labor market.

Middle class women, oppressed by the psychological mutilation and injustice of institutionalized segregation, discrimination and imposed inferiority, are most sensitive to the dehumanizing consequences of severely limited lives. Usually well educated and capable, these women are rebelling against being forced to trivialize their lives, to live vicariously through husbands and children.

Students, as unmarried middle class girls, have been most sensitized to the sexual exploitation of women. They have experienced the frustration of one-way relationships in which the girl is forced into a "wife" and companion role with none of the supposed benefits of marriage. Young women have increasingly rebelled not only against passivity and dependency in their relationships but also against the notion that they must function as sexual objects, being defined in purely sexual rather than human terms, and being forced to package and sell themselves as commodities on the sex market.

Each group represents an independent aspect of the total institutionalized oppression of women. Their differences are those of emphasis and immediate interest rather than of fundamental goals. All women suffer from economic exploitation, from psychological deprivation, and from exploitive sexuality. Within women's liberation there is a growing understanding that the common oppression of women provides the basis for uniting across class and race lines to form a powerful and radical movement.

Racism and Male Supremacy

Clearly, for the liberation of women to become a reality it is necessary to destroy the ideology of male supremacy which asserts the biological and social inferiority of women in order to justify massive institutionalized oppression. Yet we all know that many women are as loud in their disavowal of this oppression as are the men who chant the litany of "a woman's place is in the home and behind her man." In fact, women are as trapped in their false consciousness as were the mass of blacks 20 years ago, and for much the same reason.

As blacks were defined and limited socially by their color, so women are defined and limited by their sex. While blacks, it was argued, were preordained by God or nature, or both, to be hewers of wood and drawers of water, so women are destined to bear and rear children, and to sustain their husbands with obedience and compassion. The Sky-God tramples through the heavens and the Earth-

/Mother-Goddess is always flat on her back with her legs spread, putting out for one and all.

Indeed, the phenomenon of male chauvinism can only be understood when it is perceived as a form of racism, based on stereotypes drawn from a deep belief in the biological inferiority of women. The so-called "black analogy" is no analogy at all; it is the same social process that is at work, a process which both justifies and helps perpetuate the exploitation of one group of human beings by another.

The very stereotypes that express the society's belief in the biological inferiority of women recall the images used to justify the oppression of blacks. The nature of women, like that of slaves, is depicted as dependent, incapable of reasoned thought, childlike in its simplicity and warmth, martyred in the role of mother, and mystical in the role of sexual partner. In its benevolent form, the inferior position of women results in paternalism; in its malevolent form, a domestic tyranny which can be unbelievably brutal.

It has taken over 50 years to discredit the scientific and social "proof" which once gave legitimacy to the myths of black racial inferiority. Today most people can see that the theory of the genetic inferiority of blacks is absurd. Yet few are shocked by the fact that scientists are still busy "proving" the biological inferiority of women.

In recent years, in which blacks have led the struggle for liberation, the emphasis on racism has focused only upon racism against blacks. The fact that "racism" has been practiced against many groups other than blacks has been pushed into the background. Indeed, a less forceful but more accurate term for the phenomenon would be "social Darwinism." It was the opinion of the social Darwinists that in the natural course of things the "fit" succeed (i.e. oppress) and the "unfit" (i.e. the biologically inferior) sink to the bottom. According to this view, the very fact of a group's oppression proves its inferiority and the inevitable correctness of its low position. In this way each successive immigrant group coming to America was decked out in the garments of "racial" or biological inferiority until the group was sufficiently assimilated, whereupon Anglo-Saxon venom would turn on a new group filling up the space at the bottom. Now two groups remain, neither of which has been assimilated according to the classic American pattern: the "visibles"—blacks and women. It is equally true for both: "it won't wear off."

Yet the greatest obstacle facing those who would organize women remains women's belief in their own inferiority. Just as all subject populations are controlled by their acceptance of the rightness of their

own status, so women remain subject because they believe in the
rightness of their own oppression. This dilemma is not a fortuitous
one, for the entire society is geared to socialize women to believe in
and adopt as immutable necessity their traditional and inferior role.
From earliest traning to the grave, women are constrained and propa-
gandized. Spend an evening at the movies or watching television, and
you will see a grotesque figure called woman presented in a hundred
variations upon the themes of "children, church, kitchen" or "the
chick sex-pot."

For those who believe in the "rights of mankind," the "dignity of
man," consider that to make a woman a person, a human being in her
own right, you would have to change her sex: imagine Stokely Carmichael "prone and silent"; imagine Mark Rudd as a Laugh-In girl;
picture Rennie Davis as Miss America. Such contradictions as these
show how pervasive and deep-rooted is the cultural contempt for
women, how difficult it is to imagine a woman as a serious human
being, or conversely, how empty and degrading is the image of woman
that floods the culture.

Countless studies have shown that black acceptance of white
stereotypes lead to mutilated identity, to alienation, to rage and self-
hatred. Human beings cannot bear in their own hearts the contradictions of those who hold them in contempt. The ideology of male
supremacy and its effect upon women merits as serious study as has
been given to the effects of prejudice upon Jews, blacks, and immigrant
groups.

It is customary to shame those who would draw the parallel between women and blacks by a great show of concern and chest beating
over the suffering of black people. Yet this response itself reveals a
refined combination of white middle class guilt and male chauvinism,
for it overlooks several essential facts. For example, the most oppressed group within the feminine population is made up of black
women, many of whom take a dim view of the black male intellectual's
adoption of white male attitudes of sexual superiority (an irony too
cruel to require comment). Neither are those who make this pious
objection to the racial parallel addressing themselves very adequately
to the millions of white working class women living at the poverty
level, who are not likely to be moved by this middle class guilt-ridden
one-upmanship while having to deal with the boss, the factory, or the
welfare worker day after day. They are already dangerously resentful
of the gains made by blacks, and much of their "racist backlash" stems
from the fact that they have been forgotten in the push for social

change. Emphasis on the real mechanisms of oppression—on the commonality of the process—is essential lest groups such as these, which should work in alliance, become divided against one another.

White middle class males already struggling with the acknowledgment of their own racism do not relish an added burden of recognition: that to white guilt must soon be added "male". It is therefore understandable that they should refuse to see the harshness of the lives of most women—to honestly face the facts of massive institutionalized discrimination against women. Witness the performance to date: "Take her down off the platform and give her a good fuck," "Petty Bourgeois Revisionist Running Dogs," or in the classic words of a Berkeley male "leader," "Let them eat cock."

Among whites, women remain the most oppressed—and the most unorganized—group. Although they constitute a potential mass base for the radical movement, in terms of movement priorities they are ignored; indeed they might as well be invisible. Far from being an accident, this omission is a direct outgrowth of the solid male supremist beliefs of white radical and left-liberal men. Even now, faced with both fact and agitation, leftist men find the idea of placing any serious priority upon women so outrageous, such a degrading notion, that they respond with a virulence far out of proportion to the modest request of movement women. This only shows that women must stop wasting their time worrying about the chauvinism of men in the movement and focus instead on their real priority: organizing women.

Marriage: Genesis of Women's Rebellion

The institution of marriage is the chief vehicle for the perpetuation of the oppression of women; it is through the role of wife that the subjugation of women is maintained. In a very real way the role of wife has been the genesis of women's rebellion throughout history.

Looking at marriage from a detached point of view one may well ask why anyone gets married, much less women. One answer lies in the economics of women's position, for women are so occupationally limited that drudgery in the home is considered to be infinitely superior to drudgery in the factory. Secondly, women themselves have no independent social status. Indeed, there is no clearer index of the social worth of a woman in this society than the fact that she has none in her own right. A woman is first defined by the man to whom she is attached, but more particularly by the man she marries, and secondly by the children she bears and rears—hence the anxiety over sexual attractiveness, the frantic scramble for boyfriends and hus-

bands. Having obtained and married a man the race is then on to have
children, in order that their attractiveness and accomplishments may
add more social worth. In a woman, not having children is seen as an
incapacity somewhat akin to impotence in a man.

Beneath all of the pressures of the sexual marketplace and the
marital status game, however, there is a far more sinister organization
of economic exploitation and psychological mutilation. The housewife
role, usually defined in terms of the biological duty of a woman to
reproduce and her "innate" suitability for a nurturant and companionship role, is actually crucial to industrial capitalism in an advanced
state of technological development. In fact, the housewife (some 44
million women of all classes, ethnic groups and races) provides, un-
paid, absolutely essential services and labor. In turn, her assumption
of all household duties makes it possible for the man to spend the
majority of his time at the workplace.

It is important to understand the social and economic exploitation
of the married woman, since the real productivity of her labor is
denied by the commonly held assumption that she is dependent on her
husband, exchanging her keep for emotional and nurturant services.
Margaret Benston, a radical women's liberation leader, points out: "In
sheer quantity, household labor, including child care, constitutes a
huge amount of socially necessary production. Nevertheless, in a society based on commodity production, it is not usually considered
even as 'real work' since it is outside of trade and the marketplace.
This assignment of household work as the function of a special category 'women' means that this group *does* stand in a different relationship to production . . . The material basis for the inferior status of
women is to be found in just this definition of women. In a society in
which money determines value, women are a group who work outside
the money economy. Their work is not worth money, is therefore
valueless, is therefore not even real work. And women themselves,
who do this valueless work, can hardly be expected to be worth as
much as men, who work for money."

Women are essential to the economy not only as free labor, but also
as consumers. The American system of capitalism depends for its
survival on the consumption of vast amounts of socially wasteful
goods, and a prime target for the unloading of this waste is the
housewife. She is the purchasing agent for the family, but beyond that
she is eager to buy because her own identity depends on her accomplishments as a consumer and her ability to satisfy the wants of her
husband and children. This is not, of course, to say that she has any

power in the economy. Although she spends the wealth, she does not own or control it—it simply passes through her hands.

In addition to their role as housewives and consumers, increasing numbers of women are taking outside employment. These women leave the home to join an exploited labor force, only to return at night to assume the double burden of housework on top of wage work—that is, they are forced to work at two full-time jobs. No man is required or expected to take on such a burden. The result: two workers from one household in the labor force with no cutback in essential female functions—three for the price of two, quite a bargain.

Frederick Engels, now widely read in women's liberation, argues that, regardless of her status in the larger society, within the context of the family the woman's relationship to the man is one of proletariat to bourgeoisie. One consequence of this class division in the family is to weaken the capacity of men and women oppressed by the society to struggle together against it.

In all classes and groups, the institution of marriage functions to a greater or lesser degree to oppress women; the unity of women of different classes hinges upon our understanding of that common oppression. The 19th century women's movement refused to deal with marriage and sexuality, and chose instead to fight for the vote and elevate the feminine mystique to a political ideology. That decision retarded the movement for decades. But 1969 is not 1889. For one thing, there now exist alternatives to marriage. The most original and creative politics of the women's movement has come from a direct confrontation with the issue of marriage and sexuality. The cultural revolution—experimentation with life-styles, communal living, collective child-rearing—have all come from the rebellion against dehumanized sexual relationships, against the notion of women as sexual commodities, against the constriction and spiritual strangulation inherent in the role of wife.

Lessons have been learned from the failures of the earlier movement as well. The feminine mystique is no longer mistaken for politics, nor gaining the vote for winning human rights. Women are now all together at the bottom of the work world, and the basis exists for a common focus of struggle for all women in American society. It remains for the movement to understand this, to avoid the mistakes of the past, to respond creatively to the possibilities of the present.

Women's oppression, although rooted in the institution of marriage, does not stop at the kitchen or the bedroom door. Indeed, the

economic exploitation of women in the workplace is the most commonly recognized aspect of the oppression of women.

Most women who enter the labor force do not work for "pin
money" or "self-fulfillment." Sixty-two per cent of all women working
in 1967 were doing so out of economic need (i.e., were either alone
or with husbands earning less than $5000 a year). In 1963, 36 per cent
of American families had an income of less than $5000 a year. Women
from these families work because they must; they contribute 35 to 40
per cent of the family's total income when working full-time, and 15
to 20 per cent when working part-time.

Despite their need, however, women have always represented the
most exploited sector of the industrial labor force. Child and female
labor were introduced during the early stages of industrial capitalism,
at a time when most men were gainfully employed in crafts. As industrialization developed and craft jobs were eliminated, men entered the
industrial labor force, driving women and children into the lowest
categories of work and pay. Indeed, the position of women and children industrial workers was so pitiful, and their wages so small, that
the craft unions refused to organize them. Even when women organized themselves and engaged in militant strikes and labor agitation—
from the shoemakers of Lynn, Massachusetts, to the International
Ladies' Garment Workers and their great strike of 1909—male union-
ists continued to ignore their needs. As a result of this male supremacy
in the unions. women remain essentially unorganized, despite the fact
that they are becoming an ever larger part of the labor force.

The trend is clearly toward increasing numbers of women entering
the work force: women represented 55 per cent of the growth of the
total labor force in 1962, and the number of working women rose from
16.9 million in 1957 to 24 million in 1962. There is every indication
that the number of women in the labor force will continue to grow as
rapidly in the future.

Job discrimination against women exists in all sectors of work, even
in occupations which are predominantly made up of women. This
discrimination is reinforced in the field of education, where women are
being short-changed at a time when the job market demands higher
educational levels. In 1962, for example, while women constituted 53
per cent of the graduating high school class, only 42 per cent of the
entering college class were women. Only one in three people who
received a B.A. or M.A. in that year was a woman, and only one in
ten who received a Ph.D was a woman. These figures represent a
decline in educational achievement for women since the 1930s, when

women received two out of five of the B.A. and M.A. degrees given, and one out of seven of the Ph.Ds. While there has been a dramatic increase in the number of people, including women, who go to college, women have not kept pace with men in terms of educational achievement. Furthermore, women have lost ground in professional employment. In 1960 only 22 per cent of the faculty and other professional staff at colleges and universities were women—down from 28 per cent in 1949, 27 per cent in 1930, 26 per cent in 1920. 1960 does beat 1919 with only 20 per cent—"you've come a long way, baby"—right back to where you started! In other professional categories: 10 per cent of all scientists are women, 7 per cent of all physicians, 3 per cent of all lawyers, and 1 per cent of all engineers.

Even when women do obtain an education, in many cases it does them little good. Women, whatever their educational level, are concentrated in the lower paying occupations. The figures in Chart A tell a story that most women know and few men will admit: most women are forced to work at clerical jobs, for which they are paid, on the average, $1600 less per year than men doing the same work. Working class women in the service and operative (semi-skilled) categories, making up 30 per cent of working women, are paid $1900 less per year on the average than are men. Of all working women, only 13 per cent are professionals (including low-pay and low-status work such as teaching, nursing and social work), and they earn $2600 less per year than do professional men. Household workers, the lowest category of all, are predominantly women (over 2 million) and predominantly black and third world, earning for their labor barely over $1000 per year.

Not only are women forced onto the lowest rungs of the occupational ladder, they are in the lowest income levels as well. The most constant and bitter injustice experienced by all women is the income differential. While women might passively accept low status jobs, limited opportunities for advancement, and discrimination in the factory, office and university, they choke finally on the daily fact that the male worker next to them earns more, and usually does less. In 1965 the median wage or salary income of year-round full-time women workers was only 60 per cent that of men, a 4 per cent loss since 1955. Twenty-nine per cent of working women earned less than $3000 a year as compared with 11 per cent of the men; 43 per cent of the women earned from $3000 to $5000 a year as compared with 19 percent of the men; and 9 per cent of the women earned $7000 or more as compared with 43 per cent of the men. What most people do

Chart A

COMPARATIVE STATISTICS FOR MEN AND WOMEN IN THE LABOR FORCE, 1960

Occupation	Percentage of working women in each occupational category	Income of Year Round Full Time Workers		Numbers of Workers in Millions	
		Women	*Men*	*Women*	*Men*
Professional	13%	$4358	$7115	3	5
Managers, Officials and Proprietors	5	3514	7241	1	5
Clerical	31	3586	5247	7	3
Operatives	15	2970	4977	4	9
Sales	7	2389	5842	2	3
Service	15	2340	4089	3	3
Private Household	10	1156	—	2	—

Sources: U.S. Department of Commerce, Bureau of the Census: "Current Population Reports," P-60, No. 37, and U.S. Department of Labor, Bureau of Labor Statistics and U.S. Department of Commerce, Bureau of the Census.

not know is that in certain respects, women suffer more than do non-white men, and that black and third world women suffer most of all.

Chart B

MEDIAN ANNUAL WAGES FOR MEN AND WOMEN BY RACE, 1960

Workers	Median Annual Wage
Males, White	$5137
Males, Non-White	$3075
Females, White	$2537
Females, Non-White	$1276

Source: U.S. Department of Commerce, Bureau of the Census. Also see: President's Commission on the Status of Women, 1963.

Women, regardless of race, are more disadvantaged than are men, including non-white men. White women earn $2600 less than white men and $1500 less than non-white men. The brunt of the inequality is carried by 2.5 million non-white women, 94 per cent of whom are black. They earn $3800 less than white men, $1900 less than non-white men, and $1200 less than white women.

There is no more bitter paradox in the racism of this country than that the white man, articulating the male supremacy of the white male middle class, should provide the rationale for the oppression of black women by black men. Black women constitute the largest minority in the United States, and they are the most disadvantaged group in the labor force. The further oppression of black women will not liberate black men, for black women were never the oppressors of their men—that is a myth of the liberal white man. The oppression of black men comes from institutionalized racism and economic exploitation: from the world of the white man. Consider the following facts and figures.

The percentage of black working women has always been proportionately greater than that of white women. In 1900, 41 per cent of black women were employed, as compared to 17 per cent for white women. In 1963, the proportion of black women employed was still a fourth greater than that of whites. In 1960, 44 per cent of black married women with children under six years were in the labor force, in contrast to 29 per cent for white women. While job competition requires ever higher levels of education, the bulk of illiterate women are black. On the whole, black women—who often have the greatest need for employment—are the most discriminated against in terms of opportunity. Forced by an oppressive and racist society to carry unbelievably heavy economic and social burdens, black women stand at the bottom of that society, doubly marked by the caste signs of color and sex.

The rise of new agitation for the occupational equality of women also coincided with the re-entry of the "lost generation"—the housewives of the 1950s—into the job market. Women from middle class backgrounds, faced with an "empty nest" (children grown or in school) and a widowed or divorced rate of one-fourth to one-third of all marriages, returned to the workplace in large numbers. But once there they discovered that women, middle class or otherwise, are the last hired, the lowest paid, the least often promoted, and the first fired. Furthermore, women are more likely to suffer job discrimination on the basis of age, so the widowed and divorced suffer particularly, even though their economic need to work is often urgent. Age discrimination also means that the option of work after child-rearing is limited. Even highly qualified older women find themselves forced into low-paid, unskilled or semi-skilled work—if they are lucky enough to find a job in the first place.

The realities of the work world for most middle class women—that they become members of the working class, like it or not—are understandably distant to many young men and women in college who have never had to work, and who tend to think of the industrial "proletariat" as a revolutionary force, to the exlcusion of "bourgeois" working women. Their image of the "pampered middle class woman" is factually incorrect and politically naive. It is middle class women forced into working class life who are often the first to become conscious of the contradiction between the "American Dream" and their daily experience.

Faced with discrimination on the job—after being forced into the lower levels of the occupational structure—millions of women are inescapably presented with the fundamental contradictions in their unequal treatment and their massive exploitation. The rapid growth of women's liberation as a movement is related in part to the exploitation of working women in all occupational categories.

Male supremacy, marriage, and the structure of wage labor—each of these aspects of women's oppression has been crucial to the resurgence of the women's struggle. It must be abundantly clear that radical social change must occur before there can be significant improvement in the social position of women. Some form of socialism is a minimum requirement, considering the changes that must come in the institutions of marriage and the family alone. The intrinsic radicalism of the struggle for women's liberation necessarily links women with all other oppressed groups.

The heart of the movement, as in all freedom movements, rests in women's knowledge, whether articulated or still only an illness without a name, that they are not inferior—not chicks, nor bunnies, nor quail, nor cows, nor bitches, nor ass, nor meat. Women hear the litany of their own dehumanization each day. Yet all the same, women know that male supremacy is a lie. They know they are not animals or sexual objects or commodities. They know their lives are mutilated, because they see within themselves a promise of creativity and personal integration. Feeling the contradiction between the essentially creative and self-actualizing human being within her, and the cruel and degrading less-than-human role she is compelled to play, a woman begins to perceive the falseness of what her society has forced her to be. And once she perceives this, she knows that she must fight.

Women must learn the meaning of rage, the violence that liberates the human spirit. The rhetoric of invective is an equally essential stage, for in discovering and venting their rage against the enemy—and the enemy in everyday life is men—women also experience the justice of their own violence. They learn the first lessons in their own latent strength. Women must learn to know themselves as revolutionaries. They must become hard and strong in their determination, while retaining their humanity and tenderness.

There is a rage that impels women into a total commitment to women's liberation. That ferocity stems from a denial of mutilation; it is a cry for life, a cry for the liberation of the spirit. Roxanne Dunbar, surely one of the most impressive women in the movement, conveys the feelings of many: "We are damaged—we women, we oppressed, we disinherited. There are very few who are not damaged, and they rule. . . . The oppressed trust those who rule more than they trust themselves, because self-contempt emerges from powerlessness. Anyway, few oppressed people believe that life could be much different. . . . We are damaged and we have the right to hate and have contempt and to kill and to scream. But for what? . . . Do we want the oppressor to admit he is wrong, to withdraw his misuse of us? He is only too happy to admit guilt—then do nothing but try to absorb and exorcize the new thought . . . That does not make up for what I have lost, what I never had, and what all those others who are worse off than I never had. . . . Nothing will compensate for the irreparable harm it has done to my sisters. . . . How could we possibly settle for anything remotely less, even take a crumb in the meantime less, than total annihilation of a system which systematically destroys half its people. . . . "

AN INTERVIEW WITH
ABBIE HOFFMAN AND JERRY RUBIN

Paul Kurtz

Paul Kurtz.   You're both key figures in the Yippie movement. What would you say is the purpose of the Youth International party?
Jerry Rubin.   To overthrow the Government.
Abbie Hoffman.   It's not the Youth International party; that's a slogan used by *The New York Times*—which needs it. It's Yippie, and

Paul Kurtz, "An Interview with Abbie Hoffman and Jerry Rubin," *The Humanist,* May/June 1969, pp. 3–8 Reprinted by permission of *The Humanist.*

there is an exclamation point after it! Yippies are just people struggling to make a new society, one based on human values rather than property values. It's people doing that—all kinds of different people.

Rubin. Yippies are more a style than a concrete thing. It's not a card you have and say, well; I'm a member of the Yippies. It's just where your head's at and what you're doing. It involves drugs and working out your own life-style, and primarily it's saying that American society as it exists right now is immoral and has no place for its youth. Youth had to create something new and different, and Yippies are just part of that creation.

Kurtz. Now, you gave two different answers. For Jerry Rubin the purpose of the Yippies is a revolution to overthrow society, and for Abbie Hoffman to build a new society.

Hoffman. One can't be done without the other. When we talk about a system rather than a society, because a system is the machinery that holds that society together, we're talking about decision-making—how decisions are made in the country—and that's the system. And the way in which decisions are made, the kind of people, and how you get to a position where you can make a decision where you have power over another person's life—that's what we're talking about changing.

Kurtz. The first thing then is to destroy the Establishment, and then, second, to build a new society, as you've indicated.

Hoffman. Well, what do we have to do then? We *are* the new society.

Rubin. The Establishment is dead. Its myths don't have any power anymore; the people who work for the Establishment don't have their hearts in it, don't have their lives involved; it's lost the will of the majority of the world. It's on a suicide trip. Our fathers and the people who have power are on a suicide trip. And the young kids are on their own; they have to create their own thing.

Kurtz. In other words, the Yippies are both negative and positive at the same time. A lot of people, of course, think that the Yippie movement is primarily negative: destroy the Establishment, period. But do you really have a positive aim as well?

Hoffman. Well, when we went to Chicago during the Democratic Convention, we went to have a festival of life. That's a very positive thing. We're saying that nobody looks at the Democrats and says, "That's decay, that's destruction; they aren't doing anything positive." That's ridiculous. What we were doing was very positive. We are saying: "We are the new society. How are we going to survive together?"

Rubin. Let me put it in one sentence: To destroy a society that is primarily involved in destruction is a positive act.

Kurtz. All right, one destroys the Establishment. What is the next stage? Do you have some notion of what a Utopia might be?

Rubin. It's not a program, like the program they had in the '30's, or like what came out of Marxism: a 10-point program. It's a new value system that is in people's bodies. Let's just take the question of money. An old value is that a man's property is his own, and he can pass it on to his children through inheritance, and those who are poor have their own problems. And I think among the youth of America there is an entirely different attitude toward money. That it is just a means, and that it confuses and fucks up things more than anything else— we've got to get beyond it and share everything.

Hoffman. When the factory becomes a community and all the people participate in the decisions that go on in that factory, you have a new society because they are a part of it. And then the revolution becomes a whole community effort of working things out together. There is a vision.

Rubin. Let me just say one thing about the Yippie thing that is important. It says to us and to a young kid that "you have all the answers." America says, listen to the expert; the person who knows about poverty is a rich person who studied it; a person who knows how to eliminate racism is a white person who's studied it. In our heads, the people who can eliminate poverty are the poor people, the people who can eliminate racism are the people who are the victims of racism, and the only people who can build the future are the young kids. Society is constantly telling young kids: "Keep your place; listen to your teachers; listen to your parents; be good; fulfill your role."

Hoffman. Yippies try to switch it around and say, "Trust your impulses." The revolution will come out of you. It'll come out of your impulses; it will come out of your guts; and the way that it will come is when you struggle. Mao Tse-tung said that the way to learn is to do. You do, then you learn, then you do, then you learn again. I just sat down with an intellectual, and he said, "Well, we've got to think, we've got to talk, and we've got to think." Well, we did that for an hour, and I said, "Well, here we are. I haven't learned anything about you because we aren't brothers; we aren't struggling for the same things. We aren't sharing our blood together; we aren't sharing our food together. We aren't sharing our dope, we aren't living in the same area."

Kurtz. I'd like to focus first on the values in American life that you particularly find to be hypocritical or contradictory; and then let's focus on the values that you would substitute for them.

Hoffman. That's a long list.

Rubin. We'll have to be very general: America separates people. Separates blacks and whites, separates wetbacks; separates them through competition; separates them through geography. People in private homes, students, are separated from one another, students compete for exams, and when one student fucks up, another student's happy: I'm getting ahead of him. In every institution the idea is to get the people in one position to fight each other, so what's the result? The result is that there's no community, and people really have no basis for feeling an identity with each other. Also, all the energy that would go toward fighting against the Establishment for people's common goals is diverted to fighting against one another.

Kurtz. It's separation, competition, and the lack of community, then, that you particularly indict?

Hoffman. That's right.

Rubin. So black power, and youth power, and Yippie power, and Viet Cong power—all that is an attempt to get the people to recognize themselves as brothers, no matter what their small differences are, and to fight against those powers and those institutions that are dividing them.

Hoffman. And there's also one thing that Jerry left out: the fight between men and women, how they are separated. All this is done so that you can maintain a capitalist consumer economy. Once you get the people divided up like that, playing certain kinds of roles, being certain kinds of cogs in the whole machinery, then you can program them easier, and you can sell things to them quicker, and they can buy things. To be a woman, you have to buy Virginia Slims, you see? And it's easier to do that. And now you feel inadequate because you don't buy Virginia Slims and smoke them.

Rubin. That's what America says to the blacks: "Well, there's room in our society for *some* blacks." And the goal is to get some blacks into the middle class so that the majority of the blacks have as their ambition to follow those few blacks in the middle class. The black-power movement says, "We're going to advance as a total, loving community, and the benefit of the lowest guy is going to be the final judgment of all." No one guy benefits while another guy suffers.

Kurtz. You find the separation of the sexes and class distinctions to be wicked, but do you also find the consumer economy of capitalism to be a basic source of difficulty?

Hoffman. Of course it's basic, because it leads to the perpetuation of competition. It says that man is basically a competitive animal, which I believe to be incorrect fundamentally. I think man is a cooperative animal. And then there are all those studies about animals: I don't go in for all that intellectual shit, because it's there—the stuff to prove it either way. But a revolutionary attitude is one that says the people are basically good, they're basically creative, and they're basically cooperative.

Kurtz. Are you saying that you find in our society that the competition and the striving tend to destroy creativity and cooperation?

Hoffman. Well, of course. Capitalism is an economic jungle.

Kurtz. Then you also attack the system because it thwarts the ability to enjoy pleasure?

Rubin. It's a religious war; it causes ulcers.

Kurtz. This is an interesting point. Why do you view it as a religious war?

Rubin. There is no single reform that could satisfy the worldwide revolutionary movement. It's a war of ideas, and, let's say, it's against Christianity. Our Christian inheritance tells us that this life is a steppingstone to the next life; therefore, no matter what suffering we experience in this life, it is in a sense good because we're going to go to the bank when we're dead. That's a way to keep poor people down, because they're thinking about the next life. The body is bad, pleasure is bad, and out of all this comes the 8-hour day, the bank accounts, the insurance policy. The question implied that the revolution is a decision you make, which it really isn't.

Kurtz. When you say it's a religious war, does that mean that you're opposed to the Judeo-Christian system of values that we've inherited?

Hoffman. Yes, maybe like the Protestant ethic, as Max Weber has defined it: postponement of pleasure. Keep your nose clean, keep your mouth shut, upward mobility, move upward in the system, become successful, get life insurance.

Kurtz. Are you saying that you wish to enhance the present enjoyment of pleasure and not lose it, by deferring it for some future pleasure—as the Puritan does? Is this your point?

Hoffman. Sure. But let's define pleasure.

Rubin. Yes, let's not confuse it. The Viet Cong are having more fun than the American soldiers.

Hoffman. Pleasure is struggling for what you believe in.

Kurtz. You're not opposed to actual struggle or activity?

Hoffman. No, oh, no.

Kurtz. Then you're not advocating simply the contemplative withdrawal from the world of events. This is not what you mean, release from action?

Hoffman. Oh, no. We're rarely accused of that. We're talking about a change in the value system, like Christianity's struggle against the Roman Empire. You see, that also was an economic struggle, because the Christians were slaves. America is an empire, and it's dissolving. There are people all around the world who say we aren't going to put up with this anymore. And there are young people here who say we aren't going to buy that, we aren't going to participate. And there are blacks who are saying we don't want that; we don't want that honky style of life.

Kurtz. Some who have observed the Yippies are struck by the fact that the movement performs many functions of religion. It's interesting that earlier you described the revolt as a religious protest. Obviously the kids in the Yippie movement reject traditional religion. But many of the forms and functions of a new kind of religion have seemed to develop. How would you define this? Is it a kind of religion?

Rubin. It's like the churches are antireligious, because you go to church and justify that another man goes to hell. And the churches primarily divide people, and, in a sense, the churches justify the evil of the state. So the churches have failed, the schools have failed, the economy has failed, and the politicians have failed. All the experts have failed.

Kurtz. Would you call the youth movement a new religious re-awakening—not in the theistic sense, but in the humanistic sense?

Hoffman. Well, there's a religious experience involved, because there are visions, and there is magic involved, and there's belief, and there's faith in what we're doing. That's a religious experience. And we can't explain it in a nice rational way, because if we did that, we'd be like ministers in a church. We don't have the building. We're in the catacombs—in the catacomb state of religion.

Rubin. People's entire lives are involved. The revolution is people living their lives. I say the Viet Cong is a religious movement. The blacks are involved in a religious movement. The blacks are trying to redeem the culture that was destroyed, and redeeming the culture means redefining what life means, and out of that comes a search for power to implement that, because when you're working on a new way of life, you've also got to defend yourselves. As I see it, America is trying to wipe out its youth. It has no need for youth, and we feel useless, and we're on our own.

Kurtz. Would you consider your movement in some sense humanistic?

Hoffman. How could it not be? Even to call it a religion gets us a little nervous, because that's a Western concept. There's religion here, there's play here, there's work here, and all those things. We just don't relate to it that way. We relate to it as a life experience. We go to the Pentagon and we meditate, and we play, and we struggle, and we are political.

Kurtz. But in what sense is it humanistic? In that human experience, the human body, and human cooperation are fundamental, and that your ideals are primarily humanistic?

Rubin. It's humanistic in that there are no borders. A suffering thousands of miles away is my suffering. The entire life, the entire universe, is just one big planet.

Hoffman. It's also humanistic on a very specific level. We had a celebration on the first day of spring last year in Grand Central Station, at midnight. Eight thousand people came to be there and to experience community. And some kids happened to take the hands off a clock in the middle. And what happened, right after that, with no warning 200 or 300 police charged in and started beating people all over the place. I was knocked unconscious. A friend of mine came to defend me. The cops picked him up, threw him through a glass window, and broke both his hands. Now, everybody forgot this kid's hands. The only questions we'd get from people who wanted to defend the system was why did those kids take the hands off the clock? And there we are: two sets of hands. We're concerned about that guy's hands. How can you be that fucked up? Ten dollars for a lousy set of hands on a clock!

Kurtz. You emphasize the humanistic values in your movement, but Herbert Marcuse has said that humanism is "bourgeois."

Rubin. Humanism is only a word. Marcuse is relating to it in a different way. I don't know what you mean by humanism.

Kurtz. Briefly, it is antisupernatural, emphasizes the positive sphere of human experience, and expresses a genuine concern for all humans.

Hoffman. What are you saying, let's all get together and love? That's a bunch of bull.

Rubin. Brotherhood week? Is that what you mean by humanism?

Then it is not a humanistic movement. That's like keep the blacks in their place, but be nice to them one day a week. That's not the kind of humanism we're talking about.

Hoffman. When the lion gobbles up the lamb, he is at peace.

Kurtz. By humanism I mean that you're committed to a humanitarian goal of mankind, and you're interested in releasing human potentialities.

Hoffman. There's nobody struggling in the world to make a revolution that isn't.

Kurtz. How would this relate to Marxism? The early Marx was a humanist, and there is a rediscovery of Marxist humanism in Eastern Europe today. In what sense would the student movement relate to Marxism?

Rubin. I think of Marx as a myth. The myth of Marxism says people should get together and overthrow governments to improve new structures. That whole myth is part of our unconscious. It's not really relevant, because it's not like we went into a library and read a book and got a theory and then went out to implement the theory. A lot of the people who call themselves Marxists take a lot of the specific mechanisms that Marx pointed out and treat them as catechism and a religion and say that this is what we have to do. It eliminates the spontaneity and the excitement. See, you ask us a lot of questions that imply answers none of us have.

Kurtz. But the Marxist indictment of the Establishment, as viewed from the Old Left, finds in the economic structure the basic problem; and there is a very conscious effort to overthrow the structure.

Rubin. If you understand what both of us say, there is an incredible emphasis on economics. The economic system divides people, destroys them spiritually, confines them to boring work. The whole economic structure has to be changed.

Hoffman. We are for a change in the economic system because the economic system is based upon property.

Kurtz. Is it primarily the capitalist economic system, then, that is for you the main problem?

Hoffman. If we want to start there, we can start there. You can start at a lot of places because there are values that come out of that system: There's religion, the political system, and the information system.

Kurtz. But what is crucial or basic?

Rubin. I don't think that you can implement the values we're stating without a revolution in the economic structure.

Kurtz. But how do you differ from Marx?

Hoffman. I think where it differs from Marx is that we don't see the working class at General Motors ready to have the uprising. Maybe it's coming, but it isn't there right now. And what we see is a very strange phenomenon: Where people who have a relatively good materialistic deal in life, like young people—their parents had it, lived through the depression, you know, and work, and all that—they're rejecting that; they're saying, no, we don't want that kind of life. Therefore, it becomes more existential than deterministic Marxist. It's more unexplainable—you don't know why, you just know why because that thing isn't working.

Kurtz. Let's focus on what you consider to be your positive values. Obviously you're committed to the liberty of the individual. This is fundamental, as I see it. You want the individual to be free, in morality, in sex, in drugs, in enjoyment, and in appreciation of his body.

Rubin. That's only part of it. Liberty is a bad word because it implies that it's okay if the individual is part of a bad society so long as he has freedom to go by himself and do what he wants to do. We're saying that American society and Western society are societies that do not allow the individual to develop his potentiality with the other people.

Kurtz. So then you haven't abandoned the collective ideal? Many people find, you see, a kind of contradiction: on the one hand, individual freedom, and on the other hand, the collective. But can you have both at the same time?

Rubin. Now take the university. Students are working for grades and competing against one another. There are just so many places in the society they can get into. So they may have individual freedom in a certain sense, but they don't feel satisfied, because they don't feel part of a family. When you feel part of a family, then you can express your own individuality.

Kurtz. What if the family suppresses you? Or the collective suppresses you? Doesn't this occur? And if so, what happens to the freedom of the individual?

Hoffman. Then you get another collective.

Kurtz. Do you ever live outside the collective, in any sense? Is this a kind of Thoreau's *Walden* that you're emphasizing in positive terms?

Hoffman. Well, no. Say, like, dig the Beatles. They're like making a community kind of art form. But they're all individuals—we know them as individuals. They have different personalities; they maintain their individuality. There are families that work like that.

Rubin. Take a baseball team—they're all a team, and when one guy gets a home run, the other guys are happy, because the team is getting the point, but they are all doing their best within.

Kurtz. I see, so it's a kind of cooperative ideal in which you hope individual freedom will develop, but it's not individual freedom separate from the cooperative?

Hoffman. Oh, no, I don't believe there is such a thing. I think that's an illusion pumped in by a capitalist economy, a mass economy that wants to keep it that way.

Kurtz. Would your indictment of modern society also apply to socialist or communist economies?

Rubin. It would apply to Russia and Eastern Europe. It would not apply to Cuba. I was in Cuba in 1964, and I have to say that the idea that a family was possible in a society first entered my head when I was in Cuba. You'd go into a factory and every worker would say, "Hey, look at our factory!" That doesn't happen when you walk into an American factory. It's just a whole different attitude. Everyone's talking about everyone else. And if you try to explain what it's like in America, it's a foreign idea.

Kurtz. Don't you find bureaucracy there? And doesn't bureaucracy deaden both the collective and the individual? In Eastern Europe and the Soviet Union one often finds that to be the case.

Hoffman. I think every struggle has a basic respect for individuals. Even the National Liberation Front. When they go on a mission, they sit down as a group outside the town that they're going to raid and they talk about it. And the privates and the captains all talk. And they make a kind of collective thing, and they go into action. And they have their individuality. In the American Revolution it was the same way. They were standing at Lexington, and one guy in the Lexington militia said they ought to have uniforms. And they all laughed that down. And then the captain came over and said, well, the British are coming, and they said, well, nine hours, and they haven't got here. I'm going back and tend my farm. I'll stay, another guy says. It was anarchistic; it was also a very unpopular war.

Kurtz. But do the Yippies find the Eastern European countries and the Soviet Union, too, in a sense, also to be consumer economies with all their defects and problems? At the Humanist-Marxist Dialogue held last September [1968], we found that the same kind of indictment of Western capitalism also applies to Communist countries, where the individual is sacrificed to vast organizational complexes.

Hoffman.   They have state capitalism.

Rubin.   We have brothers in Russia: the young kids, fighting against the state. It is the same in Eastern Europe. Those are our brothers, you know? What's happening across the world is a rebellion of the youth against the old state governments, no matter what they are. We'd be doing the same thing if we were in Russia.

Kurtz.   What about China? Aren't there similar problems? Can one really destroy all bureaucratic organizations? Or is this an illusion?

Hoffman.   I tend to respect what's going on in China, but I think it's impossible for me to find out what's going on in China.

Rubin.   I have a positive attitude without knowing that much.

Kurtz.   If we may turn to another issue, there are many people who are disturbed at what they think is the anti-intellectualism in the Yippie movement.

Hoffman.   Hey, man, do you realize how *intellectual* this discussion has been? It's almost boring its so goddamn intellectual!

Rubin.   The university is anti-intellectual. The books that we were made to read as kids and as teenagers were anti-intellectual, because they didn't describe reality as it existed, and they got our head all fucked up with concepts and theories that made it all a mental game that never touched our bodies and never became real. What we're trying to do is work out a theory that comes right out of the body, that comes right out of blood, comes right out of guts.

Kurtz.   But what about the intellect? Are you offering a new theory or a new set of concepts?

Rubin.   It's an action.

Hoffman.   It's wasted motion to come to a university and tell people that they ought to think, they ought to analyze, they ought to consider both sides.

Kurtz.   Are you opposed to logical analysis?

Rubin.   I'm opposed to a certain kind of thinking. For example, while white cops are wiping out black people in the ghetto, I'm opposed to intellectuals sitting around and writing books and thinking about it, because that's masturbation on thinking.

Kurtz.   But you're not opposed to thinking, are you? You want a different kind of thinking related to the body or related to reality as you find it. But you're not attacking all thinking, or analyses, or concepts?

Hoffman.   The thought should be in tune with the actions of the person. You see it's not that way with the intellectual who sits in the university and makes 20 or 25,000 dollars a year and writes a book about the evils of the society. Like Galbraith: We live in an affluent society—so?

Kurtz.   Is there a literature that you refer to, are there any classics, any writers that you find to be fundamental in any sense to your position?

Hoffman.   Well, Marvel comics are great and movies are good.

Rubin.   When I was young I dug *Catcher in the Rye* by Salinger.

Hoffman.   When I was young I had a course from Marcuse on Soviet Marxism.

Kurtz.   Do you find Marcuse important, then?

Rubin.   I can't understand him.

Hoffman.   I can't understand his latest book. It's six dollars for 70 pages and I can't understand that at all. Men like Marcuse, McLuhan, Maslow—who's a great humanist: he had a lot to say about Freud and where he went off the track a little—I respect them, but I don't love them. They have good minds, and they see certain things.

Kurtz.   Do you respect good minds?

Hoffman.   I respect them because they have a way of looking at society that might be correct and there may be something to learn from that. But dammit, I don't love them; they're not participating in the struggle, and they're not going to build a new society.

Rubin.   And I don't see how you can have a good analysis if you haven't felt it, and tasted it, and experienced it. I don't know whether anybody can really write something about someone else really well. Take Eldridge Cleaver's book *Soul on Ice*. It's beautiful, it's analytical, it's poetic, it's everything. And it's coming out of his gut. It's better than all the books that have ever been written by white people about what it's like to be black. You can't study something abstractly; you can't study life in a test tube. And the university is a plastic environment that has a Chinese wall around it. And it tells people to read books, think, and out of this will come some answers. And I find that the people in the university don't know what's happening. They don't have any experience.

Kurtz.   Many liberals and members of the Old Left may sympathize with part of your critical indictment and also with some of your positive values. One of the basic values of humanism is democracy.

And this involves a commitment to tolerance and a belief in reasoned dialogue. But I take it that you are critical of the notion of toleration or of reasoned dialogue.

Rubin.   What do you mean by toleration?

Kurtz.   Tolerating different points of view. Not being tolerant of hypocrisy, in the sense that you won't criticize it, but toleration in John Stuart Mill's sense; that is, that you have an open dialogue and respect different points of view.

Rubin.   The Yippie movement is like the youth movement—there's so many differences within it. You can hardly describe it. But it's all within the family.

Kurtz.   Do you tolerate those who disagree with you?

Hoffman.   Sure.

Kurtz.   In an open society, a democratic society, there are a variety of points of view, and one who believes in democracy is willing to tolerate people expressing different points of view. Do you welcome this?

Rubin.   Do you mean tolerate in a sense that black people should tolerate white cops?

Kurtz.   I was talking about toleration in the sense of freedom of speech and discussion. Are you committed to that?

Rubin.   Oh. Yeah. I think that George Wallace should have a free hour every night on TV because he indicts himself.

Kurtz.   Yet many people in the New Left seem to deny that we should be committed to open dialogue and free speech. Marcuse even says that one should not tolerate the intolerable.

Rubin.   Yes, but he's talking about something else. He's talking about the fact that this university allows the military to come in and use it for militaristic purposes. There comes a point where you don't allow a public structure to be used for the incineration of brown people thousands of miles away. I don't tolerate that. I will not tolerate concentration camps. But anyone can say what he wants. That's fine. We're talking about tolerating people who have the power to kill, and who do kill.

Hoffman.   I was at a symposium at Dartmouth just two days ago, and there was a liberal guy who had run for Senator and had gotten beaten, and he was answering all these questions. He was good on Biafra—they're always good on Biafra, and they're good on Mississippi. But some student asked him a question: What do you think about what's going on on the campuses, and are the students right? And he paused for about 30 seconds, because there were votes there, and he came out 50-50. And the last part of his statement said, "I don't believe in violence as a means to social change." Well, that's a nice thing to say, but if he [the student] had said, are you a pacifist—oh, no, he's not a pacifist. He should give that speech to the military, he should give that speech to proponents of institutional violence, landlords. Landlords are violent people. Why doesn't he talk to them? Why doesn't he talk to the American Legion that way? You don't talk to students that way. You don't try to stem the flow of energy that's coming up to change things. You say, well, if you believe in that as a technique, okay. We're not saying you've got to use violence. You weigh 110 pounds, and you should go up and beat up that cop? You fight in your own way.

Kurtz.   Are you willing to use violence if need be?

Hoffman.   You use whatever you've got, and whatever you're good at.

Rubin.   What should the Jews have done in Nazi Germany? Should they have written letters to the editor? Should they have picketed? Should they have had legal demonstrations? What should blacks do when whites come in carrying clubs, guns, and the official uniform of the state with license to do whatever they want to do in the streets, and then the courts give their approval?

Kurtz.   In other words, you think that peaceful methods of persuasion within the established system are not adequate, and that you have to use civil disobedience, confrontation politics, and possibly violence?

Hoffman.   If we just go around living our life, doing what we think is right, and working towards a humanist society, there's confrontation.

Rubin.   Look, it's happening. The Establishment has no means that are legitimate for change. No means at all. The moment that someone challenges the Establishment effectively, the means close, and the person becomes a problem to be dealt with, through force.

Hoffman.   Even if they are reformers they are killed.

Kurtz.   But do you think that these methods will in the long run succeed? Will the youth movement, as it is now developing, be successful? Will more youth be radicalized and the system overthrown?

Rubin.   It can't lose.

Hoffman.   See, what we're talking about is the future. There are a lot of roads into the future. The future is all out there—there's a lot of space.

Kurtz.   Perhaps there is one thing that you have overlooked: the possibility that the adults may become reactionized. Many people who consider themselves to be liberal and even radical are turned off by the tactics of confrontation. There is a very startling phenomenon—a right-wing reaction—building up. In what sense will the methods you employ achieve what you want?

Rubin. Our allies are the babies being born right now. The young kids are with us. You can see it in high schools, you can see it in the colleges. The young kids are fighting for their lives; the old people are fighting for their reputations or for something else. We can't lose. The structure is illegitimate and is on a suicide trip. Private property is not going to be the future in 25 or 50 years.

Kurtz. But the adults have the power. And the question is whether or not these methods will in some sense boomerang.

Rubin. America has a lot of power, but the Viet Congs are kicking her ass.

Kurtz. Will you work cooperatively with those within the Establishment to achieve common aims?

Hoffman. No. Of course not.

Rubin. There are no common aims.

Kurtz. Do you think that either of you have been already co-opted by the system? You're both "news" for the media.

Rubin. They're trying to put us both in jail.

Kurtz. But you, Abbie Hoffman, have a book published that has a large sale.

Hoffman. Yeah, but the profits from that book—I don't even have a bank account—the profits from that get spread into the projects, and get spread into what we're doing.

Kurtz. But won't the same thing that happened to liberals, who were radicals 20 or 30 years ago and now are successful, also happen to you?

Rubin. No chance.

Kurtz. Remember the Marxists and radicals of the last generation are now professors in the universities.

Hoffman. If it happens to us—as two individuals—so what? The movement is growing. Ten years ago when I was in school, radicals went to Pete Seeger concerts; that was it. And then a struggle came that was outside the universities—somebody else's struggle in the South. About in 1964, with the free-speech movement, it came back in the universities again. People started to struggle. Now it's into the high schools. In 10 years it'll be in the grammar schools. And we know that. We know that it's happening. And we can see it: You go out to high schools and you see it. The same demands that went on in the free-speech movement in 1964 are going on in high schools today.

Rubin. You see long hair and drugs become the major issues among the teenagers, both against the parents and against school.

Kurtz. But these issues—drugs, long hair, dress—are really minor in your view, are they not? Surely they are not essential to any revolutionary movement?

Rubin. Oh, no, they're major issues, you see, because they're part of a counterculture.

Hoffman. They're major issues, but to focus your life in on one issue while not recognizing that there are other issues—

Rubin. If there had not been a Vietnam war we would have had to invent it, because the Vietnam war was our excuse to fight for our own freedom. Long hair is an expression of that; dope is an expression of that; every issue blends into the same thing, which is to fight for our own bodies and our own freedom.

Hoffman. Given our political system and our economic system, there had to be a Vietnam war. In fact there's always been. You know, the Philippines, they were our colonies and all that; I don't know when this country has had a good war.

Kurtz. Do you find any redeeming virtues at all in America? In a sense what you're saying is really an elaboration of many liberal and progressive principles, for example, as defended by Dewey and others in this country earlier.

Hoffman and Rubin. Who's Dewey—Thomas E. Dewey?

Kurtz. John Dewey, the father of progressive education in this country. Much of what you say, but surely, not all—for he had faith in the democratic process—is very much like what he argued for: his demand for liberation of individuals on the one hand and for social responsibility on the other.

Hoffman. Well, if he did, then he was right.

Rubin. We're using a lot of the ideas that we've heard against a society that doesn't implement them. We're for the underdog. The Viet Cong are the underdog; the blacks are the underdog. This society wants to wipe out the underdog. Everybody should be equal, right? But being equal within the private-property structure means that the poor can stay poor until they can solve their own individual problems. Well, we want everybody to be equal *right now.* The difference between Dewey and us is that we're part of a massive, human, social movement that is overwhelming, that can't be stopped. And so, there is no thinker we can point to and say "Here he is, here's the thinker."

It's like a river, and people flowing in the streets. And we're applying it right now.

Kurtz.   Apparently both of you have had difficulty with local, state, and Federal indictments. Where do you stand in regard to them?

Rubin.   The cops are trying very hard to put us in jail for our ideas. Not because we have them in our heads, but because we're trying to act on them. In the past eight months, I've been arrested for possession of marijuana—an alleged 3 ounces—which is intent to sell. Now, I don't know how many readers of *The Humanist* smoke marijuana, but marijuana is great, and nobody should go to jail for it. As a matter of fact, it ought to be a major thing in the schools. It's more important than textbooks. The cops had a phony search warrant and broke into my apartment; the rap is 2 to 15 years. And it's still pending. Then in Chicago, I got a state indictment—a felony for "solicitation to commit mob action," in which they charged that I incited a mob to attack cops.

Kurtz.   Are you under indictment too, Abbie Hoffman?

Hoffman.   By the time this magazine comes out, we're also both going to be indicted by the Federal Government for the crime of crossing state lines with intent to riot. I have a couple of trials under appeal—30 days in Washington for wearing a flag shirt, and 15 days for resisting arrest in Chicago, and a trial pending for Columbia University, and a lot of trials. The age of innocence is flying away. I have over 30 arrests—I used to get away with it a lot. Now, it's tough. They follow you around.

Rubin.   It's unbelievable—the FBI harassment.

Hoffman.   In the week after Chicago that I was home, I was visited no less than five times by some official Government agency.

Kurtz.   The fear is that your confrontation tactics will provoke a dangerous counterreaction.

Rubin.   If the right wing cracks down, that means all the brothers have got to get together in a united mass against the right wing. You can't go hide under a blanket if they're going to crack down.

Kurtz.   But the liberals have been polarized. I mean the Left movement has been split between the Old and New Left, liberals and radicals. Dialogue is difficult, and there is a serious hostility gap.

Rubin.   People have got to make a choice.

Kurtz.   In the present context, if you don't have any allies among the liberals, then this may provide a real opportunity for the emergence of a New Right.

Hoffman.   We have each other and we have the future.

Rubin. The liberals have got to make their choice. They either close their eyes and let fascism come down, or they put their bodies in between us and the cops.

Hoffman. They've shown for a number of years that they're going to allow the society to commit genocide on blacks, and gobble up the blacks, and they've shown for a number of years that they'll let the country gobble up other nations. Now the question is, are they going to let the country gobble up their kids? You see, we're bringing it right home. Here it is, America. We are your children. No matter what age we are, we all fly youth fare. You've got long hair, you fly youth fare, and you are young. You're a freak; you are young forever.

Kurtz. The liberals and the Old Left may be your last line of defense in this country. In vilifying them, who will be left to defend your civil liberties if and when they are attacked?

Rubin. The liberals, unfortunately, are impotent. Our only protection is ourselves. People can help us, but they really can do something only by joining us and being with us. People were very upset about Chicago, but now I stand a good chance of being put behind bars for Chicago. So I hope that people will translate the tears that they shed that week into active support.

THE HERO TODAY

Joseph Campbell

. . . The democratic ideal of the self-determining individual, the invention of the power-driven machine, and the development of the scientific method of research, have so transformed human life that the long-inherited, timeless universe of symbols has collapsed. In the fateful, epoch-announcing words of Nietzsche's Zarathustra: "Dead are all the gods." One knows the tale; it has been told a thousand ways. It is the hero-cycle of the modern age, the wonderstory of mankind's coming to maturity. The spell of the past, the bondage of tradition, was shattered with sure and mighty strokes. The dream-web of myth fell away; the mind opened to full waking consciousness; and modern man emerged from ancient ignorance, like a

Joseph Campbell, "The Hero Today." From *The Hero With A Thousand Faces,* by Joseph Campbell, Bollingen Series XVII (Princeton University Press, rev. edn. 1968) Copyright 1949 by Bollingen Foundation. Reprinted by permission of Princeton University Press, publishers of Bollingen Series.

butterfly from its cocoon, or like the sun at dawn from the womb of mother night.

It is not only that there is no hiding place for the gods from the searching telescope and microscope; there is no such society any more as the gods once supported. The social unit is not a carrier of religious content, but an economic-political organization. Its ideals are not those of the hieratic pantomime, making visible on earth the forms of heaven, but of the secular state, in hard and unremitting competition for material supremacy and resources. Isolated societies, dream-bounded within a mythologically charged horizon, no longer exist except as areas to be exploited. And within the progressive societies themselves, every last vestige of the ancient human heritage of ritual, morality, and art is in full decay.

The problem of mankind today, therefore, is precisely the opposite to that of men in the comparatively stable periods of those great co-ordinating mythologies which now are known as lies. Then all meaning was in the group, in the great anonymous forms, none in the self-expressive individual; today no meaning is in the group—none in the world: all is in the individual. But there the meaning is absolutely unconscious. One does not know toward what one moves. One does not know by what one is propelled. The lines of communication between the conscious and the unconscious zones of the human psyche have all been cut, and we have been split in two.

The hero-deed to be wrought is not today what it was in the century of Galileo. Where then there was darkness, now there is light; but also, where light was, there now is darkness. The modern hero-deed must be that of questing to bring to light again the lost Atlantis of the co-ordinated soul.

Obviously, this work cannot be wrought by turning back, or away, from what has been accomplished by the modern revolution; for the problem is nothing if not that of rendering the modern world spiritually significant—or rather (phrasing the same principle the other way round) nothing if not that of making it possible for men and women to come to full human maturity through the conditions of contemporary life. Indeed, these conditions themselves are what have rendered the ancient formulae ineffective, misleading, and even pernicious. The community today is the planet, not the bounded nation; hence the patterns of projected aggression which formerly served to co-ordinate the ingroup now can only break it into factions. The national idea, with the flag as totem, is today an aggrandizer of the nursery ego, not the annihilator of an infantile situation. Its parody-rituals of the parade ground serve the ends of Holdfast, the tyrant dragon, not the God in whom self-interest is annihilate. And the numerous saints of this anticult—namely the patriots whose ubiquitous photographs, draped with flags, serve as official icons—are precisely the local threshold guardians (our demon Sticky-hair) whom it is the first problem of the hero to surpass.

Nor can the great world religions, as at present understood, meet the requirement. For they have become associated with the causes of the factions, as instruments of propaganda and self-congratulation. (Even Buddhism has lately suffered this degradation, in reaction to the lessons of the West.) The universal triumph of the secular state has thrown all religious organizations into such a definitely secondary, and finally ineffectual, position that religious pantomime is hardly more today than a sanctimonious exercise for Sunday morning, whereas business ethics and patriotism stand for the remainder of the week. Such a monkey-holiness is not what the functioning world requires; rather, a transmutation of the whole social order is necessary, so that through every detail and act of secular life the vitalizing image of the universal god-man who is actually immanent and effective in all of us may be somehow made known to consciousness.

And this is not a work that consciousness itself can achieve. Consciousness can no more invent, or even predict, an effective symbol than foretell or control tonight's dream. The whole thing is being worked out on another level, through what is bound to be a long and very frightening process, not only in the depths of every living psyche in the modern world, but also on those titanic battlefields into which the whole planet has lately been converted. We are watching the terrible clash of the Symplegades, through which the soul must pass —identified with neither side.

But there is one thing we may know, namely, that as the new symbols become visible, they will not be identical in the various parts of the globe; the circumstances of local life, race, and tradition must all be compounded in the effective forms. Therefore, it is necessary for men to understand, and be able to see, that through various symbols the same redemption is revealed. "Truth is one," we read in the Vedas; "the sages call it by many names." A single song is being inflected through all the colorations of the human choir. General propaganda for one or another of the local solutions, therefore, is superfluous—or much rather, a menace. The way to become human is to learn to recognize the lineaments of God in all of the wonderful modulations of the face of man.

With this we come to the final hint of what the specific orientation of the modern hero-task must be, and discover the real cause for the disintegration of all of our inherited religious formulae. The center of gravity, that is to say, of the realm of mystery and danger has definitely shifted. For the primitive hunting peoples of those remotest human millenniums when the sabertooth tiger, the mammoth, and the lesser presences of the animal kingdom were the primary manifestations of what was alien—the source at once of danger, and of sustenance—the great human problem was to become linked psychologically to the task of sharing the wilderness with these beings. An unconscious identification took place, and this was finally rendered conscious in the half-human, half-animal, figures of the mythological totem-ancestors. The animals became the tutors of humanity. Through acts of literal imitation—such as today appear only on the children's playground (or in the madhouse)—an effective annihilation of the human ego was accomplished and society achieved a cohesive organization. Similarly, the tribes supporting themselves on plant-food became cathected to the plant; the life-rituals of planting and reaping were identified with those of human procreation, birth, and progress to maturity. Both the plant and the animal worlds, however, were in the end brought under social control. Whereupon the great field of instructive wonder shifted —to the skies—and mankind enacted the great pantomime of the sacred moon-king, the sacred sun-king, the hieratic, planetary state, jnd the symbolic festivals of the world-regulating spheres.

Today all of these mysteries have lost their force; their symbols no longer interest our psyche. The notion of a cosmic law, which all existence serves and to which man himself must bend, has long since passed through the preliminary mystical stages represented in the old astrology, and is now simply accepted in mechanical terms as a matter of course. The descent of the Occidental sciences from the heavens to the earth (from seventeenth-century astronomy to nineteenth-century biology), and their concentration today, at last, on man himself (in twentieth-century anthropology and psychology), mark the path of a prodigious transfer of the focal point of human wonder. Not the animal world, not the plant world, not the miracle of the spheres, but man himself is now the crucial mystery. Man is that alien presence with whom the forces of egoism must come to terms, through whom the ego is to be crucified and resurrected, and in whose image society is to be reformed. Man, understood however not as "I" but as "Thou": for the ideals and temporal institutions of no tribe, race, continent, social class, or century, can be the measure of the inexhaustible and multifariously wonderful divine existence that is the life in all of us.

The modern hero, the modern individual who dares to heed the call and seek the mansion of that presence with whom it is our whole destiny to be atoned, cannot, indeed must not, wait for his community to cast off its slough of pride, fear, rationalized avarice, and sanctified misunderstanding. "Live," Nietzsche says, "as though the day were here." It is not society that is to guide and save the creative hero, but precisely the reverse. And so every one of us shares the supreme ordeal—carries the cross of the redeemer—not in the bright moments of his tribe's great victories, but in the silences of his personal despair.

Ken Kesey: Post-Trip

Burton H. Wolfe

One sunny July day in 1967, I drove into the Skyline Mountains to see the prankster who did more than any other to create the hippie movement. He was an inmate at the San Mateo County Honor Camp, a former Boy Scout hideaway in a mountain forest that would be a fifteen-minute hike away from his former estate near La Honda if you could cut your way through the trees, bushes, and rocks. But Ken Kesey would be going there no longer. He would serve out his six-month jail sentence, get in his psychedelic bus, and return to his family in Oregon. In the meantime, he was getting whatever kicks he could at the Honor Camp.

To reach the camp, you cut off the San Francisco-San Jose Bay-shore Freeway at Redwood City, pass through the luxuriant green community of Woodside, climb into the mountains on Skyline Boulevard, swing onto Alpine Road for six miles, open a wide gate yourself and close it, then head up and down a winding one-lane road for three miles across mountain fields and through dense vegetation, praying nobody comes around a bend and hits you. The jail installation at the end of this mind-expanding trip looks like a cross between a summer camp resort and one of the better armed forces installations. There are dark frame barracks, low-slung mess hall, and log cabin shops. Kesey was working in the tailor shop when I saw him, sewing the torn blue

Burton H. Wolfe, "Post-Trip." From *The Hippies* by Burton H. Wolfe (Signet, 1965) Copyright © 1968 by Burton H. Wolfe. Reprinted by arrangement with The New American Library, New York.

denims of the inmates. There were around seventy-five of them in the
camp at the time, serving sentences of six months to two years, mostly
for dope use or lapse of alimony and child support. ("Can you imagine
a system that tries to take care of the support problem by throwing the
bread provider in jail?" Kesey asked me.) Around a dozen were hippies whose hair had been shorn by order of the camp authorities.
Otherwise, the discipline was loose. The men were detailed to specific
jobs and were called to awake, eat, and sleep over a squawk box that
rasped out orders all day long. But there were free periods to roam
around the woods or swim in a bright blue pool, and there were no
gates or guards to force anyone to remain in the camp. (Only two men
had taken off in the last two years, a deputy told me.)

No log cabin is going to remain rough-hewn for long with Kesey
around it. He had found some pieces of blue, yellow, red, purple, and
green cloth from God-knows-where and tacked them up on the beams,
rafters, and barren wood walls. He had accumulated egg cartons from
the mess hall and plastered them across the ceiling, like bee combs.
And he had wandered through the woods gathering lilacs, jasmin, blue
lupine, and other flowers and covered the jail-camp tailor shop with
them, so's all those dirty old nonsupporters and dope addicts could get
a whiff of life with wife or a pad of incense.

"One lieutenant wanted to rip all this stuff out," Kesey said, "but
a female judge came through here with a police commissioner, and
they liked it, so it stayed. Some of the deputies think I may be . . .
that way . . . because of the flowers, but they haven't tested me because
they know I wrestled in the Olympics, and they're a little afraid."

He plunked his heavy brown work boots on a desk and rocked back
and forth in his tilted wood chair, occasionally sipping coffee from an
old tin cup he had swiped from some dusty corner of the mess hall.
He was lightly tanned and his hard, hairy chest fairly burst the buttons
of his faded blue work shirt. There was an ugly horse-shoe-like mark
on his forehead, but the horse that had kicked him was inside the
power of a locomotive. "I forgot they opened up that track outside
Eugene, Oregon, the day before I got there," he said, "and the train
wracked up my car and me and my son Zane pretty bad."

That's the way he liked to talk sometimes—like a cross between a
logger, oakie, and Negro farmhand.

"I'm a troublemaker," he said. "I'll try to stir up things wherever
I go, in whatever I do. That's what the whole hippie movement is all
about: to do outrageous things that cause people to ask questions.
Whatever else comes of it, if nothing else comes of it, the hippie

movement will have had great value in that it caused the whole nation
to ask questions. This is the way that Christ went about changing the
world, by getting everybody to ask the same questions, by passing the
honey around. A lot of people don't know how to receive it yet, but
the more people we have who know how to pass it, the more will learn.
Right now, we don't have many national leaders that have this ability.
Kennedy had it. Kennedy knew how to pass the honey. It's dangerous
to have this knowledge. You saw what happened to him. Leary has this
knowledge, and I have it, and you see what's happened to us.

"It doesn't matter, though. The movement is growing and will last
a long time. One reason is it's based on a life-pulsating rhythm, an
upbeat that is vibrating through the universe, turning on people. Iam-
bic is the natural meter in all music and literature. You find it in the
temple, the Bible, Shakespeare, all the classic works. It says *life*-death,
life-death, *life*-death. There is a total impact, then decay. Well, these
kids coming up now have been born since the Bomb, and their meter
is trochaic. It goes one *and* two *and* one *and* two *and,* death-*life* death-
life death-*life*. These kids have a certain upbeat that makes them
unlike anyone else who came before them except Neal Cassady, and
they will be that way forever."

The squawk box announced lunch, and we walked up a dirt path
to the mess hall to line up for roll call. A deputy asked me if I wanted
to eat with the officers. I suppose he was surprised when I said no, I
wanted to eat with the inmates. We drew metal GI trays, went through
the chow line, and sat down at one of the dull wood tables. Kesey
downed a bowl of pea soup, slices of cheese, egg salad, three slices of
bread, tea, and stewed prunes. Between mouthfuls, he talked of the
system that separates inmates from guards, relating it to the separation
of whites from blacks, employers from employees, Catholics from
Jews, straight people from hippies.

"You know, I have a theory about all this," he said. "It relates to
there being so many Jews at the head of the hippie movement. My
theory is that the Jews were responsible for World War Two. I mean,
look at the German mentality. Here was a people conditioned for
centuries to develop their superior race concepts and penchant for
war. But there had to be a scapegoat for the Germans to start the holy
war they wanted, or else it could not have been started, and the Jews
were the perfect fall guys for it. I mean, this was a people destined to
be martyred. From their earliest Biblical stories, they prophesied it.
They were the chosen people, and they were determined to expunge
the sins from mankind. But they became a separate race, living apart

from the Christians in their own life style. And this enabled the Germans to sanctify the murder in their systems, because without this scapegoat they probably would not even have been clever enough to do that—there's no people so stupid as the Germans. In your book, if you want, you can relate this to what's happening to the hippies because of their position in the straight society."

After lunch, we walked through the woods and along a mountain stream while Kesey picked some more flowers for his tailor shop. He pulled up some plants that he called "Angel's Eucharist" or something like that, and we sucked the roots to draw out the sweet juice. As we walked back to the tailor shop with the flowers, he stopped along a bare patch of rocky soil, stooped like an Indian scout to examine the ground, and announced: "Coon tracks."

Back in the tailor shop, I took out my pen to write notes on what he was saying, so he took out his pen and waved it in imitation of my scribbling or busied himself inking a Jewish Star design on his blue denim inmates' uniform. I asked him why he had abandoned his writing after his success with *One Flew Over the Cuckoo's Nest* and *Sometimes a Great Notion.*

"I've tried on and off for the last fourteen years to write fiction," I said, "and I've always had to go back to nonfiction for a living because I just don't seem to have the creative ability. I throw my stuff away in despair. But you, on the other hand, have this wonderful gift —I'm not saying this to flatter you; *Cuckoo's Nest* is one of the most powerful novels in post-War Two literature—and yet you throw away this gift, a gift that millions of men would like to have. Why? You talk about being confined by publishers' rules. I don't think you're cramped at all. *Cuckoo's Nest* was a loose, flowing book. You set your own form in it, you said anything you wanted. I don't understand. What's bugging you?"

"There are too many things to be done," he said. "Until the final earthquake, the big zap when we're all one again, we've got to play a dual role. But it's coming, things are changing. We've already moved out of the age of Pisces into the Aquarian Age. The Millennium started some months ago."

He rambled on like that for awhile, never completing the thought, until finally I directed him back to the question.

"Yeah, well, you know, you're asking questions now like these reporters I've had to talk to. They say yes but, and yes but if. Well, like take McMurphy. He was just there, like antimatter. I didn't have to create him; the patients built him for me. But the Indian was different. I don't own the soul of that Indian. He just appeared while I was on peyote, and the first chapter of that book was written by him. So, that makes me wonder am I as talented as I might think or others think? Or am I just an instrument picked to make a statement, and after the statement is made, should I assume that I've got the right to make endless statements? Oh, I like to write. I will write a poem for a friend on the occasion of getting married and I will put everything into it. If I were to write longer things now, I wouldn't sign them. I'd just write them and send them in to the publisher and have him them out for anybody to read. See, I know now that the Indian in *Cuckoo's Nest* is not my Indian. He was brought into being by some higher power to tell America where it's at.

"Of course, I have been chosen to do that, too, and if I ever get the call to write something else, I will. But the call must come first. I will not write just for money. I don't need money. With my two books I've already earned my stripes. They have enabled me to go around and do other things that will have impact because I'm an important person, while when others do it they have no impact. Until the public knows we can take dope and paint buses and do all of these things out front and still carry on business, they will go on arresting hippies and putting them in jail. It's like running from the bogeyman. When you stop running, when you say *take* me, now you've *got* me, now what are you going to do with me—then they don't know what to do with you. This is what the hippies have got to learn. They've got to stop running and just give in, let them see how many they can arrest and what they will do about them. They watch me close here to see if I will be a shit disturber, but I play their game rules, I'm quiet, I follow orders, and then I do something like put flowers in a shop, and their minds are blown."

A member of the kitchen staff came in with a carton of ice cream he had taken out for Kesey—never believe that a celebrity outside jail ceases to become one inside. Kesey washed out his old tin cup, filled it with ice cream, and gave it to me so that I could eat politely, while he finished off the rest eating from the carton. It had been just two hours since the heavy lunch.

We talked of the irony of a thousand people smoking pot at the Human Be-in while the police looked the other way, and of his being arrested just for being in the presence of the stuff, and of the logic and rationality of a society that would then put him in jail for six months.

We talked of the press coverage and of *Ramparts'* article writing him out of the hippie movement. He was upset by much of the coverage in the newspapers and by some of the material in *Ramparts.*

"After the trial, one of the reporters said that my five-year-old, Zane, kept telling people in the court: 'I hate you.'

> . . . Young Zane diverted himself during the proceedings by turning in his front row seat, pointing at one spectator, then another and announcing: "I hate you."
>
> —*San Francisco Examiner,* June 23, 1967

That was a bummer. Zane would never say anything like that. He has been taught not to hate anyone. I've had a lot of trouble with the press."

He looked sad about that.

I read him the following statement from *Ramparts'* article: "One confounding thing about Kesey is the amorphous quality of the personal relationships in his entourage—the several attractive women don't seem, from the outside, to belong to any particular man; children are loved enough, but seem to be held in common."

"Of course that isn't true," Kesey said. "You know each woman belongs to someone. How can a writer describe an intimate relationship when he has never been there to see what's happening? Warren Hinckle never even talked to me; he was never at my place. Faye will always be my wife, and we'll always be mates. We don't have the kind of tribal relationship Hinckle was painting in his article. Romeo couldn't have made it in a tribal scene. There are people who are inevitably mated, in the stars, and when they get together, they are the lucky ones. Those not mated but married are the unlucky ones. Faye and I are among the lucky ones. She doesn't take dope; she's never used it. But we are mates.

"As for the children, I consider myself a devoted father. I've given my kids acid several times, so now they know what it is, they know where it's at, and they don't even want to take it now. They have other thing to do. But it's important to the Pranksters to know that there will be someone to take care of the kids no matter how drunk we may get. Like, we had a small calf, and the mother would have nothing to do with it, so we fed it from a bottle three times a day. We couldn't get high until we knew there would be somebody to take care of that calf; we couldn't hold our dope. So it is with the children. I've put them in with the Pranksters so I know there will always be someone to take care of them no matter how high I am, and I am often high. They think they can keep me from getting high by putting me in this jail. They don't understand that anything that gives you a sudden flash is dope. I'll take a flash wherever I can get it: from acid, pot, people, music, jail, anything.

"Besides, we can get LSD anyway. Do they think they can keep it away from us? One guy came in here with his fingernails coated with enough acid to turn on the whole camp. I let my friends know to send 'Love' in their letters; they knew what I meant. Unfortunately, one of them went a little overboard and became conspicuous enough in the letter for the cops to get wise."

He handed me a letter from one of his girl friends, handprinted in an ornate, multicolored script that must have taken hours to compose. Only one part of the letter had been censored by the camp authorities; the word "Love" had been cut out of the end. Painted into the letters were around a thousand milligrams of LSD.

"Before I took drugs, I didn't know why the guys I saw in the psycho ward at the VA Hospital were there. I didn't understand them. After I took LSD, suddenly I saw it. I saw it all. I listened to them and watched them, and I saw that what they were saying and doing was not so crazy after all. And so I was able to write about that in my first novel. Now, I don't want to tell people to take a lotta dope and then they can write a book, because it won't happen. But there comes a time when you've got to face the fact that something happens, apart from the drug itself, that no matter how pragmatic or how logical you are and the society is, you've just got to say: something supernatural is happening here.

"When we were hit by that train outside Eugene, I thought Zane was zapped out for good. The kid had stopped breathing, his heart had stopped, it seemed like he was gone. And so I knew I had to dig deep into my power and draw on every resource, yelling out: 'Don't let him die, don't let him die.' And he started breathing again. It's like we're all supermen changing clothes in the phone booth when we're called on to do a superhuman job.

"What I told the hippies was that LSD can be a door that one uses to open his mind to new realms of experience, but many hippies are using it just to keep going through the door over and over again, without trying to learn anything from it. They didn't understand, and I got hate letters. But those in the hip community who really understand, people like the Thelin brothers, know what I meant; and they will continue on. So long as people like the Thelins are there, I have confidence in this whole movement."

He looked sad again, and I asked him only one more question before I left:

"What did you want to create through the Acid Tests?"

"Ah," he said, "here's where you've got to stop writing, because you can't get this down on paper. Well, okay, I got aboard a spaceship one time, and I saw I was to be taken to outer space on a trip by myself, and I would have to spend the rest of my life in what society would consider an insane asylum, and I would be sad and lonely. So, I saw I would have to take everybody with me, I would have to turn on the whole world."

"I think I can write that down," I said, "but people will read it and take it as an explanation of you and the whole hippie movement. They will simply say: You're crazy. They're all crazy. And I don't like to give them such an easy out, but I don't know what to do about it. I don't intend to attempt any psychological evaluation of you and the hippies because I'm not a psychologist or a psychiatrist. So, unless you have some other explanation, I'm just going to write down what you say and let people think whatever they want."

"That's the way it will have to be," he said, "because you can't get this experience across to the general public. You can't write it down. They'll have to experience the whole thing themselves. They'll have to take LSD and go through the same mind-blowing experiences we have, that the hippies have, and then they'll either see it or they won't see it. To understand, they will have to turn on. The whole world will have to turn on."

As I turned to leave, he waved goodbye and said:

"Tell all my friends not to forget me. Tell them Ken Kesey is working in the tailor shop."

EPILOGUE

OF THE WORLD IN 1984

Richard E. Farson

It's all very easy, I think, to take a pessimistic view of the future of man. After all, there's a great deal of evidence of man's inhumanity to man: his creation of a technological juggernaut about to crush him; his perpetuation of present trends, which, if continued, will produce a dehumanized, depersonalized world. This evidence is certainly persuasive, and it often seems rather difficult to take a hopeful view of the future of man. But I am going to take such a view because as I assess the trends—in relation to human potentialities—the future does look quite hopeful.

Unfortunately, optimists often look foolish; pessimists look smart. Have you ever noticed that the people who are pessimistic seem realistic, hard-headed, down-to-earth, while the optimists sound grandiose, foolish, and naive? So, at some risk, let me present what I think is an optimistic view of our future, one that foresees human relationships that are more fun, more exciting, more romantic, more sexy, more intimate, more loving, more open and more honest.

Women who are pregnant today may have children who will be in the high school graduating class of 1984. If we try to imagine, as George Orwell did in his book *1984,* what life is going to be like then, about all we can be certain of is that it will be vastly different from life today. We find it difficult to think about change at all—it is even more

"Of the World in 1984" (adaptation of a speech given by Dr. Richard E. Farson at the International Design Conference, Aspen, Colorado, June 23, 1966). Reprinted from *Glamour.* Copyright © 1966 by The Condé Nast Publications Inc.

439

difficult to realize that changes are becoming increasingly frequent. In the past, we have been able to make a change and then coast for awhile before we have had to make another change. But if we plot the curve of innovation, we can see that it is an accelerating curve. This means that all the plateaus are being evened out, so that, in fact, *change will be a way of life in the future.* There will be new developments, new concepts, new values and new problems all the time. And people will be making new *demands.* These new demands have to do with the right to fulfill our human potentialities.

In discussing human potentialities, one might talk about the limitless possibilities of the human brain, about current experiments that attempt to evoke high-order behavior from people. But I would rather emphasize the realistic, practical demands that people will be making in 1984, or sooner, to help them realize their potential as human beings—a new Bill of Rights. By this I certainly don't mean a replacement of our constitutional Bill of Rights, which is concerned with living under a rule of law protecting our civil liberties. I am referring to an addition to it—one that deals with human potentialities and with the achievement of the "good life."

We need a new Bill of Rights because people are never satisfied. Once they meet their needs at one level, they move on to needs of a higher order. After their needs for survival are fulfilled, they begin to need freedom, democracy, education. There will never be an end to the developing, maturing needs of people. So my suggested Bill of Rights can be only an interim measure based upon the needs that we can now foresee.

Leisure

My first item in the new Bill of Rights is the Right to Leisure. That's a safe one to start with because we already have leisure. But, by today's definition, leisure means time off from work. I'm talking about a future society in which leisure will not mean time off, but the *right not to work* and still be considered a worthy human being. Work, to us, means receiving pay for it. But soon that kind of work will be done by a relatively small percentage of the population, perhaps only 10 percent. And that means that the chances for any of us to have jobs in the traditional sense—to "bring home the bacon"—will be quite limited. This poses a serious problem. How are people going to feel worthy without feeling useful?

For several hundred years we've been thoroughly imbued with the idea that the way to achieve self-esteem is by working hard, by being of service to others. Work has become an end in itself. Since we are caught in that value system, deriving from the Protestant Ethic, it's going to be difficult for us to imagine how we could feel worthy *just because we are fully human.* This leads to the question: What are people for anyway? To be useful? I would rather believe not.

I think that in the world of post-technical man, the whole idea of the *usefulness* of things and of people will be quite changed. We may be asking the wrong question when we ask of something or of some process, "Does it work? Is it useful?" Curiously, we don't seem to ask that about the things that are most important to us. We never ask that about a romance. We never ask that about a sunset. We never ask that about a symphony. We don't even ask that about a college education. We believe that these experiences are in some way enriching, of value in and of themselves. We only ask the "Does it work?" question of things we don't really care much about: products, training programs, advertising. It is my guess that we will ask this utilitarian question less and less, particularly when we are talking about people.

In the future we are going to see a fusion of work and play. Play will be our work, work will be our play, just as it is for children. Both must be fulfilling things that we can cry about and laugh about and do for many, many hours at a stretch. Hopefully, our homes, buildings and cities will be designed not just for work efficiency but for leisure, for delight, for romance and for play.

Health

The second right is the Right to Health. By health we have always meant the absence of illness. But we are going to have to redefine this term to mean not the *absence* of illness but the *opposite* of illness. In the future we will think of health as a positive condition of well-being, with peak moments of vigor, strength, coordination, ease. One can't help but wonder: What will be the treatment: what will be the experiences; what will be the drugs we will use to create these peak moments of health?

The same things can be said about mental health. We will no longer be talking about the mere absence of symptoms; we will be talking about emotional *wellness*—a state in which our emotions will be integrated with our behavior, giving us a feeling of potency, of euphoria. In our mental health activities we will be increasingly concerned with the normal problems of normal people—the problems of loneliness, superficiality, frustration, fear, guilt, despair, anxiety. And we will deal with these problems not only in clinics but in the basic institutions of our society—in schools, in churches, in homes, in neighborhoods, in industries. But this job can't be left to physicians and psychologists. We must use the therapeutic resources that exist in all human beings. People are very good for one another.

Beauty

The third right is the Right to Beauty. I think that right is already beginning to be recognized today, as billboards are removed, green belts established, junk yards hidden. We *need* beauty, and people are beginning to demand it. The right to beauty will be more important than the economics involved.

Truth

The fourth right is the Right to Truth. Some sociologists describe relationships between people as being either "presenting" or "sharing." You can "present" yourself to another person, that is, try to make that person form a favorable impression of you, or you can *share* yourself by letting the other person in on what it's like to be you at that particular moment. Practically all of our relationships—at work, at play, at home, at school—are of the "presenting" kind. But I believe this sharing of oneself is much more common in the younger generation—one that has been referred to as the "Honest Generation." Its members are less likely to censor what they are saying. They seem to want more of the truth from themselves and from others.

When I think of how much we censor our thoughts before saying anything, I am reminded of a little experiment conducted by a friend of mine. In this experiment he asks the people he interviews to wear earphones that feed them white noise which sounds something like a jet airplane going over. When the interviewee is talking, the noise comes on, activated by his own voice. He can hear only what the interviewer is asking. In this situation some interesting phenomena develop. For one thing, people lose some of their ability to control and censor their speech. As an example, a person who is asked, "How do you and your wife get along?" might reply, "We get along just fine," and then add very quietly, "That's a lot of nonsense." When the taped recording is played back to him he doesn't remember saying that last part.

I think that our demands for a right to truth are more and more evident as we move toward an open society. We seem less willing to go along with the deceptions and secrets that we have tolerated for so many years. We are unwilling to let manufacturers make product claims that they can't substantiate. We are concerned about truth in packaging and advertising. Many troubling questions are being raised about how we are going to deal with the significant amount of control that science has given us over heredity, over thoughts, over behavior. I believe that we must deal with this new power by reducing deception and secrecy. For example, I doubt that people will ultimately permit information about themselves to be collected and stored in computerized data banks or in thick personnel files to which they have no access. Furthermore, I doubt that people will submit to psychological testing when they are not sure that such tests are designed to benefit them. I believe there will soon be sweeping legislation that will radically change our practices of testing and investigation.

Intimacy

The fifth new right is the Right to Intimacy. In this busy, urbanized, crowded society, our complicated relations with so many people seem inevitably to lead to superficiality. Physical proximity has, paradoxically, brought emotional distance. Millions of Americans have never had and never will have in their entire lives one moment of intimacy with another human being—one moment in which they could be honestly, authentically, genuinely themselves. People have to get acquainted with their own feelings and they have to be able to share those feelings.

We need new designs for living which will make emotional intimacy possible, which will encourage it—not force it, but encourage it. As a matter of fact, we are actually embarrassed about intimacy. We have the idea that intimacy should take place only in the privacy of the family circle. The trouble is that the shared-feeling kind of intimacy seldom takes place even there.

I think that we will desperately search for authentic intimate relationships and at the same time, be relatively satisfied with relationships that may be only fleeting, transient ones. We need such experiences to remind us of our membership in the human race, to give us a sense of community, to help us be less afraid of one another, to permit us to laugh and cry with one another.

The basic philosophy in our culture holds that chance relationships are acceptable, that arranged ones are not. But that philosophy is not working. People select marriage partners by chance, and this contributes to the high divorce rate. In my community in southern California there are six divorces for every ten marriages, and that statistic assumes the proportions of a national calamity.

Perhaps it's time to get over the notion that something is wrong with arranging relationships. Actually, in many of our social practices we seem quite willing to design relationships. In business and industry, for example, we have organization charts. We don't hesitate to plan so-called intimate dinner parties. They just don't end up being intimate, that's the problem. To be successful, such designs must make use of the best that behavioral science has to offer.

I imagine you feel, as I often feel, that there is something presumptuous and naive and perhaps a little Utopian about the idea of making social arrangements, meddling in human affairs, designing society, if you will, for personal relationships. But look around you— we've *got* to meddle in human affairs.

Travel

Right number six—the Right to Travel. Soon, travel will be so inexpensive and so rapid, the exotic places of the world will be so accessible that people will insist on the right to travel. I can foresee the possibility in coming decades of union contracts which will demand as a fringe benefit the right to travel.

An inevitable consequence of large-scale travel is that we shall develop a new kind of citizen, a citizen of the world. He will return from his travels different in many ways. As an example, consider the Peace Corps volunteer. One of the major benefits of the Peace Corps is the new attitude it instills in its volunteers. Quite apart from what they are able to give to the countries in which they work, it is clear that their experiences in those countries have tremendous impact on them. It is probable that the most important changes being wrought by the Peace Corps are within the volunteers themselves. They are returning to the United States as knowledgeable citizens of the world.

Education

Right number seven is the Right to Study. I'm not talking about basic education, the right to go to school and learn basic skills; we have that right almost pinned down. I'm referring to life-long study: the enriching experience of learning as an end in itself. In the future, education will be our full-time occupation. We'll be studying and learning all the time. But education will no longer serve simply as *preparation:* it will have to stand as a worthwhile *experience* in and of itself.

Education now means *human development.* So, learning must include the effective, emotional interpersonal dimensions, as well as the cognitive, intellectual ones. We are beginning to realize that unless education encompasses all of these dimensions, people who will be graduating from our schools in the 80's and 90's are *not* going to be fully human. They will not be able to cope with increasing change, to enjoy themselves, to live creatively, or to meet the problems of that world. So we must concern ourselves with how to go about educating the emotions and the senses, how to educate for awareness, how to bring people in touch with their feelings and how to help them improve their own interpersonal competence.

Sexual Fulfillment

The eighth right is the Right to Sexual Fulfillment. We have been so plagued by ignorance and fear and guilt that we really haven't enjoyed our sexuality to its greatest extent. But I hope that my generation will be the last to settle for less than full sexuality.

Sex mores have changed, are changing, and will change much, much more. We might as well face it. There is a sexual revolution on the way. It could mean a lot more to everyone.

Altruism

The ninth right is the Right to Altruism. People always seem to want what the aristocracy has. People have demanded freedom, education, leisure, all of which used to belong only to the aristocracy. If I'm correct in my interpretation of events, people are beginning to demand beauty, travel, and the chance to study—rights which also at one time belonged almost solely to the aristocracy. As people move to needs of a higher order, one wonders if they aren't eventually going to demand the right to be altruistic, to be philanthropic. I think they will. They will demand to be in a position to extend beyond themselves, to be of help to others, to love others, to care for others. This is a genuine need, one that many of us don't even realize that we have.

Being Different

Finally, I think we will demand the Right to Be Different. We all experience enormous pressures toward conformity—and these pressures will become even greater. It is an inevitable consequence of living and working in groups. The War on Poverty has been called the war of the middle class against the lower class. It appears the middle class might win and that a homogenized society might be the result. If this happens, I think we will be very sorry. Some sociologists recently studied skid-row society in Denver and Chicago. We are used to thinking only of the failure and misery in that unfortunate segment of our population, so it was surprising to me to discover in conversations with the returning sociologists that they really liked it there. Apparently there's something that is *really* true about skid-row culture that we only *say* is true about middle-class culture. People do care about one another on skid-row. They go the distance with one another: they help one another in difficult circumstances. They regard themselves as their brothers' keepers. One sociologist said, "You know, if I didn't have a family I think I'd live there."

As we redesign our cities, our problem will be not only what to change, but what to preserve. I don't mean only historical landmarks. There are other places—charming, quaint romantic, sentimental, highly valued and highly functional places. What dingy bookshops, what smelly delicatessens, what smoky taverns, what meeting places for old people do we want to keep?

We will, in addition, certainly want to preserve some customs, practices, cultures, ethnic differences—but in depth, not just as traditional pageants that we revive once a year. A fundamental question: How can we enable people who are trapped in ghettos to improve their lives and enjoy full citizenship and, at the same time, help them retain for the benefit of all of us the richness of their culture? It may be that celebrating rather than pretending to ignore these ethnic variations will do more to achieve full citizenship, full humanity for all of us. The human potential is not only what it *is,* but it is also what we *believe* it is.

Although the subject of human potentiality demands a great deal of study, we give it very little. We seldom seem to be studying man when he is at his best. We study people in prisons and in clinics and when we run out of white rats we study college sophomores. But we don't study man when he is realizing his full potentialities. To the contrary, we bring him into our laboratories and ask him to do things he doesn't do and doesn't understand. We tend not to go out into the "real" world and observe normal people doing things that are natural to them.

We do know that environment is an important determiner of human potential. As a matter of fact, probably the best way to predict

what a person's behavior is going to be is to study the *situation,* not
the person's life history. For example, people don't smoke in church.
It doesn't make any difference what their histories are, nobody smokes
in church. The situation has determined their behavior.

As we design society, we must remember that the fundamental
element in all these designs is that they must be self-determined and
self-renewing. We must make it possible for the people who are the
components of the system to be the designers of the system.

The more progress we make, the more we must make. Perhaps
that's the most frustrating fact of life. Improvements inevitably bring
higher expectations and insistence upon more improvements. And
that's not easy to accept or to understand. We have this problem in
the civil rights movement. We keep thinking, "Okay. Now we've
provided the Negroes with equal educational benefits, we've provided
them with a chance at the polls, and that's been a difficult struggle for
all of us. Why don't they just appreciate these improvements, rest a
minute and let us catch our breath? Then we'll do something else.
Can't we just coast a little while?" And of course we can't. On the
contrary, we must, as a result of our successes, step up the pace even
more. People become increasingly anxious as they get closer to their
goals. That's why this business of trying to make life better is an
endless and frustrating task.

When people feel that their potential is not being realized, they
grumble. But these grumbles should be *valued* because they reflect
motivation toward a better life. I think we can have that better life if
we can understand that the real barrier to a better world is our own
resistance to change.

SCIENCE, SEX AND
TOMORROW'S MORALITY

Albert Rosenfeld

Wrenching changes in the nature of the ties that bind one human
being to another. Radically different meanings for old words and acts
—sex and love, for instance. Perhaps even the end of institutions such

Albert Rosenfeld, "Science, Sex and Tomorrow's Morality," *Life Magazine,* June 13, 1969, ©
1969 Time Inc. (The article is adapted from *The Second Genesis* by Albert Rosenfeld published
by Prentice-Hall, Inc.)

as marriage and the family. Startling advances in the science of reproductive biology may bring about a sweeping transformation in the style of man's life on earth. We have lived so long with our traditions, it is hard to realize how much of our morality—at least that part of it concerned with sex, marriage and the family—rests solidly on the basic and unarguable facts of reproductive biology. Long before the study of obstetrics and gynecology began, people understood that a man and a woman must unite sexually in order to produce a child; that the embryo develops on its own during the long, dark, quiet months before it is ejected into the shock of life outside; and that the helpless human infant requires an unusually prolonged period of parental protection and training before it can cope, on even a minimal basis, with its environment. An infant horned toad bursts forth from the maternal sac all ready to fend for itself. A newborn giraffe or zebra can run beside its mother within a very few hours. But the human baby is helpless.

All this being so, it was inevitable that certain sets of conventions would evolve. Thus grew our institutions of marriage and the family, buttressed by religion, law, politics, philosophy, education, commerce and the arts—an interdependent social edifice endowed with an aura of self-evident immutability.

For the rearing of the young there had to be some continuity of place and the assignment of responsibility. The mother could not give her baby the care and attention it needed to survive and, at the same time, be the one to fight and protect, to feed and clothe and shelter. So the father had to be discouraged from straying. Society channeled sexual urges toward one goal—procreation—devising complicated systems of prescriptions and proscriptions.

Everyone in the family, from infants to uncles to grandmothers, had his assigned role and was aware of his rights, duties and privileges. Courtship was ritualized, wedding vows were solemnized, family support was enforced. Parents were to be obeyed, elders respected, children protected. Spouses were to be the exclusive sexual property of one another. Theologians labored to inculcate in man and woman alike a deep sense of sin regarding the pleasures of the flesh. But if religious taboos were insufficiently inhibiting, more practical fears were at hand: the fear of impregnating or of becoming pregnant, the fear of contracting a venereal disease, the fear of losing a spouse's devotion, the fear of earning the disapproval of one's friends and the condemnation of society.

Exceptions to convention were never uncommon, human powers

of self-discipline being what they are, but such departures have, on the whole, fared rather badly. Romantic love and other cultural variants have influenced people's attitudes from time to time and from place to place, yet at no time and in no place—not, at any rate, until modern times—has there existed for very long a widespread belief that a stable society of responsible citizens could be maintained without marriage and the family.

True, these institutions clamped undeniable restrictions on individual freedom (or at least on individual license), but they also served the individual's essential needs. For a man, they served his need for sex, his need for a mate who would provide progeny to carry on his name, his need for status, his need to be needed, his need for a physical and psychical base of operations. For a woman, they served her need for security during her periods of maximum vulnerability—pregnancy and child-rearing—her need for a man and a mate to provide her with children, her need for status, her perhaps even greater need than a man's to be needed.

The system was never perfect, but it worked better than any other that men had been able to devise—and most of us have been raised in the belief that things would always go on more or less the same way. It was possible to believe this—almost impossible to believe otherwise —because there was no reason to doubt that the facts of life on which the whole moral structure rested would also remain essentially unchanged forever.

But in the sciences forever has a way of turning out to be not so everlasting after all. We are now entering an era when, as a result of new scientific discoveries, some mind-boggling things are likely to happen. Children may routinely be born of geographically separated or even long-dead parents, virgin births may become relatively common, women may give birth to other women's children, romance and genetics may finally be separated, and a few favored men may be called upon to father thousands of babies.

What has been far less widely discussed, however, are the implications of this approaching revolution, particularly the fact that traditional morality will experience a far more severe and far more profound shaking up than most people have yet. Imagined if the biological foundations of present-day morality are removed, can it not logically be argued that this morality, every last time-honored shred of it, has become nothing but a useless anachronism?

Consider, as an indication of the current rapid pace of change, the matter of birth control. The potentialities for control are better understood than ever before. In addition to techniques for the *prevention* of conception, techniques are now available for the *encouragement* of conception. Where other therapies have failed, the doctor can intervene directly in two ways to promote conception. He can implant in the wife the husband's own sperm or that of an anonymous donor—a commonplace procedure these days; or he can implant an egg taken from the tubes or uterus of another woman—a technique so far applied only in animal experiments. The further refinement of freezing techniques will, moreover, permit the establishment of sperm banks and egg banks. Long-term storage would mean that proximity in space and time of donor, recipient and middleman (doctor) would no longer be required.

Beyond artificially assisted fertilization, there could be (and has been, experimentally) fertilization *in vitro*—*i.e.,* in laboratory glassware. An egg thus prefertilized could be implanted in any woman. Furthermore, it might well be possible eventually to grow babies entirely *in vitro,* with the protecting and nourishing presence of a human mother nowhere in evidence.

There are also other variations to be played upon this theme, variations which nature has already played spontaneously, at least with the lower orders of animals, and which biologists can now duplicate in the laboratory. There is, for one, the phenomenon of parthenogenesis or virgin birth, in which, without the presence of a male sperm, the egg spontaneously doubles its supply of chromosomes, thus in effect fertilizing itself. When parthenogenesis takes place, all the child's genetic traits are maternal and there is only one true parent. And a bit of microsurgery could easily make the father the one true genetic parent. In that case the resulting child would have no genetic mother at all.

Among other controls bestowed by medical science will be the power to determine in advance the sex of one's offspring. There are two kinds of sperm—one (androsperm) that produces males, the other (gynosperm) females. Several scientists have claimed success in separating the two—and, after artificially inseminating animals with the separated sperm, getting a significantly higher portion of the desired sex.

Finally, there is the distinct possibility of raising people without using sperm or egg at all. Could people be grown, for example, in tissue culture? In a full-grown, mature organism, every normal cell has within itself all the genetic data transmitted by the original fertilized egg cell. There appears therefore, to be no theoretical reason why a means might not be devised to make all of a cell's genetic data accessible. And when that happens, should it not eventually become possible to grow the individual all over again from any cell taken from anywhere in the body? A number of scientists believe so.

Even more startling would be the production of human beings whose characteristics can be specified in advance. Breakthroughs in genetic knowledge make speculations anything but preposterous, and when this kind of biochemical sophistication has been attained, man's powers will have become truly godlike. Just as he has been able, through chemistry, to create a variety of synthetic materials that never existed in nature, so may he, through genetic surgery, bring into being new species of creatures never before seen or imagined in the universe —beings better adapted, if he wishes, to survive on the surface of Jupiter, or on the bottom of the Atlantic Ocean.

If, then, the so-called facts of life are going to be subject to change in these startling ways, we can expect a chain reaction of related changes in social attitudes and institutions. This means, of course, that if we are to manage the new controls that scientists will soon be handing us, the nature of human relationships must be thoroughly re-examined—and, some think, radically reconstructed.

All this may sound unduly alarmist to those who assume that people would automatically resist as bizarre the idea of subjecting themselves to bio-engineering. But would they really? Take *in vitro* embryology. While it is not likely to be available to us soon, the technical obstacles to its attainment are surely surmountable. And when they *are* surmounted, someone somewhere is going to produce *in vitro* offspring. Once the first full and safe success has been achieved, it will not be long before some couples in special circumstances start raising babies in this fashion. Imagine what the reaction must have been to the first outlandish suggestions that human beings might one day be conceived through artificial insemination. Yet, today husbands and wives by the thousands collaborate in this manner with doctors and anonymous sperm donors to produce progeny.

So would it be with *in vitro* babies. Research in this direction will undoubtedly be accelerated by the new interest in prenatal medicine —doctoring the fetus while still in its mother's womb. Many medical scientists believe they could do much more than they now can, perhaps preventing hundreds of thousands of birth defects, if the embryo and fetus could be developed *in vitro,* as visible and accessible to diagnosis and therapy as any other patient is. Hitherto reluctant parents might opt for *in vitro* babies to increase their chances of having a healthy child. Some mothers, too, might simply find it more convenient to skip the whole process of pregnancy and childbearing. There would, of course, remain staunch, old-fashioned types who consider this more a deprivation than a convenience—but have very many women ever turned down labor-saving devices? Besides, sex as recreation, as opposed to sex as procreation, is not exactly a new idea.

A quick look around confirms that a startling transformation is already taking place in our attitudes toward sex—long in advance of most of the techniques we have been talking about. In fact, where sex is concerned it is hard to say any more what is "normal" and what is not. All sorts of behavior which only a few years ago were considered wrong, or at least questionable, now seem reasonable. Playwrights and novelists do not hesitate to describe any kind of sexuality they can imagine in whatever terms seem suitable to them. Books once available only by mail in plain brown wrappers now flourish on paperback racks in card shops and at your local pharmacy. Sex in the movies leaves little to the imagination. And if sex is talked about much more openly these days, there is no reason to doubt that it is practiced much more uninhibitedly, too. On the college campus, where a goodnight kiss at the dormitory door was once considered a bit wicked, premarital sex—while not indulged in universally—is now taken for granted. (It is difficult to remember that as recently as 1960 the University of Illinois fired a biology professor for suggesting that premarital sex might be ethically justifiable.) Around a few campuses free-sex clubs featuring nude parties have sprung up. In the scientific laboratory sexual activity is studied clinically, recorded and measured by instruments and photographed in color by motion-picture cameras, and many people already accept this as logical: men and women of various ages, alone or with partners, with or without the aid of artificial devices, are willing to perform sexually and even earn a modest fee for their contribution to scientific knowledge.

If all this has taken place in the context of the familiar facts of life, essentially unaltered by science, what even greater change will occur when the new facts of life take over? Chances are we haven't seen anything yet.

Even before the current sexual revolution, there were problems aplenty in interpersonal relationships. Today, however, the problems are more evident than ever. The divorce rate is high and would be even higher if many couples did not work hard to "make a go of it." Unfortunately, the "go" they make of it frequently amounts to nothing more than a borderline accommodation to a minimally tolerable arrangement. Under the best of circumstances the chronic failure of communication that besets so many marriages creates a nagging sense of discontent and insecurity. Add an ingredient—the prevailing liberalized attitudes toward sex—and you compound all the existing confusions and insecurities. Dependable standards of fidelity are getting harder to come by. How are married couples to fix them, even for themselves, with convincing validity, let alone arrive at standards that apply to other people? And in their own state of uncertainty, what standards do they fix for their growing children—and how do they make their criteria credible? It is difficult enough even for confident parents, in a stable era, to impart what is traditionally assumed to be their superior, experience-based wisdom. In a chaotic time like ours, how do you persuade teen-agers to "behave"—or even that they ought to?

The moral sanctions of religion once served as a sufficient guide for most people. But those sanctions, and the grounds on which they are based, have been increasingly called into question, even by theologians, so that more and more laymen have come to feel that sexually they are on their own.

But if the wrath of God is no longer to be feared, what then? We may soon reach a time when venereal disease is no longer any threat, and when contraception is so cheap and easy as to remove any risk of an unwanted pregnancy. Once physiological immunity is thus assured, we can suppose that, with changing attitudes, there may also be social immunity; that is, if one is found out, no one will care. In fact, there would be no point in secrecy at all.

Any man or woman living in this changed moral environment will clearly have greatly increased opportunities for sexual adventures— though enhancing the opportunities may diminish the adventure. For any husband or wife so inclined, the temptation to philander may be overpowering. The man or woman who is not personally tempted, but who is subject to jealous apprehensions, is bound to become more uneasy with the awareness that the second party may not be resisting temptation with equal success. A jealous person traditionally has at least had the sympathy of friends. But he might find that most of his friends think it absurd to expect anyone to be faithful. The effect of all these pressures would vary with the individual, of course, but in the case of a marriage already precarious these added concerns could easily finish it.

With old fears replaced by new freedoms, do the foundations of fidelity then fall? Does fidelity become an outmoded concept? And if sex outside the marriage bed is O.K., what happens to marriage itself?

Do we marry for love, companionship, security? And are these lasting? Should we be prepared to change partners whenever there is a feeling on the part of either one that it's time for a change? Are the legal bonds of marriage nonsense? Is the ideal to be a purely personal arrangement without law or ceremony, a companionate arrangement such as those that are becoming increasingly common among college students?

Dr. Margaret Mead, an anthropologist who has long studied the folkways of marriage, underscores the relevance of such questions by pointing up the enormous obstacles to staying married for life, especially in the U.S. where marriage undergoes extraordinary strains because of the romantic expectations it must uphold. "The ideal is so high," says Dr. Mead, "and the difficulties so many . . . that a very rigorous re-examination of the relationship between ideals and practice is called for."

But what about the rearing of children? Is it not vital to maintain marriage and the current family structure for that reason alone? Not necessarily. Many observers have raised serious questions about how well children fare under current circumstances anyway. They may fare considerably less well as biology begins to displace tradition. That tradition has been to regard a child as a product of the marriage bed —and therefore, in some way, sacred. "Moved by the force of love," Père Teilhard de Chardin, the priest-scientist, once wrote "fragments of the world seek out one another so that a world may be." The fragments of the world he was talking about were the sperm and the egg—the sperm fresh-sprung from the father's loins, the egg snug in its warm, secret place, the propelling force being conjugal love, the new world being the child itself.

But the force of love may henceforth have little to do with the process. The crucial fragments of the world may simply be taken out of cold storage on demand. Even if the scientist or technician who brings the fragments together in the laboratory managed to maintain an attitude of reverence toward the life he was thus creating, love in the old sense would no longer be a part of the procreative process.

Assuming that the father's own sperm and the mother's own egg were used, the mere fact of conception outside themselves—conception in which they did not personally participate—might make a vast difference in their later attitudes toward their children. If the sperm or egg—or both—belonged originally to someone else, it would add to the impersonality of the transaction. How much of any mother's feeling toward a child is bound up in the physical fact of having carried it inside the womb for those long months, providing nourishment with her own body, fulfilling herself physiologically and spiritually as a woman? With this gone, would her maternal feelings be the same?

There are, of course, some people for whom this question is quite irrelevant: those who are capable of giving genuine love and affection to a child who has been adopted, who is not their genetic product at all. Might the answer—or a partial answer—then be to restrict child-rearing privileges to couples who really want them? "People brought up without parental love," A. S. Makarenko, the Soviet counterpart of Dr. Spock, reminds us, "are often deformed people."

When family units were larger—in older, less urbanized days, when there were grandparents in the house, or even aunts and uncles—a child had alternate sets of adults to turn to, and therefore a wider chance of getting the kind of love and attention he needed, at the time he needed it. Even when there was not a large family living under one roof, people used to stay put longer in their communities, so that lots of long-time friends, who were almost like relatives, were in the immediate neighborhood during the years when a child was growing up. Among the many peoples she has studied, Dr. Mead believes the Samoans are by far the best adjusted sexually and maritally, for the very reason that "the relationship between child and parent is early diffused over many adults. . . . He is given food, consoled, carried about, by all the women of the large households, and later carried about the village by child nurses who cluster together with their charges on their hips."

In the U.S. today, however, the typical family is a "nuclear" one, with only the married couple and their immediate children living in a separate house or apartment. They probably have not lived there very long and may contemplate moving again soon. Chances are that no relatives live with them—or even close by—and that they are not really "involved" with their friends and neighbors. The result is that the children are dependent for emotional sustenance solely on their single set of parents, and their human experience is thus considerably restricted.

Except in our nostalgic fantasies, the large, tribal, multiparental household or community is a thing of the past. But one day might friends or relatives arbitrarily decide to live together in groups again, sharing expenses, households and parental duties (just as neighbors now trade around babysitting chores on occasion)? In Sweden as well as in the U.S. and Canada today a few groups are currently experimenting with such arrangements, and many communes in this country have been trying it. But could this form of tribalism ever really work in our highly mobile, technological society? Farfetched though the idea may be, it is perhaps not to be dismissed out of hand.

If we were to enter an era when permanent marriages became a rarity and children were raised only by volunteer parents, what would happen to the children when the parents separated? Whose children would they be? Would they be reassigned to some other group or couple for a while? Or, for stability's sake, would they have to be raised by the state—perhaps in small, familylike units? And in the new era what would be the role of sex? If it were as casual as any other harmless pleasure (assuming the harmlessness of it), what would be wrong with anyone having sex with anyone else for no other reason than their mutual desire? Some people have been saying, in effect, "Good! It's about time sex was devalued and put in its place. Now maybe people will marry for more sensible reasons." But this kind of freedom could bring about a drastic decline in the quality of sexual experience—as well as a drastic reversal in the roles of both the male and the female.

Such a reversal would give neither sex much to rejoice at. Traditionally the male has been much more free about sex than the female. He was expected to delight in sex, to be the aggressor, the panting pursuer, the sower of wild oats. In the sex act it was the woman who bestowed the favors, the man who won them. The woman treasured her chastity, used it as a lure to marriage. One of the reasons a man married was to assure himself secure possession of a pleasure that was otherwise hard to get. The woman submitted to his passion as her wifely duty.

Women have increasingly emancipated themselves from this mystique. They hear and read a great deal about the female orgasm, what a monumental experience it can and should be, their inalienable right to intense and frequent sexual pleasure—yea, even into their 70s and 80s. We now know that the sexual needs of women are at least as great as those of men, and that the female climax is more intense and longer-lasting.

The male sexual capacity, despite the Casanovas and Don Juans of history, seems to be essentially more limited than the female's and his need more easily satisfied. It will be satisfied even more easily if the female goes on the prowl. He will not have to pursue at all. Soon, in fact, he may find himself fleeing as opportunities surpass his ability to deal with them.

The woman, who formerly competed for males as marriage partners, may find herself competing for them as sexual partners. She will have become the aggressive pursuer of coy, hesitant males (even if the coyness and hesitancy are due merely to satiation—or to boredom with a commodity so totally available). Even today, as a woman grows older, she finds there are fewer and fewer men to go round. (For one thing, they tend to die earlier than women do.) With so many enhanced opportunities for dissipation, the men may begin to wear out even sooner. To preserve them longer, women—especially if they can begin to have their babies without having to carry them, thus freeing them from their ancient bondage—may wind up working while the more delicate male stays home and takes care of himself. And as the supply of available males dwindled in a world where sexual satisfaction was every woman's right, what would women do? Would there be a return of polyandry? Would they turn to each other?

However it all went, the concept of adultery would disappear, words like "premarital" and "extramarital" would become meaningless, and no one would think of attaching a label like "promiscuity" to sex activities. After all, why not be as free to experiment with a variety of sexual partners as with a variety of foods and restaurants? Love, marriage and the family have been around a long time and have served us very well. But it is clear that they may not survive the new era unless we really want them to.

Whatever our attitude, a more liberalized sexuality does seem to be here to stay, and it finally seems to be established, even among many churchmen, that sex is, or ought to be, a good and joyous thing. In this atmosphere most authorities tend to agree with the judgment of Dr. Joseph Fletcher, an Episcopal theologian: "It is doubtful that love's cause is helped by any of the sex laws that try to dictate sexual practices for consenting adults." It looks very much as if we will have to abandon our old habit of insisting that sex must serve the same purpose for everyone, or even for the same person at different times of his life. As long as sex is practiced in private between fully consenting adults who do no physical harm to one another, is it really a matter for the police or for criminal statutes?

A good many authorities have suggested that it might help, too, if we stopped thinking of sex as consisting only of intercourse, if we thought, instead, of sex as something a person *is* rather than something he *does,* as something incidental to his or her total sexuality—that is, to all the experiences and all the thoughts, from childhood to old age, that have contributed to his or her maleness or femaleness. Sexual feeling does not, after all, invariably or even usually involve only sexual intercourse; rather, it involves a whole range of attitudes and actions, from a mother's tenderness to a father's pride in the development of a child.

A man of our time, feeling overburdened by his confusions and responsibilities, might see distinct advantages in the more carefree kind of world that the new biology could make feasible. He might even envy his imaginary counterpart in one of the possible societies of the not-too-far-off future—a man grown *in vitro*, say, and raised by a state nursery. Such a man, it is true, might never know who his genetic parents were, nor would he have any brothers or sisters he could call his own. On the other hand, if he considered all men his brothers, what need would he have for a few specifically designated siblings who happened to be born in the same household? Think how carefree he might be: no parents to feel guilty about neglecting, no parental responsibilities of his own, no marriage partner to whom he owes fidelity —free to play, work, create, pursue his pleasures. In our current circumstances the absence of a loved one saddens us, and death brings terrible grief. Think how easily the tears could be wiped away if there were no single "loved one" to miss that much—or if that loved one were readily replaceable by any of several others.

And yet if you (the hypothetical *in vitro* man) did not miss anyone very much, neither would anyone miss you very much. Your absence would cause little sadness, your death little grief. You too would be readily replaceable.

A man needs to be needed. Who, in the new era, would need you? Would your mortality not weigh upon you even more heavily, though your life span were doubled or tripled?

"Which of us has known his brother?" wrote Thomas Wolfe. "Which of us has looked into his father's heart? Which of us has not remained forever prison-pent? Which of us is not forever a stranger and alone?"

The aloneness many of us feel on this earth is assuaged, more or less effectively, by the deep and abiding relationships we have with other human beings—with our parents, our children, our brothers and sisters, our wives, husbands, sweethearts, lovers, closest friends. These relationships are not always as close as we would like them to be, and communication is often distressingly difficult. Yet there is always the hope that each man and woman who seeks this special warmth will eventually find it.

But in the *in vitro* world, the tissue-culture world, even this hope might be difficult to sustain. Could society devise adequate substitutes? Could the trans-humans of post-civilization survive without

love as we have known it in the institutions of marriage and the family?
If each of us is "forever a stranger and alone" here and now.

DAY MILLION

Frederik Pohl

On this day I want to tell you about, which will be about ten
thousand years from now, there were a boy, a girl and a love story.

Now, although I haven't said much so far, none of it is true. The
boy was not what you and I would normally think of as a boy, because
he was a hundred and eighty-seven years old. Nor was the girl a girl,
for other reasons. And the love story did not entail that sublimation
of the urge to rape, and concurrent postponement of the instinct to
submit, which we at present understand in such matters. You won't
care much for this story if you don't grasp these facts at once. If,
however, you will make the effort you'll likely enough find it jam-
packed, chockful and tiptop-crammed with laughter, tears and poignant sentiment which may, or may not, be worthwhile. The reason
the girl was not a girl was that she was a boy.

How angrily you recoil from the page! You say, who the hell wants
to read about a pair of queers? Calm yourself. Here are no hot-breath-
ing secrets of perversion for the coterie trade. In fact, if you were to
see this girl you would not guess that she was in any sense a boy.
Breasts, two; reproductive organs, female. Hips, callipygean; face hair-
less, supra-orbital lobes nonexistent. You would term her female on
sight, although it is true that you might wonder just what species she
was a female of, being confused by the tail, the silky pelt and the gill
slits behind each ear.

Now you recoil again. Cripes, man, take my word for it. This is a
sweet kid, and if you, as a normal male, spent as much as an hour in
a room with her you would bend heaven and Earth to get her in the
sack. Dora—we will call her that; her "name" was omicron-Dibase
seven-group-totter-oot S Doradus 5314, the last part of which is a
color specification corresponding to a shade of green—Dora, I say, was
feminine, charming and cute. I admit she doesn't sound that way. She
was, as you might put it, a dancer. Her art involved qualities of intel-

Frederick Pohl, "Day Million." From *Day Million* by Frederick Pohl. Reprinted by permission
of the author.

lection and expertise of a very high order, requiring both tremendous natural capacities and endless practice; it was performed in null-gravity and I can best describe it by saying that it was something like the performance of a contortionist and something like classical ballet, maybe resembling Danilova's dying swan. It was also pretty damned sexy. In a symbolic way, to be sure; but face it, most of the things we call "sexy" are symbolic, you know, except perhaps an exhibitionist's open clothing. On Day Million when Dora danced, the people who saw her panted, and you would too.

About this business of her being a boy. It didn't matter to her audiences that genetically she was a male. It wouldn't matter to you, if you were among them, because you wouldn't know it—not unless you took a biopsy cutting of her flesh and put it under an electron-microscope to find the XY chromosome and it didn't matter to them because they didn't care. Through techniques which are not only complex but haven't yet been discovered, these people were able to determine a great deal about the aptitudes and easement of babies quite a long time before they were born—at about the second horizon of cell-division, to be exact, when the segmenting egg is becoming a free blastocyst—and then they naturally helped those aptitudes along. Wouldn't we? If we find a child with an aptitude for music we give him a scholarship to Juilliard. If they found a child whose aptitudes were for being a woman, they made him one. As sex had long been dis-sociated from reproduction this was relatively easy to do and caused no trouble, and no, or at least very little, comment.

How much is "very little"? Oh, about as much as would be caused by our own tampering with Divine Will by filling a tooth. Less than would be caused by wearing a hearing aid. Does it still sound awful? Then look closely at the next busty babe you meet and reflect that she may be a Dora, for adults who are genetically male but somatically female are far from unknown even in our own time. An accident of environment in the womb overwhelms the blueprints of heredity. The difference is that with us it happens only by accident and we don't know about it except rarely, after close study; whereas the people of Day Million did it often, on purpose, because they wanted to.

Well, that's enough to tell you about Dora.It would only confuse you to add that she was seven feet tall and smelled of peanut butter. Let us begin our story.

On Day Million, Dora swam out of her house, entered a transporta-tion tube, was sucked briskly to the surface in its flow of water and ejected in its plume of spray to an elastic platform in front of her—

ah—call it her rehearsal hall. "Oh, hell!" she cried in pretty confusion, reaching out to catch her balance and finding herself tumbled against a total stranger, whom we will call Don.

They met cute. Don was on his way to have his legs renewed. Love was the farthest thing from his mind. But when, absentimindedly taking a shortcut across the landing platform for submarinites and finding himself drenched, he discovered his arms full of the loveliest girl he had ever seen, he knew at once they were meant for each other. "Will you marry me?" he asked. She said softly, "Wednesday," and the promise was like a caress.

Don was tall, muscular, bronze and exciting. His name was no more Don than Dora's was Dora, but the personal part of it was Adonis in tribute to his vibrant maleness, and so we will call him Don for short. His personality color-code, in angstrom units, was 5290, or only a few degrees bluer than Dora's 5314—a measure of what they had intuitively discovered at first sight: that they possessed many affinities of taste and interest.

I despair of telling you exactly what it was that Don did for a living. I don't mean for the sake of making money, I mean for the sake of giving purpose and meaning to his life, to keep him from going off his nut with boredom—except to say that it involved a lot of traveling. He traveled in interstellar spaceships. In order to make a spaceship go really fast, about thirty-one male and seven genetically female human beings had to do certain things, and Don was one of the thirty-one. Actually, he contemplated options. This involved a lot of exposure to radiation flux—not so much his own station in the propulsive system as in the spillover from the next stage, where a genetic female preferred selections, and the sub-nuclear particles making the selections she preferred demolished themselves in a shower of quanta. Well, you don't give a rat's ass for that, but it meant that Don had to be clad at all times in a skin of light, resilient, extremely strong copper-colored metal. I have already mentioned this, but you probably thought I meant he was sunburned.

More than that, he was a cybernetic man. Most of his ruder parts had been long since replaced with mechanisms of vastly more permanence and use. A cadmium centrifuge, not a heart, pumped his blood. His lungs moved only when he wanted to speak out loud, for a cascade of osmotic filters rebreathed oxygen out of his own wastes. In a way, he probably would have looked peculiar to a man from the 20th century, with his glowing eyes and seven-fingered hands. But to himself, and of course to Dora, he looked mighty manly and grand. In the course of his voyages Don had circled Proxima Centauri, Procyon and the puzzling worlds of Mira Ceti; he had carried agricultural templates to the planets of Canopus and brought back warm, witty pets from the pale companion of Aldebaran. Blue-hot or red-cool, he had seen a thousand stars and their ten thousand planets. He had, in fact, been traveling the starlanes, with only brief leaves on Earth, for pushing two centuries. But you don't care about that, either. It is people who make stories, not the circumstances they find themselves in, and you want to hear about these two people. Well, they made it. The great thing they had for each other grew and flowered and burst into fruition on Wednesday, just as Dora had promised. They met at the encoding room, with a couple of well-wishing friends apiece to cheer them on, and while their identities were being taped and stored they smiled and whispered to each other and bore the jokes of their friends with blushing repartee. Then they exchanged their mathematical analogues and went away. Dora to her dwelling beneath the surface of the sea and Don to his ship.

It was an idyll, really. They lived happily ever after or anyway, until they decided not to bother any more and died.

Of course, they never set eyes on each other again.

Oh, I can see you now, you eaters of charcoal-broiled steak, scratching an incipient bunion with one hand and holding this story with the other, while the stereo plays d'Indy or Monk. You don't believe a word of it, do you? Not for one minute. People wouldn't live like that, you say with a grunt as you get up to put fresh ice in a drink.

And yet there's Dora, hurrying back through the flushing commuter pipes toward her underwater home (she prefers it there; has had herself somatically altered to breathe the stuff). If I tell you with what sweet fulfillment she fits the recorded analogue of Don into the symbol manipulator, hooks herself in and turns herself on . . . if I try to tell you any of that you will simply stare. Or glare; and grumble, what the hell kind of love-making is this? And yet I assure you, friend, I really do assure you that Dora's ecstasies are as creamy and passionate as any of James Bond's lady spies', and one hell of a lot more so than anything you are going to find in "real life." Go ahead, glare and grumble. Dora doesn't care. If she thinks of you at all, her thirty-times-great-great-grandfather, she thinks you're a pretty primordial sort of brute. You are. Why, Dora is farther removed from you than you are from the australopithecines of five thousand centuries ago. You could not swim a second in the strong currents of her life. You don't think progress goes in a straight line, do you? Do you recognize that it is an ascending, accelerating, maybe even exponential curve? It takes hell's own time to get started, but when it goes it goes like a bomb. And you, you Scotch-drinking steak-eater in your relaxacizing chair, you've just barely lighted the primacord of the fuse. What is it now, the six or seven hundred thousandth day after Christ? Dora lives in Day Million. Ten thousand years from now. Her body fats are polyunsaturated, like Crisco. Her wastes are hemodialyzed out of her bloodstream while she sleeps—that means she doesn't have to go to the bathroom. On whim, to pass a slow half hour, she can command more energy than the entire nation of Portugal can spend today, and use it to launch a weekend satellite or remold a crater on the Moon. She loves Don very much. She keeps his every gesture, mannerism, nuance, touch of hand, thrill of intercourse, passion of kiss stored in symbolic-mathematical form. And when she wants him, all she has to do is turn the machine on and she has him.

And Don, of course, has Dora. Adrift on a sponson city a few hundred yards over her head or orbiting Arcturus fifty light-years away. Don has only to command his own symbol-manipulator to rescue Dora from the ferrite files and bring her to life for him, and there she is; and rapturously, tirelessly they love all night. Not in the flesh, of course; but then his flesh has been extensively altered and it wouldn't really be much fun. He doesn't need the flesh for pleasure. Genital organs feel nothing. Neither do hands, nor breasts, nor lips; they are only receptors, accepting and transmitting impulses. It is the brain that feels; it is the interpretation of those impulses that make agony or orgasm, and Don's symbol-manipulator gives him the analogue of cuddling, the analogue of kissing, the analogue of wild, ardent hours with the eternal, exquisite and incorruptible analogue of Dora. Or Diane. Or sweet Rose, or laughing Alicia; for to be sure, they have each of them exchanged analogues before, and will again.

Rats, you say, it looks crazy to me. And you—with your aftershave lotion and your little red car, pushing papers across a desk all day and chasing tail all night—tell me, just how the hell do you think you would look to Tiglath-Pileser, say, or Attila the Hun?